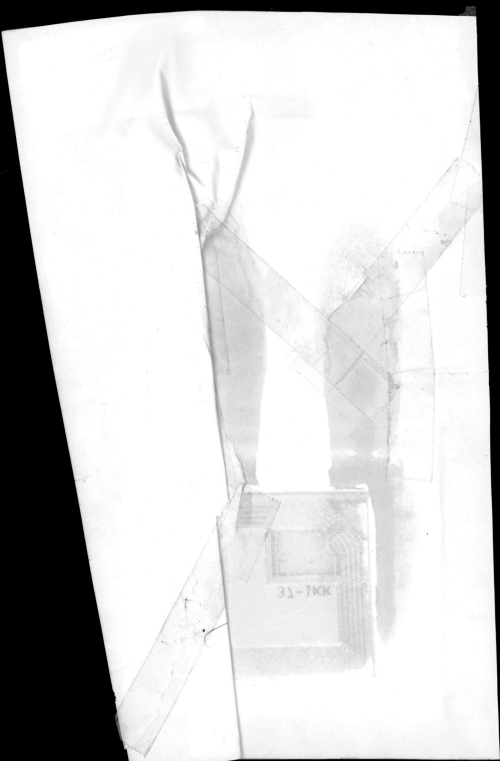

The
MUSHROOM HANDBOOK

The

MUSHROOM HANDBOOK

by

LOUIS C. C. KRIEGER

*Illustrated by photographs and
drawings by the author*

WITH A NEW PREFACE AND APPENDIX ON

NOMENCLATURAL CHANGES BY

ROBERT L. SHAFFER

*University Herbarium
The University of Michigan
Ann Arbor, Michigan*

DOVER PUBLICATIONS, INC.
NEW YORK

This Dover edition, first published in 1967, is an unabridged republication of the second edition, as published by The Macmillan Company in 1936. The work
was originally published by The University of the State
of New York in 1935 under the title *A Popular Guide
to the Higher Fungi (Mushrooms) of New York State*.
The publisher is grateful to The Horticultural Society
of New York for supplying a copy of this work for the
purpose of photographic reproduction.

Standard Book Number 486-21861-9
Library of Congress Catalog Card Number: 67–28792

Manufactured in the United States of America
Dover Publications, Inc.
180 Varick Street
New York, N. Y. 10014

PREFACE TO THE DOVER EDITION

Louis Charles Christopher Krieger, the finest painter of North American fungi, was born in Baltimore, Maryland, on February 11, 1873.[1] After receiving his basic education and studying art in that city, he became an assistant to Dr. Thomas Taylor of the Division of Microscopy, United States Department of Agriculture. Taylor's hobby was mushrooms, and he had Krieger paint fungi found in the vicinity of Washington, D. C., and copy plates from European mycological books. When the Division was disbanded in 1895, Krieger went to Munich for a year of study at the Royal Bavarian Academy of Fine Arts. Following his return to Baltimore, he taught drawing and painting at the Maryland Institute of Fine Arts, where he had once been a student.

In 1902 Krieger became artist to Professor William G. Farlow, the famous cryptogamic botanist of Harvard University. Farlow had for some years been collecting and studying higher fungi in New England, New York, and New Brunswick with a view toward publishing a work with good illustrations and full descriptions of common species. Mr. Joseph Bridgham at first did the paintings; and then, in the period 1902-1912, Krieger made some 400 water colors of both fungi and algae for Farlow. Although Farlow died in 1919, *Icones Farlowianae,* edited and with descriptions by Professor E. A. Burt, was published in 1929. Most of the plates were Bridgham's; only 23 were from paintings done by Krieger. The artist of each plate is not identified in the *Icones,* but once one is familiar with Krieger's work, his plates can easily be picked out. Their superiority is obvious.

Bibliography was another major part of Krieger's mycological interest, and it was during his time with Farlow that

---

[1] The major sources consulted for biographical information on Krieger are the following: KANOUSE, BESSIE, "Doctor Howard Atwood Kelly," *Mycologia* 35: 383-384, 1943. KELLY, HOWARD A. Preface to *Catalogue of the Mycological Library of Howard A. Kelly, by* L. C. C. Krieger, Baltimore, privately published, 1924. STEVENSON, JOHN A., "Louis Charles Christopher Krieger, 1873-1940," *Mycologia* 33: 241-247, 1941.

he began indexing the literature on the higher fungi. This index eventually contained nearly 400,000 entry cards.

Krieger returned to the Department of Agriculture in 1912 and worked at the Plant Introduction Garden in Chico, California, where he mainly painted cacti. In 1918 he accepted the invitation of Dr. Howard A. Kelly, a wealthy Baltimore physician, to resume studying and painting fungi. Krieger's ten years with Kelly were the high point of his career. He painted, of course; but also during this time he published several brief papers on fungi and on aspects of their illustration. He wrote the well-known article on mushrooms that appeared in the May, 1920, issue of *The National Geographic Magazine* and that was illustrated, in part, by 16 plates of his paintings. He assisted Kelly in obtaining a choice mycological library of approximately 12,000 items and compiled a catalogue of the library, which is still a useful bibliographical aid.

Kelly's library and specimens of fungi were presented to the University Herbarium of the University of Michigan in 1928 and designated The L. C. C. Krieger Mycological Library and Collections. Krieger was named honorary curator. Included also in the Kelly gift were many of Krieger's paintings of fungi. Of these, 331 remain at the University, including some of those used for the *National Geographic* article and some done during the years with Farlow.

Krieger left Kelly's employ in 1928 and the following year was appointed mycologist at the New York State Museum in Albany. During his brief stay there, he prepared *A Popular Guide to the Higher Fungi (Mushrooms) of New York State,* which was eventually published in 1935 as the Museum's Handbook 11. With only slight alterations, the book was reissued as *The Mushroom Handbook* by the Macmillan Company in 1936 and again in 1947. And now, Dover Publications, Inc., is reprinting the book with a new appendix listing nomenclatural changes since 1935.

In a biography published soon after Krieger's death, Mr. John A. Stevenson, of the United States Department of Agriculture, wrote that *The Mushroom Handbook* "was well written, carefully illustrated, and scientifically accurate and is one of the most satisfactory of the popular mushroom manuals ever issued in this country." This judgment remains valid. The book still will serve in the identification of edible and poisonous mushrooms. However, I consider it more than a field guide. With its intelligent and interestingly written discussions of many varied aspects of the biology and importance of fungi, it is really a mycological textbook for amateurs. Its bibliography and illustrations are especially helpful, and the 32 plates reproduce some of Krieger's excellent paintings. (Unfortunately, the paintings themselves, loaned by the University of Michigan Herbarium to the New York State Museum during the preparation of the book, disappeared and have never been found.)

Krieger once again returned to the Department of Agriculture as a botanical artist in 1929. His paintings were now of flowers and other horticultural and plant pathological subjects. Little time could be spent on mycology, but he was planning an atlas of paintings of fungi, another book on mushrooms for amateurs, and an illustrated monograph of *Boletus,* a genus of special interest to him. These plans were unfulfilled when he died on July 31, 1940.

Krieger's paintings of fungi stand above all else that he did. The published plates, in *The Mushroom Handbook* and elsewhere, are good, but they give only an incomplete idea of Krieger's abilities as an artist and as an observer of fungi. The paintings themselves are wonderful (in the true sense of that often misused word), and to see them is an unforgettable experience for anyone interested in fungi or in painting. Their beauty, their detail, and their accuracy are astounding. We should regret that so many of them were not published, while feeling fortunate that a few of them, at least, were.

ROBERT L. SHAFFER

Ann Arbor, Michigan
May 31, 1967

CONTENTS

[1]

ILLUSTRATIONS

The colored plates (excepting pls. 1 and 18) are from drawings by the author, prepared directly from nature. The two exceptions are imaginative productions based upon observations made in forests.

FIGURES

[5]

Figure 116 Sheep Polyporus, *Polyporus ovinus.*
Figure 117 Top of the cap of the Scaly Polyporus, *Polyporus squamosus.*
Figure 118 Umbellate Polyporus, *Polyporus umbellatus.*
Figure 119 Abruptly Bulbous Mushroom, *Psalliota abruptibulba.*
Figure 120 The well-known Meadow Mushroom, *Psalliota campestris,* brown, scaly variety.
Figure 121 Flat-capped Psalliota, *Psalliota placomyces.* Top view of caps showing the great number of fine, dark scales.
Figure 122 Flat-capped Psalliota, *Psalliota placomyces.* A splendid collection showing the double ring, the lower one radiately split.
Figure 123 Spatulate Sparassis, *Sparassis spathulata.*
Figure 124 *Spathularia clavata.*
Figure 125 Cone-like Boletus, *Strobilomyces strobilaceus.*
Figure 126 *Urnula craterium.* A stalked, *Peziza*-like fungus.

COLORED PLATES

*Plate 1 Frontispiece; Mushrooms in their natural habitat. The species shown are: *Clavaria stricta, Boletus versipellis, Cantharellus cibarius,* and *Amanita muscaria,* scarlet form.
Plate 2 Caesar's Mushroom, *Amanita caesarea.*
Plate 3 Fly Mushroom, *Amanita muscaria.*
*Plate 4 Panther Amanita, *Amanita pantherina.*
Plate 5 Destroying Angel, *Amanita virosa.*
*Plate 6 Sheathed Amanitopsis, *Amanitopsis vaginata* var. *fulva,* and *Amanitopsis vaginata* var. *plumbea.*
Plate 7 Edible Boletus, *Boletus edulis.*
*Plate 8 Bitter Boletus, *Boletus felleus.*
*Plate 9 Granulated Boletus, *Boletus granulatus.*
*Plate 10 Rough-stemmed Boletus, *Boletus scaber.*
Plate 11 Orange Chantrelle,* *Cantharellus aurantiacus,* and Chantrelle, *Cantharellus cibarius.*
Plate 12 Jack-o'-lantern or False Chantrelle, *Clitocybe illudens.*
*Plate 13 Abortive Clitopilus, *Clitopilus abortivus,* and its abortive form.

---

* Published here for the first time.

* Published here for the first time.

INTRODUCTION AND ACKNOWLEDGMENTS

In recent years considerable interest in mushrooms has become manifest. Even clubs for their study, so-called mycological clubs, have been formed in various parts of the country, particularly in the large cities. The Federal and most State governments have issued literature advising which kinds to eat and which to avoid. New York State may be said to have done not only pioneer but effective work in the accumulation and dissemination of knowledge concerning mushrooms. For more than forty years the late Dr. Charles H. Peck, former State Botanist, studied this group intensively from the purely scientific as well as from the gastronomic standpoint. His publications (Peck, 1872–'12), many of them long since out of print, may for the most part be found in the reports, bulletins and memoirs of the New York State Museum. Since these thoroughly informative writings are to be seen at the present time only in well-stocked libraries, it was thought advisable to publish a popular, illustrated guide to the higher fungi (in which are included the so-called mushrooms), a book which, convenient in size, would give reliable information about these plants.

It is not surprising that the public is interested in mushrooms. Several reasons exist. First and foremost, many are good to eat, as everyone knows who consults the bills-of-fare of the better restaurants. Some people, especially our Italian and Bohemian fellow-citizens, search woods and meadows for the spontaneous crop that is to be had for little more than the effort required in the picking. True, there are poisonous, even deadly, kinds, but these one can learn to avoid by acquiring a little knowledge such as this book is intended to convey.

Another attractive feature about mushrooms is that they take us into the great out-of-doors (Eyre, '04; Rayner, '06). Collecting the wild kinds is a truly fascinating sport. With a modicum of interest in their biological status and their classification, and with an appreciation of their beauty, both of form and color, one will return home thoroughly satisfied at having had a profitable outing, without gun or golf-stick.

What are fungi and of what importance are they in the economy of nature and in that of man? How do they compare with the green plants we see about us?

Fungi, of which the common mushroom is the most familiar example, are plants of a lowly kind. Yet they are of prime significance, not only in nature's economy but in man's as well. Where sufficient moisture and a favorable degree of heat are present they forthwith appear, be it as mushrooms in forests and fields, as moulds on cheeses, bread and other foodstuffs, as yeasts in the making of bread and alcohol, or as disease producers in plants, animals, and, alas, also in man. At every turn we meet them. Indeed, we cannot escape them if we would, either as our friends or as our enemies. The very soil itself, one of the chief supporters of life, would be sterile were it not for the continuous enrichment (humus) furnished by the fungi in their disintegrating effect upon the living and dead bodies of plants and animals. It has been well said that if fungi were suddenly to cease their destruction of the dead remains of plants and animals, these remains would, in a short time, clutter the earth to such an extent that there would be no getting about (Smith, A. L., '17).

The microscopic bacteria (also fungi, though they do not especially concern us in a purely popular work) are among the chief agents in this disintegrating process. No less important a service is rendered by certain kinds of bacteria in their work of gathering, or "fixing", the free nitrogen of the air in little nodules on the roots of certain leguminous plants used as green-manure crops (vetches, etc.). Farmers and orchardists need not be told of the

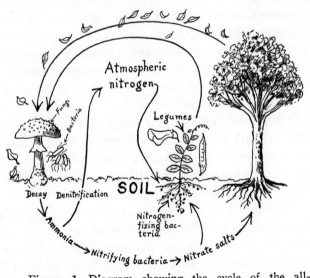

Figure 1 Diagram showing the cycle of the all-important nitrogen in its course through plants, soil and air

value of such plants in revivifying exhausted soils (figure 1). A curious relationship between certain fungous elements and higher plants, of value to man, also exists in a "fifty-fifty" arrangement entered into by fungus mycelia and some higher plants (see Mycorrhizas, p. 34, and Symbiosis, p. 36).

Fungi are plants, of course, but they are of a peculiar nature in that they lack the green particles (chlorophyll grains) found in the leaves of trees, shrubs, herbs and grasses. Only rarely do we find green fungi, and in such this color is due to other substances (pp. 32, 92). Certain plants, the lichens — those dry, sometimes grayish-green, crusty patches one sees on barren rock—would seem to form an exception to the rule. But lichens are not fungi alone, they are fungi that have formed another fifty-fifty arrangement, not with higher plants, but with microscopic, green, chlorophyll-containing algal (seaweed) cells which they hold in close imprisonment. Working together for their mutual benefit, these two organisms, aided by weather conditions, initiate the first steps in soil-making by breaking up the hardest rocks.

It is thus easily evident that fungi, and more especially mushrooms, are well worth the attention of all who wish to have somewhat more than a merely hazy notion of things in this interesting world into which, for so short a span, we are placed.

Little that is new to science is told in these pages, the various chapters and the descriptions of the species being based upon the authoritative writings of professional mycologists. Among the works drawn upon are those of Dr. Charles H. Peck; indeed, his descriptions are in most cases cited verbatim. Other writings freely consulted are those of Drs. H. J. Banker, A. H. R. Buller, F. E. Clements, W. C. Coker, E. T. Harper, C. G. Lloyd, W. A. Murrill, W. Phillips, J. Ramsbottom, and F. J. Seaver. Special papers and books are credited in the text by reference to the bibliography. To the late Dr. C. H. Kauffman, for many years the director of the Herbarium of the University of Michigan, and to Dr. Gilbert Grosvenor and Mr. John Oliver La Gorce, President and Vice-president, respectively, of the National Geographic Society, the author owes especial thanks for permission to reproduce many of the colored plates and some of the half-tone engravings, while to Dr. C. E. Cummings, of the Buffalo Society of Natural Sciences, he is no less indebted for allowing the publication of his beautiful photographs of a great variety of mushrooms. Dr. C. L. Shear coöperated most cheerfully by contributing from the files of the U. S. Department of Agriculture two colored plates and several photographs, and also by permitting the republication of various engravings. The chapter on mushroom culture gives a resumé of the researches of Dr. B. M. Duggar and Dr. E. B. Lambert, published by the same Government Department. For cooking recipes, Messrs. Harper and Brothers very graciously permitted the writer to draw upon William Hamilton Gibson's still unsurpassed book on mushrooms. Dr. H. D. House, the State Botanist of New York, not only constantly helped with advice, but made available for illustration, photographs by himself and by Dr. W. A. Murrill.

Though mentioned last, most important of all was the aid and unflagging encouragement received by the writer from the gentlemen who made the book possible: Dr. Howard A. Kelly, the writer's cherished friend and patron, Dr. Charles C. Adams, Director of the New York State Museum, and Mr. Charles M. Winchester, President of the J. B. Lyon Company, Printers. It is hoped that the execution of the task of writing and illustrating the book measures up, in some degree, to their expectations.

ABBREVIATIONS

p.=page or pages.

Fig.=figure (line engraving or half-tone).

Pl.=plate (in colors).

sp.=species.

μ (Greek letter m)=micron or micromillimeter (see glossary for definition).

in.=inch or inches.

Mon.=Monograph.

The Bibliography (p. 456) is referred to by authors' names, and date of publication of books or papers, as: (Harshberger, '17). All dates are given in full except those beginning with nineteen hundred. For these only the last two figures are given.

The reader is advised to consult the Glossary (p. 494) for definitions of unfamiliar, technical terms, and the Alphabetic Index to the Literature for the Identification of the Higher Fungi (p. 168) for references to books, papers and monographs treating of the classes, orders, families and genera.

FIELD STUDY OF MUSHROOMS AND OTHER FUNGI

A HUNT FOR MUSHROOMS

Man's interest in the plant world was at first, and for that matter still is, largely utilitarian. His first thoughts when regarding a plant were often: "What can I do with it? Will it nourish me, house me, clothe me or cure my ills?" In the world of green plants, of trees, shrubs and herbs, he soon found materials in plenty for food, shelter, clothing and medicine. But coming upon those seemingly unplant-like plants called mushrooms, he doubtless stopped short until through sheer curiosity, and urged by hunger, he made a meal of the first pretty cluster of mushrooms he found in the woods, and—was killed. It is not at all improbable that the fear of mushrooms, innate in most of us, is traceable to these early and oft-repeated sad experiences. The ancients called these plants excrescences of the earth. Even today, if anyone familiar with edible and poisonous kinds returns home from a collecting trip, his open basket laden with choice bits of fungous food, he is likely to be taken by the average person whom he meets for either a fool, or for some poor despondent who has ulterior motives on his own life, or, worse still, for one who wishes to dispose of others.

Enlightenment on their nature and uses was slow to develop. Early Greek and Roman writers, such as Dioscorides, Galen and Pliny, having only their food value in mind, divided them into edible and poisonous kinds, a classification still popular with people who distinguish only between mushrooms and toadstools (Buller, '14).

If one may judge from the remarks of persons of intelligence and education, one realizes that little is generally known of the classification of these plants and of the fact, that they have been, and are still being studied, with the same care as flowering plants. Foolish questions are frequently asked: "Is the peeling of the cap a sign of edibility?" "Do poisonous mushrooms blacken silver?" One, a mushroom wizard, went so far as to suggest that poisonous kinds always grow where rusty iron or rotten rags lie buried in the ground, and that venomous snakes, too, have something to do with their pernicious quality; that these animals, in winding their way through the woods, occasionally stop to breathe upon a mushroom and that, as a consequence, such a mushroom is instantly converted into a toadstool. Curiously, this legend goes straight back to the writings of the ancient Greeks and Romans, and to the herbalists of the sixteenth and seventeenth centuries, the latter slavishly copying from the former. It was not until early in the nineteenth century that serious efforts were made to classify fungi (Harshberger, '17).

To give the reader an idea of the broad lines of this classification, let us assume that on some fine autumn day, when mushrooms abound everywhere if weather conditions have been at all favorable, he is taking a walk in the country, accompanied by his inquisitive little son and by a friend well versed in mushroom lore (Charles, '31; Cummings, '33; Graham, '33; Krieger, '20, '20-a; McKenny, '29; Stover, '30; Thomas, W. S., '28).

Even before leaving his lawn he notes a clump of inkcaps (figures 2d, 83, plate 15) that was not there when he returned from his office the day before. His son, imaginative lad that he is, remarks upon the similarity of the caps to the egg of Columbus, sitting on end as they do before the stem lengthens.

"What do you call them?"

"Shaggy-manes, *Coprinus comatus*. Fine, fluffy, white things when young and fresh, they are delectable eating when stewed in cream and served on crisp, buttered toast. When old they are unsightly objects, as the caps dissolve into a black, dripping mass, only the besmirched stems remaining to indicate the spot where they grew. Shelley somewhat gruesomely describes this *passé* stage:

> 'Their mass rotted off them flake by flake,
>   Till the thick stalk stuck like a murderer's stake,
>   Where rags of loose flesh yet tremble on high,
>   Infecting the winds that wander by.' "

Around a spot where years ago a tree stood, in the far corner of the lawn near the street, a circle of pale mushroom bonnets has sprung up, each bonnet supported on a delicate, white stem.

"*Hypholoma* species (figure 95, plate 21); also good to eat," whispers his mushroom mentor. "There is not much substance in a single specimen, but coming in masses as this kind does, a saucepan is easily filled."

Even the old Elm, near the curb, has something growing upon the upper part of its trunk. Lifting little laddie so that he can reach the bunch of good-sized mushrooms, the eager hands tear it loose.

"The Elm-tree Mushroom; a species of *Pleurotus* (see *Pleurotus ostreatus,* figures 2f, 114); *also* fine for the table," from the mentor. "Now, you see, we are not ten yards from your doorstep, and you have already found enough mushrooms to afford you quite a respectable snack. But what's that under the old oak?"

Near the base of the tree stands a tall, stately mush-

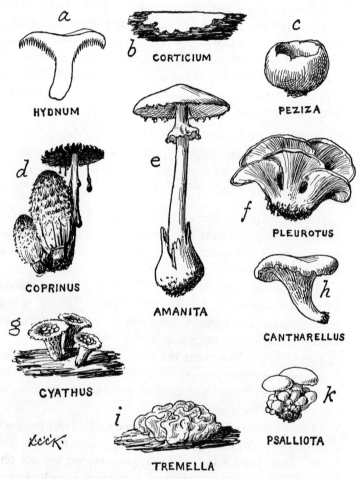

a
HYDNUM

b
CORTICIUM

c
PEZIZA

d
COPRINUS

e
AMANITA

f
PLEUROTUS

h
CANTHARELLUS

g
CYATHUS

k
PSALLIOTA

i
TREMELLA

Figure 2 Selected generic types of fleshy fungi

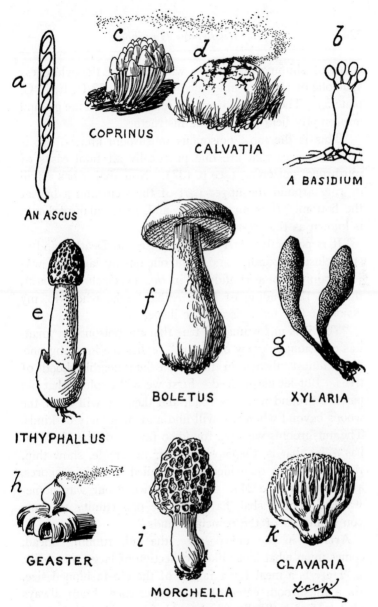

a

c
COPRINUS

d
CALVATIA

b
A BASIDIUM

AN ASCUS

e
ITHYPHALLUS

f
BOLETUS

g
XYLARIA

h
GEASTER

i
MORCHELLA

k
CLAVARIA

Figure 3 Selected generic types of fleshy fungi

[21]

room of shimmering, satiny whiteness, of the whiteness symbolic of absolute innocence (figures 2e, 37 D, E, F, G, plate 5). The lad who wants to remove it from the ground is promptly held back by the instructor.

"This is the most poisonous mushroom known. It is to this species that are due practically all fatal cases of mushroom-poisoning (see p. 137). Note that it has a frill or ring around the upper part of the stem and a bag at the bottom. It is an *Amanita,* and, in popular parlance, is known as the Destroying Angel."

"It is perfectly terrifying that Life and Death stand in such close proximity, and right out on my lawn. I was just gaining some confidence in *this mushroom business,* through the finding of these edible kinds, when, lo, my vision of fine feasts is at once dispelled."

"Yes, it is unfortunately true that the poisonous Amanitas occasionally grow on lawns," replies the knowing one, "but almost always in the immediate neighborhood of trees. But let us proceed. First we will explore that old pasture ground near the road, and then we will enter the woods beyond where we will find a great variety of kinds. The mushrooms we have found so far are of the kind that has gills; that is, the caps, on their underside, show thin, radiating plates on which the so-called 'seeds' or spores, are borne (figure 24). Before we wend our way homeward, I hope I shall have had the opportunity to show you examples of the principal kinds."

Arrived in the old pasture, the lad, running ahead, comes upon what looks like a collection of large snowballs.

"Here is a meal for a family of the old-fashioned size. As a mushroom eater of long experience, I am always glad to find puffballs (figures 3d, 74). The white flesh, as white as cottage cheese, should be cut into thin slices, dipped into egg batter and quickly fried in very hot butter, seasoning with a little salt and pepper."

"That sounds appetizing. But, tell me, are puff-balls also mushrooms? They are so utterly unlike the growths on the lawn and on the elm, that I am nonplussed."

"Yes, they are mushrooms, but of an entirely different kind. Whereas gill-mushrooms have stem, cap and gills, these are nothing more than large, more or less globular, bodies that develop their spores inside. At first the interior is solid and white, but with age it becomes soggy and of a brownish color. In the last stage, after the moisture has disappeared, there is nothing left but a dirty, tattered, dust-filled bag, the dust being the ripe spores. If you kick such a bag—." But the mushroom man is not permitted to finish his explanation; little laddie is already showing by actual and vigorous pedal demonstrations how the microscopic spores can be made to leave the bag in great brown clouds.

"Since I am particularly anxious to impress upon you this afternoon the different kinds of mushrooms, I am glad we encountered this Puffball, or Devil's Snuffbox. Puffballs form a very large group called the stomach mushrooms, because of the enclosed cavity in which they develop their spores. Over there, on that trash-heap under the willow, is another of the tribe. It is known as the Stinkhorn (figures 3e, 4, 59c), its odor being atrocious, carrion-like. Here—smell!" (figure 4).

"Brrr—*terrible!* But why all the flies about the green, slimy head? They are buzzing about it; great blowflies."

"They are attracted by the stench, and the spore-mass —that green, slimy, semi-fluid covering you noted—hav-

Figure 4 *Dictyophora ravenelii,* one of the stinkhorns

ing a sweetish taste, offers a further invitation to a meal. Incidentally, the object of this clever ruse of nature is spore-dissemination. The flies, in getting about, carry the spores on their bodies and in their excreta. Result,— more stinkhorns for more flies (see also p. 48). Dead Men's Fingers (figure 59a) are also stinkhorns.

"But see, here at our very feet, another of the Puff-ball group. This time, an Earthstar. This species is a veritable barometer. If wet weather impends, the points of the star open up and recurve, exposing the central spore-containing 'stomach'; if the weather promises to be fair, the points close (figure 62e). Now, to the woods."

The party has not entered far into these when the mushroom guide points out a *Boletus*. We will let him describe the plant, as his concise way of explaining so involved a subject as mushrooms is more effective, for the present, than scientific characterization.

"Indeed, what luck! Another kind to illustrate my open-air lecture. This is a true *Boletus* (figure 3f, plate 7). Note the underside of the cap; it is like an old, much-used pin-cushion in grandmother's sewing box; full of little holes, each hole the mouth of a little tube (figure 20g). See, how with ease, I can remove the entire layer of tubes from the cap. The general shape is not unlike that of a substantial gill-mushroom, that is, there is a cap and a stem. This species happens to be one of the most desirable, the justly celebrated *Cèpe* of the French; the *Stein-* or *Herren-Pilz* of the Germans. Note the exquisite, white network on the stem. You see, mushrooms address themselves to our esthetic nature, quite as much as do flowers and birds. Before we move on, turn around. Just back of you, on that Pine, is another tube-bearing fungus, one of the so-called bracket fungi (*Cryptoporus,* fig. 56d). It is a rather small species, but one of the most interesting. The tube layer being covered by a rather tough tissue, the liberation of the spores is effectually prevented until a small hole appears in this tissue, produced by tearing or perhaps, through the agency of a weevil (House, '14; Zeller, '15). In contrast with Boleti, which are fleshy, bracket fungi are hard, tough, and almost wood-like."

A few more steps and the three halt in mute admiration before growths that cover almost the entire length of a huge, well-rotted, mossy pine log.

"Coral," shouts the boy.

"Yes, coral mushrooms (plate 1, and figures 3k, 76, 78). If we were not absolutely certain that we are not dreaming, I should say that instead of traversing this forest, we are in divers' suits at the bottom of some tropical sea, viewing those animal growths your son has in mind."

"You say that these, too, are mushrooms?"

"Yes, but of a comparatively simple structure. The one on this log is very much branched, as you see. There is a still simpler sort that consists of a single club (figures 54b, 77). To give you a real surprise, I wish one of the Hedgehog fungi would favor us by appearing in our path. But we are not yet finished with this log. See what's growing here, under the far end of it. Feel how slippery it is, and how the light seems to penetrate the interior of its substance. We call these gelatinous fungi, owing to their peculiar consistency. This one is a *Tremella* (figures 2i, 5, 6). The group, a fairly large one, stands quite apart from those we have so far encountered, though

Photo by C. E. Cummings. Courtesy
Buffalo Society of Natural Sciences

Figure 5 *Tremella vesicaria*. Its white, alabaster-like body,
seen against a dark background, is a beautiful object to behold

Figure 6 *Tremella lutescens.* Witches' Butter well describes these little dabs of yellow, gelatinous fungus matter

[28]

related. Yes!!—your son is shouting over there. What is it?"

"Oh, dad! look! See what's on this log! Some more Coral!"

"Ah, my wish has been answered. This is one of the Hedgehog mushrooms and one of the most startlingly beautiful of the group—the Bear's-head Hydnum, *Hydnum caput-ursi* (plate 18). It is a close relative of *Hydnum coralloides,* a plant which so impressed one of the illustrious masters of the study of mushrooms, when he was a boy, that he decided to devote his life to mycology. Fries, his name—Elias Fries; like Linnaeus, a Swede.

"Notice the spines or teeth (figure 20h) hanging down from the multitudinous branches, and the pure whiteness of the plant, as it stands in relief against the dark, mossy, beech log on which it is growing. Some teeth fungi, like gill mushrooms and Boleti, have cap and stem (figure 2a, plate 19).

"The sun is getting low, so we had better be going homeward. Oh, good! here is still another group, represented by this queer, trumpet-like specimen, the Trumpet of Death, or Horn of Plenty (figure 86, plate 17). It has nothing whatever to do with death, as it is good to eat. Its group stands low down in the scale of mushroom development, for, as you see, it has neither gills, tubes nor teeth, but merely a smooth, or somewhat wrinkled, surface on which to bear its spores."

Returned home, the reader, guided by the advice of his friend, enjoyed such edible kinds as were found.

The following key, taken from Clements' admirable book ('10), presents in simple form the classification of mushrooms into families (for a more elaborate key, see p. 203).

KEY TO THE MUSHROOM FAMILIES BASED ON READILY OBSERVABLE CHARACTERS

I. Plant cap-like to shelf-like, with gills, pores or teeth, usually on the lower surface

  1. Cap with gills   *Gill fungi*

        (Agaricaceae, figures 2d, e, f, h, k, 3c)

  2. Cap with pores or tubes   *Pore fungi*

        (Polyporaceae, figure 3f)

  3. Cap with teeth or spines   *Teeth fungi*

        (Hydnaceae, figure 2a)

II. Plants without gills, pores or teeth; shelf-, coral-, club-, saddle-, cup- or ball-like

  1. Plant cup-shaped or saucer-shaped

    a. Cup leathery, with seed-like bodies inside

                   Bird's-nest fungi

        (Nidulariaceae, figure 2g)

    b. Cup fleshy, hollow   *Cup fungi*

        (Pezizaceae, figure 2c)

  2. Plant coral-, fan-, club-, saddle-, shelf- or ball-like

    a. Cap without minute pits or cavities in cross section

      (1) Cap jelly- or cartilage-like   *Jelly fungi*

        (Tremellaceae, figures 2i, 5, 6)

      (2) Cap fleshy to leathery, not jelly-like

        (a) Cap coral-, club-, saddle-, shelf-, or layer-like, rarely funnel-form

          x. Cap coral-, club-, or saddle-like

            (x) Cap coral-like   *Coral fungi*

        (Clavariaceae, figure 3k)

            (y) Cap club- or saddle-like

              m. Cap club-like, not distinct from stem; spores on basidia (figure 3b)

                   Coral fungi

        (Clavariaceae, figure 54b)

n. Cap saddle-like or club-like, distinct
from stem; spores in sacs (figure
3a) *Saddle fungi*
(Helvellaceae, figure 3i)

y. Cap shelf- or layer-like, rarely funnel-
form *Leather fungi*
(Thelephoraceae, figure 2b, plate 17)

(b) Cap ball-like, then broken by the lengthening stem, or cracking to expose the
powdery spores

x. Cap broken by the stem which carries at
the tip a more or less sticky, strong-smell-
ing spore mass
Stinkhorns or *Carrion fungi*
(Phalloideae, figure 3e)

y. Cap opening by cracks or by a mouth to
expose the powdery mass of spores
Puffballs
(Lycoperdaceae, figure 3d)

b. Cap with minute pits or cavities in cross section,
usually black and hard, or bright-colored and
fleshy when parasitic *Black fungi*
(Pyrenomycetes, figure 3g)

CONDITIONS UNDER WHICH MUSHROOMS GROW AND THRIVE

FOOD REQUIRED

Unable, because of the lack of chlorophyll, to manufacture for themselves out of the carbon dioxide of the air, out of water, and out of certain mineral salts the food they require, fungi, in order to grow and thrive, attack the higher, green plants that alone possess this power. In this respect they resemble animals. Like these, they must have starch, sugar, and other substances. Such fungi as are parasitic invade living tissues (see Parasitism, p. 33); others, the saprophytic kinds, are content with dead remains (see Saprophytism, p. 32).

SAPROPHYTISM

With few exceptions all fleshy mushrooms are saprophytes, that is, they settle upon and disintegrate plants already dead. A walk in the woods in the autumn will show them at work. Great tree trunks, lying prostrate, will be found covered with species belonging to a variety of genera (plate 1). Species of *Collybia, Mycena, Omphalia, Pluteus, Pholiota, Armillaria, Tricholoma, Flammula, Hypholoma, Boletus, Clavaria, Hydnum* and *Thelephora* find nutriment here. Scattered over the débris of the forest floor—on and amongst thoroughly rotted wood, branches, twigs and leaves—are troops of fungi, ranging from gorgeously colored and stately Amanitas to ever-so-tiny species of *Marasmius*. One of the latter genus, *M. rotula,* is always a pleasure to behold (figure 106). Upon a black stem, as fine as horsehair, is poised a delicately fluted cap, on the underside of which are gills so curiously attached to a collar around the stem that one is reminded of the workmanship of an extraordinarily skilled mechanic. Russulas, of a red so deep and transparent that a Titian or a Rubens would find himself outdone, stud the pathway as one wanders about regarding the wealth of fungus forms. It fills one with wonder that this scavenger work of disposing of vegetable trash is done to the accompaniment of so much unseen or unregarded beauty. Man, if he would, could take a lesson here.

One saprophytic species, *Lentinus lepideus* (figure 57e), specializes in the destruction of railroad ties. Very appropriately, it has been called "the train wrecker." Railroad men have, however, taken steps to combat this enemy of the unsuspecting passenger by impregnating the wood with preservative materials that prevent the development of destructive mycelia.

Polystictus versicolor, a common polypore growing in dense, shelving masses on standing tree trunks, may be parasitic as well as saprophytic. Its velvety Jacob's-coat-of-many-colors, marked with conspicuous zones, ought to recall it to the forest rambler (figure 44).

PARASITISM

Whereas the saprophytic, scavenger activities of mushrooms are necessary and welcome in nature's colossal laboratory, the parasitic, life-destroying activities, though equally necessary, are not so welcome, at least to man, in so far as plants of economic value are concerned. But destruction alternating with reproduction (construction) are the two great and eternal principles of the organic world as well as of the rest of the universe. The little, "hopeful" acorn of the White Oak, as it germinates, is not aware of the existence of a host of fungus species already lying in wait to kill and destroy the mighty tree of which it is the humble beginning (Farlow and Seymour, 1888; Saccardo, 1882–'26, vol. 13; Seymour, '29). By far the worst of the oak's enemies is the Root-rot, caused by the Honey Mushroom, *Armillaria mellea* (figure 69), a species equipped with an insatiable hunger for woody tissues, including those of our prized fruit trees.

Where are our chestnut trees that represented two hundred million dollars worth of lumber? With few isolated exceptions one and all fell prey to a fungus of insignificant size, introduced into our country from Asia. All that remains now of those magnificent trees are gray skeletons, naked and desolate.

The ravages of the Wheat Rust are so enormous that our annual output of this precious cereal is considerably reduced (p. 105). For the entire world the toll levied on our economic plants by parasitic fungi is almost beyond computation. Plant breeders and students of plant diseases, by their incessant activities, attempt to hold these ravages in check.

MYCORRHIZAS OR MUSHROOM ROOTS

Collectors and students have long known that certain kinds of mushrooms are constantly found under or near trees and other green plants. *Boletus laricinus* and *B. elegans,* for example, are always found under larches; *Boletus granulatus* (plate 9) and *B. luteus* (figure 70), under pines. Others do not limit themselves to specific trees, but occur either in coniferous or deciduous woods, or in both, while ubiquitous and omnivorous kinds, like the detested *Armillaria mellea* (figure 69), grow wherever there is wood to be devoured.

Some forty years ago, a German mycologist (Frank, 1885), after examining into the nature of this association between mushrooms and higher plants, found that the mycelia of the species studied form mantles of fine hairs or "mushroom roots" (hyphae) on the roots of their "hosts." He also stated that the relationship between the two plants is not one of parasitism, but rather one of mutual interdependence. These mushroom root-hairs he called mycorrhizas (p. 34); the relationship between the plants concerned, symbiosis (p. 36).

The question as to whether there is a perfect equilibrium in the life processes, working for the preservation of both fungus and flowering plant, is still a matter of controversy.

Mycologists distinguish between two kinds of mycorrhizas, one kind living on the outside of the roots (ectotrophic), the other within (endotrophic). It is conceded that the latter are beneficial to the invaded plants; indeed, certain orchids are absolutely dependent upon their assistance, as will be learned further on. The former are held to be mildly parasitic, at least by one school of workers.

The following mushrooms have been found to form ectotrophic mycorrhizas on the roots of trees:

Amanita muscaria, on Birch, Larch, Pine and Spruce.
Boletus badius, on Pine.
Boletus edulis, on Birch.
Boletus elbensis, on Tamarack.
Boletus granulatus, on Pine.
Boletus scaber, on Birch and Poplar; var. *fuscus,* on Birch.

Boletus versipellis, on Birch and Poplar.
Cantharellus floccosus, on Fir.
Cortinarius camphoratus, on Larch.
Hygrophorus russula, on Beech.
Lactarius deliciosus, on Pine and Spruce.
Lactarius piperatus, on Beech and Oak.
Russula emetica, on Oak.
Russula fragilis, on Pine.
Scleroderma vulgare, on White Oak.
Tricholoma flavobrunneum, on Birch.
Tricholoma terreum, on Pine and Beech.
Tricholoma transmutans, on Oak.

Consultation of the list of mushroom species under Habitats (p. 50) will offer further suggestions to the student interested in possible mycorrhiza associations (Hatch and Doak, '33; Hatch & Hatch, '33; Henry, '32; Kauffman, '06; Kelly, '32; Mason, '30; Masui, '27; McDougall, '14; Melin, '30; Mimura, '33; Rayner, '22).

SYMBIOSIS

Coöperation is the present-day watchword among enlightened individuals, corporations and societies, and, apparently, among nations. Competition, sooner or later, means the end of one or more, or perhaps of all competitors. Some plants learned to coöperate many eons ago. In considering the mycorrhizas, or mushroom roots, it was learned that orchids and certain fungus mycelia are dependent one upon the other. This is particularly true of a Japanese orchid, *Gastrodia elata,* which produces no flowers on the offsets of its tuberous rhizomes unless these have been infected by mycorrhizas produced by the rhizomorphs (cord-like strands of mycelium) of that arch tree-enemy, *Armillaria mellea* (Ramsbottom, '23). Frank's term, symbiosis, aptly describes this coöperative effort in plants, being derived from two Greek words meaning, "living together." Another well-known instance of symbiosis—the coöperation of fungi and algae in the lichens—was mentioned in the introduction.

TEMPERATURE REQUIREMENTS; SEASONAL OCCURRENCE

Every mushroom grower knows that temperature is one of the chief factors in the successful production of a crop. In fact the limits are very narrow, between 50 and 60 degrees Fahrenheit (see Growing Mushrooms, p. 121).

In the case of wild mushrooms there is a greater tolerance for both high and low temperatures. In the coolness of early spring—rarely in late autumn—we get morels, Pezizas and other Ascomycetes. Some, such as Boleti, occur in the hot summer months. (Is it possible that their capacity to endure the direct rays of the sun in midsummer is due to the unusually thick flesh of the caps?) The great majority of mushrooms grow in late summer and autumn. A sure sign of the approach of the latter season is the appearance of troops of Cortinarii. At the end of autumn and until well into the frosty days of November certain species of *Hygrophorus* of the Limacium group still hold their own. But these Hygrophori, especially *H. fuligineus* (for descriptions of species, consult the index), are well protected against cold by the thick slime which completely envelops the plants. One fleshy species, *Collybia velutipes,* grows in winter, the velvety coat of its stem and the glutinous exterior of the cap keeping out the nipping cold of December and January days (Graham, '26).

So much for mushrooms of temperate regions. In regions of a torrid or semi-torrid climate, like the hot inner valleys of California, fungi keep well under ground until their structural parts are fully formed and the spores are ready for dissemination. In *Podaxon* (figure 60b), for example, the cap, after having been perfected deep under the surface of the hot soil, is pushed up by a tough, almost wood-like, stem. In the tropics fungi of a tender, fleshy nature are rare, or they appear at high altitudes in the mountains. Extreme cold has an inhibitive effect upon fungous growth, though Buller ('24) finds that *Schizophyllum commune* is not killed by the lowest temperatures. Extreme heat, on the other hand, long enough applied, will kill the life-plasm.

Photo by C. E. Cummings.   Courtesy Buffalo Society of Natural Sciences

Figure 7 *Mitrula phalloides* as one finds it in its natural surroundings, in cold, boggy places in the Adirondacks

SEASONAL OCCURRENCE OF FLESHY FUNGI

	Dec.–Mar.	Apr.	May	June	July	Aug.	Sept.	Oct.	Nov.
Amanita					.....	.....	.....	.....	
Amanitopsis			.....	.....	.....	.....	.....	.....	
Armillaria					.....	.....	.....	.....	.....
Boletus					.....	.....	.....	.....	
Calvatia					.....	.....	.....	.....	
Cantharellus			.....	.....	.....	.....	.....	.....	
Clavaria					.....	.....	.....	.....	
Clitocybe				.....	.....	.....	.....	.....	
Clitopilus					.....	.....	.....	.....	
Collybia				.....	.....	.....	.....	.....	
Collybia velutipes	.....	.....	.....	.....	.....	.....	.....	.....	.....
Coprinus		.....	.....	.....	.....	.....	.....	.....	
Cortinarius			.....	.....	.....	.....	.....	.....	.....
Crepidotus					.....	.....	.....	.....	
Entoloma					.....	.....	.....	.....	
Flammula					.....	.....	.....	.....	
Galera			.....	.....	.....	.....	.....	.....	
Hebeloma				.....	.....	.....	.....	.....	
Helvella		.....	.....					.....	
Hydnum					.....	.....	.....	.....	
Hygrophorus puniceus, virgineus, etc.				.....	.....	.....	.....	.....	
Hygrophorus fuligineus, etc.								.....	.....
Hypholoma incerium, etc.				.....	.....	.....			
Hypholoma perplexum, etc.				.....	.....	.....	.....	.....	.....
Inocybe					.....	.....	.....	.....	
Laccaria					.....	.....	.....	.....	
Lentinus					.....	.....	.....	.....	.....
Lepiota					.....	.....	.....	.....	
Lycoperdon					.....	.....	.....	.....	.....
Marasmius			.....	.....	.....	.....	.....	.....	
Morchella		.....	.....					.....	.....
Mycena				.....	.....	.....	.....	.....	
Naucoria			.....	.....	.....	.....	.....	.....	
Omphalia			.....	.....	.....	.....	.....	.....	.....
Panaeolus			.....	.....	.....	.....	.....	.....	.....
Panus	.....	.....	.....	.....	.....	.....	.....	.....	.....
Peziza		.....	.....	.....	.....	.....	.....	.....	.....
Phallus					.....	.....	.....	.....	
Pholiota			.....	.....	.....	.....	.....	.....	
Pleurotus					.....	.....	.....	.....	.....
Pluteus				.....	.....	.....	.....	.....	.....
Psathyrella			.....	.....	.....	.....	.....	.....	.....
Psilocybe					.....	.....	.....	.....	.....
Schizophyllum	.....	.....	.....	.....	.....	.....	.....	.....	.....
Stropharia			.....	.....	.....	.....	.....	.....	.....
Tricholoma					.....	.....	.....	.....	.....
Volvaria					.....	.....	.....	.....	

WATER; MOISTURE CONDITIONS

As with all organisms, mushrooms must have water. The very low, almost alga-like, Phycomycetes actually live in water and in the juices of potatoes, fruits, etc. But ordinarily, mushrooms grow when the water supply is just sufficient for growth. Too much or too little effectually prevents or stops it (see Growing Mushrooms, p. 128). Every hunter of the common Meadow Mushroom knows that it is useless to look for this delicacy during a time of drought. He also knows that, given a favorable season of moderate rain and heat, it is equally useless to seek specimens in low, wet places, as, almost invariably, they are to be found on more or less elevated ground in meadows.

An old Italian investigator, and a modern one (Farlow), found that small *Coprinus* species sometimes grow in water, and certain Ascomycetes (species of *Vibrissea* [figure 49a] and *Mitrula* [figures 7, 47d]) grow on water-soaked sticks and leaves that have long lain in the cold water of mountain brooks and swamps.

LIGHT; PHOTOTROPISM

Though mushrooms as a class, unlike green plants, are relatively independent of light, there are some species that are unable to form caps and hymenial surfaces in its absence. A certain species of *Lentinus* (figure 57e), when growing in the dark, produces no caps but only oddly-formed stems; other species fruit freely in cellars, mines and caves (figure 29). As will be seen by consulting the list of species cited under Habitats (p. 50), some grow in the open, others in the more or less dense shade of woods and forests. One small dung-inhabiting fungus, *Pilobolus crystallinus,* is provided with a tiny, transparent bladder that functions as an eye. At the terminal end of the bladder is a black spore-case that is shot off with considerable force, but the shooting does not begin until the longitudinal axis of the bladder is in perfect alignment with the source of light (figure 8). Since this interesting little species grows on horse-dung, anyone can verify this phenomenon (Allen and Jolivette, '14; Buller, '21).

GRAVITY

If a large gill-mushroom in perfect condition—say, an *Amanita*—be left lying on a table in the horizontal position over night, it will be found by the next morning to have changed its shape. The straight stem will be curved, the upper end having assumed an approximately vertical position. The cap, which was left with its margin touching the table, will have resumed the horizontal position (figure 9). The cause of this spectacular phenomenon is gravity. Every plant must adapt its structures to the steady pull of this force. Just as the engineer, in constructing a bridge, must design its parts in such a manner that it will not be pulled down by the earth's attractive force, so a mushroom that similarly essays to construct parts above the earth's surface must arrange those parts so that the entire structure will not topple over. The problem with a gill-mushroom of the type of *Amanita,* in which a perfectly circular disk, the cap, is to be elevated above the soil in the horizontal position, is to have the straight, columnar stem attached to the exact center of the cap. Now, when such a specimen is laid on its side, the straight stem no longer serves this purpose. In order to bring the cap back again to the horizontal position, the

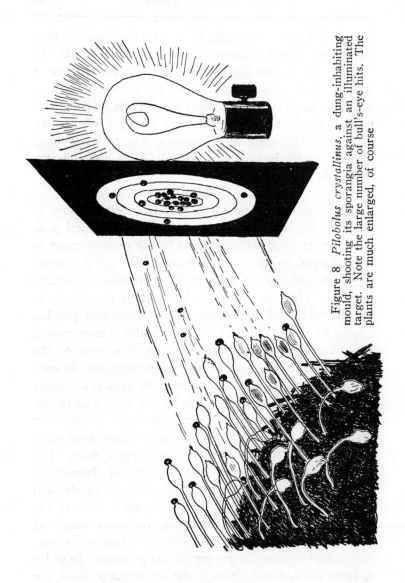

Figure 8 *Pilobolus crystallinus*, a dung-inhabiting mould, shooting its sporangia against an illuminated target. Note the large number of bull's-eye hits. The plants are much enlarged, of course

stimulus of gravity reasserts itself by curving the stem sufficiently to accomplish this.

The gills exhibit a like response to this force. In order that the spores may fall without coming in contact with the gill-sides on which they were produced, the gills hang down from the underside of the cap in the absolutely perpendicular position (figure 20a; Buller, '09, '22, '24). They do this so long as the specimen remains erect. When it is laid on its side, the gills, to regain the closest approximation to the **vertical,** fall over sidewise, those to the right falling to the right, those to the left falling to

Figure 9   A specimen of *Amanita muscaria* that has lain in the horizontal position over night.   Note the effect of gravity in causing the stem to bend so that the cap will again be horizontal

the left.   In viewing the gills of a cap that has lain undisturbed on its margin for a few hours, it will be seen that the uppermost gills have parted from each other, whereas those lowermost are closely pressed together to form what appears like the crest of a wave.   Artists, who wish to give their mushroom pictures a natural appearance, will do well to heed these truths.

The phenomenon of a plant's response to the earth's pull is called *geotropism,* that is, turning towards the earth. Botanists distinguish between two kinds of geotropism, viz., *positive geotropism,* which draws tissues or organs such as roots and gills toward the earth, and its negation, *negative geotropism,* which causes plant-parts, such as the plumules of seeds and the stems of mushrooms, to grow upwards and away from the earth.

FAIRY-RINGS

Some mushrooms have the habit of growing in circles called fairy-rings. Among these are such well-known New York species as *Psalliota arvensis* (plate 29), *P. campestris* (plate 29), *Amanita caesarea* (plate 2), *A. muscaria* (plate 3), *A. phalloides, Calvatia cyathiformis* (figure 73), *C. gigantea* (figure 74), *Cantharellus cibarius* (plate 11), *Clitocybe infundibuliformis, Clitopilus orcella, Cortinarius armillatus* (plate 16), *Hebeloma crustuliniforme, Hydnum repandum* (plate 19), *Hygrophorus virgineus, Lactarius piperatus* (figure 98), *L. torminosus, Lepiota procera* (plate 25), *Lycoperdon gemmatum* (figure 102), *Marasmius oreades* (figure 105) *Morchella esculenta* (figure 50b), *Paxillus involutus, Pluteus cervinus, Psalliota placomyces* (figures 121, 122), *Tricholoma equestre, T. panaeolum, T. personatum, T. terreum,* etc., etc.

Quite a formidable list, but best known are the rings formed by *Marasmius oreades* (figures 10, 11).

To be seen almost anywhere where there are extensive areas of grass, these rings have attracted the attention of man from earliest times. In the absence of a scientific explanation of the phenomenon, the imagination was

Figure 10 Fairy-ring formed by *Marasmius oreades*

drawn upon. Fairies were supposed to step "the light fantastic" on misty, moonlit nights, whirling around in circles as they danced, thus wearing down the grass. Gnomes and hobgoblins buried their treasure within the confines of such rings. Dragons, resting momentarily from the labor of scaring simple folk out of their wits, breathed living fire, thus scorching the greensward about them. Even "old Nick," when not at his usual devilish work, sometimes churned butter in such places, and so forth, endlessly. Later, seeking more natural causes, the then "scientists" thought that the rings marked the spots where thunderbolts had struck in the open, where a whirlwind had passed, where ants or moles had been active, or where haystacks had stood. It was not until the latter part of the eighteenth century that an English botanist (Withering, 1796) hit upon the real cause, the aforementioned mushroom, *Marasmius oreades* (Ramsbottom, '27; Rolfe, '25).

A fairy-ring is in reality a grass disease. Beginning from a point of infection, where spores of this fungus have started the growth of a mycelium, it spreads steadily outward (unless interrupted by lack of food), sometimes attaining a diameter of great dimensions (300 to 800 feet; this in the case of another species). In Colorado, rings, or segments of rings, have been found that must have taken anywhere from 250 to 600 years to form. The rate of advance of a ring varies according to conditions, the minimum being three inches in a year, the maximum about thirteen. The effect of fairy-ring mycelia on grass has been recently studied (Shantz and Piemeisel, '17). The initial stimulation experienced by the grass through the liberation of nitrogenous materials is shown in figure 11 at *d*. The grass becomes very tall and dark green. Following this zone is a bare one (at *c*) in which, owing to the packing of the mycelium, the ground is rendered impervious to water. Lacking this essential, the vegetation languishes. In the third, innermost zone (at *b*), the mycelium having here died off, water again becomes available and growth is luxuriantly resumed, even the bare zone being eventually recovered. At *e* and at *a*, normal grass before and after the attack, respectively. The active mycelium is shown at *f*.

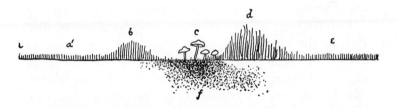

Figure 11 Cross-section of a fairy ring produced by *Marasmius oreades*. *a*, center of ring; *á*, grass in central portion; *b*, inner stimulated zone; *c*, bare zone showing fruit-bodies of the *Marasmius*; *d*, outer stimulated zone; *e*, normal grass outside of ring; *f*, the mycelium. Adapted from Shantz and Piemeisel ('17) who reproduce Molliard's figure

Three types of fairy-rings are known, the one just described, another in which the verdure is stimulated without the production of a bare zone, and a third in which no effect is visible.

The mycelia of fairy-rings are excellent illustrations of the perennial type of mycelium as opposed to that formed anew each year (see p. 80).

ANIMAL EATERS OF MUSHROOMS

Man is inclined to rate himself rather highly, especially in the realm of gastronomics, but, "there are others", creatures quite as selective, when it comes to "tickling the palate".

To begin near the bottom of the scale of animal life, the common slug does not pass by a mushroom that happens to stand in its slimy path; it halts and gormandizes until there is nothing left of the plant but a complete wreck, sometimes much to the disgust of the student who may have wanted the specimen for his scientific collections. Buller ('22) tells of the wonderful "smeller" these lowly animals have for a certain fungus.

Insects, too, are no despisers of a mushroom diet. Indeed, the larvae of some kinds may be regarded as among the happiest creatures on earth, for the mother, in depositing her eggs, seeks out especially tasty mushrooms that will serve as a food-bed for her progeny (Johannsen, '09–'12; Weiss, '22).

Certain large tropical ants, the termites, even go so far as to cultivate little, mycelial bodies as food for themselves. The "compost" is made of green leaves which are brought in by hosts of these intrepid mushroom growers. During a recent visit to Cuba, the writer saw a long procession of "bibijaguas"—*Atta insularis,* a termite peculiar to the island—advancing, Indian fashion, toward their nest, each individual holding a leaf-fragment aloft, like an umbrella, from which habit they get their popular name, "umbrella-ants".

The original observations on these mushroom-cultivating ants were made on Brazilian species of *Acromyrmex* and *Atta* (Forel, '28; Möller, 1893).

Advancing up the line of animal life, the tortoise occasionally stops in its leisurely peregrinations to take more than a look at the mushroom it meets. A friend of the writer once surprised this animal "red-handed" at the business of devouring an *Amanita!* He did not actually see it eating, but there was the *Amanita* with fresh evidences of having been picked at, and there was the tortoise, its beak still retaining tell-tale fragments of the meal! A jury would hang a man on evidence so conclusive.

But the prime mushroom eaters, short of discriminating humans, are the red squirrels (Buller, '20; Cram, '24; Hatt, '29). Specimens of Boleti are frequently found, their caps showing distinct signs of having been nibbled at by these rodents. When satiated, they store specimens in the forked branches of trees for future use (figure 12).

Figure 12 Red squirrel storing mushrooms in the forks of a tree branch. After W. E. Cram ('24)

They seem to prefer the substantial Boleti, but other kinds are also eaten. According to one observer (Metcalf, '25), even the poisonous Fly Agaric, *Amanita muscaria* (plate 3) is not despised. To the forester it is not news that deer and cattle are also fond of mushrooms.

Animals, in eating mushrooms, unconsciously aid in the distribution of the various kinds eaten, for in devouring the fungi they also take within themselves the spores which are later scattered far and wide in the excreta (see Spore Dissemination, pp. 23, 85).

HABITATS; WHERE MUSHROOMS GROW

General remarks. To say where mushrooms—and fungi generally—do not grow would be easier than to give even a few of their numberless habitats. That they grow everywhere except in fire and in boiling water would be a statement approximating the truth. The lower forms, bacteria and the ferment-producers, being omnipresent, fill the air with their tiny cells and spores that are ever ready to pounce upon both living and dead plants and animals. Sticky culture-plates, carried into the upper atmosphere by airplanes and there exposed, have caught up spores of the rust of wheat. The larger fungi, or mushrooms, occur on all substances that offer nourishment.

In a general way it may, therefore, be said that the places where their food plants grow, are also the places of their occurrence. Some grow only in the open, while others require sheltered, shady ground. Some grow under or on certain kinds of trees, while others are to be found in mixed woods. Many may be sought only on dung, while others prefer association with mosses, lichens and ferns. In a few cases they even parasitize each other (Graham, '27, '28).

The appended tabulation, in which a large number of

the species of fleshy mushrooms are classified according
to their habitats and hosts, should prove useful to the
beginner who, finding himself in any one of the situations
where the plants or plant associations indicated grow,
would like to know what mushrooms he is apt to encounter.
The principal omissions in the list consist of species that
occur either generally in woods the character of which is
not specifically indicated in the literature, or of species that
are too rare to be taken note of in this general account.

KINDS OF MUSHROOMS GROWING MORE OR LESS IN THE OPEN

On Mossy Rocks and in Rocky Soil

Hebeloma pascuense
Lycoperdon calyptriforme

Pholiota duroides
Psilocybe fuscofolia

In Gravelly Soil

Amanita spreta
Entoloma scabrinellum
Hebeloma velatum

Inocybe subtomentosa
Tricholoma infantile

In Sand or Sandy Soil

Amanita spreta
Boletus cyanescens
Boletus scaber
Boletus subluteus
Boletus versipellis
Cortinarius tricolor
Gyromitra esculenta
Hebeloma colvini
Hebeloma excedens
Hebeloma gregarium
Hebeloma parvifructum
Hebeloma sordidulum
Hygrophorus immutabilis

Inocybe maritimoide
Inocybe serotina
Inocybe subfulva
Laccaria laccata
Laccaria trullisata
Lactarius chelidonium
Lepiota arenicola
Naucoria arenaria
Naucoria lenticeps
Polysaccum pisocarpium
Psalliota halophila
Psilocybe arenulina
Tricholoma equestre

In Clayey Soil

Clavaria argillacea
Eccilia housei
Helvella infula

Inocybe rigidipes
Inocybe unicolor

In Alluvial Soil

Lepiota alluviina

Psilocybe limophila

Grassy Grounds Such as Lawns, Gardens, etc.

Amanita virosa
Amanitopsis pusilla
Calvatia cyathiformis
Calvatia gigantea
Clavaria inaequalis
Clitocybe dealbata
Clitocybe multiceps
Clitocybe sudorifica
Galera coprinoides
Hebeloma sarcophyllum
Hebeloma sociale
Hygrophorus limacinus
Hygrophorus pratensis
Hygrophorus virgineus
Hypholoma candolleanum
Hypholoma incertum

Lepiota americana
Lepiota cretacea
Lepiota cristata
Lepiota naucinoides
Leptonia hortensis
Lycoperdon pusillum
Lycoperdon wrightii
Marasmius oreades
Naucoria semiorbicularis
Naucoria sororia
Pholiota praecox
Pleurotus petaloides
Polysaccum pisocarpium
Psilocybe foenisecii
Stropharia coronilla
Tricholoma brevipes

In Pastures, Meadows and Fields

Amanita muscaria
Amanitopsis nivalis
Calvatia caelata
Cantharellus pruinosus
Clavaria vermicularis
Clitocybe aperta
Clitocybe compressipes
Clitocybe vilescens
Clitopilus caespitosus
Clitopilus novaeboracensis
Clitopilus orcella
Clitopilus pascuensis
Cortinarius vernalis
Entoloma grayanum
Entoloma sericeum
Flammula halliana
Hebeloma pascuense
Hebeloma sociale
Hygrophorus borealis
Hygrophorus coccineus
Hygrophorus laetus
Hygrophorus psittacinus

Inocybe subfulva
Laccaria laccata
Lactarius affinis
Lactarius piperatus
Lactarius subdulcis
Lepiota procera
Lycoperdon atropurpureum
Lycoperdon frostii
Lycoperdon gemmatum
Lycoperdon molle
Omphalia pyxidata
Panaeolus retirugis
Pholiota angustipes
Pholiota vermiflua
Psalliota arvensis
Psalliota campestris
Psilocybe semilanceata
Stropharia johnsoniana
Tricholoma albiflavidum
Tricholoma infantile
Tricholoma microcephalum

Along Streets, Roadsides, Old Wood Roads, Railroad Ties, etc.

Amanitopsis pulverulenta
Clitocybe aperta
Coprinus atramentarius
Coprinus micaceus
Entoloma grayanum
Hypholoma incertum
Inocybe diminuta
Laccaria laccata
Laccaria tortilis
Lentinus lepideus (on railroad ties)
Lentinus sulcatus
Lepiota procera
Pholiota aggericola
Pholiota temnophylla
Psalliota rodmani
Psathyrella atomata
Psathyrella graciloides
Psilocybe castanella
Stropharia bilamellata

On Burnt Ground

Clitocybe sinopica
Flammula carbonaria
Flammula highlandensis
Morchella esculenta
Omphalia fibuloides
Omphalia olivaria
Various species of *Peziza*

On Dung or Rich Grassy Manured Grounds

Bolbitius vitellinus
Coprinus comatus
Coprinus plicatilis
Deconica coprophila
Deconica subviscida
Galera lateritia
Galera tenera
Lepiota cepaestipes and its var. lutea
Naucoria semiorbicularis
Naucoria sororia
Panaeolus campanulatus
Panaeolus papilionaceus
Panaeolus solidipes
Pholiota vermiflua
Pluteolus coprophilus
Psalliota campestris
Psathyrella hirta
Psathyrella minima
Psathyrella odorata
Psathyrella tenera
Stropharia melasperma
Stropharia semiglobata
Stropharia umbonatescens
Tricholoma sordidum
Volvaria speciosa

KINDS COMMONLY FOUND IN CONIFEROUS WOODS

Arbor Vitae

Collybia fuliginella
Tricholoma thujinum

Balsam Fir

Clavaria abietina
Cortinarius coloratus
Cortinarius ochraceus
Inocybe albodisca
Mycena flavifolia
Omphalia olivaria
Pleurotus mitis
Russula abietina

Hemlock (see also under Pine)

Amanita frostiana (also in mixed woods)
Cantharellus cibarius
Collybia abundans
Collybia familia
Cortinarius castaneoides
Craterellus clavatus
Hydnum cyaneotinctum
Lactarius deceptivus

Lactarius plumbeus (also under Spruce and Balsam Fir
Mycena atroumbonata
Omphalia lilacifolia
Omphalia oculus
Psalliota placomyces
Russula sordida
Russula viridella
Tricholoma terraeolens

Pine

Boletus albus (also under Hemlock)
Boletus americanus
Boletus badius
Boletus granulatus
Boletus hemichrysus (on the roots of *Pinus palustris*)
Boletus luteus
Boletus pachypus (also under Beech)
Boletus subluteus
Clitocybe metachroa
Clitocybe patuloides
Clitocybe pinophila
Clitocybe pithyophila
Clitocybe subconcava
Clitocybe tumulosa
Clitopilus unitinctus
Collybia albipilata
Collybia colorea
Collybia conigena
Collybia expallens
Cortinarius autumnalis
Cortinarius distans
Flammula sapinea
Gomphidius nigricans
Gomphidius viscidus
Hebeloma excedens
Hebeloma parvifructum
Hygrophorus flavodiscus
Hygrophorus fuligineus
Hygrophorus purpurascens
Hypholoma capnoides (also under Spruce)
Inocybe agglutinata
Inocybe squamosodisca
Lachnocladium vestipes
Lactarius chelidonium

Lactarius cilicioides
Lactarius fuligineus
Lactarius indigo
Lentinus lepideus (also common on railroad ties)
Lentinus spretus
Lepiota fuscosquamea (also under Hemlock)
Lycoperdon glabellum
Marasmius androsaceus
Mycena epipterygia
Mycena filopes (under *Pinus rigida*)
Mycena pulcherrima
Mycena pura
Mycena splendidipes
Mycena tenerrima
Mycena vulgaris
Paxillus atrotomentosus (also under Hemlock)
Paxillus panuoides (also under Hemlock)
Pleurotus porrigens (also under Hemlock)
Pleurotus striatulus (also under Hemlock)
Pluteus umbrosus
Psilocybe atomatoides
Russula turci
Spathularia clavata
Tremellodon gelatinosum
Tricholoma equestre
Tricholoma flavescens
Tricholoma leucocephalum
Tricholoma putidum
Tricholoma rutilans
Tricholoma terreum, small umbonate-papillate form

Spruce

(Most of them also under Balsam Fir)

Clavaria abietina
Clitocybe sulphurea
Cortinarius biformis
Cortinarius castaneus
Craterellus dubius
Entoloma griseum
Entoloma salmoneum
Hygrophorus pudorinus

Inocybe castanea
Lactarius sordidus
Omphalia austini
Omphalia striipilea
Psathyra conica
Scleroderma aurantium (also under Hemlock and Pine)
Tricholoma fallax

Tamarack

Boletinus cavipes
Boletus clintonianus
Boletus elbensis (also under Spruce and Balsam)

Hygrophorus laricinus
Hygrophorus speciosus

In coniferous woods, but trees not indicated. (Those marked with an asterisk also grow in deciduous woods.)

Amanitopsis farinosa
*Boletus edulis**
*Cantharellus cibarius**
*Clavaria flava**
Clavaria ligula
Clitocybe decora
*Eccilia housei**
Flammula magna
*Geaster triplex**
Gomphidius glutinosus
Gyrocephalus rufus
*Gyromitra esculenta**
Hydnum auriscalpium

Hydnum imbricatum
Omphalia campanella
Omphalia rugosidisca
*Panus salicinus**
*Panus stipticus**
*Pholiota squarrosoides**
*Scleroderma aurantium**
Sparassis crispa
*Strobilomyces strobilaceus** (usually in deciduous woods)
Tricholoma imbricatum
Tricholoma vaccinum

KINDS COMMONLY FOUND IN DECIDUOUS WOODS

Alder

Calvatia saccata
Clitocybe subcyathiformis (also under birches)
Flammula alnicola

Russula palustris
Schizophyllum commune (also on other trees)
Trogia alni

Basswood

Crepidotus tiliophilus

Hebeloma velatum

Beech

Boletus pachypus (also under
    Pine)
Clavaria formosa
Hydnum caput-ursi
Hydnum coralloides (also on
    Hickory)
Hydnum septentrionale (also
    on Black Gum and Sugar
    Maple)

Hygrophorus russula (also un-
    der other deciduous trees)
Mycena cyaneobasis (also on
    Birch, etc.)
Mycena leaiana
Pholiota limonella
Pleurotus atrocaeruleus (also
    on alders and poplars)
Tricholoma columbetta var. C

Gray Birch

Boletus scaber

White Birch

Entoloma jubatum

Yellow Birch

Pholiota luteofolia

Birch, Kinds not Indicated

Pleurotus minutus
Pleurotus serotinus (also on
    Beech, etc.)

Tricholoma columbetta var. A
Trogia faginea (also under
    Alder and Beech)

Chestnut

Clitocybe illudens (also on Oak)

Elm

Lentinus vulpinus
Morchella esculenta
Mycena corticola
Pleurotus sapidus (also on

    Beech, Birch, and Horse-
    chestnut)
Pleurotus subareolatus
Pleurotus ulmarius

Hickory

Exidia glandulosa (also on
    Elm, Poplar and Cherry)

Mycena luteopallens (often at-
    tached to the nuts)

Red Maple

Lentinus approximans (also on the Groundsel Tree or Bush)

Striped Maple

Lentinus haematopus

Sugar Maple

Clitocybe truncicola
Hydnum septentrionale
Lepiota acerina

Naucoria firma
Pholiota albocrenulata

Maple, Kinds not Indicated

Crepidotus herbarum
Mycena adirondackensis
Pleurotus ulmarius var. *acericola*

Volvaria bombycina (also on other deciduous trees)

Mulberry

Pleurotus campanulatus

Oak

Armillaria mellea (also in orchards)
Boletus indecisus
Boletus separans
Calocera cornea
Helvella crispa
Hirneola auricula-judae
Hydnum erinaceus (also on Locust and Beech)
Lycoperdon leprosum

Morchella esculenta (also in apple orchards and near Elms)
Omphalia corticola
Pleurotus ostreatus
Russula ochrophylla
Sparassis herbstii (=*S. spathulata*)
Tremella frondosa

Poplar

Cortinarius alboviolaceus
Crepidotus croceitinctus (also on Beech)
Crepidotus fulvotomentosus (also on Maple)

Crepidotus haustellaris
Pleurotus ulmarius var. *populicola*
Tremella mesenterica

Rhododendron

Omphalia rhododendri

Willow

Galera inculta (also under alders)
Inocybe vatricosoides
Lentinus suavissimus

Panus salicinus
Pleurotus salignus
Psilocybe limophila

Also in orchards

Armillaria mellea
Exidia glandulosa

Morchella esculenta
Psilocybe conissans

KINDS COMMONLY FOUND IN SWAMPS OR IN LOW, WET PLACES IN WOODS

Boletinus cavipes
Boletinus paluster
Boletinus pictus
Boletinus spectabilis
Boletus scaber
Calvatia saccata
Cantharellus infundibuliformis
Clitocybe multiformis
Collybia lentinoides
Cortinarius squamulosus
Craterellus lutescens
Deconica semistriata
Entoloma cuspidatum
Entoloma flavoviride
Entoloma peckianum
Entoloma variabile
Flammula squalida
Hebeloma palustre
Hygrophorus basidiosus
Hygrophorus miniatus
Hygrophorus psittacinus
Hygrophorus subviolaceus
Hypholoma rugocephalum

Inocybe paludinella
Laccaria amethystina
Laccaria laccata
Lachnocladium ornatipes
Lactarius camphoratus
Lactarius deliciosus
Lactarius paludinellus
Lactarius rufus
Lactarius subpurpureus
Lepiota solidipes
Leptonia subserrulata
Naucoria temulenta
Nolanea clintoniana
Omphalia gracillima
Pholiota caperata
Pluteolus callisteus
Psilocybe limophila
Psilocybe nigrella
Psilocybe uda
Russula emetica
Russula fragilis
Russula palustris
Tricholoma thujinum

KINDS FOUND ON OR AMONG MOSSES, USUALLY IN SWAMPY WOODS

Hypnum

Galera hypnorum

Polytrichum

Deconica bryophila
Pholiota minima

Psathyra polytrichophila

Sphagnum

Eccilia sphagnophila
Entoloma clypeatum
Entoloma cuspidatum
Entoloma variabile
Galera sphagnorum
Hygrophorus m i n i a t u s var.
  sphagnophilus

Laccaria laccata
Mycena palustris
Mycena praelonga
Naucoria elatior
Nolanea delicatula
Omphalia gerardiana
Psilocybe uda

Among Mosses of which the Genera are not Indicated

Calvatia saccata
Cantharellus infundibuliformis
Cantharellus muscigenus
Cantharellus umbonatus
Clitocybe fragrans
Clitocybe media
Clitocybe sinopicoides
Collybia myriadophylla
Cortinarius coloratus
Entoloma salmoneum
Galera aquatilis
Hebeloma frmum
Helvella palustris
Hygrophorus ceraceus

Hygrophorus conicus
Hygrophorus chlorophanus
Inocybe infida
Lactarius paludinellus
Lactarius subpurpureus
Lepiota amianthina
Lycoperdon leprosum
Lycoperdon molle
Mycena odorifera
Pleurotus tremulus
Russula rugulosa
Tricholoma columbetta var. *A*
Tricholoma silvaticum

KINDS FOUND AMONG FERNS

Hygrophorus peckianus
Hygrophorus psittacinus (often under brakes, *Pteris aquilina*)
Inocybe nigridisca

Lepiota pusillomyces (ground under brakes)
Mycena amabillissima

KINDS FOUND AMONG LICHENS

Clitocybe peltigerina (among *Peltigera*)

Mycena corticola (among mosses and lichens on trunks of elms)

KINDS FOUND ON OTHER MUSHROOMS

Boletus parasiticus (on *Scleroderma*)
Collybia tuberosa (on old, blackened fungi, etc.)
Cordyceps capitata (on *Elaphomyces,* an underground mushroom)
Exobasidium mycetophilum (on *Collybia dryophila*)
Hypomyces chrysospermum (usually on *Boletus chrysenteron* which it turns bright yellow)
Hypomyces hyalinus ([=*H. inaequalis*] on young speci-

mens of *Amanita rubescens* which are completely whitened by it)
Hypomyces lactifluorum (commonly on *Lactarius*)
Hypomyces transformans (on *Cantharellus*)
Nyctalis asterophora (especially on *Russula, Lactarius, Cantharellus* and *Clitocybe*)
Stropharia epimyces (on *Coprinus*)
Volvaria loveiana (on *Clitocybe nebularis*)

KINDS FOUND INDOORS, IN MUSHROOM BEDS, HOUSES, HOTHOUSES, CELLARS, AND IN MINES, ETC.

Clitocybe dealbata (in mushroom beds)

Cortinarius intrusus (in mushroom beds)

Lepiota acutesquamosa (woods and conservatories)

Lepiota amanitiformis (in conservatories)

Lepiota cepaestipes (in greenhouses)

Lepiota cretacea (in hotbeds, etc.)

Lepiota rhacodes (in gardens and greenhouses, also on spent tan-bark in stables, etc.)

Merulius lacrymans (on building timbers in houses and ships)

Panaeolus venenosus (in mushroom beds; poisonous)

Peziza vesiculosa (in mushroom beds)

Poria vaporaria (indoors, on timbers)

Psalliota campestris

Pseudobalsamia microspora (in mushroom beds)

Volvaria volvacea (usually in hothouses or in cellars)

Xylaria species

FOREST TYPES WITH REFERENCE TO THE DISTRIBUTION OF FLESHY FUNGI

The forested region of the eastern United States and Canada offers a rich collecting ground for the student of mushrooms. The forests, still large in total area, though for the most part not primeval, are the characteristic form of native vegetation in ordinary soils except the most poorly drained. They vary in composition with differences in latitude, altitude, soil, etc. The most general types, correlated apparently with differences in climate, are the Alpine Meadows of the highest mountains of New England, New York, northeastern Canada and the Rocky mountains; Spruce-Balsam forest in Canada, across the northern border of the eastern states and locally southward on the highest elevations; Hardwood-Spruce forest, a semi-mountainous type widely distributed northward especially in the mountainous sections; Beech-Maple-Hemlock forest forming the main forest type of the Appalachian plateau in the east and extending northward into New England, New York, and the Lake States; Oak-Hickory-Chestnut forest, typical of the Piedmont plateau region, northward into southern New England and westward across the Ohio valley, Kentucky and Tennessee to the Great Plains; and the Oak-Sweet Gum-Persimmon forest of the coastal plain in the east and south.

The following tabulation gives the tree species most characteristic of the forest types mentioned. Numerous other species often occur associated with them but are less characteristic, less common, or not so useful in designating the particular forest type.

Oak-Sweet Gum-Persimmon Forest

Willow Oak   Sweet Gum
Black-jack Oak   Persimmon

Oak-Hickory-Chestnut Forest

Red Cedar   Hackberry
Hickories   Tulip Tree
Black Walnut   Sassafras
Oaks   Sycamore
Black Birch   Tupelo
Chestnut (where it has survived
   the blight)

Beech-Maple-Hemlock Forest

White Pine   Wild Black Cherry
Hemlock   Sugar Maple
Yellow Birch   Striped Maple
Beech

Hardwood-Spruce Forest

White Pine   Beech
Hemlock   Mountain Ash
Red Spruce   Wild Black Cherry
Balsam Fir   Sugar Maple
Yellow Birch   Striped Maple

Spruce-Balsam Forest

Red Spruce   Paper Birch (also abundant
Balsam Fir   elsewhere)
                              Mountain Ash

Alpine Meadows
No trees

On poorly drained soils the native vegetation is usually some form of swamp, either open marsh or wet meadow, or a shrubby or forested swamp or bog. In the latter cases the forest may be a mixture of Elm, Red Maple, and other species, or it may consist of more or less pure stands of Arbor Vitae (also found on dry limestone soils, and elsewhere), Tamarack, Balsam Fir, Black Spruce, etc. Alders and Willows are conspicuous components of a shrubby swamp nearly everywhere in the eastern and southern states, as well as in the region of the Great Lakes.

Still another special type of forest is that found on sterile sandy soil, widespread on the coastal plain, where drainage is usually exceptionally good. Such forests are often conspicuous for their abundance of pines, oaks, and chestnut.

Except in the northern and mountainous regions and in a few other smaller areas there has been a great deal of clearing of the forest for agricultural and other purposes, but the fragments of forest for the most part remain true to the foregoing types when the disturbances by man have not been too great. Total clearing, however, occasioned either by logging or fire, often results temporarily, at least, in an entirely different type of forest. In the Hardwood-Spruce region this may be of nearly pure Spruce or Balsam or of mixed poplars (aspens), birches, Wild Red Cherry, and other species. Further south and at lower altitudes the aspens, cherry, etc., are prominent, with oaks, pines, and Gray Birch especially abundant on sandy soil.

From the preceding paragraphs on forest types it might be inferred that, except where agriculture, lumbering, or fire have interfered, the vegetation is, in its general composition on any particular site, decidedly static. In many situations, however, the conditions seem to be just the opposite, and it is apparently only the most widespread forest types which are really stable over long periods of time. In less favorable situations (such as swamps, where drainage is poor; sandy land, where the soil is sterile, porous, and so well aerated that nutritive organic matter accumulates very slowly; or cleared land, where conditions of shade, moisture, and humus have been very much altered) the vegetation is often quite different, as has been indicated, but it is by no means stable. The level of swamps is gradually built up by the accumulation of the remains of the plants themselves until the soil becomes much less saturated with water; humus eventually *does* accumulate on sand, thus improving the moisture-holding qualities of the soil, and much the same thing is true of the cleared land, with the result that the plants of these situations are gradually replaced by different species, until finally the whole composition of the forest has changed and it has become, eventually, one of the types first outlined, or, in other words, a climax forest. Changes in the mushroom flora, of course, parallel these successional changes in the higher vegetation.

A summer rainfall of from six to twenty inches descends upon this vast land of forests and fields, causing fungi to appear in such numbers that the beginner is fairly bewildered. The habitat list (p. 51) indicates roughly what species might be expected to grow on or under the respective trees, and elsewhere. The kinds occurring in the open are to be sought, of course, mostly in settled sections of the country; those which grow on rocks or in rocky soil being most common, however, in the hilly or mountainous regions. Ferns and lichens may be looked for in woods or brush land.

HOW TO COLLECT, STUDY, AND PREPARE MUSHROOMS FOR THE HERBARIUM

Some collectors who at first go out merely to fill their baskets with edible kinds find that they would like to secure accurate knowledge about other species they encounter. But the study of mushrooms, if it is to serve scientific ends, must be done with precision, with a certain amount of equipment, and with a view toward the preservation of the specimens so that they may be consulted later in critical identification work. Suggestions for such work will be found in several papers (Burlingham, '17; Burt, '98; Cooke, '95; Morgan, 1885; Underwood and Earle, '97).

To do really effective work, the student should pick out a distinct area. If he is in the habit of spending his summer or autumn vacation in some camp or resort, let that be his collecting ground, not for one season only, but for as many as possible. In this way he becomes thoroughly familiar with the species occurring there, and should he leave a record in writing or in print (and, *nota bene,* preserve his specimens), that record will constitute a contribution to science.

In his room, preferably one with a northern exposure, he should have a plain working table large enough to hold the necessary books and a microscope, with enough space left over for a water-color paint-box and drawing board. It is also advisable to have a rough table on which he can spread out his freshly collected specimens, make spore-prints, and do the odds and ends. A loose-leaf notebook in which to enter observations must always be handy both in the field and in the laboratory.

For transporting specimens from the field to the laboratory, an ordinary splint basket with hinged cover and handles is suitable (figure 14).　Small tin boxes of the kind in which afternoon-tea cakes are commonly sold will be found useful in caring for very delicate specimens—Mycenas, Omphalias, Psathyrellas, Coprini, and the like. The bottom should be covered with wet moss to conserve the moisture in the specimens, and the lid perforated to

Figure 14　A convenient basket to take along on collecting trips

maintain aëration.　A stout knife will prove of service in digging out larger plants or in cutting away others that grow on wood.　For the tough, woody polypores even a hammer and a chisel will be wanted.

After a specimen with all its parts, above and under ground, has been removed, notes should at once be made on a little slip of paper giving the habitat, date, and serial number for that season. If the fungus grew on or under a tree, the kind of tree should be stated. Before placing the find in the basket, it is well to wrap it up with care in a sheet of wax paper of the sort used for lunches, not forgetting to enclose the habitat slip. In placing the specimens in the basket, the heavier should go in first, as otherwise the more fragile ones will be crushed beyond recognition. In going about in the woods, the basket must be kept closed to prevent injury from branches and twigs to the material collected. Before starting on the homeward journey, moistened ferns should be laid on top of the collections to slow down evaporation.

Arrived at the laboratory, the basket must be emptied without delay, the smaller, evanescent plants receiving attention first. Species of *Marasmius, Lentinus, Panus,* etc., can be laid aside for a while, as they are not perishable. The first can even be revived by the application of water. But Mycenas and Collybias should be studied at once, especially with regard to the nature of the margin of the cap. Note should be taken as to whether it is straight or incurved. The same applies to the smaller rosy-spored agarics, *Leptonia* and *Nolanea.* For further detailed note-taking the reader is referred to p. 226.

Whenever there is a sufficiency of specimens of a species, a fairly mature one should be laid aside immediately for the securing of the all-important spore-print. To determine a mushroom generically, it is not only necessary to make notes on the structure and external characters generally, but the color of the spores must be ascertained as well. To infer this color from that of the gills is likely to lead to grievous errors, and as these must be avoided in so fundamental a matter, a deposit of the spores themselves should be obtained (figure 15). As examples of species that are likely to mislead the beginner, *Amanita caesarea, Clitocybe illudens, Tricholoma equestre,* and *Tricholoma rutilans* may be mentioned. *All are yellow-gilled, but throw down white spores!*

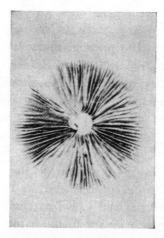

Figure 15   Spore-print of
an *Entoloma* species

A good print may be had by proceeding as follows: A freshly mature or maturing specimen should be selected, the stem removed by cutting it off as close as possible to the cap, and this laid, gill-side lowermost, on two sheets of paper, one white, the other black, the sheets being so disposed that both receive equal amounts of the spore-rain. The length of time required for the formation of a sufficiently dense deposit varies somewhat, but in an hour or two enough spores will have fallen to enable one to decide as to their color. A finger bowl can serve as a cover, otherwise the microscopic spores are likely to be blown about by air currents (figure 16). Some mycologists "fix" the spore-prints to the paper by gently spraying artists' fixatif on them with an atomizer, a fluid which is nothing more than white shellac dissolved in alcohol. At best, a spore-print loses its color, or gets

Figure 16 Cap of a mushroom placed on black and white paper under a finger-bowl, to secure a deposit of the spores liberated by the gills

rubbed and blurred. As it is very important to have a record of the color of the freshly deposited spores, it is advisable to match the print immediately with color-samples in a standard color-nomenclator (Maerz and Paul, '30; Ridgway, '12). This matching must be done by holding the area covered by the spores directly over and parallel to the color-samples, for the eye is readily deceived by color (Krieger, '14). The print may then still be kept, not fixed, however, but in a small, corked, glass vial. Preserved in this manner, microscope slides can be prepared with little delay at any time later.

The spore color definitely known, the determination of the specimen can begin. With a microscope having a magnifying power of from 100 to 700 diameters at hand, a fine cross section of one of the long gills should be made, mounted dry on a slide and placed under the objective. Water may be added later. The shape and surface characters of the spores, the basidia (figure 20c), and the presence or absence of cystidia, crystals, etc., can now be ascertained. It is also necessary to measure the spores, but in order to do this a small circular, glass micrometer (figure 24v), the value of the rulings of which having previously been carefully determined by comparison with a stage micrometer, must be inserted into the ocular or eye-piece of the microscope. This is easily done by unscrewing the upper glass of the eye-piece. In slipping in the bit of glass, one must always be certain that the rulings are on the upper side of the disk, and this side should be made easily recognizable by pasting a tiny bit of paper near the margin. In order to reveal exceedingly fine markings on a spore, an oil-immersion lens, magnifying about 1200 diameters, should be secured. This is especially true for the study of the spores of Russulas (Crawshay, '30). For the objectives giving magnifications from 400 diameters upward, the sections need to be exceedingly thin. Proficiency in cutting such thin sections with a very sharp razor can be acquired with practice. For the oil-immersion lens, the crushing of a thin section on the slide is the usual practice in the field, where an elaborate microtome is neither accessible nor wanted.

After one is familiar with both the external and internal characters of the mushroom in hand, the next requisite is literature (p. 164) in which to make a search for a description that tallies. The desirable monographs and books for the identification of North American species are listed in the bibliography (p. 456), while an analysis of these publications by classes, orders, families and genera is presented on p. 168.

A record of a species will be all the more complete if accompanied either by water-color sketches or by photographs. Sketches need not be masterpieces of art. All that is required for scientific purposes is a faithful rendering of the shape and the colors of cap, gills and stem, and of the various details present on these. If the student has little or no aptitude for free-hand sketching, a camera lucida of the hinged—not pivot—type can be used to advantage. When properly set up and adjusted to avoid distortion, anyone with a slight amount of patience and skill can secure the correct outlines (Krieger, '22, '26). Photographs should show different stages of growth, various views of mature plants, and of the gills, not omitting a good picture of a longitudinal section. Care must also be taken to get a correct rendition of the color values. Color filters and color sensitive plates will give these. When such filters and plates are used, exposure must be longer, but the time spent is well worth while, as an ordinary photograph is misleading as to these values.

No record receives full scientific recognition, however, unless descriptions and pictures are accompanied by the original specimens. Especially true is this if a student has been fortunate enough to discover what later may prove to be a new species. The preservation of specimens can be accomplished either by drying or by placing them in alcohol or formaldehyde. For herbarium purposes drying is commonly preferred. In the field the apparatus should be simple and effective. The best in both respects is a galvanized wire tray, suspended by strong cords from a suitable support. The tray should measure about 14 x 20 inches and should be 2 inches deep (figure 17). Ordi-

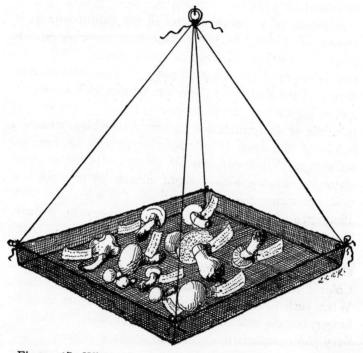

Figure 17 Wire tray for drying mushrooms. It may be suspended over lamps

nary kerosene hand-lamps, the flames adjusted so that the specimens will not bake or burn, should be placed under the wire tray in sufficient number to dry the several piles of specimens. No more than three lamps are required for a tray of the size recommended. The lamps should be kept lighted under the tray until all plants are thoroughly dry. Occasionally specimens that are nearly so may be shifted to positions where they will receive less heat. When completely dry they are ready for placement in small pasteboard boxes of which it is well to have a variety of sizes to take care of specimens of different size. The species boxes can then be stored away in larger genera boxes.

Some form of herbarium label (figure 18), giving only the most necessary data, should be adopted. By a num-

MYCOLOGICAL HERBARIUM
OF

ALBANY, N.Y.

No. *104*
NAME *Agaricus campestris*
HABITAT *Old pasture*
LOCALITY *Keene Valley, Essex Co., N.Y.*
DATE *August 20, 1928*
COLLECTOR *Arthur Smith*
DETERMINED BY *John Doe*
REMARKS *Grew in rich soil. About 20 specimens formed a fairy ring. Basidia of some specimens bisporigerous. See spore-print, painting, and 2 photos.*

Figure 18 Form for an herbarium label

ber, which should be the same for specimen, description, spore-print, drawing and photograph, the species can at any time later be studied or compared with others.

In drying, most of the insects and larvae inhabiting the specimens will have been killed. But it happens not infrequently that such enemies invade the herbarium later, in which case it becomes necessary to subject all collections to the vapors of carbon bisulphide. Five cubic centimeters of this poison in a saucer placed in an air-tight, tin box for three days will effectually kill the unwelcome visitors. Ordinarily, a pinch of naphthalene flakes in each box will prevent their molestations. The flakes should be renewed once a year, preferably in the winter.

The best arrangement of specimens in an herbarium is the systematic one. Then, at any time, the various species of a particular genus can be compared and studied. For a key to such an arrangement, see p. 203.

LIFE HISTORY AND GENERAL CHARACTER-
ISTICS OF MUSHROOMS

LIFE HISTORY

If, in a walk through the woods, one disturbs the leaf-mold, or rips away a piece of bark on an old rotting log, one is very apt to uncover a tangle of white, microscopic threads (hyphae), which may be loosely scattered, mould-like, feathery, or compacted into cords or flat, kid-leather-like sheets. This tangle of threads is the mycelium (figure 19). Commercial growers of mushrooms know

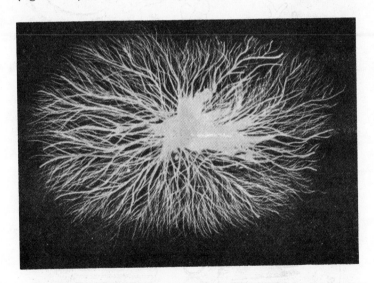

Figure 19   Feathery type of mycelium (spawn). In the center it is solidly compacted into the sheet-like type

it as "spawn" (figure 31). Timbers in old coal mines are often festooned with great streamers of it. In rare instances it is colored.

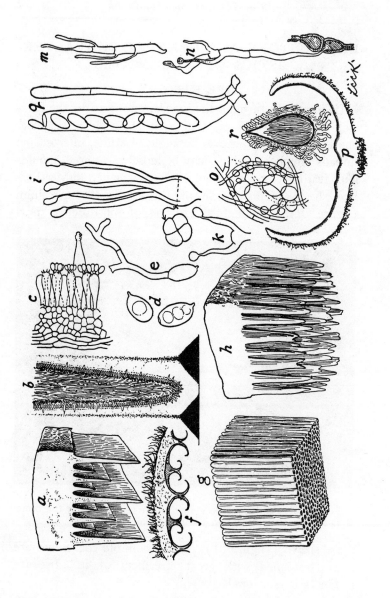

Figure 20 Diagrams of both gross and microscopic details of fleshy fungi, with a figure of a germinating teliospore of the Wheat Rust Fungus, *Puccinia graminis*, included. *a*, Section of the lower part of the cap of a gill mushroom showing long and dimidiate gills. *b*, One of the long gill sections somewhat enlarged to show the central, parallel-running hyphae of the trama, and on the exterior, the hymenial layer. The two black heaps are spore-deposits formed by the falling spores (directions for making a spore-print are given on p. 68. *c*, A part of the hymenial layer further enlarged. Proceeding from the left to the right one sees the long hyphae of the trama, the polygonal cells of the subhymenial layer, the club-shaped bodies (basidia) bearing little projections (sterigmata) which in turn bear a spore each. Intermingled with the basidia are the sterile paraphyses (shown in dotted outlines). The single, long body extending beyond the basidia and paraphyses, and bearing encrusted matter at its apex, is a cystidium. *d*, Two spores showing droplets (guttulae) within, as well as the small points (apiculi) which once connected them with the sterigmata of the basidia. The lower spore also shows a germinating pore at the upper end opposite the apiculus. *e*, A spore germinating and producing a single hypha, the beginning of a new mycelium. *f*, Section through the cap of *Schizophyllum commune*, showing gills divided along their edges. *g*, Tubes of a *Boletus*. Its spores are borne on the inner tube walls. *h*, Teeth of *Hydnum repandum*. The spores are produced on the exterior of the teeth. *i*, Basidium of *Exidia*, a genus of the gelatinous fungi. The cross-section at the lower left of this figure shows the four separate chambers into which the basidium is (cruciately) divided. *k*, Basidium of a *Dacryomyces*, another genus of the gelatinous fungi. *m*, Basidium of *Auricularia*, a genus related to the gelatinous fungi. Note the relationship in structure to the promycelium issuing from a teliospore of the wheat rust fungus, *Puccinia graminis* (*n*). Both basidium and promycelium are transversely septate, instead of longitudinally divided, as in the true gelatinous fungi. *o*, Vesiculose cells found in the fruit-bodies of *Lactarius* and *Russula* species. *p*, Section through the fruit-body (ascophore) of a *Peziza* showing the layer of closely-packed asci lining the concave inner side. *q*, An ascus enlarged. Asci usually bear eight spores, which in some species escape after a little lid (operculum) has been forced open. Immediately adjoining, on the right, is a single, sterile paraphysis. *r*, Perithecium containing asci. For microscopic details of some genera of the Gasteromycetes, see fig. 63; for figures of spores of some gill mushrooms and Boleti, see fig. 24

This mycelium, or spawn, originates from the spores (figures 20d, e), the "seeds" of a matured mushroom, but it may also be cultured from the tissues of a fresh, young plant. Formerly, in the production of commercial spawn, this tissue-culture method was followed (Duggar, '05). The mycelium is not the root system of a mushroom, as the layman might be led to conclude from comparison with the structural parts of higher plants; it is the plant itself, the mushroom above ground being the fruit-body, developed to produce and scatter more spores (see Spore Dissemination, p. 85). When conditions of moisture and heat are propitious, it grows and feeds on whatever substances it happens to be invading. Later, it proceeds to form a fruit-body or mushroom.

The first indication of a fruit-body is the appearance on the mycelium of little knots or knobs. As these knots or knobs grow in size, it is not long before one can discern a differentiation into stem (stipe) and cap (pileus). Usually the stem portion grows (in the case of conspicuous kinds of mushrooms) into a large globular body, with the cap, very much smaller and hemispheric, perched on top. It is at about this stage that the fruit-body is first noticed by inquisitive eyes. Mushrooms do not grow over night as is generally supposed. Much growth takes place in the soil and out of view. Development follows very quickly, however, after the new plant has become visible. The globular stem, a regular food reservoir, puts forth its energies in forming the cap (figure 37G) and its parts, the while becoming longer itself, in order that the cap may be elevated above the level of the leaf-mold or earth in which the plant is growing.

By following out the development of the common

Meadow Mushroom, after its appearance above ground, an idea may be gained of the development of all mushrooms of its type.

Once the elongation of the stem has begun, the next step is the expansion of the cap into a more or less flat disk. If one watches this step with care, it will be seen that a tissue, extending from the margin of the cap to the upper part of the stem, has been ruptured and torn. This tissue is the ring or annulus (figures 37Aa, Ba, Da, Ea). It is also called the partial veil because it hides from view a limited area of the cap, the underside, where the gills (or lamellae) are situated. In certain kinds, notably in the Amanitas (which include the most poisonous species known), there is an additional veil, the so-called universal veil or volva. This tissue, sometimes distinctly bag-like and again more or less loosely woven and crumbly, at first envelops the entire plant, just as the egg-shell envelops the egg. Through the extension of the stem this universal veil is burst open at the top to make room for the emerging cap (figures 37F, G, Db, Eb). Many species, on the other hand, lack both veils.

With the rupturing of the partial veil the gills become visible. These are knifeblade-like plates that hang down from the underside of the cap (figure 20a). In the Meadow Mushroom they are rather closely placed side by side, and are colored a beautiful shade of pink that slowly changes to chocolate-brown as the spores ripen.

The spores ripened, the development of a mushroom has run its full course; that is, starting from a germinating spore, the mycelium was produced, the mycelium formed a fruit-body (the mushroom proper), and the fruit-body—on its gills—gave rise to new spores ready to repeat the cycle, *ad infinitum*. Occasionally, in some species, the cycle is interrupted, and that at the mycelial stage. If, for example, conditions should become untoward (lack of nourishment, unfavorable moisture supply, or too little or too much heat), the mycelium may then go into a resting stage, forming small or large hard bodies known as sclerotia (figure 48a, at the base of the plants; 52c, base). A well known, very large sclerotium is the Indian Bread or Tuckahoe of the Southern states. It is usually found attached to Pine roots. Favorable conditions returning, the sclerotia proceed to form fruit-bodies.

Students of mushrooms (mycologists, they are called) also distinguish between annual and perennial mycelia, between such as are formed afresh annually from spores, and such as hibernate and resume their activities with the advent of the growing season (see under Fairy-Rings, p. 44).

If one has a compound microscope at one's disposal, interesting observations can be made on the manner in which the spores are borne on the gills. A thin slice of a gill—the cut made crosswise—will show that the surface (the hymenium) is made up of a number of structural elements (figures 20b, c). In the central portion are fine threads (the hyphae, in this position collectively called the trama) that curve outwards toward the surface of each side of the gill. The extremities of these threads, becoming intricately interwoven, form a layer (the subhymenial layer) upon which, in close array, club-shaped bodies (the basidia) appear. These basidia are the actual spore producers, each basidium bearing on its rounded end from two to eight (usually four) spores. The spores do not, however, rest directly on a basidium, tiny projections (the sterigmata) forming the connection. Scattered between the basidia are sterile cells (paraphyses, and sometimes cystidia), but these are of no particular concern in this rather sketchy survey of the structure of a mushroom, both gross and minute. It is important, though, to know about the basidia, as they play a fundamental part in the first division of all fungi into great classes. But of this, more further on (pp. 203, 230).

Gill mushrooms are not the only basidia-bearing mushrooms. There are others. First, there are the polypores, that bear them on the inside of fine tubes, the tubes taking the place of gills. Boleti (figure 20g), and the bracket fungi (figures 41, 56b, c) one sees projecting from the trunks of trees, are familiar examples of polypores. Then there are the hedgehog fungi or Hydnums (plates 18, 19). These grow their basidia on small, fleshy, spine- or teeth-like projections (figure 20h). Another family, the Clavarias, or coral fungi (figures 76, 77, 78), present either a single club or a mass of erect branches on which to rear their basidia. Still another group, the Thelephoras (figure 21), lacking gills, tubes, and teeth, give rise to the basidia on either perfectly smooth or merely wrinkled surfaces. The only representatives of this group we shall consider in the descriptive part are three common species, two in *Craterellus* (plate 17, figure 53a), the other in *Sparassis* (figure 123). (Cotton, '12.)

In the families just mentioned, the basidia-bearing surface (the hymenium) is naked and exposed almost from the beginning of the life of the fruit-body. These families are collectively known as Agaricales or Hymenomycetes, one of the orders of fungi. Opposed to them are the Lycoperdales or Gasteromycetes, the stomach fungi. In these the basidia are borne and matured within a sac. Some of the members of this order are very common in our woods and fields, so much so that there are few people who can say that they have not, at some time or other,

Photo by W. A. Murrill

Figure 21 *Thelephora anthocephala*

kicked a Puffball, or Devil's Snuffbox, to make it puff. This order is quite large, including plants of most varied form. Besides the puff-balls (figure 74), there are the stinkhorns (atrocious smelling objects, figure 4), the fairy-purses (figure 2g), the earthstars (figure 22), and many of equally unique structure.

Though differing in the manner in which the basidia are borne, the Agaricales and Lycoperdales have this in common, their basidia are invariably simple, and more or less inverted bottle-shaped, the interior being devoid of any partitions. In certain fungi of a gelatinous consistency, the Tremellineae, however, the basidia are divided

*Photo by C. E. Cummings. Courtesy
Buffalo Society of Natural Sciences*

Figure 22   An earthstar, *Geaster triplex*

by partitions, that is to say, the space within each basidium is composed of four elongated, separate chambers (figure 20i).   In *Auricularia* the basidium is divided into four successive cells (figure 20m).

Taken together, the Agaricales, Lycoperdales and Tremellineae constitute a vast assemblage of plants known to science under the class name Basidiomycetes, or basidia-bearing mushrooms (see classification, p. 203).

Contrasting with the Basidiomycetes is another equally large class of species, known as Ascomycetes (p. 203). In these we find an entirely different state of affairs, when we view the spore-bearing surface under the microscope. Instead of basidia that bear their spores on the outside, we find a layer of minute, densely packed, cylindric sacs (the asci, figure 20q), each sac containing from two to eight spores (usually eight). Common examples of Ascomycetes are the Sponge Mushroom, or Morel (*Morchella*), the Helvellas, and the cup fungi (Pezizas, figure 111).

The key and tabulation (p. 203, and the chart opposite p. 183) will give the reader an idea of the classification of the Eumycetes (or true fungi) to which the Basidiomycetes and Ascomycetes belong.

REPRODUCTION

Fungi, along with the seaweeds, mosses, ferns and liver-worts, are known as flowerless plants or cryptogams, the latter a word derived from two Greek roots, meaning concealed marriage. Flowering plants, in which special, usually conspicuous parts, the flowers, function in reproduction, are called phenogams or phanerogams, a word, also of Greek origin, meaning visible marriage. When fungi were studied with the same care as flowering plants, it was found that, though "concealed", sexual reproduction, in some form, is present.

Most seaweeds, long before there were any land plants,

had already developed so far as to possess two distinct, sexual elements, the egg, and the free-swimming, fertilizing sperm-cell. In the fleshy fungi, except in some Ascomycetes, and in those Basidiomycetes having two strains of mycelium, the method of reproduction through two structurally distinct, sexual elements was lost, only cell division and intracellular migration of cell-nuclei remaining, a simpler mode harkening back to the division (fission) of bacteria and to the budding of those tiny fungi (Saccharomycetes) which convert sugar into alcohol. Those species possessing two mycelial strains are known as heterothallic, the single-strained ones as homothallic. The very complex phenomena of nuclear division and migration are at present engaging the attention of an ever-increasing number of scientists (Buller, '09, '22, '24; Gäumann, '28; Gwynne-Vaughan, '22, '27).

Vegetative reproduction, that is, the formation of fruit-bodies from cells of the plant other than the spores, is readily induced among the gill-mushrooms. Duggar's ('05) tissue culture, for the production of commercial mushroom spawn, is based upon this mode of propagation (see Growing Mushrooms, p. 124).

SPORE DISSEMINATION

The spores of the fleshy fungi (figure 24) are tiny life units of exceedingly small dimensions. They are not quite as small as bacteria, but so diminutive in size that it would take a goodly number, placed end to end, to span the diameter of a human hair. Figure 23 shows a human hair placed (under the microscope) side by side with some spores of the Fly Mushroom, *Amanita muscaria*, and some bacteria. The fine dots near the spores are the bacteria. Some idea of the excessive minuteness of fungus spores is conveyed by this sketch. It will be realized why these little bodies are omnipresent. Every cubic foot of air, up to thousands of feet above the earth's surface, is alive with them, each and every one ready to fall upon some tree wound, on the soil, or on vegetable and animal débris.

Spores are produced in incredible numbers. Buller ('09, '24) has found that a good-sized specimen of the Giant Puff-ball, *Calvatia gigantea* (figure 74), pro-

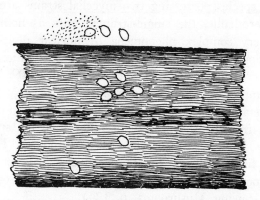

Figure 23 Part of a human hair, spores of *Amanita muscaria,* and a colony of bacteria, shown to illustrate relative size

duces 7,000,000,000,000 spores. A single specimen of the Meadow Mushroom, *Psalliota campestris* (figure 120), developed 16,000,000,000. According to these computations, the meadows of the world (under favorable conditions for spore germination) would be covered with a dense mass of these delectable delicacies. Spores evidently have their "up-and-downs" in this "cruel" world, otherwise we would not be able to get about for all the fungous growth.

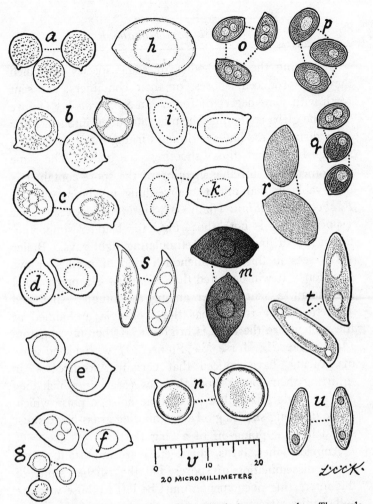

Figure 24 Spores of various fleshy fungi drawn to scale. The scale (of 20 micromillimeters, sometimes called microns, and designated in the descriptions with the Greek letter, μ) is included at the bottom of the plate. *a, Amanita verna,* 8 μ; *b, Amanita citrina,* 9–7.5 μ; *c, Amanita muscaria,* 7.6–7.5–10 x 7.6–6.3 μ; *d, Amanita caesarea,* 7.6–10 μ; *e, Amanita crenulata,* 7.5–10 μ; *f, Amanita russuloides,* 10–10.5 x 6.3–6.5 μ; *g, Clitocybe illudens,* 4–5 μ; *h, Lepiota procera,* 14–18 x 9–11 μ; *i, Lepiota morgani,* 9–12 x 6–8 μ; *k, Lepiota brunnea,* 10–12 x 6–8 μ; *m, Panaeolus subbalteatus,* 13–14 x 6.5–8.5 μ; *n, Amanitopsis vaginata,* the very dark, brown form, 11.6–12 x 8.5–11 μ; *o, Psalliota campestris,* 6.3–7.6 x 4–5 μ; *p, Psalliota arvensis,* 6–7 x 4–4.5 μ; *q, Psalliota rodmani,* 5–6.3 x 4–5 μ; *r, Naucoria semiorbicularis,* 12–13.2 x 7.5–8.8 μ; *s, Lepiota clypeolaria (= L. metulaespora),* 12.7–20.3 x 6–7.6 μ; *t, Boletus gracilis,* 12.7–17.8 x 5–6.3 μ; *u, Boletus ornatipes,* 11.4–14 x 4–5 μ; *v,* micromillimeter scale which is placed in the eye-piece (ocular) of the compound microscope. The values of the smallest spaces must be ascertained in terms of micromillimeters for each combination of ocular and objective (see p. 44). For microscopic details of other fungi, see Figs. 20 and 63

In leaving the fruit-bodies of some species on which they are produced, spores, or their containers, are sent forth with some degree of force. In *Sphaerobolus* (figure 61c) the gleba containing them is catapulted into space for some distance, the inner peridium turning inside out with a sudden movement, thus "shooting" the gleba. The same phenomenon of forcible shooting of the spore container is observable in that minute, horse-dung inhabiting species, *Pilobolus crystallinus* (figure 8). Here, the black spore sac (sporangium) is not "shot" until the bladder supporting the sac is in line with the stimulating light rays. Buller ('21) sees in this phenomenon a kind of ocellus or eye function. It will be noted that *Pilobolus* is a pretty good marksman, a sharpshooter among the fungi. Allen and Jolivette ('14) found that the sporangia are aimed at the spot where the light is brightest. Other investigators (Johnstone, '21; Morse, '34; Stone, '20), with a keen sense of hearing, have noticed that certain Ascomycetes, in squirting their spores from the sacs (asci) in which they are borne, do this with a perceptible noise, a noise which, to the little bug snoozing on a neighboring grass-blade, must sound like the going-off of a "big Bertha."

Animals (flies, birds, slugs, etc.) are important agents in the dissemination of spores, but the further study of this interesting phenomenon must be left to those who are sufficiently attracted to peruse the literature of fungi. (See Animal Eaters of Mushrooms, p. 48; also pp. 23 and 85).

GROWTH

Like all living things, fungi grow by increasing in number the cells that compose their bodies. A bacterium consists of but one cell. There is no further growth except by the division of this cell into two cells, through the formation of a separating wall. After this wall is completed, the two cells part company. In the mushroom, beginning with the spore, there is at once evident a growth by the accretion of cells to form a more or less complex body. The spore, falling upon a suitable nutriment-furnishing substratum, germinates, that is, it sends forth a single hypha (figure 20e), the beginning of the much-branched mycelium proper (figure 19), which then forms a fruit-body. By the production of more cells this body increases in size until the mushroom, as we know it, is finished in all its parts.

If, during its growing period, a mushroom is confined within a given space, as, for example, in *Amanita,* where the young plant is surrounded by a tissue called the universal veil or volva, then, with a steady increase of cells, such pressure is exerted that the volva bursts at the top to give freedom to the developing plant (figure 37G). In stinkhorns we have a like bursting of an enveloping tissue, the peridium or bag, containing the embryo (figure 58e). But in this case, what is nothing more nor less than a spring-like stem is held tightly compressed so long as the peridium can withstand the pressure. At length this pressure becomes so great that the peridium bursts open and releases the rapidly extending stem. This extension is sometimes mistaken for real growth, whereas it is only apparent.

The pressure exercised by growing mushrooms is often so great that strong materials are unable to resist it. It has happened that dense clusters of tender ink-caps have broken up concrete sidewalks. This is not an infrequent occurrence in newly laid out suburbs, where such sidewalks have been put down on ground but recently denuded of its arboreal covering. Mycelia are thus suddenly covered up, only to assert themselves in the production of fruit-bodies later on, to the great distress of realtors and suburbanites. *Scleroderma geaster,* to the writer's knowledge, made havoc in the cellar of a house in the District of Columbia by raising and breaking up the concrete flooring. An interesting case of drain-blocking by a fungus has also been reported (Smith, A. L., '20).

Another odd manifestation of growth is the inclusion of other vegetation within the tissues of fruit-bodies of fungi. In scouring the woods for specimens, not infrequently one sees a woody polypore, such as *Polyporus (Ganoderma) lucidus,* growing at the base of a tree stump, its substance apparently forcibly penetrated by grass, stems of herbage, and by fallen branchlets and twigs. Sometimes one has the good luck to see how this inclusion is accomplished. The soft margin of the cap of this species, in growing outward, meets a blade of grass, and, without disturbing it in the least, the tissues of the polypore slowly surround it until, after some weeks, the foreign object is well imbedded within the fungus. Compressed, the force of fungous growth seems well-nigh irresistible; acting unrestrained, it touches with the lightness of a pickpocket's fingers.

SIZE

Mushrooms range in size from almost pin-like species of *Mycena* and *Marasmius* (figure 106), to puffballs measuring as much as six feet in circumference (figure 74), and to bracket fungi (polypores) that extend out from tree trunks two feet or more (figure 25).

Great dimensions are a matter of comparison. In genera in which few species ever exceed half an inch or an inch in height, it is customary to speak of those exceptional species that are from six to ten inches tall as giants.

Photo by C. E. Cummings. Courtesy
Buffalo Society of Natural Sciences

Figure 25 A giant polypore, *Polyporus berkeleyi*

Lepiota procera, the Parasol Mushroom, sometimes has a cap measuring seven inches across, with a stem-length of twenty inches or more (plate 25). This is unusual in a genus where most species keep well within much smaller dimensions. Hence *Lepiota procera* is a giant species. The same applies to *Pholiota spectabilis, Boletus versipellis* (plate 1), *Clitocybe gigantea,* to *Psalliota arvensis* (plate 29), and to many others. Also, a mushroom that would be a giant in one genus might be a pigmy in another. Gulliver was a giant among the Lilliputians, but very much of a pigmy when he came among the Brobdingnagians.

COLORS, COLOR CHANGES AND SURFACE TEXTURES

Colors, bright colors, are commonly associated with flowers and the gay plumage of birds. It is not realized that mushrooms offer a gamut quite as rich and varied. Beginning with Russulas, all shades of red are to be had, from the deep-red of *Russula rubra* to the pale-pink of *R. fragilis*. The European form of *Amanita muscaria* has a cap painted bright-carmine upon which, like jewels, are set the white, wart-like fragments of the volva. A celebrated Scotch authority on mushrooms describes its beauty with the enthusiasm of an artist: "In the highlands of Scotland it is impossible not to admire it, as seen in long perspective, between the trunks of the straight fir trees; and should a sunbeam penetrate through the dark and dense foliage and rest on its vivid surface, an effect is produced by this chief of a humble race which might lower the pride of many a patrician vegetable." (Greville, 1823; see plate 1).

The oranges are to be seen in their full glory in such species as *Clitocybe illudens* (plate 12), *Amanita caesarea* (plate 2), *Cantharellus cibarius* (plate 11), *Clavaria fusiformis* (figure 54a), and in *Peziza aurantia*.

Yellows occur in all tints—from true spectrum-yellow to the faintest washes—in *Clavaria inaequalis*, *Hygrophorus marginatus*, *Hygrophorus ceraceus*, *Entoloma cuspidatum*, and in *Lepiota cepaestipes* var. *lutea*.

Green, so rare a color in mushrooms, is to be found in *Hygrophorus psittacinus, Stropharia aeruginosa, Russula virescens,* and in *Chlorosplenium aeruginosum,* which latter stains oak wood a beautiful shade of this color.

Blue, nearly as rare as green, colors the fruit-bodies of *Cortinarius cyanites, Mycena cyaneobasis, Entoloma cyaneum* and *Lactarius indigo.*

Lavender and violet, in various shades and tints, may be looked for in *Cortinarius alboviolaceus, Cortinarius violaceus, Tricholoma personatum, Tricholoma nudum, Laccaria amethystina* (plate 23), and in the gills of *Omphalia lilacifolia.* Purple, with a velvety shimmer, appears on the caps of *Russula mariae.*

White and black kinds are not infrequent, the former including the notoriously poisonous *Amanita virosa* (plate 5), as well as the innocuous *Tricholoma resplendens,* together with *Hygrophorus virgineus, Hygrophorus eburneus* (figure 93), *Lepiota naucinoides,* and the white form of the Meadow Mushroom (plate 29). Black, that is, jet-black, is known only in the Pyrenomycetes, in such genera as *Xylaria* (figure 48b), *Hypoxylon,* and *Daldinia* (figure 47f).

Color changes are equally attractive features in the fungi. Boleti, especially, are notable in this respect. If a specimen of *Boletus cyanescens* be broken, the white flesh changes on the instant to deep-blue. The same is true of *Boletus luridus.* The flesh of *Lactarius theiogalus* changes with equal rapidity from white to bright-canary-yellow; *Amanita rubescens,* the Blusher, and *Lepiota americana* (plate 24), slowly turn dark-red. Blackish tints are assumed by *Russula nigricans* and *Hygrophorus conicus.*

Gills also show color mutation, due to the ripening of the spores. Those of *Lepiota morgani* change from white, through dirty-green, to sordid brown; *Coprinus* (plates 14, 15) gills, from white to black; in *Cortinarius* (plate 16) species startling changes from violet or yellow to cinnamon-color are quite usual. The change of color in the gills of the common Meadow Mushroom, from "baby-pink" to chocolate-brown, is well known to all who gather this delicacy for the table. The flesh (gleba) of puffballs also exhibits a marked change of color as the spores mature.

Added to the colors and color changes, mushrooms have coats of all degrees of texture. Some, like the viscid *Hygrophorus* species, are covered with a glutinous slime, whereas *Amanita virosa* and *Tricholoma resplendens* have satiny caps. Velvet, soft to the touch and deep-brown. clothes *Lactarius lignyotus, Lentinus velutinus,* and the stem of *Collybia velutipes. Panus strigosus* and certain tropical species of *Hexagona* bristle with hairs, whereas *Boletus ravenelii, Lepiota cepaestipes* (figure. 101), and *Amanita wellsii* are dusted with powder. Tufts, or pyramid-shaped warts, arise from the caps of *Lepiota acutesquamosa, Amanita strobiliformis* and *Strobilomyces strobilaceus* (figures 55c, 125). Indeed, the colors and textures of mushrooms are so varied and beautiful that an artist cannot well resist their portrayal in terms of paint.

ODORS

In the matter of odors, mushrooms vie with the fragrance of flowers and with the insupportable effluvium of Limburger cheese raised to the nth degree. It is always a pleasure to treat the olfactories to the delicate anise-like aroma of *Clitocybe odora*, whereas the horrible odors of stinkhorns (figure 4), and of *Hygrophorus mephiticus*, are nothing less than an insult to these organs.

Species whose odors have been more or less definitely described are:

Amanita chlorinosma, like chloride of lime.

Amanita virosa, like an old potato cellar.

Clitocybe odora, like anise.

Cortinarius argentatus, like chestnut blossoms.

Entoloma nidorosum, alkaline.

Hygrophorus mephiticus, like skunk.

Ithyphallus impudicus, like carrion.

Lactarius camphoratus, like dried melilot.

Lactarius glyciosmus, alcoholic.

Lactarius volemus, when old, like rotting fish.

Lentinus suavissimus, sweet, agreeable.

Lepiota acutesquamosa, like old oil-rags.

Lepiota cristata, fishy.

Lepiota procera, when dried, agreeable, not unlike Slippery Elm.

Marasmius scorodonius, like garlic.

Mutinus caninus, nauseating.

Mycena alcalina, alkaline.

Nolanea suaveolens, agreeable, like dried melilot.

Psalliota arvensis, sweet, like almonds.

Psalliota campestris, agreeable.

Psalliota subrufescens, sweet, like almonds.

Psathyrella odorata, like Poison Elder.

Russula xerampelina, when old, like rotting fish.

Strobilomyces strobilaceus, strong when old, not unlike camphor.

Mycologists would welcome an instrument that automatically registers odors—an *odorimeter.* A *saporimeter* would also find a place in the laboratory, for tastes are even more elusive, when it comes to defining them in scientific language.

TASTE

If odors are difficult to describe, taste—except as to mildness, sweetness, sourness, and peppery quality—is almost impossible. There is an old German adage—tastes differ, otherwise moths would not eat cloth—which points out rather quaintly the element of personal equation that enters into any attempt to state in words what the palate experiences. To group a few mushrooms roughly into mild, sweet, and peppery kinds, the following classification may serve:

MILD

Coprinus comatus	*Pleurotus ulmarius*
Lepiota naucinoides	*Polyporus frondosus*
Lepiota procera	*Polyporus umbellatus*
Lepiota rhacodes	*Psalliota campestris*
Morchella esculenta	*Russula alutacea*
Pleurotus ostreatus	

In short, all species that are ordinarily recommended as edible.

SWEET

Psalliota arvensis	*Psalliota subrufescens*

PEPPERY OR OTHERWISE OBJECTIONABLE

Amanita muscaria (said to produce a peculiar, indefinable, raw sensation when swallowed)

Armillaria mellea (tastes markedly of tannic acid, when eaten in the uncooked state)

Lactarius piperatus (very peppery when eaten raw)

Lentinus velutinus (sharper even than Cayenne pepper)

Russula emetica, and certain other species of the genus,—very peppery

Taste, it must be remarked here with emphasis, is not a safe guide as to edible or poisonous qualities. Peppery kinds, such as *Lactarius piperatus,* lose their sharp taste in cooking, while the deadliest of all mushrooms, *Amanita phalloides,* is said to give no forewarning to the eater of his almost certain doom.

EXUDATIONS

Some species exude a watery or milky juice. This is especially true of all members of the genus *Lactarius* (figure 97). The degree of copiousness, the taste, the color, and the change in color of this milk, or latex, constitute characteristics that help materially in the identification of the species. In *Lactarius volemus* the fluid is white, mild, sticky, and so abundant that, on the slightest injury to the plant, it gushes forth instantly in large drops. *Lactarius piperatus* also has white, rather plentiful milk, which is so extremely peppery that a tingling sensation is felt by the tongue for some time after the last morsel of the fungus has been spat out. Other *Lactarius* species have colored milk. In *Lactarius indigo* it is deep-blue, in *L. subpurpureus* dark-purple, in *L. deliciosus* orange, in

L. chelidonium saffron-yellow. Species noted for color changes in the milk are *Lactarius uvidus* (white to lilac), *L. theiogalus, L. chrysorrheus* and *L. resimus* (white to bright-yellow).

Certain Mycenas contain juice that readily exudes. If the stems of *Mycena haematopus* (figure 108), *M. sanguinolenta,* and *M. anomala* be broken, a dark-red fluid promptly appears in droplets. *Mycena galopus* has a white, *M. crocata* a yellow-orange exudate. The edges of the gills in *Hypholoma velutinum* and *H. lacrymabundum* are beautifully beaded with minute, gem-like droplets (figure 57k). In *Coprinus* species the gills, on the ripening of the spores, liquefy, or deliquesce (figure 2d). This is not decay, as one might be led to suppose, but a natural physiological process, called autodigestion (Buller, '09, '24). The gills of *Russula foetens* often bear large, ruby-red globules of moisture.

Boleti of the Viscipelles group show resinous granules on tube-mouths and stems (plate 9).

The Dry-rot Fungus, *Merulius lacrymans,* does what its specific name indicates, it weeps. It is the common enemy of building timbers where these are exposed to moisture that has no chance to evaporate, as in damp cellars. It belongs to the polypores and is of a gelatinous consistency. Among the tough, woody kinds, *Polyporus berkeleyi* (figure 25) and *P. schweinitzii* sometimes have their tube-surfaces studded with glistening drops of moisture.

In the puffballs, the above mentioned phenomenon of deliquescence is a marked feature that accompanies the ripening of the spores. The interior mass or gleba, is at first white, but as the ripening process begins, drops of a yellowish-brown fluid issue forth when the fruit-body is cut. Continued deliquescence makes the entire gleba wet and soggy. Finally it dries, and the spores are then ready to escape into the air, either through a single apical mouth (*Lycoperdon,* figure 61a), or through cracks and fissures extending over the entire upper part of the plant (*Calvatia,* figure 3d).

BIO-LUMINESCENCE

Much has been published of late, in scientific books and journals, as well as in the popular press, about the production of light by various organisms, including mushrooms. Bacterium lamps, powerful enough to see by, may come to be a reality. *Bacterium phosphoreum,* for example, when cultured in flasks, gives out a light strong enough to enable one to recognize a person about six feet away (Buller, '09, '24). Meat, fish, and cabbage sometimes develop luminous spots due to bacteria. But conspicuous for light production is the mycelium of *Armillaria mellea* (figure 69), the so-called Honey Mushroom. In removing the bark from rotting logs in the forest, at night, bright, flashing areas of this mycelium may be uncovered —the so-called Fox Fire. The fruit-bodies themselves are not luminescent. To see such, one must secure young specimens of the Jack-o'-lantern, *Clitocybe illudens* (plate 12). Placed in a dark room, a soft, greenish light is seen to emanate from the gills. It is not very strong, but if one remains in the room until the eyes have adapted themselves to the darkness, it becomes clearly visible. A stronger light issues from the gills of a Japanese species, *Pleurotus japonicus,* a single fruit-body giving enough illumination to enable one to see Roman letters about four-tenths of an inch wide.

Other American species that possess the power of generating light, either from their mycelium or from parts of the fruit-body, are: *Boletus edulis* (plate 7), *Collybia longipes, Collybia tuberosa, Corticium caeruleum, Fomes annosus, Panus stipticus* forma *luminescens, Polyporus caudicinus, Polyporus sulphureus* (plate 28), *Trametes pini,* and *Xylaria hypoxylon* (Murrill, '15).

MUSHROOM MONSTROSITIES

As with all organisms, mushrooms are given to the production of occasional, abnormal forms called monstrosities, which may be due to the attack of parasites, or to just natural, misdirected or wild growth—a kind of mushroom cancer. *Collybia maculata* (Alb. and Schw.), normally provided with the usual radiating gills, has been known to produce them in tiers encircling the stem, after the fashion of the genus *Cyclomyces* (figure 56a). For this *Collybia,* the writer ('27) has reported another abnormality, which consisted of a single club with no gill development whatever. *Armillaria mellea* and *Clitopilus abortivus* (figure 80, plate 13) frequently exhibit such deformations. *Collybia dryophila* has been seen to produce minute, gilled caps on the inner extremities of the regular gills. *Cantharellus cibarius* (plate 11) and certain species of *Russula* (plate 31) sometimes have additional gills or caps on the top of the original cap. Also, it is not an infrequent occurrence to see two specimens fused or grown together, like the noted Siamese twins. Two stinkhorns are sometimes found growing in one "egg", and a *Cortinarius* species (*C. scutulatus*) is on record as having produced a cap so deformed as to resemble the pitted cap of a morel (plate 26). *Lactarius* species are frequently disguised beyond recognition by the attack of *Hypomyces* species (figure 46a). The same is true of *Amanita rubescens* and *Boletus chrysenteron*. A case of adhesion of two specimens of *Boletus pallidus* is shown in figure 26. The normal development of the younger specimen was entirely prevented. *Clavaria fusiformis* (figure 54a), is also subject to malformation. More instances of malformation could be adduced, but enough have been mentioned to show that mushrooms have "bodily troubles", just as we have ours (Ulbrich, '26).

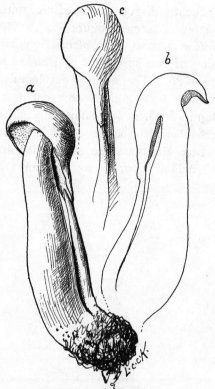

Figure 26 *Boletus pallidus*, malformed. What was to be the cap of
the younger specimen adhered to the
margin of the older one. *a,* view
showing the tube surface of the older
specimen. *b,* longitudinal section
showing how the flesh of the two
specimens became continuous. *c,*
another view showing how the marginal portion of the cap of the older
specimen was pulled down. Specimens in the herbarium of the University of Michigan (The Louis C. C.
Krieger Mycological Library and Collections, No. 41)

ECONOMIC IMPORTANCE OF FUNGI

EDIBLE SPECIES

The wild-growing kinds are not of economic importance in this country, except with certain recent immigrants, chiefly from Russia and southern Europe. The average American of "Nordic" stock either does not care for mushrooms at all, or he stands in such mortal fear of the wild kinds that nothing could tempt him to eat one of these. In most continental European cities of any size, the wild forms are sold in the public markets, being brought there by country people. But before they are offered for sale, each lot is carefully looked over by an official expert for the purpose of excluding any poisonous or deleterious kinds. The number sold each season runs into thousands of pounds, the price varying with the desirability of the species. In Munich, during the summer and fall of 1901, 1,850,000 pounds of wild-growing mushrooms were sold (Duggar, '15).

With us the consumption of mushrooms is restricted to the French "champignons", to certain dried *Boletus* species (mainly from Russia), to those brought in from China, and to the home-grown Meadow Mushroom. Of these, vast quantities are used both in restaurants and homes. The importations alone, during a period of five years, were well over 38,000,000 pounds. It is to be hoped that our people will in time learn to know, collect and eat at least a few of the common wild edible species, vast quantities of which go to waste in our fields and forests every season.

Formerly it was the habit of writers on mushrooms to call attention to the tons of mushroom food—"equal to so much beef"—that go unutilized. This was an over statement regarding their food value. It is mainly as condiments that they are valuable. Beef, bread, and beans are very nourishing, but who wants to eat these at all times? Occasionally appetizers prove acceptable, even though they may not contain the calories and vitamins present in the common food staples (Mendel, 1898).

POISONOUS SPECIES

These are of no economic value whatever, viewed from the standpoint of the mushroom-eater, but in so far as they help along, with thousands of other species about whose edible qualities nothing is known, in the formation of humus, they, too, serve man, as without humus the whole biological experiment of nature on this planet would soon come to a complete halt.

MICROSCOPIC FERMENT FUNGI, AND MOULDS, VALUABLE IN THE INDUSTRIES

Some of the microscopic fungi serve most useful purposes. Dough can be raised with baking powder, without the aid of yeast, but in order to have "the kind of bread mother used to bake", the old-fashioned yeast must still be used. This fungous article is also highly recommended in advertisements as a regulating tonic for maltreated digestive tracts. Other industries based upon the action of ferment fungi, or moulds, are the production of alcohol, buttermilk, and cheese, leather tanning, tobacco curing, and the fermentation of vegetables (sauerkraut, fodder in silos, etc.)

FUNGI DESTRUCTIVE TO ECONOMIC PLANTS

In the chapter on Wood Destroying Fungi (p. 150), an account is given of the pernicious and costly activities of fungi that attack and destroy trees, with incidental reference to those that, living part of their lives on woody plants, later, in another phase, destroy crop plants such as wheat. Massee ('11), quoting estimates as to the annual losses in economic plants due to fungi throughout the world, says that the grand total amounts to at least ten billion dollars. In Ceylon, for example, the coffee-leaf disease demands a tribute aggregating eighty-five million dollars. Cereals, in Prussia, are damaged by rust to the extent of one hundred million dollars. The Bitter-rot of apples costs our citizens the round sum of twelve million dollars. The bill for the ravages of Wheat Rust in the year 1916, in the United States and Canada, which totaled two hundred and eighty million dollars (280,000,000 bushels at $1.00 a bushel—an underestimate of value) would go far toward paying the annual cost of the public school system of the State of New York, which, for the year 1926–27, was two hundred and ninety-four million dollars.

COMMON EDIBLE MUSHROOMS
KINDS SAFE FOR THE BEGINNER

The account of the poisonous mushrooms (p. 134) is likely to dampen the ardor of the budding mycophagist. But he who will have roses must look among thorns. In the mushroom world, fortunately, "thorns" are few and "roses" plentiful. At most there are not more than a baker's dozen of poisonous kinds that must be avoided at all cost, whereas those that are known to be edible run into the hundreds. Professor Peck, in the 139th bulletin of the New York State Museum, lists close to two hundred species that have an unblemished reputation for edibility. The question then for the enthusiast resolves itself into this: "How may I pluck the mushroom 'roses', the while escaping the mushroom 'thorns'?"

The answer is, first learn to know the killers, that you may recognize them instantly on sight, and then make the acquaintance of the edible kinds, one by one, beginning with such as have an unmistakable identity. There are in fact not a few highly desirable and common species possessed of such marked characteristics that a child can be taught to pick them from an assortment of good, bad, and indifferent. This is not a rhetorical flourish, but a statement based on experience.

The Amanitas, the killers referred to above, are singled out on page 136. Here the attempt will be made to counterbalance these by selecting more than an equal number of kinds that are excellent for the table, fairly common, and easily distinguished. In going over the Peck list, not less than twenty stand out conspicuously because of special ear-marks by means of which a beginner may learn to know them. The purpose here is not to describe the selected kinds but merely to call attention to those botanical characters that set them apart from the poisonous Amanitas and other undesirables. For further details, the descriptions and figures should be consulted.

The prospective collector, having familiarized himself with the Amanitas and false morels (*Gyromitra,* figure 50a), may begin by learning to know the large puffballs. When in prime condition their interior is solid and pure white. Indeed, the substance of the plants looks very much like a good-sized ball of cottage cheese surrounded by a skin that later bursts open to give freedom to the spores. When the spore-ripening process starts, yellowish brown droplets appear the moment the knife is passed through the body of the plant. At this stage, the substance is no longer fit for food, a distinct bitterness having developed. There are four species of sufficient bulk to merit attention, viz.: *Calvatia cyathiformis* (figure 73), *C. craniiformis* (figure 72), *C. saccata,* and *C. gigantea* (figure 74)'. Of these the first, the smallest of the four, is the commonest, while the last, unfortunately not common, attains such huge dimensions (up to 18 or 20 in. in diameter) that, occasionally, photographs of exceptionally large specimens appear in the rotogravure sections of our metropolitan dailies.

There is not the slightest danger of collecting poisonous kinds among these puff-balls, yet, it must be stated, a young *Amanita,* before it bursts the volva or bag that encloses it, somewhat resembles a Puff-ball (figure 37f, g). A longitudinal cut through the middle of the plant, however, will at once disclose the young embryo, should one have found an *Amanita*. Also, these large puffballs usually grow in more or less open (pasture) grounds, whereas Amanitas nearly always occur in woods. The smaller puff-balls, *Lycoperdon gemmatum* (figure 102), and *L. pyriforme* (figures 103, 104), are also sought, but in these the spore-ripening begins very soon and, as a consequence, it is not often that one finds them in proper condition for food.

With the exception of *Clavaria dichotoma,* a slender, regularly-branched, flaccid, pinkish-white species, all Clavarias are as safe to eat as puffballs. In one type, *Clavaria pistillaris* (figure 77), the plant consists of a simple club; in another, *C. fusiformis* (figure 54a), the clubs arise in tufts, while in still another, there are many branches, emanating from a common stem: *C. botrytis,* etc. (figures 76, 78). They are not of the very best (some have a bitter taste), but in the absence of better kinds, or as bulk makers with others, they are not to be ignored. The last named species is plainly marked by the pink or reddish tips of the uppermost branches. When very young, the branches form a rather compact and fleshy mass. As with all fungi that are to serve as food, they must be free from insect attack and in the best condition.

Perhaps the easiest of all edible mushrooms to recognize is the Morel or Sponge Mushroom, *Morchella esculenta.* Such a great favorite was it with the peoples of Central Europe in medieval times that forests were burnt down to secure the substratum which it seems to prefer, though it also grows in old apple orchards and under elms. In some regions of this country, notably in western Maryland and in Pennsylvania, it is the kind meant when the farmers speak of mushrooms. In the latter State, they are referred to as "merkels", and are prepared as a potpie (Herbst, 1899). The only poisonous species that might be collected in its place is the False Morel, *Gyromitra esculenta.* A comparison of the pictures (figures 50a, b, plate 26), will enable anyone to recognize the two plants. The True Morel, it will be seen, has a pitted head, whereas the false one has that part convoluted, like a brain. The caps of old stinkhorns (figure 59b, c), after the greenish spore mass has been either lapped up by blow flies or washed off by rains, somewhat resemble those of morels, but the net-like, perforated wall of the stem in the former will decide the matter beyond peradventure.

The Trumpet-shaped *Craterellus, C. cornucopioides,* is another fungus that can be gathered and eaten without trepidation. Some species of *Cantharellus* (plate 11), have a similar shape, but as these are also edible, no danger can ensue. *Craterellus cantharellus* (figure 53a), is very much like a *Cantharellus.* The Trumpet-shaped Craterellus—also called Horn of Plenty, or Trumpet of Death; the latter name without cause—has a dingy violet-pinkish-gray to dark-brown coloring, the former being present on the outer or hymenial side, which is also covered with a multitude of wrinkles. Cooked slowly as a stew it makes an acceptable dish. The trouble is to find the plants. Owing to their inconspicuous coloring, they are difficult to discern amid the dead leaves in woods (plate 17).

The tube fungi, especially the fleshy kinds, constitute another safe group for the nouveau in the fine art of mycophagy. World-renowned is the *Cèpe* of commerce, *Boletus edulis* (plate 7). Its mild-tasting, white flesh does not turn blue, the stem is covered with a fine, white network, and the creamy-white, stuffed tubes of young plants finally become greenish. The pale zone on the very margin of the cap is conclusive in the determination. *Boletus scaber* (plate 10), and *B. versipellis* (pl. 1, figure 55e), have stems rough with coarse, blackish points, and the latter species has, in addition, a margin that overlaps the layer of tubes. *Strobilomyces strobilaceus* (figures 55c, 125), a great favorite with Bohemian people, is unforgettable after it, or a picture of it, has once been seen. Cap and stem are almost black, the former exhibiting very coarse, erect scales. The tube-mouths are lighter colored, and hexagonal in shape. Old specimens sometimes have a strong musky-camphorous odor. It is advisable to discard all Boleti that turn blue, even though many of these are eaten by some people without fear, and, apparently, without untoward consequences (see Collins, 1899).

Among the tough-fleshed polypores (bracket fungi), only young specimens of three or four species are sufficiently tender to serve as food. Perhaps best known is the Beefsteak or Poor-man's Mushroom, *Fistulina hepatica* (figure 87). It cannot be overlooked in any woods where there are old stumps of Oak and Chestnut. The upper surface is darkish-blood-red; the lower, porous one, pinkish-creamy. A sure sign that one has the species, is the odd movability of the skin of the upper surface. Due to an underlying gelatinous layer, this skin can be shoved about, exactly like the skin on the back of the open hand. The upper surface of young specimens, on close inspection, also shows a multitude of fine, reddish dots or papillae. The interior is stringy and mottled, not unlike beef streaked with thin layers of white fat.

The Chicken Mushroom, *Polyporus sulphureus* (plate 28, figure 42), cannot be missed, once it is encountered. Large, bright lemon-yellow to orange clusters, one cap growing above the other, tile-fashion, grow out from the trunks of oaks and other trees, the lemon-yellow color being confined to the lower surface. Nothing in the fungus line looks like it. Only the young, knob-like beginnings of caps should be eaten, as the rest of the plant is tough.

Polyporus frondosus (figure 115), the Hen of the Woods (*Poule de Bois,* as the French call it), looks much like a hen squatting, with feathers spread, protecting her chicks. The resemblance is due to the overlapping of a great number of small, dimidiate caps that go to make up a fruit-body about the size of a large hen. Like *Polyporus sulphureus,* it is quite unique.

In *Polyporus umbellatus* (figure 118), numberless small, cup-shaped caps grow from a common central core, each cap the termination of a little stem. It is such a pretty plant that one hesitates to put it to use as food. *Polyporus ovinus* (figure 116) and *P. pes-caprae* are also sought by the informed hunter.

Coming to the white-spored gill-mushrooms the danger zone is entered, for the deadly Amanitas belong to this group. Yet, even in this close proximity to the man-killers, there is one kind, the Umbrella Mushroom, *Lepiota procera* (plate 25), that can be placed on the list from which the beginner may select with safety. It is a tall mushroom, and though, in common with Amanitas, it has white spores, there are other pronounced features which characterize it so definitely that the writer feels no hesitation in recommending it as an esculent of the first quality. The botanical ear-marks are: the prominently umbonate cap, the scales (*not warts!*) on the surface of this part (figure 65b), the deep socket on the under side into which the rounded upper end of the stem fits, the extreme remoteness of the gills from the long, equal, hard stem the exterior of which is cracked into innumerable, speck-like dark spots, and, most important, the thick ring, which in older plants, after the stem has contracted a little from loss of moisture, can be moved up and down, like an encircling bracelet. The base of the stem, though enlarged, bears no trace of crumbs, scales, or bag-like volva. For those who have a microscope, the spores (figure 24h) offer a further means of identification, these unusually large bodies measuring as much as 18 microns in length. Their shape is almost exactly ovate. The deadly Amanitas, on the other hand, have round, or almost round, spores (figures 24a, b, c) of a diameter half the length of the major axis of those of *Lepiota procera*. Compare the description of *Lepiota morgani,* a closely related deleterious species (p. 373).

Collybia velutipes has a stem encased in a coat of dark-brown velvet. Growing on trees, even in the cold winter months, it furnishes a mess to the enthusiast who must have his mushrooms. Its taste, however, is rather insipid.

Living Elm and other deciduous trees bear clusters of *Pleurotus ulmarius* and *P. ostreatus,* both high in favor with mycophagists. The descriptions (p. 409), and the figures (figures 2f, 114), will acquaint the reader with their general appearance.

Lactarius deliciosus and *L. volemus,* of the milk-bearing kind, are not permitted to rot where they grow if a mushroom-lover happens by, as they are reckoned among the choicest of fungus tid-bits. The orange milk of the former, and the very profuse white milk of the latter will enable anyone to spot them.

Cantharellus cibarius, the Golden Chantrelle (plate 11), too, must be mentioned. Bearing not less than two hundred pet names in the countries of continental Europe, it has been a favorite for more than four centuries. It is a small plant with a trumpet-like shape, but with a solid, unperforated body, with blunt-edged, much intergrown gills, and with a color like that of the yolk of an egg fried hard. The False Chantrelle, *Clitocybe illudens* (plate 12), is large and has keen-edged, non-intergrown gills, and *Cantharellus aurantiacus* (plate 11), an undesirable species, has very close gills that fork regularly, always in twos (dichotomously).

Among the Russulas, *Russula virescens* will offer no difficulties in the matter of identification, its green, cracked cap being a sufficient mark. *Russula crustosa* (plate 31), a related plant, looks somewhat like it.

Ordinarily, it is wise to let rosy-spored mushrooms strictly alone, as some *Entoloma* species bear a bad reputation in the annals of mycophagy, but if a whitish, fleshy species of moderate size, with *very decurrent,* permanently reddish gills is found, it is perfectly safe to put it in the basket along with others that are intended for the saucepan. Its description appears on p. 302 under the name of *Clitopilus prunulus.* Another of the same genus, *Clitopilus abortivus* (figure 80, plate 13), has similar esculent qualities. It is larger than *Clitopilus prunulus,* has a gray exterior, the same decurrent gills, and is usually accompanied by roundish white masses, the abortive form.

The purple-brown spored series is the haven of safety

for the timid. This is true, above all, of the genus *Psalliota* which contains the Meadow Mushroom, *Psalliota campestris* (plate 29). For a comparison of this species with the deadly Amanitas see p. 136.

Hypholoma sublateritium, when not bitter (*H. perplexum,* plate 22), is good to eat. One advantage is its commonness. In the autumn it cannot be overlooked, growing at the base of deciduous trees, in dense clusters. The color is a dark brick-red, hence its popular name, the Brick-top. *Hypholoma fasciculare,* the Sulphur-top, not often met with, should be avoided because of its dubious reputation in Europe.

Coprinus species require no doctor's dissertation to explain their unmistakable identity. A small child that once overheard the writer point out the peculiarities of *Coprinus comatus,* the Shaggy-mane (figures 2d, 83, plate 15), ever afterwards picked out the plant unerringly from a great variety of species. With equal readiness the same child invariably pointed its tiny finger at the death-dealers saying, "those are Amaniters; they will kill you; don't eat them!" Moral: If a child can learn to separate good from bad kinds, there ought to be hope for adults.

RECIPES FOR COOKING MUSHROOMS

The preparation of wild mushrooms for the table (Atkinson, '00; Gibson, '95; Peck, '95) should really begin in the field, the moment they are picked. If one is out to collect specimens for both study and the stewpan, the two collections should be placed in separate baskets. The identity of those to be eaten definitely settled on the spot, the stems, with adhering earth, leaves, twigs, etc., should be cut off close enough to the cap to remove the hard, inedible parts. If this precaution is not taken, bits of gritty earth and other objectionables are likely to appear in the dish later on. Some viscid species, such as certain Boleti and Hygrophori, will require the removal of the slimy pellicle that covers the caps and, in some cases, the stems. The peeling of mushrooms is no sign of edibility (see p. 135), serving merely in the cleaning process, to get rid of a skin too tough, too dirty, or too slimy, to eat.

After the dirt has been removed, the specimens should be rinsed in water by placing them in a colander under a faucet. When perfectly clean, they are left for a few moments on a towel or clean dish-cloth until all moisture has been absorbed, after which they are ready to be cut into small pieces the size of a large chinquapin.

The flavor of mushrooms is so delicate that the addition of strong spices is inadvisable. A method commonly employed by those who prefer their mushrooms cooked in simple style, is to put the specimens into a double-boiler, adding a sufficient amount of butter, and then seasoning with pepper and salt to taste. The cooking should be continued over a slow fire for about fifteen minutes after the mass has become hot. As mushrooms contain from 70 to 90 per cent water there will be much of this fluid, which can be thickened with flour previously browned in a skillet. Serve hot on toast. This method is well adapted to the cooking of the Meadow Mushroom.

Mushrooms lend themselves, however, to a great variety of culinary treatments. They may be baked, stewed, fried, broiled, creamed, roasted, pickled, and (in the case of morels) stuffed. They may also be made into catsups, soups, purées, ragoûts, fritters and salads.

Baked mushrooms

Russulas and *Lactarius* species are delicious baked. Butter, olive oil, or, better still, strips of fat bacon should be added. Sprinkle over them fine herbs, dry bread crumbs, and season to taste. Especially tempting to the palate is *Lactarius volemus,* treated in this way.

Stewed mushrooms

Follow the directions given in the third paragraph under Recipes (p. 115), but add a few black peppers, some mace or powdered nutmeg, not overdoing the seasoning, of course. Use cream or milk in thickening with unbrowned flour.

The Chantrelle, *Cantharellus cibarius,* needs to be stewed slowly, as it is rather tough. Place over a very slow fire; too much heat destroys the delicate flavor.

Lactarius deliciosus, Hydnum repandum, and perfectly crisp and fresh *Hydnum coralloides* are also good when stewed. The same applies to the Clavarias, to the large polypores, *Polyporus sulphureus, P. frondosus, P. umbellatus,* and to the Oyster and Elm-tree Mushrooms, *Pleurotus ostreatus* and *P. ulmarius,* respectively.

Fried mushrooms

If one has found a great number of fairy-ring mushrooms, *Marasimus oreades,* or large *Clavaria* clusters, frying is in order. The butter or oil should be very hot before the mushrooms are added. The stems of the *Marasmius* should be discarded. Season to taste with salt and pepper. See also Mushroom Fritters, p. 119.

Broiled mushrooms

This style of cooking is recommended for the camper. If he has been so fortunate as to find a goodly number of parasols (*Lepiota procera*), he should revolve the caps over a lively fire until hot and slightly crisped. The addition of a dab of butter and the usual simple seasonings convert this woodland species into a fit accompaniment for wild game of any sort. A green, decorticated twig or branchlet may serve as spit or broiler. If enough specimens and a couple of pheasants are at hand, the birds might be stuffed with the mushrooms.

Creamed mushrooms

Worthington Smith's recipe is tempting to the gourmet. It reads: "Trim and rub half a pint of button-mushrooms, *Agaricus* [*Psalliota*] *campestris;* dissolve two ounces of butter rolled in flour in a stewpan; then put in the mushrooms, a bunch of parsley, a teaspoonful of salt, half a teaspoonful each of white pepper and powdered sugar; shake the pan around for ten minutes, then beat up the yolks of two eggs with two tablespoonfuls of cream, and add by degrees to the mushrooms. In two or three minutes you can serve them in the sauce.

Roasted mushrooms

Follow the directions given in the third paragraph under Recipes (p. 115), except that the specimens should be placed in a small covered dish and roasted in the oven for about fifteen minutes. A little water should be added at first, to prevent burning. Roasts of beef are improved by a garnishing of mushrooms.

Stuffed morels

Morels, being completely hollow within, may be stuffed like green peppers with forced meats of any kind. Before placing them in the oven, they should be moistened with a little olive oil and seasoned with salt and pepper. Serve with parsley and lemon sections. Morels, like spinach, must be thoroughly washed in cold water (outside and inside) to remove adhering sand and débris.

Pickled mushrooms

This treatment, a favorite with Bohemians and Russians, is especially applicable to Boleti. After the tubes have been removed and the caps peeled, the specimens (caps and stems) should be sliced into long strips and these spread on brown paper until ready for the pickling. In the absence of a good dry white wine, vinegar may be used. Boil the wine or vinegar and add salt, grated nutmeg, bay-leaves, and red peppers to taste. Put in the mushrooms, boil three times on successive days over a slow fire, each time for thirty minutes, after which decant into glass jars previously sterilized by boiling in hot water. The mushrooms and other ingredients should be equally distributed so as to present an appetizing appearance. Cover with sterilized jar-tops until cool and then screw these down securely.

In Russia, during the war, nearly every peasant pickled mushrooms of the edible sorts known to him by throwing them into a large barrel of strong brine. The supply was then drawn upon during the long and lean winters of those terrible years when other food was scarce. The preservation of wild mushroom is described by Pernot ('08).

Dried mushrooms

Such species as are not too juicy may be easily dried and kept for winter use. Central European peoples collect Boleti, chantrelles, parasol mushrooms and other species for this purpose. The plants are divided into pieces of suitable size, and these are strung on threads and suspended over a stove until bone-dry. Before cooking, it is only necessary to soak them in water to restore them to their pristine pliancy. Thoroughly dried mushrooms, when pulverized, make tasty flavorings for soups and gravies.

Mushroom soup

Cook the mushrooms after the simple fashion previously mentioned (p. 115), then take them out, cut them up very fine, and add beef- or veal-stock. Boil again and serve.

Mushroom fritters

Fleshy caps of Boleti or large puffballs are cut into slices about half an inch thick, dipped into egg batter, and fried till brown in very hot butter, fat, or oil. Add pepper and salt at the table.

Mushroom catsup

When mushrooms are put up as a catsup, the delicate flavor is apt to be entirely lost, unless one exercises great care in the seasoning. To make catsup, the mushrooms are placed layer upon layer in a crock, with a sprinkling of salt on each layer. The next day, the mass is crushed with a potato-masher. On the third day it is pressed through a colander lined with cheese-cloth. The resulting liquor, after the desired spices have been added, is boiled for fifteen minutes, then strained through clean cheese-cloth. Boiled again for a quarter of an hour on each of the two succeeding days, it is ready for bottling and sealing. It is understood, of course, that kitchen utensils, cheese-cloth, bottles, etc., must be sterilized before operations are begun.

Mushroom salad

The Beefsteak Mushroom, *Fistulina hepatica,* young, mild Russulas, and *Polyporus sulphureus* are sometimes used as salads with French dressing. The first is likely to prove a little too acid for some tastes, in which case the lemon or vinegar of the dressing should be omitted. The *Polyporus* should be parboiled and then cooled. Served with Shrimp or Lobster, its colors join with those of the crustaceans in a delightful Whistlerian symphony of orange, pink, lemon, and white.

GROWING MUSHROOMS

In the United States there is a great demand for the cultivated mushroom, a fact demonstrated by our large importations (from seven to nine million pounds per annum), and by the presence of the home-grown product in our markets and better class stores. In New York State alone, the cultivation of mushrooms in specially constructed buildings, in old ice houses (in the Hudson valley), in abandoned mines, tunnels, quarries, and in other places, has in the past few years steadily increased. At the present time, of course, commodity prices are at a low ebb, and one pays correspondingly low prices for mushrooms —from twenty-five to fifty cents a pound, the average being about forty cents. However, if the producer could secure the average price for himself by dealing directly with the consumers (through mail orders, or through some other method of personal solicitation), his business might still be made to yield a fair profit, were it not for the scarcity and consequent high cost of good manure, and the ever-present factor of chance in the actual growing of the mushrooms. The reasons for the last statement will appear in the following. (Duggar, '05, '15, '22; Falconer, 1897, '10; Lambert, '32; Robinson, no date.)

Time for growing mushrooms. Mushrooms can be grown the year round, if the temperature suitable for their proper development can be had and maintained. In deep caves and mines this is possible without artificial heat in winter, or refrigeration in summer; above ground, the expense would be too great to apply the latter. It is for this reason that the small grower begins operations in fall, when there is no longer any danger of a return of summer heat. Another advantage in beginning late lies in the fact that insects reproduce more slowly at lower growing temperatures. However, in composting small heaps of manure in the open in winter, freezing must be guarded against.

Manure. The best results in growing mushrooms are obtained when manure from healthy, grain-fed horses is used, that from grass- or hay-fed animals being much less valuable. Manure from veterinary hospitals, or from stables that are kept clean by the use of disinfectants, should be rejected. Bedding straw, when from cereals, is a welcome addition, if not too long. Shavings are less desirable. Sawdust is not to be tolerated at all as the beds pack too solidly, a reason that also precludes the use of cattle manure as a substitute or addition. Well trampled stable manure is to be preferred to any other, provided it is free from medicaments and disinfectants.

Composting. Before the manure is used in the beds, it must first be fermented, or composted. This is accomplished by piling it in heaps from four to five feet deep, preferably under cover, and where there is little loss of moisture through leaching into the soil. After four or five days, the heaps should be turned by forking over. In from seven to ten days this operation should be repeated, water being added if there is a tendency to dryness. The heaps should be kept merely moist, then there will be no danger of burning or sour fermentation. Three or four days after each turning the heaps shrink to about three feet in height. Two or three weeks later (depending upon conditions of moisture, packing, and weather), the temperature of the heaps ought to be down to a point where decomposition through fermentation takes place less violently, and the making of the beds can be thought of. To prevent the compost from drying out excessively between turnings, some growers mix about one-fourth to one-third loam with unfermented manure, while others prefer to compost the manure without soil. The compost should not be too much rotted, as the mushrooms will be small and will lack solidity. It is ready for the construction of the beds, when the so-called "sweet fermentation" has set in, when it has lost most of its objectionable odors, has acquired a chocolate-brown color, and when, on being pressed in the hand, it holds together without being pasty. *Under no circumstances should it be wet.*

The mushroom house or cellar, and preparation of the beds. Success in growing mushrooms is dependent upon a number of factors, not least among which is the selection of the place in which the crop is to be raised. To go at the venture in the wrong way, one would choose warm weather, a drafty barn, with no provision for temperature control, and with many holes in the roof for the leakage of water onto the beds. To go at it in the right way, operations should begin in the cool weather of fall, a cellar should be selected in which the temperature can be held continuously between 50 and 55 degrees Fahrenheit, and where provisions can be made for ventilation and moisture control. The structural units—boards, beams, etc.—should be removable in order that they may be thoroughly cleaned and disinfected after each crop, or if disease or insect troubles should break out (Charles & Lambert, '33; Thomas, C. A., '31). When the growing season is over, the cellar, too, should be cleaned and fumigated with formaldehyde, or by burning sulphur. One of the objections to the use of extensive mines and caves, is the difficulty experienced in maintaining perfect cleanliness, and in controlling draughts.

There are three types of beds, the flat floor-bed (figure 27), the shelf-bed (figure 28), and the ridge-bed (figure 29). In this country, the shelf-bed is used almost exclusively, the floor-bed having been discarded because it proved to be a breeding place for insects. The ridge-bed is found only in Europe, notably in the mushroom-caves of France. Shelf-beds should be from eight to ten inches deep, the manure being dumped in until that depth is obtained, about one bushel sufficing for every two square feet of surface. A range of mushroom houses, with a diagram for a heating plant, is shown in figure 30.

Spawning. Spawn, obtained from selected varieties by the tissue culture method (perfected by Duggar), and sold in "brick" form, was used for many years, but at present experienced growers universally employ the kind obtained by pure culture from germinated spores and grown on suitable solid media in glass bottles (figure 31).

About forty square feet can be spawned from the contents of a bottle, the egg-sized lumps of spawn-material being inserted into holes from one to two inches deep, and about a foot apart. After closing the holes with manure, the beds are firmed down.

Spawning must not be undertaken until the temperature in the beds, after a sudden rise due to a secondary fermentation, has gradually fallen during a week or so to seventy or seventy-five degrees Fahrenheit. Eighty degrees would prove fatal to the spawn.

Figure 27 Cellar with a single floor-bed. After B. M. Duggar

Figure 28 Shelf-beds in a warm cellar. After B. M. Duggar

Figure 29 Ridge-beds in a mushroom cave. After B. M. Duggar

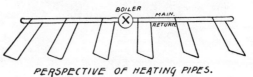

BOILER

MAIN.

RETURN

PERSPECTIVE OF HEATING PIPES.

Figure 30 A range of mushroom houses, showing heating arrangement and general construction. After B. M. Duggar

Figure on left by courtesy of U. S. Dep't of Agriculture. Figure on right, original

Figure 31 Manure "bricks" impregnated with the mycelium or spawn of the cultivated Meadow Mushroom, *Psalliota campestris*; also a bottle of spawn. After B. M. Duggar

Casing. If moisture conditions in the beds and in the house are normal, casing can begin in about two weeks. Before doing this, however, the beds should be examined to ascertain whether the spawn has begun to "run", and whether there is enough moisture present. Water in the form of a fine spray should be applied only when absolutely necessary, as wet beds will most certainly cause the spawn to damp off and die.

The casing should be neither of heavy clay, nor of sandy soil, but of a good, rich, moist, loamy earth that has been thoroughly screened in order to exclude stones, large pebbles, and trash of all kinds. The layer of loam should be from one to one and a half inches deep.

Watering. While the spawn is spreading through the beds, no water should be applied, unless, through too great heat in the house, the beds show unmistakable signs of drying. If the moisture and temperature conditions of beds and house have been properly maintained from the beginning of the operations, watering should not be necessary until the crop begins to appear, after which a light sprinkling once or twice a week is advisable, owing to the extraction of moisture by the mushrooms, and by evaporation. At no time, however, should the beds be drenched (see p. 38). The sprinkling should be done after the gathering of the mushrooms.

Picking. In picking the mushrooms the demand of the market should be kept in view. At the present time a preference is shown for mushrooms that have attained their full weight, but in which the veil is still intact. At their first emergence, the mushrooms spring up in dense clusters from the places where the spawn was inserted (figure 2k). Such clusters will contain individuals ranging from "buttons" of the smallest size to fully developed mushrooms. These clusters should be removed *en bloc* by cutting them out, but the cutting must be done in such a way that the spawn beneath will suffer the least possible disturbance. The clean hole left should then be filled with fresh loam. The large marketable buttons are put in a shallow basket, while the smaller ones are held for canning, an industry that, of late, is making remarkable strides in this country. Very tiny buttons, or very large mushrooms in which the veil is torn, or such in which it is about to tear, need not be thrown away, but may be converted into catsup, or canned by the usual method of sterilization. A market is likely to develop for a tasty mushroom catsup. It could be sold at a moderate price for flavorings, and, most important, losses due to wastage would be practically eliminated. Even mushrooms in which the gills have become dark might be included, for dark-colored flavorings are not objectionable.

Later on, when the mushrooms come up singly, or in clusters containing only a few specimens of nearly the same size (figure 120), the removal from the bed should be by a twisting motion, the individuals being grasped by the cap, or, if quite large, by cap and stem. Under no circumstances should parts of stems, or other fleshy masses, be left in the bed to decay, and so cause the destruction of the spawn.

After the picking, the mushrooms are ready for grading as to size, the stems having been cut off just below the veil, and any adhering loam removed by brushing with a soft brush.

Packing. Attractive looking packages help to sell an article. This is also true of mushrooms (figures 32, 33). The mushrooms should be clean, unopened, and of

Courtesy U. S. Dep't of Agriculture

Figure 32 How to pack the cultivated mushrooms for the market.
After B. M. Duggar

Courtesy U. S. Dep't of Agriculture

Figure 33 Basket of cultivated
mushrooms ready for shipment. After
B. M. Duggar

approximately the same size, and there must be no "top layer for the eye", with the bottom layers made up of scrubs of all kinds. The grower is selling to customers who are perfectly willing to pay a good price, provided the offerings are of first-class quality throughout. Baskets ("Climax" baskets) holding three pounds, and lined with paraffin paper, make ideal containers for shipment. For the smaller buttons, crated strawberry boxes are suitable (figure 34). As mushrooms are a very perishable crop, the baskets and crates must be kept cool and placed on the nearest market without delay. In refrigerator cars, mushrooms can be shipped for a considerable distance.

Courtesy U. S. Dep't of Agriculture

Figure 34　A convenient crate for shipping cultivated mushrooms. After B. M. Duggar

Beds, properly made and cared for, ought to come into bearing in from six to eight weeks, and should continue to produce fine solid mushrooms for some months (from two to five), the length of time depending upon the growing temperature. The yield per square foot varies from a half pound to two pounds.

When the beds are no longer profitable they should be thrown out, and the house and structural wood of the beds cleaned and fumigated, as previously indicated. The manure and loam casing often can be sold to truck-farmers and gardeners, as it is excellent fertilizer but useless for further mushroom production.

A certain large and heavy species, *Psalliota villatica,* grown by at least one producer, is not suitable for the market, as it soon exudes a dark-brown, highly odoriferous liquid, even when shipped a short distance.

Care must also be exercised that other kinds, such as *Panaeolus* species (figure 35), are not included in the picking. For a list of species likely to appear in mushroom beds, see p. 60.

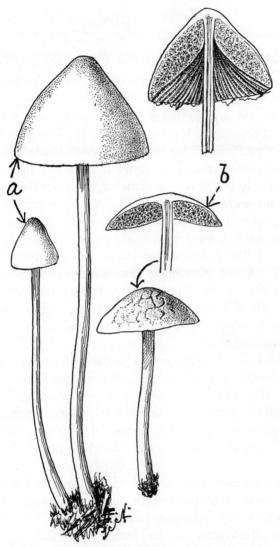

Figure 35 *Panaeolus* species. *a, Panaeolus campanulatus; b, Panaeolus papilionaceus.* Note the
spotted gills and the long, narrow stems. These deleterious plants are apt to come up in beds of the cultivated mushroom

POISONOUS MUSHROOMS ("TOADSTOOLS")

(For references to the descriptions of most of the species discussed here, consult the index)

It is an old saying, that a little knowledge is not good for us. Fortunately, it does not apply to those who wish to collect mushrooms for the table, as but "little" of this commodity is necessary to avoid those kinds that slay, provided only that it is true knowledge and not the superstitious nonsense one hears on all sides when mushrooms are the topic of conversation. Almost the first question broached when a mushroom is shown is, "Does it peel?" A glance at the picture of the top of the cap of *Amanita muscaria* (figure 36), ought to convince any one of the utter falsity of this "test". The picture demonstrates clearly that this deadly species peels as readily as the common Meadow Mushroom. Equally fallacious are all other so-called tests.

But what is this little knowledge that will prevent those dire accidents of which we read all too often in the daily press? It is this: to know how to recognize Amanitas when you encounter them, be it out in the open in the collecting grounds, or in the kitchen of a friend, who is about to introduce you to the "delights" of mushroom eating.

It must by now have become evident, even to the most casual reader, that mushrooms, like other plants, have individuality. A poisonous *Amanita* is not the edible Meadow Mushroom, for the same reason that a peach tree is not an apple tree. There are easily understood differences by which one can, in either case, distinguish one from the other.

What, then, are the differences between the deadly

Amanitas and the edible Meadow Mushroom? Both, as with apple and peach trees, have certain things in common. Just as the two trees have roots, trunks, branches, leaves, blossoms, fruits and seeds, so the mushrooms have stems, gills, caps and spores. But, also, just as the parts

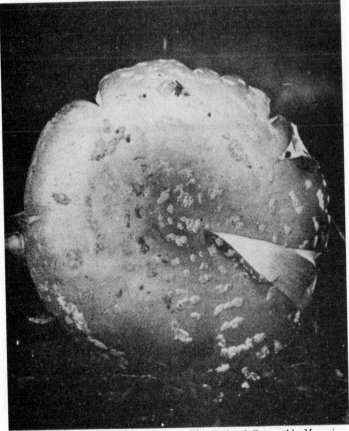

Reproduced by special permission from The National Geographic Magazine

Figure 36 Top of the cap of *Amanita muscaria*, showing that this deadly mushroom can be peeled just as easily as the Meadow Mushroom. It is commonly believed that *peeling* is a sign of edibility. Copyright The National Geographic Society

of the trees are different, so are the parts of the mushrooms. To contrast the differences, nothing is so effectual as a side-by-side demonstration in word and picture (plates 29, 3, 4, 5, figure 120).

HOW TO DISTINGUISH DEADLY AMANITAS FROM THE EDIBLE MEADOW MUSHROOM

Amanitas	Meadow Mushroom
1. Grow in woods, very rarely in old meadows or lawns.	1. Grows in old meadows, *never in woods.* (Some species of *Psalliota* grow in wooded areas, but the Meadow Mushroom, *Psalliota campestris,* holds to meadows.)
2. They are usually quite tall and conspicuous.	2. Is short and squatty in stature.
3. The caps in *Amanita muscaria* are bright-lemon to orange-color; in *Amanita phalloides,* from w h i t e, t h r o u g h yellowish and brownish-grays, to olive-brown and blackish.	3. Cap white to brownish.
4. Surface of cap usually bears traces of the volva in the form of detachable warts or patches.	4. Surface of cap either smooth or fibrillose to appressedly scaly, the scales being difficult to remove as they are due to the tearing of the cuticle.
5. Gills free, usually white though some have reddish or lemon-yellow gills.	5. Gills free, *pink at first,* soon *dark chocolate-brown.*
6. The spore-deposit *always white*.	6. Spore-deposit *dark purplish-brown.*
7. Stems usually quite long, and, in most species, bulbous at the base. Ring rather pronounced and pendulous. Remains of the volva nearly always present, either in the form of crumbs, concentric scales, or as a more or less distinct bag (figure 39).	7. Stem short, tapering slightly at the base, *not bulbous.* A very slight, soft ring present above. *Base always devoid of any trace of crumbs, scales or bag.*
8. Spores *hyaline (white)*, globose to broad-ovate, comparatively large (figures 37 D, E, F, G, 38a, b, c, d).	8. Spores *p u r p l i s h-b r o w n,* broadly elliptical, comparatively small (figures 37, A, B, C).

To sum up the essentials: *Amanitas have white spores, are rather tall, and possess, on their stems, both ring and volva. The Meadow Mushroom, Psalliota campestris, has purple-brown spores, is short and squatty, and possesses only a slight ring, and no volva.*

How any one who has had impressed upon his mind these marked differences can confound the Amanitas with the Meadow Mushroom, passes comprehension!

If Amanitas are conscientiously avoided, the danger from mushroom poisoning is practically eliminated, as most deaths due to this cause can be traced to them, more especially to the worst of them all, *Amanita phalloides,* or to one of its varieties. There are others that may cause death, but these are not so likely to be eaten, partly on account of their rarity, partly because of their small size or unfamiliar appearance.

Many investigations have been carried on in this country to determine the specific poisons present in the deadly and deleterious species, notably by Ford and his associates (Ford, '09, '11, '23; Ford and Clark, '14, '14a). A summary of their conclusions with regard to the poisons, symptoms and treatment, species by species, follows (see also Kauffman, '18).

Amanita phalloides, including A. verna (figure 68), and A. virosa (plate 5, figures 37D, E, F, G)

This, one of the commonest species, is met with almost immediately one enters any wooded area. Especially is this true of the white variety, *Amanita virosa* (for the descriptions see pp. 241, 243, 245).

It is a particularly insidious plant as the symptoms of poisoning do not appear until its deadly work has been

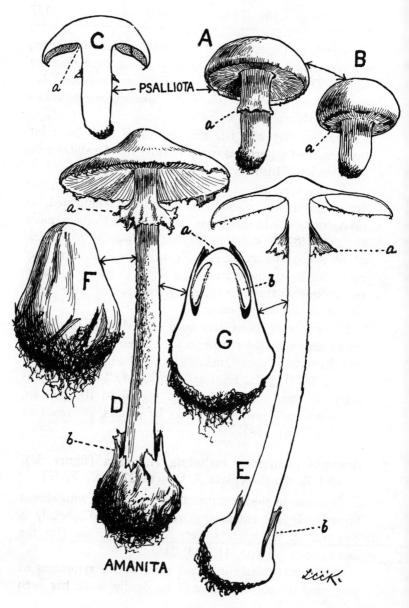

PSALLIOTA

AMANITA

all but completed. The active principle is known as Amanita-toxin, a constituent indestructible in the ordinary process of cooking, only boiling acids accomplishing its final disintegration. Time also has little effect upon its virulence, as specimens kept for nine years have been found to be actively poisonous. Its exact chemical nature has not been definitely ascertained. The symptoms, however, are fairly characteristic. In from six to fifteen hours after the fungi have been eaten, the unsuspecting and unfortunate victim is suddenly seized with violent pains in the abdomen, the pains being accompanied by excessive vomiting, thirst, and by either diarrhea or constipation. The pains may be so severe that the face becomes drawn, pinched, and of a livid color. The attacks coming on periodically, the patient soon loses strength, jaundice may set in, and coma develops, followed by death, apparently

Figure 37 The edible Meadow Mushroom (*Psalliota campestris*) and one of the deadly Amanitas (*Amanita virosa*) contrasted. *A. Psalliota campestris*, after the veil (*a*) has torn, and the young, pink gills have become visible. *B*, the same in the "button" stage; the veil (*a*) is just beginning to separate from the margin of the cap. *C*, section of the plant figured under *A*, the pink gills (which later become chocolate brown) are seen to be free at *a*, *D, Amanita virosa*, the Destroying Angel, fully matured; *a*, the tattered veil, with remains of it left on the margin of the cap; *b*, the volva or death cup; *E*, section of plant figured under *D*, veil, at *a*, volva at *b*; the gills are free and their edges fimbriate. The gills are white and remain so throughout the plant's existence. *F*, the young plant still enclosed in the intact volva. At this stage the plant might be mistaken for a Puff-ball, but if it be cut open lengthwise (*G*), the embryo will be seen within; *a*, the top of the cap about to emerge through the opening torn into the volva; *b*, the gills, still lying closely appressed to the stem. The development of this *Amanita* is also that of the other species, except that the volva is not always present in the form of a distinct bag. In some species it breaks up into warts or crumbs. Compare the development of the deadly Fly Mushroom (Fig. 38), and the stem bases of three deadly Amanitas (Fig. 39). Figures *A, B* and *C* from the Therapeutic Gazette, Philadelphia

due to the extreme fatty degeneration of the liver. Convulsions may or may not occur toward the end. The death rate is from 60 to 100 per cent, depending upon the amount eaten and upon the age of the patient. A child is known to have been killed by eating a fragment of a cap. The duration of the illness varies from three to eight days. No antidote is known that will counteract

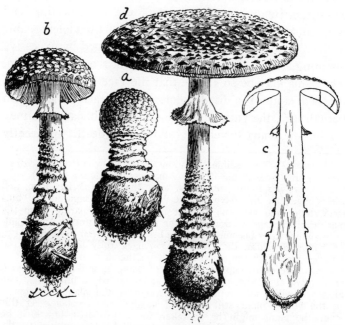

From the Therapeutic Gazette, Philadelphia

Figure 38 The development of the deadly poisonous Fly Mushroom, *Amanita muscaria* (see also pl. 1 and 5, figs. 36 and 24c). *a.* Young plant showing the formation of the warts on the cap, and of the concentric volva remains on the base of the stem. *b,* More advanced stage. *c,* Section of *b.* *d,* Mature plant. For the development of the Destroying Angel (*Amanita virosa*), see fig. 37, d, e, f, g

the dreadful poison. (At the Pasteur Institute, Paris, however, an antitoxic serum has recently been prepared. It is reported to be effectual in cases of human intoxication by this *Amanita*.) A physician should be called on the slightest suspicion, as it is important to remove, as

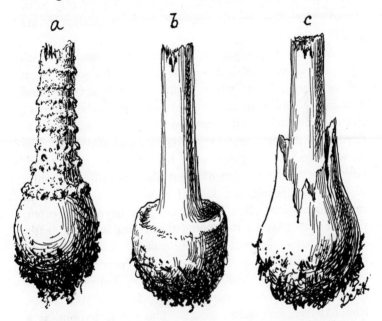

Figure 39 Bases of the stems of three deadly species of Amanita: *a, Amanita muscaria,* showing scaly type of volva. *b, Amanita mappa,* circumscissile type. *c, Amanita virosa,* bag-like type. Like the triangular shape of a rattlesnake's head, these danger signs of deadly mushrooms should be well heeded

soon as possible, every bit of the material from the digestive tract. Alcohol is of no use whatever in the treatment, for it is a powerful aid in the diffusion of the poison through the system.

Amanita muscaria

(Plates 1, 3, figures 36, 38a, b, c, d, 67)

Poisoning by this species, though it may eventuate in death in grave cases, is not so much to be feared as that caused by *Amanita phalloides,* for reasons presently to be stated (for the description of *Amanita muscaria,* see p. 237).

A complex of poisons is present in the fungus of which muscarin appears to be the most active. Its action is on the nervous system, which it affects most severely and quickly. Almost immediately (from one to six hours) the victim exhibits an excessive flow of saliva, perspiration, tears, nausea, retching, vomiting, and diarrhea. The pulse becomes irregular and breathing is accelerated. Giddiness and confusion of ideas also prevail. Delirium, violent convulsions, and loss of consciousness develop in rapid succession when large quantities have been eaten, the patient sinking into a coma that is followed by death. In light cases, the patient, after attacks of vomiting and diarrhea, falls into a deep sleep, from which he awakes several hours later, profoundly prostrate, but on the road to recovery. Within two or three days, in such cases, complete recovery takes place. The drug, atropin, is a perfect antidote for muscarin. It should not be administered, however, except by a physician, as it is itself a poison.

The early appearance of the symptoms is characteristic of poisoning by this species, those caused by *Amanita phalloides* coming on much later. The spores, to be had from vomits and excreta (Offner, '05), are also indicative, *A. phalloides* spores (or those of its close allies) being almost globose, whereas those of *A. muscaria* incline toward elliptic-globose (figures 24a, b, c).

Amanita pantherina

(Plate 4)

This species produces a mild form of *Amanita muscaria* poisoning, death occurring rarely. It contains muscarin. Related species of *Amanita pantherina* are, *A. cothurnata*, *A. velatipes,* and *A. pantherinoides.* The latter, a Pacific coast species, has been found by Murrill to be definitely poisonous (for the description of *A. pantherina,* see p. 240).

Amanita spreta

Coker ('17) reports that this species has been eaten in the form of a soup. As he did not see actual specimens from lots that were cooked and eaten, the writer prefers to join Ford ('09) in classing the plant as deadly poisonous, since this investigator has found the terrible Amanita-toxin present, even though only in minute quantities.

Amanita porphyria, A. strobiliformis, A. radicata, and A. chlorinosma

Ford ('09) states that these four species contain a heat-resistant substance, which has an effect on animals similar to that produced by the Amanita-toxin, when administered in small doses. He adds, that they should be strictly avoided by mushroom-eaters. Another species, *Amanita solitaria,* one of the *strobiliformis-radicata-chlorinosma* group, should also be regarded with suspicion.

Russula emetica, Boletus satanas, and B. luridus

The presence of muscarin having been demonstrated in these species, it would seem wise for the mushroom-eater to avoid their consumption.

Boletus miniato-olivaceus var. sensibilis

Some years ago, Palmer (1885) published a colored figure which he labeled *Boletus subtomentosus,* an edible species. It turned out to be a good picture of the poisonous *B. miniato-olivaceus* var. *sensibilis,* a correction of a misdetermination that we owe to the sad experience of Collins (1899), who ate some specimens which he identified as *"Boletus subtomentosus"* by means of this figure. The symptoms, which appeared within two hours after the meal, indicate that muscarin was present. There were recurrent attacks of nausea, purging, exhaustion, a feeling of cold as from a sudden icy wind, and narrowing of the pupils of the eyes. After several days recovery was complete.

Gyromitra esculenta: False Morel, or Lorel

(Figure 50a)

The False Morel, like the True Morel, is enjoyed and highly praised by many who regularly make a practice of eating it. The literature of mushroom-poisoning shows, however, that up to 1907 over 160 cases of poisoning were recorded as due to this species. Its poisonous principle, helvellic acid, has been isolated. It is completely soluble in hot water, and parboiled specimens, therefore, should be innocuous, provided the water is poured off (but see Dearness, '24, for a death due to parboiled specimens). The poisonous properties disappear, or are much lessened, in dried specimens.

It is difficult to come to a conclusion with regard to the edibility of this species. The writer has had letters recommending it as one of the very best mushrooms, yet, in view of its record, it would appear that extreme caution should be used in preparing it for the table. It is possible that the amount of poison varies in plants from different localities. It is also possible that there are two, different, closely allied species or varieties concerned, one edible, the other poisonous. Of *Panus stipticus,* for example, it is known that there are two forms, one luminescent, the other non-luminescent, and yet the two are indistinguishable by their structure (Buller, '24). Natural insensitivity of the eaters to the poison, may be the explanation.

Pink-spored mushrooms: Volvaria and Entoloma

Volvaria gloiocephala, and the closely related *V. speciosa,* should not be eaten, as several deaths have been ascribed to the former. All members of the genus *Entoloma* also stand under suspicion, one species especially, *E. sinuatum,* having had almost fatal effects upon Worthington G. Smith, the English mycologist, who ate about a quarter of an ounce of the substance of the plant (for a figure of *Volvaria bombycina,* an edible species, see plate 32).

Ocher-spored mushrooms

In this group, three species stand forth as definitely poisonous, viz.: *Inocybe infida, I. infelix,* and *Pholiota autumnalis* (=*P. marginata*) the latter having caused the death of two children (Murrill, '09; Peck, '12). They are rather inconspicuous plants and are therefore not likely to be gathered for food.

Lactarius species

Lactarius torminosus is very acrid to the taste, produces gripes, and is a powerful purgative. In eastern Russia, and in Sweden, it is nevertheless eaten, preserved in salt and seasoned with oil and vinegar. *Lactarius piperatus* (figure 98), a very common, large species, is peppery, but this quality is lost in cooking. They should not be eaten raw. The same applies to the peppery Russulas.

Hygrophorus species

This genus is safe except for one species, *H. conicus,* which is reported to have caused the deaths of four individuals in China. It is easily recognized by the blackening of its parts.

Clitocybe illudens

(Plate 12)

Vomiting, diarrhea and great prostration follow the eating of this brilliantly-colored, luminescent agaric. The illness lasts but a short time, and after a day or two the patient again enjoys normal health. It has not been known to cause death in man.

Clitocybe sudorifica appears to harbor a muscarin-like substance. When eaten by man, it causes profuse perspiration, but no ill effects.

Purple-brown-spored species: Hypholoma and Stropharia

Hypholoma fasciculare, the Sulphur-top, is rated as undesirable because of its bitter taste. Most species of *Stropharia* are also looked upon askance by expert mushroom-eaters. The genus is closely related to *Psalliota,* which includes the precious Meadow Mushroom. The two genera are easily distinguished, if attention is paid to the manner in which the gills are attached to the stem. In *Stropharia* they are adnate; in *Psalliota* they are free.

Black-spored mushrooms

Panaeolus species (figure 35) look harmless enough, but it is well to keep them out of the cooking utensils for, though not violently poisonous, they can be the cause of considerable, momentary, anxiety. The effects of the poison become evident almost instantaneously. The symptoms are not unlike those of alcohol-intoxication. Conspicuous are, failure of muscular coördination, difficulty in standing, inability to walk, drowsiness, lack of control of the emotions, bloodshot eyes, dilated pupils, incoherent or inappropriate speech (the afflicted laughing inordinately at his own foolish remarks), and visions of dancing, wobbly. furniture, combined with glorious color combinations. Prostration is usually absent. Temporary but complete paralysis of the arms or legs may also appear (Douglass, '17; Krieger, '11).

One species, *Panaeolus venenosus* Murr. (=*Psathyra helobia* [Kalchbr.]?) is known to come up in beds of the cultivated mushroom, *Psalliota campestris* (Murrill, '16).

TYPES OF MUSHROOM POISONING

Ford ('23) recognizes five different types of mushroom poisoning which he classifies as follows:

Gastro-intestinal type. Characterized by early appearing symptoms of nausea, vomiting, and diarrhea. The symptoms terminate rapidly and, usually spontaneously, the patients being restored to health in a day or two. Rarely fatal. Causative mushrooms: *Russula emetica, Boletus satanas, B. miniato-olivaceus* var. *sensibilis, Lactarius torminosus, Entoloma lividum* and *Lepiota morgani.*

Choleriform type. Gastro-intestinal symptoms develop in from ten to fifteen hours, followed by rapid loss of strength and weight. The death rate is high. Causative mushrooms: *Amanita phalloides, A. virosa* (and closely related species), and, perhaps, *Pholiota autumnalis* and *Hygrophorus conicus.* It is reported that an antitoxic serum against the poisons of *Amanita phalloides* has been produced (see p. 141).

Nerve-affecting type. Early, gastro-intestinal symptoms, appearing in two or three hours after the fungi have been eaten, terminating in violent convulsions, delirium, coma, and often in death. The active poisonous principle is muscarin, for which the perfect antidote is atropin. Causative mushrooms: *Amanita muscaria, A. pantherina,* various Inocybes, like *Inocybe infelix* and *I. infida,* and *Clitocybe illudens. Clitocybe sudorifica,* while producing nothing more serious than profuse perspiration, also belongs here because the active principle is muscarin, which is present in small quantities.

Blood-dissolving type. Abdominal distress, with jaundice developing in four or five days. Death may occur. Blood transfusion is suggested by Ford as the logical treatment. Causative mushroom: *Gyromitra esculenta.*

Cerebral type. The transient symptoms appear shortly

after the meal. They are, exhilaration, staggering gait, and queer disturbances of vision. The patients are soon normal again. Causative mushrooms: various species of the genus *Panaeolus*.

It ought to be needless to emphasize that only perfectly fresh, non-water-soaked, insect-free specimens should be selected for the table. Also, that mushrooms, deteriorating very rapidly as they do, must not be kept until it is convenient to cook them, but should be cleaned, and at least parboiled, immediately after they have been bought or collected.

THE WOOD-DESTROYING FUNGI

(For references to the descriptions of some of the species discussed here, consult the index)

Man has a sentimental, as well as an economic, interest in trees. It, therefore, touches his heart to see the tree the woodman spared fall prey to the ravages of a fungus parasite. Tree surgeons are engaged to save a particularly fine Oak that for generations has stood near the ancestral home. Millions of dollars were spent in a futile effort to save our splendid chestnut trees from destruction through the blight. State and Federal moneys are at present being expended to prevent the five-needle pines from sharing a similar fate at the hands of the Blister Rust, and, within very recent years, the *Dutch Elm Disease* has entered our country, threatening to destroy another noble tree.

Starting in the nurseries, trees are beset from their very "babyhood" with diseases due to fungi. Coniferous and other trees have scarcely sprouted when the mycelia of certain soil fungi cause them to "damp off". Protection of the seedlings by maintaining temperature and moisture conditions inimical to the fungi, together with the application of soil disinfectants, will hold the trouble in check. Later, as the trees develop their own defenses, life for them becomes a little more certain, until finally, with age, they succumb to the attacks of fungi, insects, and other agencies. The structures of these defenses and the means nature employs to break them down, preliminary to the onset of diseases due to fungi, are noteworthy.

Von Schrenk ('00) says: "In any consideration of the life and growth of trees one must not forget that every tree, after it has reached a certain age, which varies with different trees, is composed of two distinct parts, the living part and what may for the sake of convenience be called the dead part. The former consists of the leaves, the younger branches, and the smaller roots, and of a thin layer, including the most recently formed wood and the inner bark, while the latter includes the old wood of the trunk, larger roots and branches, inclosed by the newer wood, and the bark. The living parts are renewed at short intervals, while the old wood, known as heartwood, becomes permeated with certain preservative and coloring materials, and serves mainly as a support for the growing parts of the tree. Fungi which cause disease may so affect the living parts that they cease to perform their functions, or they may destroy the dead parts so that they can no longer support the living wood and the leaves."

Trees are thus seen to be provided with natural means of protection. In addition, the upper, more exposed surface of the leaves is covered with a thickened layer that gives toughness to that part. The breathing pores, usually on the lower surface, are provided with guard cells that close when respiration is not going on. The trunk, branches, and twigs are encased in bark, and wounds to the larger of these parts are readily healed by gums or resins. Yet, withal, the fungi gain entrance. In this they are assisted by man and animals, and by the elements. Woodpeckers make holes and lovers cut their initials into the bark; insects bore extensive galleries into the heartwood; larger animals such as deer, bears, and horses rip the bark; storms and heavy snow break off branches, and lightning and forest fires add their damaging effects. Once a tree has been injured, the way stands open for invasion by hosts of wood-hungry fungi (Farlow and Seymour, 1888; Seymour, '29).

A fungus enters by means of its spores. These tiny bodies, ever present in the air, or on or in insects and other tree visitors, gain lodgment in an exposed part and proceed to form a mycelium (see Spore Dissemination, p. 85). The mycelium, continuing to grow, travels under the bark and between the annual wood-layers and the

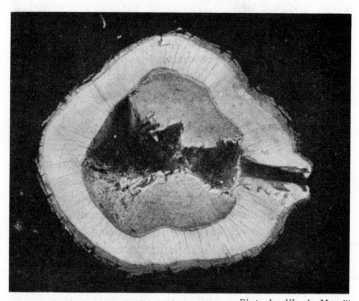

Photo by W. A. Murrill

Figure 40   Cross section of a hickory log, showing the effect of *Hydnum septentrionale*. The fruit-body (fig. 95) grew from the hole shown on the right

medullary rays, feeding all the while, until the entire structure is reduced to a punky, soggy, or powdery mass (figure 40). Occasionally, in order to propagate itself, the fungus forms fruit-bodies, and it is these one sees projecting from trees like brackets (figures 41, 42), or as mushrooms with teeth or gills (figures 91, 114).

Figure 41 *Fomes applanatus* destroying a tree

Figure 42 Sulphurous or Chicken Mushroom, *Polyporus sulphureus,* growing from a wound in an oak tree. See also plate 28

Diseases of trees due to fungi may be divided into groups, according to the parts affected by them. Some, mostly microscopic forms, attack leaves; others are to be found at work in the tissues of the roots or in the sapwood or heartwood.

Of the leaf diseases, common examples are: the Leaf Blight of sycamores, due to *Gloeosporium nervisequum,* the Tar Spot of maple leaves (irregularly shaped, black blotches occurring in late summer, and caused by *Rhytisma acerinum*), the various mildews (one of which is often seen on lilacs), the rusts on conifers, and the Peach Leaf curl, familiar to the orchardist.

Of the root diseases there are several, but the worst by far is the so-called Oak Root-rot due to the gill mushroom, *Armillaria mellea.* Its effect upon a great variety of trees is deadly in the extreme. Working on the roots and on the sapwood under the bark, it soon kills the tree. After removing the bark of a tree afflicted with the *Armillaria* (figure 69) disease, one can pull loose long, black cords of compacted mycelium, the rhizomorphs of the fungus, by means of which the trouble is carried into further feeding grounds (Shoestring Disease). Although the *Armillaria* rot is one of the worst of all tree diseases, especially where oaks and orchard trees live in close proximity, there are few serious tree infections that can be laid to gill mushrooms, most of these being saprophytes, or consumers of dead plant tissues. *Pholiota adiposa* may be mentioned as a wound parasite on maple, and *Collybia velutipes* causes sapwood rot in basswood, in the buckeye, and in the horse-chestnut. Two species of *Pleurotus,* the edible *Pleurotus ulmarius* and *P. ostreatus* (figure 114), produce wood- and sap-rot, respectively, in various deciduous trees.

Coprinus micaceus (figure 84), *Hypholoma sublater-itium, H. incertum* (plate 21, figure 95), and *Clitocybe illudens* (plate 12) are generally found at the base of frondose trees, but their action does not appear to be of a parasitic nature. *Schizophyllum commune* (figure 20f) likewise invades dead bark-tissue. *Cantharellus floccosus,* on the other hand, has been found to be mildly parasitic on firs in Japan (Masui, '27), on the roots of which it forms mycorrhizas. *Lenzites, Lentinus* (figure 57e), *Daedalea* (figures 43, 56e), *Poria,* and *Merulius* species are destructive to building timbers, the rot caused by *Merulius lacrymans* being especially feared.

The fleshy polypores (*Boletus,* plates 1, 7, 8, 9, 10), are saprophytes. *Boletus hemichrysus,* however, grows attached to the roots of conifers, but whether parasiti-cally or not has not been determined. The really destruc-tive parasites of living trees among the higher fungi are the tough, woody polypores or bracket fungi, the "punks" or "conchs" of the forester. They are members of the genera *Trametes* (figure 56b), *Fomes* (figures 41, 56c), and *Polyporus* (plate 28, figure 42). Foremost as an enemy of timber stands *Trametes pini.* Its fruit-bodies are large, cinnamon-brown on the lower side, black, charcoal-like and cracked on the upper. It is thought to be responsible for about four-fifths of the havoc wrought in timber by fungi. Most of the conifers which furnish lumber are subject to the disease, which consists of a white-spotting of the wood.

Polyporus schweinitzii, a yellow-brown, stipitate species, starts its destructive work at the roots of hemlocks, spruces, pines and other conifers, continuing upward into the trunk. Its mycelium travels through the soil and may invade a number of close-standing trees.

Polyporus sulphureus (plate 28, figure 42), the polypore whose young fruit-bodies are prized by the mushroom-eater, is also a most persistent enemy of coniferous as well as deciduous trees. It is found on oaks, chestnuts,

Photo by W. A. Murrill

Figure 43 *Daedalea quercina,* a woody fungus common on oak stumps. A view into the labyrinthine structure of the tubes is shown in figure 56 at *e*

locusts, maples, alders, walnuts, pines, hemlocks and spruces, even apple trees being attacked. The fungus easily attracts attention by its vivid colors, the tops of the overlapping caps being bright pinkish-orange, the lower side, lemon-yellow.

Polyporus betulinus is well known to all who scour the northern woods, its white, rounded, semicircular fruit-bodies protruding from the trunks of the Canoe Birch. It causes a powdery rot of the sapwood. Other sapwood rots are due to *Fomes fomentarius* (on Birch and Beech), and to *Fomes pinicola* (on firs and other evergreens). The former is rather large and hoof-shaped, with a hard, grayish upper surface and a ferruginous lower one, whereas the latter, similarly shaped, is brighter colored, reddish-brown and yellow tints predominating.

Fomes igniarius, hoof-shaped and colored light cinnamon-brown, induces a white soft-rot in the wood of willows, walnuts, poplars, oaks, maples, alders, and other frondose trees. Apple trees are also made to suffer.

Fomes applanatus (figure 41), one of the best known representatives of the polypore family, causes a white butt-rot of Beech, Birch, Maple, Oak and Poplar. The upper surface of the fruit-body is colored grayish-brown. The lower one, being nearly white, and (when perfectly fresh) easily darkened by scratching with a knife or other sharp implement, is sometimes used by artists as a sketching ground. When thoroughly dry the drawing is permanent, and the fungus can be set up over the fireplace of one's cabin as an ornament.

At the base of oaks grows *Polyporus frondosus* (figure 115), a species which enjoys a reputation for edibility. It is not very common, nor is it especially destructive.

Polyporus rimosus destroys the wood of the Locust, a tree ordinarily free from fungous attack.

Polyporus roseus affects many evergreens with a heartwood rot, reducing the wood to a charcoal-like powder.

Two species of *Polystictus, P. versicolor* (figure 44), and *P. pergamenus,* are of economic importance in that they are the cause of the destruction of much of the wood of deciduous trees used for railroad ties. Occasionally

Photo by W. A. Murrill

Figure 44 *Polystictus versicolor,* "at work"

they assume a parasitic rôle by attacking the sapwood. The latter species usually follows in the wake of forest fires.

Among the teeth fungi (Hydnaceæ) few enemies of living trees exist. *Hydnum erinaceus* produces a white rot in both the Red and White Oak, as well as in other frondose trees. The diseased wood is rendered wet and soggy by the fungus, and, sometimes, moisture exudes from the fruit-bodies themselves. These are rather conspicuous white objects, measuring up to twelve inches in diameter. The body of the fungus usually grows from holes made by the Oak Borer. Hanging down from the underside are long, white, pointed teeth or spines that bear the spores.

Hydnum septentrionale (figures 40, 91) forms large, white masses of overlapping fruit-bodies on Hickory, Maple and Beech trees, causing a white sapwood rot. The teeth are white, narrow, long, and closely placed, side by side.

Another species, *Echinodontium tinctorium,* induces very destructive heartwood rot in the White Fir throughout California. It gets its specific name, *tinctorium,* from the use to which Indians put the rusty-red interior of the fruit-bodies in making their war paint.

In the Thelephoraceæ, the *Rhizoctonia* (mycelial) stage of *Corticium vagum* is a pest on a number of valuable plants, including the potato. It is also reported as causing the Brown Patch on golf links. In tree nurseries it is one of the important factors in the damping-off disease. *Stereum purpureum* is well known as the cause of the Silver Leaf in fruit trees, while *Thelephora terrestris* strangles to death the young seedlings of conifers, Hard Maple, and those of other trees.

The smaller branches of some trees (Maple and fruit trees) frequently exhibit small, pink, elevated spots (Coral-spot disease) due to a species of *Nectria,* a genus of the Hypocreaceæ. The so-called Witches' Brooms, erect bunches of thin branchlets seen on a variety of trees, are also, at times, of fungous origin. These Brooms, when caused by fungi, are alterations in the normal mode of branching of a tree, and are due to stimulation from mycelium that spreads into twigs and branches. One *Peziza*-like species, *Rhizina inflata* (figure 51a), is antagonistic to the roots of conifers. It is somewhat puffed out, of a rusty-brown color, with whitish margin, and with root-like projections on the underside.

Cedar Apples, those unusual-looking, roundish, chocolate-brown galls one sees on cedars (*Juniperus*) in autumn, are the product of a fungus (*Gymnosporangium*) which undergoes part of its development on apple trees, on the leaves, fruits and twigs of which it causes the characteristic Cedar Rust spots. The life cycle of this fungus offers an illustration of what is known as alternation of generations, one phase of the development taking place on the Apple tree, the other on the Cedar, with spores of a different character borne in each phase. Such alternation, from one host to another, is also to be observed in the Pine Blister Rust and in the Wheat Rust. In the former the alternative hosts are *Ribes* species (gooseberries and currants), in the latter, the Common Barberry. The eradication of the Barberry is, therefore, compulsory in most wheat-growing regions. According to a recent report of the United States Department of Agriculture, more than 18,500,000 barberry bushes have been destroyed in this country in the last fifteen years.

In 1916, the losses from Wheat Rust in the United States and Canada reached the gigantic total of 280,000,000 bushels (for a diagram illustrating the life cycle of the Wheat Rust, see figure 45. For an account of the losses due to fungi, see p. 105).

TREATMENT OF TREE DISEASES

Except where forestry is carried out in a thoroughly scientific way, little can be done to combat the diseases of forest trees beyond cutting down badly infected stands. Early recognition of disease by trained men, before the timber has been rendered unmarketable, is expensive and, therefore, for the present at least, uneconomic. Improving the living conditions of trees by a systematic thinning of stands is the true solution. Once the punks or mushrooms make their appearance on the bark, treatment is useless, except in so far as single trees are concerned that one wishes to preserve for sentimental reasons, in which case really expert tree surgeons, not "tree butchers," should be engaged to make the necessary excisions, and to apply the proper disinfectants.

Where white pines and other five-needled species are concerned, currants and gooseberries should be kept at a safe distance. Apple orchards and cedars should likewise be as far as possible from each other, and the Common Barberry must be exterminated altogether and replaced by a Japanese variety that is not an alternative host to the Wheat Rust Fungus.

For the preservation of wood which is to be exposed to the elements (railroad ties, telegraph poles, etc.), impregnation of the cellular structure with creosote, or other preservative materials, is resorted to. Proper ventilation (to control moisture conditions) will prolong the durability of indoor, structural timbers (Atkinson, '01; Freeman, '05; Galloway and Woods, 1896; Harshberger, '17; Heald, '26; Meinecke, '14, '30; Rankin, '18; von Schrenk, '00, '02; von Schrenk and Spaulding, '09; Spaulding, '09; Stevens, '13).

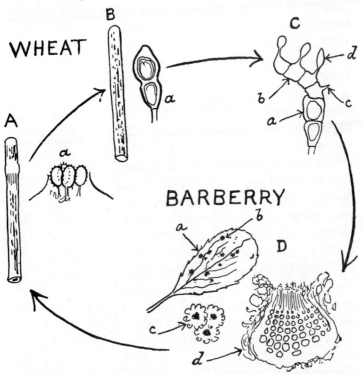

Figure 45   Cycle of the Wheat Rust Fungus, *Puccinia graminis*. *A,* Red rust; *a,* uredineospores. *B,* Black rust; *a,* teliospore. *C,* teliospore at *a,* germinating and producing a promycelium (basidium), *b;* the latter sending forth sporophores (sterigmata), *c;* each sphorophore bearing a sporidium (basidiospore), *d.*   *D,* barberry leaf with cluster-cups (aecia), *a, b,* started by germinating sporidia; *c,* cluster-cups enlarged; *d,* longitudinal section through a cluster-cup showing the aeciospores which, carried over to the wheat, complete the cycle

THE LITERATURE ON MUSHROOMS AND THEIR ALLIES

The most creditable, popular discussion of mushrooms ever published in this country is Gibson's work (1895). The text is informative and well written and the accompanying illustrations, some of which are colored, combine scientific accuracy and artistic rendering. A more recent work, published in England (Rolfe, '25), is also valuable as introductory reading. Cooke and Berkeley's little volume (1875), though issued many years ago, is still acceptable as a treatise on the nature and uses of fungi. Massee's book ('11) will also prove of interest to the beginner. Underwood's Moulds, Mildews and Mushrooms (1899), gives a view of the entire field of study.

For the identification of mushrooms, illustrated books will be found necessary, preferably such as give colored figures. With the exception of Farlow's Icones ('29) there is no extensive American work that offers colored pictures. Europe, more fortunate, has many such (see p. 167). Of the more popular books, one of the reports of Peck (1895) can be recommended. Sixty-seven New York species are described in language not too technical, and the illustrations are sufficiently good to aid in the recognition of species. The memoir by this author ('00a) and succeeding bulletins continue the description and illustration of New York's edible species. Atkinson's publication ('00) is well illustrated with half-tone engravings, and many species are discussed. The bulky tome of McIlvaine and Macadam ('00) describes one thousand American species, not a few of which are adequately figured by half-tones. The colored illustrations are not so good, and the advice as to the edibility of certain kinds might be questioned. Miss Marshall's less pretentious book ('10) gives a few colored plates and many half-tones. A useful feature is the key to the genera, each genus being characterized by an outline sketch. Hard's work ('08) will also assist in placing species. The pictures are uncolored but fairly numerous, and the text is clear. Government bulletins (Charles, '31; Patterson and Charles, '15) cover the common species with thoroughness, and give many fine illustrations. McDougall's two publications ('17, '25), and Moffat's writings ('09, '23), should be added to one's collection, as also three recent, desirable publications by New Yorkers (Cummings, '33; McKenny, '29; Thomas, W. S., '28). Most important of all is Kauffman's thoroughly scientific treatment of the gill-mushrooms of Michigan ('18). Very recently the Canadian government has put forth an admirable presentation of the mushrooms of that country (Güssow and Odell, '27). The writer's article in the National Geographic Magazine (with sixteen colored plates), and his key to the Genera of the Gill Mushrooms (Krieger, '20, '20a), may also prove instructive. In the latter work small ink-sketches illustrate the genera.

Two foreign works (Ramsbottom, '23; Rea, '22, '27, '32) are to be highly recommended as many of the species described occur also in this country. For those who wish to delve deeper, Clement's Genera of the Fungi ('09) will be necessary. See also the new, much enlarged edition of this work (Clements and Shear, '31). Saccardo's Sylloge Fungorum (1882–'26) presents the descriptions of the fungi of the entire world.

The student interested in the ecological aspect of fungi should consult the writings of Buller ('31), Graham ('27,

'28), Lange ('23) and McDougall ('17, '25). Very little work has been done on this phase of mycology, and valuable observations can be made by anyone familiar with both flowering plants and fungi. The literature on mycorrhizae has been listed by Kelly ('32).

A very helpful guide to the literature of the fungi, by families and genera, is Bessey's paper ('20). Burt (1899) likewise points out where the principal treatises on the genera are to be found. Indexes to the descriptions of genera and species will be found in Farlow ('05), Guba and Young ('24), Plunkett ('23), Solheim, Young, and Plunkett ('27), and in volumes 12, 16 and 18 of Saccardo's work (1882–'26). Published illustrations in the world's literature are made accessible through Laplanche's convenient little volume (1894) and, on a comprehensive scale, through volumes 19 and 20 of Saccardo's Sylloge. The history of mycological illustrating is briefly reviewed in a paper published by the writer (Krieger, '22). For a history of the mycology of the ancient Greeks and Romans, Buller's paper ('14) is authoritative. Mycological history in general should be read in Harshberger's book ('17), and Whetzel ('18) gives the development of the science of phytopathology or plant diseases. Occasionally the student meets with obsolete fungus names, names no longer in use (synonyms). These he will find in volume 15 of Saccardo's Sylloge, where they are referred to accepted names.

The world's literature on fungi (the individual papers and books published) is recorded by Jackson (1881), Krieger ('24), Lindau and Sydow ('08–'18), and Pritzel (1872). Barnhart's index ('16) will also be found useful. The literature pertaining directly to United States species is listed by Farlow and Trelease (1887; continued by Farlow alone, 1888). Books and papers on the New York species have been enumerated by House ('16). A concise list of works dealing with edible and poisonous fungi was prepared by Clark (1898).

Farlow and Seymour (1888), Saccardo (in volume 13 of his oft-referred-to work), and Seymour ('29), enable the student to approach the parasitic fungi (the large and conspicuous, as well as the microscopic, species) from the standpoint of their hosts. Fossil species of fungi (the few that are known) are listed in volume 10 of the Saccardo work. Many fungi, even the higher ones, have several fruit-forms. Lyman's paper on polymorphism ('07) is a scientific treatise on the known forms.

The morphology of fungi presents many interesting features. Buller ('09, '22, '24, '31, '33, '34) has illumined this phase of the study with his innumerable and original investigations in which he shows, down to the most minute details, the operation of the physical forces of nature in shaping the forms, and in initiating and controlling the functions, of the fruit-bodies of fungi. See also Gwynne-Vaughan ('22, '27), and Gäumann ('28). Ulbrich ('26) presents the subject of malformations in fungi (teratology).

A glossary of terms used in describing fungi will be found on p. 494. It is based on the one published by Daniels (1899). Jackson's ('16) is even more comprehensive. Clement's Genera of Fungi ('90) and the new edition, by Clements and Shear ('31), also contain lists of defined terms.

The most important of the great, illustrated works of the world are *all foreign*. They are: Barla, 1859, 1888; Boudier, '05–'10; Bresadola, '27–33; Bulliard, 1809;

Cooke, 1881; Flora Batava (date not ascertainable);
Flora Danica, 1761–1871; Fries, 1867–1884; Gillet, 1878;
Gramberg, '21; Greville, 1823; Hollós, '04; Hussey, 1847–
1855; Kalchbrenner, 1873–1877; Kallenbach, '26–'34;
Krombholz, 1831–1847; Michael, '18–'19; Richon and
Roze, 1888; Schäffer, 1762–1770; Sowerby, 1797–1809,
and Vittadini, 1835.

When the writer began the study of the higher fungi,
many years ago, he often wished for a guide to the larger
and more comprehensive books, papers and monographs.
Nothing of the kind was available. For the benefit of the
present-day student he has included an extensive, though
by no means complete bibliography (p. 456) to which the
following alphabetically arranged index is the key, in so
far as the names of classes, orders, families and genera
are concerned. Papers and books pertaining to poisoning
cases, tree diseases, etc., etc., are referred to where these
subjects are discussed.

ALPHABETIC INDEX TO THE LITERATURE FOR IDENTIFICATION OF THE HIGHER FUNGI

Agaricaceae. Atkinson, '00 (N. Amer. sp.); Boudier,
'05 (French sp.); Clements, '09 (key to the genera);
Coker, '19b (N. Car. sp.); Davidson, '30; Day, 1882
(N. Y. sp.); Earle, '09 (genera); Engler and Prantl,
Teil 1, Abt. 1 * *, '00, and second edition, '28 (genera);
Hard, '08 (N. Amer. sp.); Kauffman, '18 (Mich. sp.);
Krieger, '20a (key to the genera), '27; Lange, '14, '15,
'17, '21, '23, '26, '28 (Danish sp.); Massee, '02 (Europ.
sp.); McIlvaine and Macadam, '00 (N. Amer. sp.);
Morgan, 1885a, '07a, '08 (N. Amer. sp.); Murrill, '06,
'10, '14, '15a, '16b, '17a, '22, '22a, b, c, '23, 24 (N.
Amer. sp.); Peck, 1872, etc. (N. Y. sp.); Rabenhorst,

vol. 1, Abt. 1, 1884 (Central Europ. sp.) ; Rea, '22 '27
(British sp.) ; Ricken, '15 (Central Europ. sp.) ; Sac-
cardo, vols. 5, 6, 9, 11, 14, 16, 17, 21, 23, 1882–'26
(world sp.) ; Sass, '29; Smith, A. H., '34, '34b; Stover,
'12 (Ohio sp.) ; Sumstine, '18 (N. Y. sp.) ; White, E. A.,
'05, '10 (Conn. sp.). **Agaricus** (see *Psalliota*). **Aleuria.**
Seaver, '14 (N. Amer. sp.). **Aleurina.** Seaver, '14 (N.
Amer. sp.). **Aleurodiscus.** Burt, '18 (N. Amer. sp.).
Alpova, Dodge, C. W., '31. **Amanita.** Beardslee, '08 (N.
Car. sp.) ; Coker, '17 (Eastern U. S. sp.) ; Gilbert, '18;
Kavina and Pilat, '34; Lange, '15 (Danish sp.) ; Lloyd,
1898 (U. S. sp.) ; Morgan, 1887 (N. Amer. sp.) ; Murrill,
'13 (Eastern U. S. sp.) ; '14 (N. Amer. sp.) ; Peck, 1880
(N. Y. sp.) ; Quélet and Bataille, '02. Seyot, '30;
Veselý, '33. **Amanitopsis.** Beardslee, '08 (N. Car.
sp.) ; Coker, '17 (Eastern U. S. sp.) ; Lloyd, 1898 (U. S.
sp.) ; Murrill, '14 (N. Amer. sp.) ; Peck, 1880 (N. Y.
sp.). **Annularia.** Murrill, '17 (N. Amer. sp.). **Aposte-
midium** (see *Geoglossaceae*). **Arcangeliella.** Dodge,
C. W., '31; Zeller and Dodge, '19 (N. Amer. sp.).
Armillaria. Kauffman, '22 (U. S. sp.) ; Murrill, '14 (N.
Amer. sp.) ; Peck, 1890a (N. Y. and U. S. sp.) ;
Zeller and Togashi, '34. **Ascomycetes.** Bell, '33; Fink
and Richards, '15; Fischer, 1897 (See also *Discomycetes*
and *Pyrenomycetes*). **Asterodon.** Banker, '14 (N.
Amer. sp.). **Asterostroma.** Burt, '24 (N. Amer. sp.).
Atylospora. Murrill, '22c (N. Amer. sp.). **Auriculariae.**
Lindau, '00; Neuhoff, '24 (See also *Tremellaceae*).
Barrett, '10; Burt, '21 (N. Amer. sp.).

Basidiomycetes (see also *Hymenomycetes* and *Gasteromycetes*). Bell, '33; Burt, 1899 (Vt. genera) ; Clements, '09 (key to the genera) ; Coker, '20; Day, 1882

(N. Y. sp.) ; Engler and Prantl, Teil 1, Abt. 1 **, '00 (genera) ; Lindau, '28; Massee, '92 (Brit. sp.) ; Migula, '31 (German sp.) ; Rabenhorst, vol. 1, Abt. 1, 1884 (Central Europ. sp.) ; Rea, '22, '27, '32 (British sp.) ; Sumstine, '18 (N. Y. sp.) ; Saccardo, vols. 5, 6, 7, 9, 11, 14, 16, 17, 21, 23, 1882–'26 (world sp.) **Bolbitius.** Murrill, '17 (N. Amer. sp.). **Boletinus.** Murrill, '10 (N. Amer. sp.) ; Peck, 1889a (U. S. sp.). **Boletus.** Bataille, '08; Boudier, '05; Collins, 1899; Gilbert, '31; Kallenbach, '26; Kienholz, '34; Murrill, '10, '14a, '19 (the latter, Conn. sp.) ; Peck, 1887c (N. Y. viscid sp.), 1889a (U. S. sp.) ; Rea, '22, '27 (British sp.) ; Sartory and Maire, '31; Snell, '32–'34; Yates, '16 (histology of certain Calif. sp.). **Bovista.** Massee, 1888b (Mon.). **Bovistella.** Lloyd, '02 (Mon).

Calostoma (See *Mitremyces*). **Calvatia.** Coker and Beardslee, '23 (N. Car. sp.) ; Coker and Couch, '28 (U. S. and Canada sp.) ; Peck, 1879b (U. S. sp.). **Cantharellus.** Coker, '19b (N. Car. sp.) ; Murrill, '10, '16b; Peck, 1887a (N. Y. sp.). **Cladoderris.** Burt, '24 (N. Amer. sp.) ; Lloyd, '13 (Mon.). **Clathrus.** Burt, 1896. **Claudopus.** Murrill, '17 (N. Amer. sp.) ; Peck, 1886 (N. Y. sp.). **Clavaria.** Burt, '22 (N. Amer. sp.) ; Coker, '23 (U. S. and Canada sp.) ; Cotton and Wakefield, '19 (British sp.) ; Harper, '18 (*C. fistulosa* group) ; Huber, '34; Kauffman, '27 (N. Amer. sp.) ; Peck, 1872i (key to N. Y. sp.). **Clavariaceae.** Bourdot and Galzin, '09–'23 (French sp.) ; Clements, '09 (key to the genera) ; Coker, '23 (U. S. and Canada sp.) ; Cotton and Wakefield, '19 (British sp.) ; Day, 1882 (N. Y. sp.) ; Engler and Prantl, Teil 1, Abt. 1 **, '00 (genera) ; Rabenhorst, vol. 1, Abt. 1, 1884 (Central Europ. sp.) ; Saccardo, vols. 6, 9,

11, 14, 16, 17, 21, 23, 1882–'26 (world sp.) ; Sumstine, '18 (N. Y. sp.). **Clitocybe.** Coker and Beardslee, '22 (N. Car. sp.) ; Kauffman, '27a (U. S. sp.) ; Lange, '30 (Danish sp.) ; Murrill, '15a, '16b (N. Amer. sp.) ; Peck, '12 (N. Y. sp.). **Clitopilus.** Murrill, '17 (N. Amer. sp.) ; Peck, 1889 (N. Y. sp.). **Collybia.** Arnold, '34; Coker and Beardslee, '21 (N. Car. sp.) ; Corner, '34; Lange, '17 (Danish sp.) ; Murrill, '15a, '16a (N. Amer. sp.) ; Peck, 1896 (N. Y. sp.) ; Sartory and Maire, '18. **Colus.** Seaver, '31, '34; Sumstine, '16. **Coniophora.** Burt, '17 (N. Amer. sp.). **Coprinus.** Daniels, '01; Earle, '02a (N. Amer. sp.) ; Lange, '15 (Danish sp.) ; Massee, 1896 (Mon.) ; Peck, 1872f (N. Y. sp.). **Cordyceps.** Cooke, 1892; Jenkins, '34; Massee, 1895 (Mon.). **Corticium.** Burt, '26, '29 (N. Amer. sp.). **Cortinarius.** Bataille, '11; Earle, '02e (U. S. sp.) ; Kauffman, '05, '06, '32; Krieger, '25; Peck, 1872g (N. Y. sp.). **Cortinellus** (see *Tricholoma*). **Craterellus.** Burt, '14a, 15 (N. Amer. sp.) ; Coker, '19b (N. Car. sp.) ; Peck, 1887b (N. Y. sp.). **Creolophus.** Banker, '13c (N. Amer. sp.). **Crepidotus.** Murrill, '17 (N. Amer. sp.) ; Peck, 1886 (N. Y. sp.). **Cryptoporus.** House, '14; Zeller, '15. **Cymatella.** Burt, '24 (N. Amer. sp.). **Cyphella.** Burt, '15 (N. Amer. sp.). **Cytidia.** Burt, '24 (N. Amer. sp.).

Dacryomycetae. (See also *Tremellaceae*.) Burt, '21 (N. Amer. sp.) ; Fischer, '32; Hennings, '00; Martin and Fisher, '33 (Iowa sp.). **Daldinia.** Child, '29, '32. **Deconica.** Morgen, '07a (N. Amer. sp.) ; Murrill, '22c. **Discina.** Seaver, '17a, '21 (N. Amer. sp.). **Discomycetes.** Bachman, '09 (Ohio sp.) ; Boudier, '05 (French sp.) ; '07 (key to the genera) ; Buller, '34; Cummins, '30 (Montana sp.) ; Day, 1882 (N. Y. sp.) ; Engler and Prantl, Teil 1, Abt. 1, 1897 (genera) ; Fairman, 1896 (N. Y. sp.) ; Lagarde, '06; Morgan '02a (Ohio sp.) ; Phillips, 1887 (British sp.) ; Saccardo, vols. 8, 10, 11, 14, 16, 18, 22, 24, 1882–'28 (world sp.) ; Seaver, '09 (N. Dakota sp.), '10 (Iowa sp.), '28 (N. Amer. sp.) ; Sumstine, '18 (N. Y. sp.). **Drosophila** (See *Hypholoma*).

Eccilia. Murrill, '17 (N. Amer. sp.). **Echinodontium.** Banker, '13c (N. Amer. sp.). **Eichleriella.** Burt, '15b (N. Amer. sp.). **Elaphomyces.** Dodge, C. W., '29. **Entoloma** (see also *Rhodophyllus*). Murrill, '17 (N. Amer. sp.) ; Peck, '09a (N. Y. sp.). **Eomycenella.** Atkinson, '02. **Epithele.** Burt, '20 (N. Amer. sp.). **Exobasidiineae.** Hennings, '00. **Exobasidium.** Burt, '15a (N. Amer. sp.).

Flammula. Kauffman, '26 (U. S. sp.) ; Lange, '28 (Danish sp.) ; Murrill, '17 (N. Amer. sp.) ; Peck, 1897a (N. Y. sp.). **Fomes.** Lloyd, '15 (Mon.).

Galera (=*Galerula*). Atkinson, '18 (N. Amer. sp.) ; Earle, '03d (N. Amer. sp.) ; Murrill, '17 (N. Amer. sp.) ; Peck, 1893b (N. Y. sp.). **Galerula** (see *Galera*). **Ganoderma.** Haddow, '31 (See also *Polyporaceae*). **Gasteromycetes.** Clements, '09 (key to the genera) ; Coker and Beardslee, '23 (N. Car. sp.) ; Coker and Couch, '28 (U. S. and Canada sp.) ; Day, 1882 (N. Y. sp.) ; Dodge, '34; Engler and Prantl, Teil 1, Abt. 1 **, '00 (genera) ; Fairman, 1896 (N. Y. sp.) ; Hollós, '04 (Hungarian sp.) ; Johnson, '29 (Ohio sp.) ; Lloyd, '02 (genera) ; Massee, 1889, 1891 (British sp.) ; Moffatt, '23 (Ill. sp.) ; Morgan, 1889a, 1890, 1891, 1892 (N. Amer. sp.) ; Rabenhorst, vol. 1, Abt. 1, 1884 (Central Europ. sp.) ; Saccardo, vols. 7, 9, 11, 14, 16, 17, 21, 23, 1882–'26 (world sp.) ; Sumstine, '18 (N. Y. sp.) ; Trelease, 1888 (Wisc. sp.) ;

Zeller, '34. **Gautieria.** Zeller and Dodge, '18a (N. Amer. sp.). **Geaster** (including *Myriostoma*). Coker, '24 (U. S. and Canada sp.); Lloyd, '02a; Longnecker, '27 (Iowa sp.); Morgan, 1885 (N. Amer. sp.). **Geoglossaceae.** Durand, '08, '21 (N. Amer. sp.); Imai, '34; Lloyd, '16; Massee, 1897. **Geopyxis.** Kupfer, '02. **Gloiodon.** Banker, '13c (N. Amer. sp.). **Gloeostereeae.** Imai, '33. **Gomphidius.** Kauffman, '25 (U. S. sp.); Murrill, '22a. **Gymnomyces.** Zeller and Dodge, '19 (N. Amer. sp.). **Gyromitra.** Dearness, '24 (poisoning case); Seaver, '20, '28 (N. Amer. sp.).

Hebeloma. Murrill, '17 (N. Amer. sp.); Peck, '10a (N. Y. sp.). **Heliomyces.** Murrill, '15a (N. Amer. sp.); Morgan, '06a (N. Amer. sp.). **Helvellaceae.** Anderson and Ickis, '21 (Mass. sp.); Bataille, '11; Burt, 1899a (Vt. sp.); Hone, '04, '06 (Minn. sp.); Morse, '34; Peck, 1879 (key to N. Y. sp.); Schroeter, 1897; Seaver, '20, '28, '30, '31a (N. Amer. sp.); Underwood, 1896 (N. Amer. sp.). **Hemiasceae.** Fischer, 1897. **Hexagona.** Lloyd, '10a (Mon.) **Hiatula.** Murrill, '16b (N. Amer. sp.). **Hydnaceae.** Banker, '01, '02, '04, '06, '12a, '13a, b, c, '14, '29 (N. Amer. sp.); Beardslee, '24 (scaly sp. of *Hydnum*); Cejp, '31a; Clements, '09 (key to the genera); Coker, '19a (N. Car. sp.); Day, 1882 (N. Y. sp.); Engler and Prantl, Teil 1, Abt. 1 **, '00 (genera); Miller, '33, '34, '34a; Rabenhorst, vol. 1, Abt. 1, 1884 (Central Europ. sp.); Saccardo, vols. 6, 9, 11, 14, 16, 17, 21, 23, 1882–'26 (world sp.); Sumstine, '18 (N. Y. sp.). **Hydnellum.** Banker, '13b (N. Amer. sp.). **Hydnochaete.** Banker, '14 (N. Amer. sp.). **Hydnodon.** Banker, '13c (N. Amer. sp.) **Hydnum.** Banker, '02, '04, '06, '12a, '13a, b, c, '14 (N. Amer. sp.); Beardslee, '24 (scaly sp.); Coker,

'19a (N. Car. sp.). **Hygrophorus.** Bataille, '10 (Europ. sp.); Earle, '02b (N. Amer. sp.); Lange, '23 (Danish sp.); Murrill, '16b (N. Amer. sp.); Peck, '07 (N. Y. sp.). **Hymenochaete.** Burt, '18a (N. Amer. sp.). **Hymenogastraceae.** Bataille, '23 (Europ. sp.); Fischer, '00; Zeller and Dodge, '18a, '19, '24 (N. Amer. sp.). **Hymenomycetes** (see also *Agaricaceae, Polyporaceae, Hydnaceae, Clavariaceae, Thelephoraceae*). Bell, '33; Boughton, '17 (N. Y. sp.); Bourdot and Galzin, '09–23 (French sp.); Buller, '34; Clements, '09 (key to the genera); Day, 1882 (N. Y. sp.); Engler and Prantl, Teil 1, Abt. ******, '00 (genera); Fairman, 1893 (N. Y. sp.); Kalchbrenner, 1873 (Hungarian sp.); Killermann, '28; Lyman, '07 (Polymorphism); Moffat, '09 (Ill. sp.); Overholts, '29; Rabenhorst, vol. 1, Abt. 1, 1884 (Central Europ. sp); Saccardo, vols. 5, 6, 9, 11, 14, 16, 17, 21, 23, 1882–'26 (world sp.); Stevenson, 1886 (British sp.); Sumstine, '18 (N. Y. sp.); Togashi and Oda, '34; White, E. A., '05, '10 (Conn. sp.). **Hypholoma** (=*Drosophila*). Earle, '02 (N. Amer. sp.); Harper, '14, '16 (Great Lakes region sp.); Lange, '23 (Danish sp.); Morgan, '08 (N. Amer. sp.); Murrill, '22; Peck, '11 (N. Y. sp.). **Hypochnus.** Burt, '16 (N. Amer. sp.). **Hypocreaceae.** Cooke, 1892; Massee, 1895 (Mon.); Seaver, '10 (N. Amer. sp.). **Hypodendrum** (see *Pholiota*). **Hypogaei.** Bucholtz, '03 (Morphology); Fischer, '08 (Morphology); Hesse, 1891–1894 (German sp.). (See also *Hymenogastraceae, Rhizopogonaceae, Tuberaceae*.) **Hypolyssus.** Burt, '24 (N. Amer. sp.). **Hysterangium.** Zeller and Dodge, '29. **Hysteriales.** Bisby, '23; Lindau, 1897 (world genera).

Inocybe. Bataille, '10 (Europ. sp.) ; Earle, '03e (N. Amer. sp.) ; Heim, '31 (world sp.) ; Kauffman, '21 (N. Y. sp.), '24 (N. Amer. sp.) ; Lange, '17 (Danish sp.) ; Massee, '04 (Mon.) ; Peck, '10 (N. Y. sp.). **Irpex.** Cejp, '31 (see also *Hydnaceae*).

Laccaria. Coker and Beardslee, '22 (N. Car. sp.) ; Murrill, '14 (N. Amer. sp.) ; Peck, '12a (N. Y. sp.). **Lachnocladium.** Burt, '20 (N. Amer. sp.) ; Coker, '23 (U. S. and Canada sp.). **Lactarius.** Bataille, '07 ; Burlingham, '07, '08, '10, '13, '32 (U. S. sp.) ; Coker, '19 (N. Car. sp.) ; Earle, '02d (N. Amer. sp.) ; Lange, '28 (Danish sp.) ; Peck, 1885 (N. Y. sp.). **Laternea.** Linder, '28. **Lentinus.** Earle, '03a (N. Amer. sp.) ; Harper, '22 (Great Lakes region sp.) ; Murrill, '15a (N. Amer. sp.) ; Peck, '09 (N. Y. sp.). **Lepiota.** Kauffman. '24a (U. S. sp.) ; Lange, '15 (Danish sp.) ; Morgan, '06b, '07 (N. Amer. sp.) ; Murrill, '14 (N. Amer. sp.) ; Peck, 1884 (N. Y. sp.) ; Quélet and Bataille, '02. **Lepista** (see *Tricholoma*). Murrill, '15a, '17 (N. Amer. sp.). **Leptonia** (see also *Rhodophyllus*). Murrill, '17 (N. Amer. sp.) ; Peck, 1872b (N. Y. sp.). **Leucogaster.** Dodge, C. W., '31 ; Zeller and Dodge, '24 (N. Amer. sp.). **Leucophlebs.** Zeller and Dodge, '24 (N. Amer. sp.). **Lycoperdon.** Coker and Beardslee, '23 (N. Car. sp.) ; Coker and Couch, '28 (U. S. and Canada sp.) ; Fischer. '00; Lloyd, '02 (U. S. sp.) ; Lohman, '27 (Iowa sp.) . Massee, 1887a (Mon.) ; Peck, 1879b (U. S. sp.).

Macowanites. Zeller and Dodge, '19 (N. Amer. sp.). **Manina.** Banker, '12 (N. Amer. sp.). **Marasmius.** Bataille, '19 (Europ. sp.) ; Kühner, '33 ; Lange, '21 (Danish sp.) : Morgan, '06 (N. Amer. sp.) ; Murrill, 15a

(N. Amer. sp.) ; Peck, 1872h (N. Y. sp.) ; Pennington, '15a (N. Y. and U. S. sp.). **Matruchotia.** Burt, '24 (N. Amer. sp.). **Merulius.** Bourdot and Galzin, '09–'23 (French sp.) ; Burt, '17a, '19 (N. Amer. sp.). **Microstroma.** Burt, '24 (N. Amer. sp.). **Mitremyces** (=*Calostoma*). Lloyd, '05 (Mon.) ; Massee, 1888a (Mon.). **Mitrula** (see *Geoglossaceae*). **Morchella.** Bataille, '11; Morgan, '02; Seaver, '28 (N. Amer. sp.) ; Trelease, 1888 (Wisc. sp.). **Mutinus.** Martin, '31 (see also *Phallaceae*). **Mycena.** Beardslee and Coker, '24 (N. Car. sp.). Höhnel, '13, '14 (new system of classifying the species) ; Lange, '14 (Danish sp.) ; Murrill, '16a (N. Amer. sp.) ; Peck, 1872a (N. Y. sp.). **Mycobonia.** Burt, '20 (N. Amer. sp.). **Myriostoma** (see *Geaster*).

Naucoria. Murrill, '17 (N. Amer. sp.) ; Peck, 1872c (N. Y. sp.). **Nidulariaceae.** Fischer, '00; Lloyd, '06; Martin, '27; White, V. S., '02 (N. Amer. sp.). **Nolanea.** Murrill, '17 (N. Amer. sp.). **Nyctalis.** Murrill, '10 (N. Amer. sp.).

Odontia. Peck, '00 (key to N. Y. sp.). **Omphalia.** Lange, '30 (Danish sp.) ; Murrill, '16a (N. Amer. sp.) ; Peck, 1893 (N. Y. sp.).

Panaeolus. Morgan, '07a; Peck, 1872d (N. Y. sp.). **Panus.** Earle, '03b; Forster, 1888; Murrill, '15a (N. Amer. sp.). **Paxillus.** Kauffman, '26 (U. S. sp.) ; Murrill, '17 (N. Amer. sp.) ; Peck, 1887 (N. Y. sp.). **Peniophora.** Burt, '25 (N. Amer. sp.). **Peziza.** Seaver, '09, '10, '14, '15a, '16a, '17a, '21, '28 (N. Amer. sp.). **Pezizaceae.** Durand, '00 (classification). **Pezizales.** Hone, '09 (Minn. sp.) ; Seaver, '28 (N. Amer. sp.) ; Lindau, 1897 (world genera). **Phallaceae.** Burt, 1896a,

1897 (U. S. sp.); Fischer, 1890, '00; Lloyd, '09 (Mon.); Long, '07 (Texas sp.); Seaver, '34; Sumstine, '16. **Phellodon.** Banker, '13a (N. Amer. sp.). **Pholiota** (=*Hypodendrum*). Harper, '13a, '16 (Great Lakes region sp.); Lange, '21 (Danish sp.); Overholts, '24 (N. Amer. sp.), '27 (U. S. sp.), '32; Peck, '08 (N. Y. sp.). **Pilobolus.** Allen and Jolivette, '14; Buller, '34. **Pilosace.** Morgan, '07a; Murrill, '22. **Pistillaria.** Burt, '16b; Killerman, '34. **Pleurotus.** Lange, '30 (Danish sp.); Murrill, '15a, '16a (N. Amer. sp.); Peck, 1886 (N. Y. sp.). **Pluteolus.** Earle, '03c (N. Amer. sp.); Murrill, '17 (N. Amer. sp.); Peck, 1893a (N. Y. sp.). **Pluteus.** Lange, '17 (Danish sp.); Murrill, '17 (N. Amer. sp.); Peck, 1885a (N. Y. sp.). **Podaxon** (=*Podaxis*). Fischer, '34; Massee, 1890 (Mon); Morse, '33. **Polyporaceae.** Ames, '13 (structure in relation to genera); Baxter, '24, '25, '27, '29, '32, '32a, '34; Clements, '09 (key to the genera); Day, 1882 (N. Y. sp.); Engler and Prantl, Teil 1, Abt. 1 **, '00 (genera); Lowe, '34 (N. Y. sp.); Murrill, '08, '14b, 15b, c, '24 (N. Amer. sp.); Neuman, '14 (Wisc. sp.); Overholts, '11, '14, '15a (Ohio sp.) '33 (Penn. sp.); Rabenhorst, vol. 1, Abt. 1, 1884 (Central Europ. sp.); Rea, '22, '27 (British sp.); Saccardo, vols. 6, 9, 11, 14, 16, 17, 21, 23, 1882–'26 (world sp.); Sharp, '33; Shope, '31 (Colorado sp.); Smith, '31 (N. England sp.); Sumstine '18 (N. Y. sp.); Wolf, '31 (Iowa sp.). **Polyporus.** Atkinson, '08 (Europ. and N. Amer. sp.); Baxter, '24, '25, '32a, '34; Lloyd '11, '12, '15a (Mon.); Lowe, '34, 34a (N. Y. sp.); Overholts, '33; Zeller, '15 (on *Polyporus volvatus*). **Polysaccum.** Massee, 1887, 1888 (Mon.). **Polystictus.** Lloyd, '10 (Mon.). **Poria.** Baxter, '27, '29, '32a, '34; Ling, '33. Overholts, '19, '22, '23, '23a, '31 (U. S. sp.).

Poronia. Ellis and Everhart, 1887. **Protocoronospora.** Burt, '24 (N. Amer. sp.). **Protogaster.** Zeller, '34. **Psalliota** (=*Agaricus*). Coker, '28 (N. Carol. sp.); Lange, '26 (Danish sp.); Murrill, '22b; Peck, 1884a (N. Y. sp.); Smith, C. O., 1899 (Champlain Valley sp.). **Psathyra.** Morgan, '07a (N. Amer. sp.); Murrill, '22c (N. Amer. sp.); Peck, '11a (N. Y. sp.). **Psathyrella.** Morgan, '07a (N. Amer. sp.); Murrill, '22c (N. Amer. sp.); Peck, 1872e (N. Y. sp.). **Psilocybe.** Morgan, '07a (N. Amer. sp.); Murrill, '23 (N. Amer. sp.); Peck, '12b (N. Y. sp.). **Pyrenomycetes.** Clements, '09 (key to the genera); Ellis and Everhart, 1887, 1888–1889, 1892 (N. Amer. sp.); Engler and Prantl, Teil 1, Abt. 1, 1897 (genera); Lloyd, '17a, '19 (the larger *Pyreno.*); Rabenhorst, vol. 1, Abt. 2, 1884 (Central Europ. sp.); Saccardo, vols. 1, 2, 8, 10, 11, 14, 16, 18, 22, 24, 1882–'28 (world sp.).

Queletia (see *Tylostoma*).

Radulum. Lloyd, '17 (Mon.); **Rhizopogon.** Zeller and Dodge, '18 (N. Amer. sp.). **Rhizopogonaceae.** Dodge, C. W., '31; Zeller and Dodge, '18, '18a, '19, '24; **Rhodophyllus** (=*Entoloma* and *Leptonia*). Lange, '21 (Danish sp.). **Russula.** Bataille, '07; Beardslee, '18 (N. Car. sp.); Burlingham, '15, '17 (U. S. sp.), '18 (Long Island, N. Y. sp.), 18a (Mass. sp.), '21, '24; Crawshay, '30; Denniston, '05 (Wisc. sp.); Earle, '02c (N. Amer. sp.); Kauffman, '09 (Mich. sp.); Lange, '26 (Danish sp.); Macadam, 1889 (N. Amer. sp.); Maire, '10; Peck, '07a (N. Y. sp.); Schaeffer, '33; Singer, '32.

Sarcodon. Banker, '13 (N. Amer. sp.). **Schizophyllum.** Linder, '33; Murrill, '15a (N. Amer. sp.).

Scleroderma. Fischer, '00 (see also *Gasteromycetes*). **Sclerotinia.** Whetzel, '26. **Sebacina.** Burt, '15b (N. Amer. sp.). **Septobasidium.** Burt, '16a (N. Amer. sp.); Couch, '29. **Sepultaria.** Seaver, '15a. **Skepperia.** Burt, '24 (N. Amer. sp.). **Solenia.** Burt, '24 (N. Amer. sp.). **Solenopeziza.** Seaver, '30; **Sparassis.** Cotton, '12 (systematic position of). **Spathularia** (see also *Geoglossaceae*). Peck, 1897 (key to N. Y. sp.). **Sphaeriales,** Wehmeyer, '26. **Sphaerobolus.** Buller, '33; Lorenz, '33. **Steccherinum.** Banker, '12a (N. Y. sp.). **Stereum.** Bergenthal, '33; Burt, '20a (N. Amer. sp.); Lloyd, 13a (Mon.). **Strobilomyces.** Murrill, '10 (N. Amer. sp.); Peck, 1889a (U. S. sp.). **Stropharia.** Earle, '03 (N. Amer. sp.); Harper, '13a, '16 (Great Lakes region sp.); Lange, '23 (Danish sp.); Morgan, '08 (N. Amer. sp.); Murrill, '22a (N. Amer. sp.).

Thelephora. Burt, '14 (N. Amer. sp.). **Thelephoraceae.** Bourdot and Galzin, '09–'23 (French sp.); Burt, '14a, '15a, b, '16a, '17, '18a, '20a, '24, '25, '26 (N. Amer. sp.); Clements, '09 (key to the genera); Imai, '33; Coker, '19b, '21 (N. Car. sp.); Day, 1882 (N. Y. sp.); Emmons, '27 (Iowa sp.); Engler and Prantl, Teil 1, Abt. 1 **, '00 (genera); Rabenhorst, vol. 1, Abt. 1, 1884 (Central Europ. sp.); Saccardo, vols. 6, 9, 11, 14, 16, 17, 21, 23, 1882–'26 (world sp.). **Tilletia.** Buller, '33. **Trametes.** Peck, '01 (key to N. Y. sp.). **Tremellaceae** (including *Auriculariae* and *Dacryomycetes*). Burt, '21 (N. Amer. sp.); Clements, '09 (key to the genera); Engler and Prantl, Teil 1, Abt. 1 * *, '00, and second edition, '28 (genera); Gilbert, '10 (Wisc. sp.); Killermann, '28; Looney, '33 (Iowa sp.); Martin, '27 (Iowa sp.); Neuhoff, '24; Rabenhorst, vol.

1, Abt. 1, 1884 (Central Europ. sp.) ; Saccardo, vols. 6, 9, 11, 14, 16, 17, 21, 23, 1882–'26 (world sp.). **Tremellodendron.** Burt, '15b (N. Amer. sp.). **Tremellodon** (see *Tremellaceae*). **Tricholoma** (including *Cortinellus* and *Lepista*). Murrill, '14 (N. Amer. sp.) ; Peck, 1891 (N. Y. sp.) ; Sartory and Maire, '18a. **Trogia.** Murrill, '10 (N. Amer. sp.). **Tubaria.** Murrill, '17 (N. Amer. sp.). **Tuberaceae.** Bataille, '21; Fischer, 1897, 1897a; Gilkey, '16 (Calif. sp.) ; Harkness, 1899 (Calif. sp.) ; Hone, '09 (Minn. sp.) ; Massee, '09 (Brit. sp.) (See also *Hypogaei*). **Tulasnella.** Burt, '20 (N. Amer. sp.). **Tylostoma** (including *Queletia*). Lloyd, '06a; White, V. S., '01 (N. Amer. sp.). **Tylostomaceae.** White, V. S., '01 (N. Amer. sp.). **Typhula.** Killerman, '34.

Underwoodia. Seaver, '18, '28. **Urnula.** Kupfer, '02.

Veluticeps. Burt, '20 (N. Amer. sp.). **Verpa.** Brébinaud, '31. **Vibrissea** (see *Geoglossaceae*). Phillips, 1881 (Mon.). **Volvaria.** Lange, '28 (Danish sp.) ; Lloyd, 1898 (U. S. sp.) ; Murrill, '17 (N. Amer. sp.).

Xylaria. Ellis and Everhart, 1887; Peck, 1879a (key to N. Y. sp.) ; Tulasne, 1863.

SYSTEMATIC ACCOUNT OF SELECTED LARGER FUNGI

WHAT ARE SPECIES, GENERA, FAMILIES, ORDERS AND CLASSES?

In previous paragraphs, dealing with the general characteristics of mushrooms and their allies (p. 17), the broad lines of classification of these plants were indicated, based in the main on the shape of the fruit-bodies. Figures (figures 2, 3) were given to illustrate the principal forms. In the following pages (and on a chart following p. 183) a classification along scientific lines is offered, beginning with certain microscopic details that divide the bewildering number of genera and species into great groups. Following this classification, which takes the form of a key to the classes, orders, families and genera, more than two hundred species are described and discussed, especially with regard for their relationship with other species, so that most of the commonly encountered mushrooms are brought to the notice of the reader.

A few introductory remarks, explaining the terms: species, genera, families, orders and classes, may not be amiss.

Man is a classifier. Going out into nature's mighty museum he encounters a great variety of objects, some alive, like plants and animals, others "lifeless", like rocks and minerals. After seeing an object he says to himself, "You have seen this or something very like it before." The writer distinctly recalls the impression he received when, as a small boy, going to his first circus, he saw lions, leopards and cougars for the first time. "You have seen a similar animal before," he said to himself. On returning home, "pussy" happened to pass through the room—there, *there* was the model of that collection of glorified cats in the circus! The shape, though on a smaller scale, was the same, so were the eyes with that unforgettable, uncanny glow, so was the stealthy walk, and so were—the whiskers! "Yes, they are *all* cats," was the conclusion reached, a conclusion which he found verified later when reading his first elementary book on zoölogy. In that little treatise, cats—"tabby," and the glorified ones—bore high-sounding, Latin names: *Felis domestica,* the text said, is just plain pussy; *Felis leo,* the "King of Beasts"; *Felis pardus,* the Leopard, and so on. The classic names mattered not, a more valuable lesson was learned—*a real kinship, a classifiable kinship, exists among nature's creations.* Beginning with individuals of a given brood (of animals or plants), it was found by naturalists that, although differing in minor points, there is a very close likeness among them. Among several broods a similar likeness was observed. This led to the conception of species, to a grouping of organisms having certain features in common. As other individuals were scrutinized that differed markedly from those already brought together under the term species, and yet showing a degree of likeness too, they were designated as another species. This process continued until it led to the grouping of several species into what is called a genus. As observation was extended still further, genera were found to be sufficiently closely related to form other groups called families; families were assembled to form orders; and finally came the still larger groups called classes, which embrace individuals, species, genera, families, and orders. Pussy, at home, is just an individual cat, but taken together with all pussies, in all homes, the world over, she forms a species. When compared with lions, leopards, and cougars, she becomes a member of a genus, *Felis*. Tracing likenesses still further among cats of other genera, she belongs in the family Felidae. These, with dogs, horses, elephants, man, etc., comprise the mammals, and the mammals, grouped with all animals having a back-bone, are vertebrates.

Mushrooms are classified in the same way. The common Meadow Mushroom, *Psalliota campestris,* forms a species. Together with other species of *Psalliota,* it becomes a member of that genus. The genus, along with many others, goes to make up the family Agaricaceae (the gill mushrooms). The Agaricaceae, the Polyporaceae (the tube-bearing fungi), the Hydnaceae (the teeth-bearing kinds), etc., belong in the order Agaricales, or Hymenomycetes (fungi with the spore-bearing surface exposed from early youth), and that huge order, together with the Lycoperdales, or Gasteromycetes (fungi that bear their spores within containers until maturity), is one of the grand divisions of the class Basidiomycetes (fungi in which the spores are borne on the ends of tiny clubs, or basidia). The Basidiomycetes may be contrasted with another vast assemblage of species, genera, families, and orders comprising the class Ascomycetes (fungi in which the spores are borne in tiny sacs, or asci), of which the common Morel (*Morchella*) is a familiar example.

By means of the following key (page 203), the reader, now forearmed and forewarned (and aided by a compound microscope, and the descriptive characters noted on p. 226), will doubtless be able to undertake the identification of most of the mushrooms he finds. A few genera, hitherto not reported from the State, have been included in order to give a more complete survey of the great variety that exists among fungous structures.

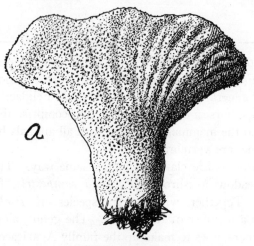

HYPOMYCES
ON LACTARIUS

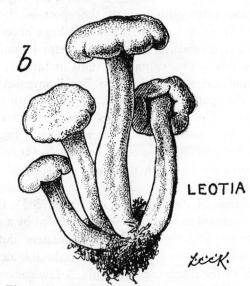

LEOTIA

Figure 46 Selected generic types of the Ascomycetes. a, *Hypomyces lactifluorum* on
Lactarius. b, *Leotia lubrica*

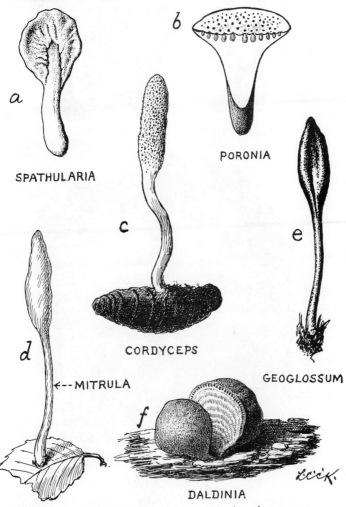

Figure 47 Selected generic types of the Ascomycetes. *a,*
Spathularia clavata. b, Poronia punctata (After Greville). *c,*
Cordyceps militaris. d, Mitrula phalloides. e, Geoglossum glabrum.
f, Daldinia concentrica

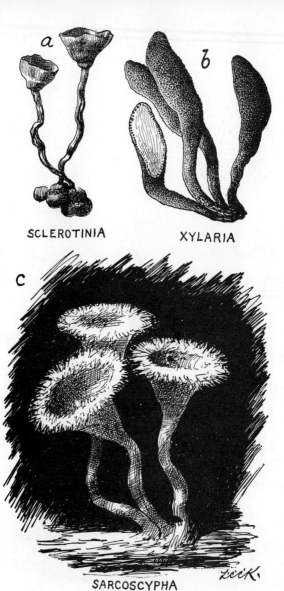

SCLEROTINIA   XYLARIA

SARCOSCYPHA

Figure 48 Selected generic types of the Ascomycetes. *a, Sclerotinia tuberosa,* showing sclerotia at the base of the plants. *b, Xylaria polymorpha,* the perithecia visible in the white stroma of the plant on the left. *c, Sarcoscypha floccosa*

[186]

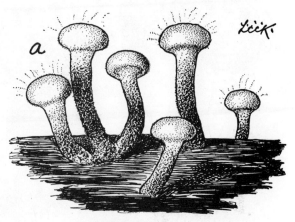

VIBRISSEA

APOSTEMIDIUM

Figure 49 Selected generic types of the Ascomycetes. *a,
Vibrissea truncorum. b, Apostemidium guernisaci. c, Apostemidium turbinata.* All after W. Phillips

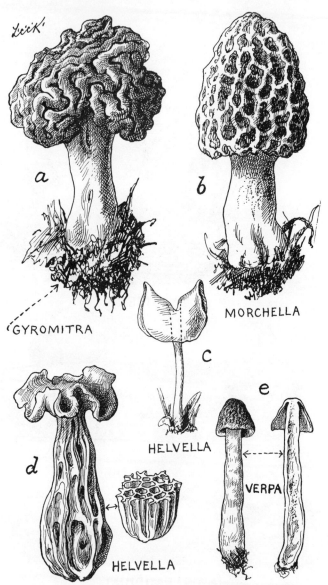

Figure 50 Selected generic types of the Ascomycetes. *a, Gyromitra esculenta* (Poisonous). *b, Morchella esculenta* (Edible). *c, Helvella elastica. d, Helvella crispa* and section of stem. *e, Verpa digitaliformis* and section. *b,* from Therapeutic Gazette, Philadelphia; *d,* after Greville

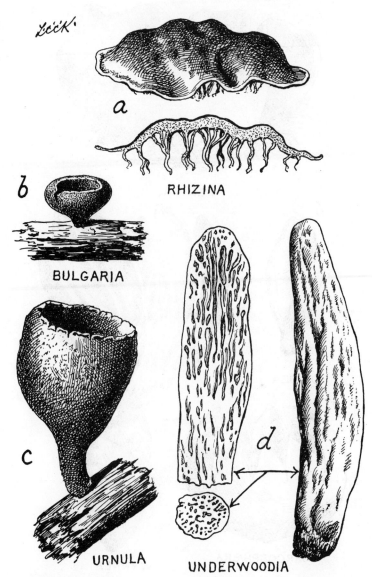

Figure 51 Selected generic types of the Ascomycetes. *a, Rhizina inflata. b, Bulgaria inquinans. c, Urnula craterium. d, Underwoodia columnaris.* The last after Harper

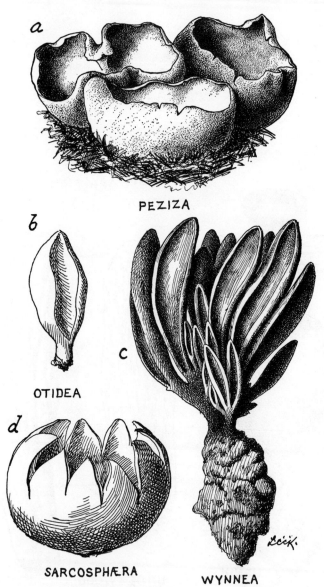

PEZIZA

OTIDEA

SARCOSPHÆRA

WYNNEA

Figure 52 Selected generic types of the Ascomycetes.
*a, Peziza vesiculosa. b, Otidea onotica. c, Wynnea
americana* (After Thaxter). *d, Sarcosphaera coronaria*

[190]

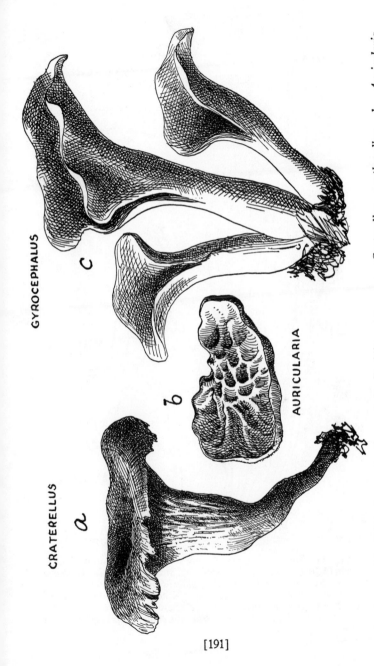

CRATERELLUS

AURICULARIA

GYROCEPHALUS

a

b

c

Figure 53 Selected generic types of the Basidiomycetes. *a*, *Craterellus cantharellus*. *b*, *Auricularia auricula-judae*. *c*, *Gyrocephalus rufus*. *a*, one of the Thelephoraceae; *b*, and *c*, members of the Tremellaceae

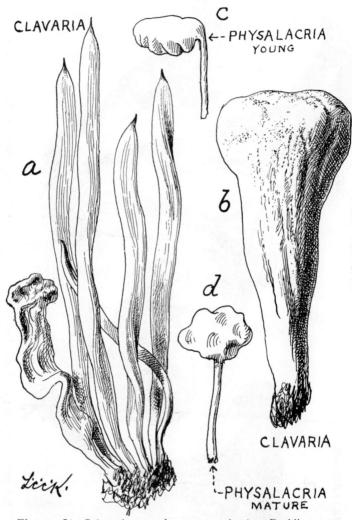

CLAVARIA

C
←– PHYSALACRIA
YOUNG

a

b

d

CLAVARIA

¦–PHYSALACRIA
MATURE

Figure 54 Selected generic types of the Basidiomycetes. *a, Clavaria fusiformis.* One club is malformed. *b, Clavaria pistillaris,* truncate form. *c, Physalacria inflata,* young, before the erection of the bladder-like cap. Note the gill-like folds of the lower, hymenium-bearing part. *d,* Same as *c,* after the erection of the cap (Krieger, '23). For the much-branched type of *Clavaria,* see figs. 80 and 82

[192]

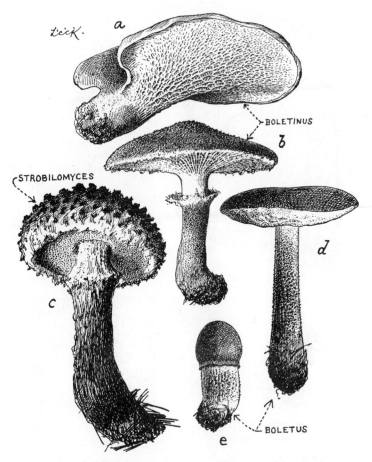

Figure 55 Selected generic types of the Basidiomycetes. *a,
Boletinus porosus. b, Boletinus cavipes. c, Strobilomyces
strobilaceus. d, Boletus duriusculus. e, Boletus versipellis,* young,
showing the overlapping margin of the cap peculiar to this species

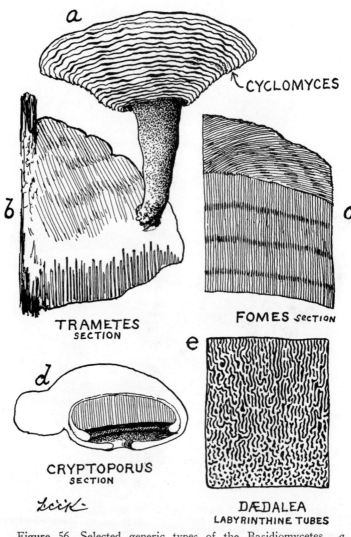

CYCLOMYCES

a

b

TRAMETES
SECTION

c

FOMES *section*

d

CRYPTOPORUS
SECTION

e

DÆDALEA
LABYRINTHINE TUBES

Figure 56 Selected generic types of the Basidiomycetes. *a,
Cyclomyces greenei. b, Trametes pini,* section. *c, Fomes fomentarius,* section. *d, Cryptoporus volvatus,* section. *e, Daedalea
quercina,* view into the labyrinthiform tubes. For a picture showing the growing plant, see fig. 43

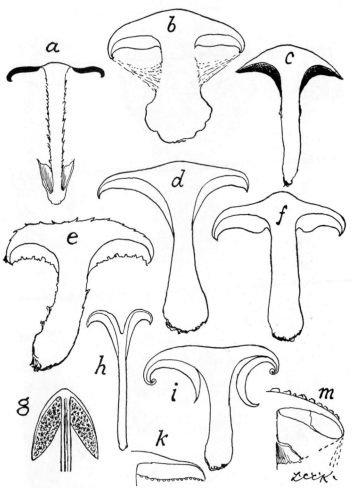

Figure 57 Selected generic types of the Basidiomycetes. Diagrams showing structural details of some genera of the Agaricaceae (gill mushrooms). *a, Montagnites,* flesh of cap membranous, volva present at base of stem. *b, Cortinarius,* note cobwebby ring stretching from the margin of the cap to the stem, the latter with a margined bulb. *c, Gomphidius,* if spores are blackish; *Hygrophorus* (of the Limacium group), if spores are white. *d, Clitocybe,* if spores are white; *Clitopilus,* when they are rosy. *e, Lentinus,* substance tough, gills coarsely serrate. *Panus,* also tough-fleshed, has the gill-edges even, and so has *Pleurotus,* but in that genus the substance is fleshy. *f, Tricholoma,* with white spores; *Entoloma,* if the spores are rosy. Note the umbo in the center of the cap, and the emarginate (sinuate) gills, descending upon the stem with a tooth (uncinate). *g, Panaeolus,* cap campanulate, gills mottled. *h, Omphalia,* with white spores; *Eccilia,* when the spores are rosy. Note decurrent gills and the deep umbilicus (navel) in the center of the cap. *i, Paxillus,* like *Clitocybe* (*d*), but spores yellowish brown and gills detachable from the cap (tubes detachable in *Boletus!*). Note also the extremely involute margin of the cap. *k, Hypholoma,* gills adnate, the edges beaded with little droplets of moisture. Last character present in some species. *m, Amanita (muscaria).* Note warts on top of cap, free gills, and ring on stem (see Krieger, '20)

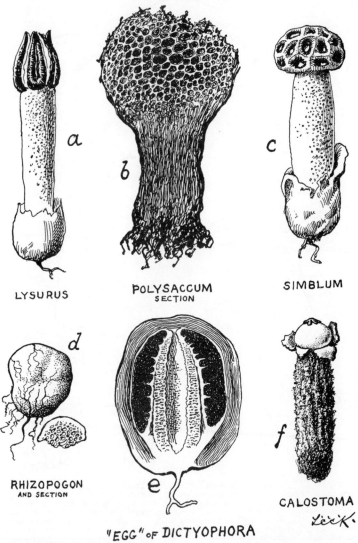

LYSURUS

POLYSACCUM
SECTION

SIMBLUM

RHIZOPOGON
AND SECTION

CALOSTOMA

"EGG" OF DICTYOPHORA

Figure 58 Selected generic types of the Basidiomycetes. *a,
Lysurus borealis. b, Polysaccum pisocarpium* (see also fig. 63*g*).
c, Simblum sphaerocephalum. d, Rhizopogon rubescens and
section. *e, Dictyophora ravenelii,* "egg" (see also fig. 59*b*.) *f,
Calostoma cinnabarinum* (see also fig. 63*d* for basidium and spores
of a species)

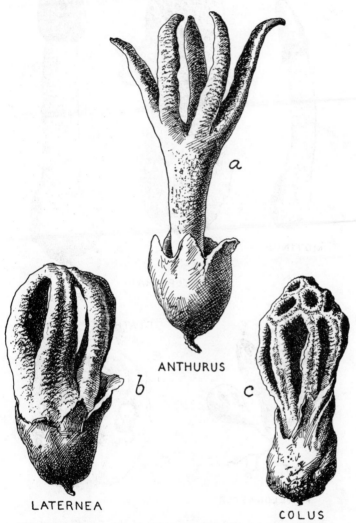

ANTHURUS

LATERNEA

COLUS

58* Selected generic types of the Basidiomycetes. *a, Anthurus aseroëformis. b, Laternea columnata. c, Colus hirudinosus*

[197]

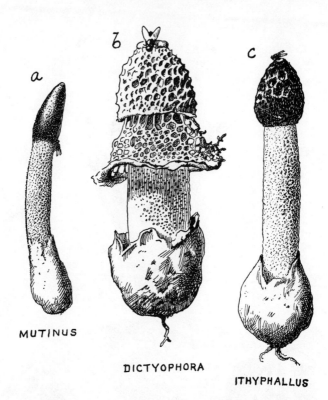

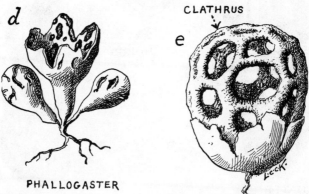

Figure 59   Selected generic types of the Basidiomycetes.
a, Mutinus curtisii.   b, Dictyophora duplicata (see also
fig. 58*e*).   *c, Ithyphallus impudicus.   d, Phallogaster saccatus.   e, Clathrus cancellatus*

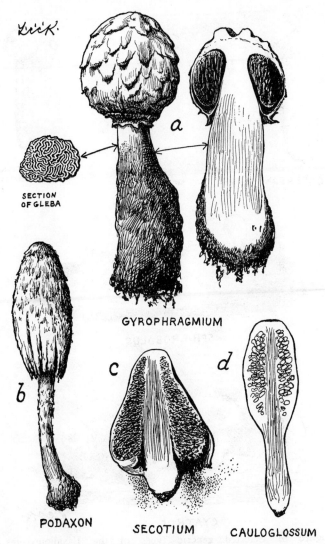

SECTION
OF GLEBA

GYROPHRAGMIUM

PODAXON   SECOTIUM   CAULOGLOSSUM

Figure 60 Selected generic types of the Basidiomycetes. *a,*
Gyrophragmium delilei, showing longitudinal section on the right
and cross section of the gleba on the left. According to Lloyd,
this is a rather scaly-topped specimen. Collected by the writer
at Chico, Calif. *b, Podaxon carcinomalis. c, Secotium acuminatum,*
section, showing escaping spores. *d, Cauloglossum transversarium,*
section

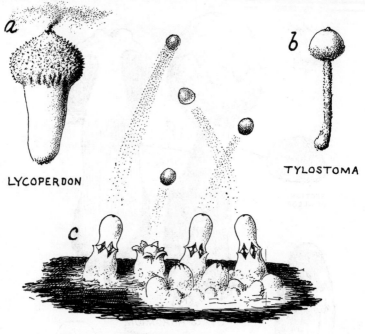

LYCOPERDON

TYLOSTOMA

c

SPHÆROBOLUS

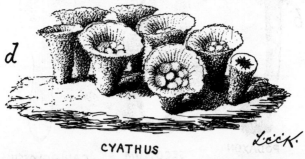

Lick.

CYATHUS

Figure 61 Selected generic types of the Basidiomycetes. *a, Lycoperdon gemmatum,* showing the spore-cloud escaping by the single, apical mouth. In *Calvatia,* the spores escape through many fissures in the peridium. *b, Tylostoma mammosum* (see also fig. 63*a*). *c, Sphaerobolus stellatus,* showing the forcible catapulting of the gleba, or spore-container. *d, Cyathus striatus.* The peridioles are shown within. Each peridiole attached to the fruit-body by a little string (funiculus)

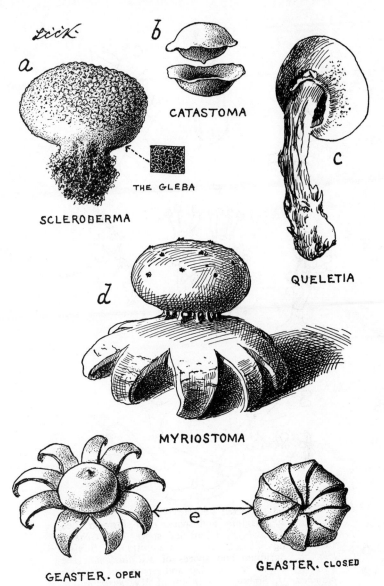

Figure 62 Selected generic types of the Basidiomycetes.   *a,
Scleroderma   verrucosum.   b,   Catastoma   circumscissum.   c,
Queletia mirabilis. d, Myriostoma coliforme. e, Geaster hygrometricus* (see also fig 63*b* for basidium and spores of *Geaster*).
c, after Dr. C. G. Lloyd

[201]

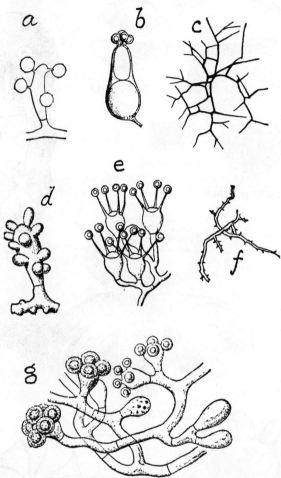

Figure 63 Selected generic types of the Basidiomycetes. *a,* Basidium and spores of *Tylostoma* (see
also fig. 61*b*). *b,* Basidium and spores of a *Geaster*
(see also figs. 3*h,* 22, 62*e*). *c,* Capillitium of *Bovista
pila. d,* Basidium and spores of a *Calostoma* (see
also fig. 58*f*). *e,* Basidia and spores of *Bovista
plumbea. f,* Spinose capillitium of *Mycenastrum. g,*
Basidia and spores of a *Polysaccum* (see also fig.
58*b*). For microscopic details of other fungi, see figs.
20 and 24. Figures *c* and *d* after Lloyd, the rest
also after Lloyd who reproduced them after Engler
and Prantl

Class	Sub=class	Orders	Sub=Orders	Families
		Sphaeriales.............................		
	As-co-my-ce-tes		Helvellineae..	Geoglossaceae.
				Helvellaceae...
		Pezizales........		Rhizinaceae....
			Pezizineae...	Bulgariaceae...
				Helotiaceae....
				Pezizaceae.....
Eu-my-ce-tes (which include the higher fungi)		Agaricales.................... (Hymenomycetes)		Tremellaceae...
				Clavariaceae...
				Thelephoraceae.
				Hydnaceae....
				Polyporaceae...
	Ba-sid-i-o-my-ce-tes			Agaricaceae.....
				Hymenogastrace
				Phallaceae......
		Lycoperdales.................. (Gasteromycetes)		Lycoperdaceae..
				Nidulariaceae....

Sub=Families	Genera
....	Hypomyces, Cordyceps, Poronia, Xylaria, Daldinia
Geoglosseae....	Mitrula, Geoglossum, Spathularia
Cudoniae......	Leotia, Vibrissea, Apostemidium
....	Morchella, Verpa, Helvella, Gyromitra, Underwoodia,
....	Rhizina
....	Bulgaria
....	Sclerotinia, Sarcoscypha, Chlorosplenium
....	Plicariella, Peziza, Otidea, Wynnea, Sarcosphaera, Urnula
....	Auricularia, Gyrocephalus, Exidia, Tremella, Tremellodon, Tremellodendron, Dacryomyces, Guepinia, Calocera
....	Clavaria, Physalacria, Lachnocladium
....	Thelephora, Craterellus, Sparassis
....	Hydnum, Phlebia, Radulum, Odontia
....	Fistulina, Strobilomyces, Boletinus, Boletus, Cryptoporus, Cyclomyces, Favolus, Daedalea, Fomes, Polyporus, Polystictus, Trametes, Hexagona, Merulius
....	Amanita, Amanitopsis, Lepiota, Armillaria, Clitocybe, Laccaria, Omphalia, Collybia, Tricholoma, Lactarius, Russula, Hygrophorus, Mycena, Hiatula, Cantharellus, Nyctalis, Pleurotus, Lentinus, Marasmius, Heliomyces, Xerotus, Panus, Schizophyllum, Trogia, Lenzites, Metraria, Volvaria, Annularia, Pluteus, Entoloma, Clitopilus, Eccilia, Leptonia, Nolanea, Claudopus, Rozites, Locellina, Pholiota, Cortinarius, Flammula, Bolbitius, Paxillus, Tubaria, Inocybe, Hebeloma, Naucoria, Pluteolus, Galera, Crepidotus, Hypholoma, Pilosace, Deconica, Agaricus (Psalliota), Stropharia, Psilocybe, Psathyra, Montagnites, Anthracophyllum, Coprinus, Anellaria, Gomphidius, Psathyrella, Panaeolus
....	Rhizopogon
....	Dictyophora, Ithyphallus, Mutinus, Simblum, Clathrus, Anthurus, Laternea, Lysurus, Phallogaster
Podaxae.......	Gyrophragmium, Cauloglossum, Secotium, Podaxon
Geastrae......	Tylostoma, Queletia, Calostoma, Geaster, Myriostoma
Lycoperdae....	Bovista, Mycenastrum, Catastoma, Bovistella, Lycoperdon, Calvatia, Hypoblema
Sclerodermatae.	Scleroderma, Polysaccum, Arachnion
....	Sphaerobolus, Cyathus, Crucibulum, Nidula, Granularia

KEY TO THE CLASSES, ORDERS, FAMILIES AND GENERA

(For the most part only those families and genera have been presented which contain large, conspicuous species. For a complete key to all fungus genera, see Clements and Shear, '31, and for a chart giving a tabulation of the genera, following page 202).

Spores borne in asci.................	Class **Ascomycetes.**
Spores borne on more or less club-shaped basidia	Class **Basidiomycetes.**

ORDERS OF THE ASCOMYCETES

Asci in tiny containers (perithecia) which may be superficially imbedded in a fruit-body produced by the fungus itself (stroma), or in other fungi	Order **Sphaeriales.**
Asci in a hymenium which clothes a part of the fruit-body	Order **Pezizales.**

Order SPHAERIALES

Perithecia superficially imbedded in the substance of other fungi......	Genus *Hypomyces* (figure 46a)
Perithecia imbedded in the substance of the fungus itself (stroma) Stroma growing on fungi or on dead insects....................	Genus *Cordyceps* (figure 47c)
Stroma growing on dung.........	Genus *Poronia* (figure 47b)
Stroma growing on wood or on other remains of higher plants Stroma usually more or less clavate	Genus *Xylaria* (figure 48b)
Stroma more or less globose and concentrically zoned within....	Genus *Daldinia* (figure 47f)
Stroma effuse..................	Other Xylariaceae, as *Hypoxylon*, etc.

Order PEZIZALES

Fruit-body pileate and stipitate (rarely
flattened and sessile, as in *Rhizina*),
never cup-shaped or discoid; pileus
subglobose, columnar, saddle-shaped,
or bell-shaped..................... Sub-order **Helvellineae**.
Fruit-body urn-shaped, cup-shaped or
discoid, stipitate or sessile......... Sub-order **Pezizineae**.

Families of the Helvellineae

Cap borne on a stem (except in *Apostemidium* [family Geoglossaceae]
and *Underwoodia* [family Helvel-
laceae])
    Cap clavate, spathulate, compressed
laterally or subglobose. Asci non-
operculate. Plants not large.... Family **Geoglossaceae**.
    Cap irregularly globose to elongate-
conic or bell-shaped, saddle-
shaped to more or less lobed, convolute or ridged or columnar and
stemless; asci operculate. Plants
usually fleshy and large........ Family **Helvellaceae**.
Cap sessile, spread out more or less
flat, inflated .... Family **Rhizinaceae**.

Family Geoglossaceae

Plants clavate, spathulate, or fan-
shaped, the hymenial portion
usually more or less compressed. Sub-family **Geoglosseae**.
Plants clavate, the hymenial portion
not at all or only slightly decurrent on opposite sides of the
stem.
    Spores small, elliptical, cylindri-
cal or fusiform, one-celled
(rarely with one septum),
hyaline. Plants bright-colored. Genus *Mitrula* (figures 7,
                          47d)
    Spores cylindrical or clavate-
cylindrical, three- to many-
septate when mature (rarely
one-celled in one species),
brown or smoky. Plants black
or blackish .... Genus *Geoglossum* (figure
                          47e)

Plants spathulate or fan-shaped, hymenial portion decurrent on opposite sides of the stem...... Genus *Spathularia* (figure 47a, 124)

Plants with a more or less globose cap (turbinate and sessile in *Apostemidium*) .... Sub-family **Cudoniae.**

Spores elliptical fusiform; plants gelatinous .... Genus *Leotia* (figures 46b, 100)

Spores filiform or filiform-clavate. Plants stipitate .... Genus *Vibrissea* (figure 49a)

Plants sessile or turbinate....... Genus *Apostemidium* (figure 49b, **c**)

Family **Helvellaceae**

Cap ridged longitudinally and laterally, subglobose to elongate-conic, distinct but not separate from the stem (except in *Morchella hybrida* and *M. bispora*).................. Genus *Morchella* (figure 50b)

Cap smooth or merely wrinkled longitudinally, bell-shaped, separate from the stem .... Genus *Verpa* (figure 50e)

Cap saddle-like, more or less lobed.. Genus *Helvella* (figures 50c, d)
See under **Pezizaceae**

Cap more or less irregularly globose, convolute, like brain.............. Genus *Gyromitra* (figure 50a)

Cap stemless, plant columnar........ Genus *Underwoodia* (figure 51d)

Family **Rhizinaceae**

Fruit-body somewhat flattened out or inflated, under side provided with root-like cords .... Genus *Rhizina* (figure 51a)

Families of the **Pezizineae**

Fruit-body waxy-fleshy to leathery.. Family **Helotiaceae.**

Fruit-body fleshy (except in *Urnula*), usually growing on the ground.... Family **Pezizaceae.**

Fruit-body gelatinous-elastic........ Family **Bulgariaceae.**

Family **Helotiaceae**

Fruit-body growing from a sclerotium Genus *Sclerotinia* (figure 48a)

Fruit-body more or less green, growing on decaying wood............. Genus *Chlorosplenium.*

Family **Pezizaceae**

Fruit-body somewhat buried in the ground, margin deeply incised...... Genus *Sarcosphaera* (figure 52d)

Fruit-body growing on the ground or on rotten wood

　Fruit-body leathery................ Genus *Urnula* (figures 51c, 126)

　Fruit-body fleshy

　　Spores globose.................. Genus *Plicariella*

　　Spores elliptical

　　　Fruit-body more or less distinctly hairy or setose, usually brightly colored (red)...... Genus *Sarcoscypha* (figure 48c)

　　　Fruit-body smooth or nearly so, yellow or brown

　　　　Fruit-body eventually cup-, plate-, or urn-shaped (some of the more or less stipitate species should be carefully separated from *Helvella*).. Genus *Peziza* (figures 52a, 111)

　　　　Fruit-body eventually more or less rabbit-ear-shaped

　　　　　Growing singly or gregariously .... Genus *Otidea* (figures 52b, 110)

　　　　　Growing in a fascicle from a more or less well-defined stem, the latter sometimes emerging from a sclerotium............. Genus *Wynnea* (figure 52c)

Family **Bulgariaceae**

Spores one-celled................... Genus *Bulgaria* (figure 51b)

Spores many-celled................. Genus *Coryne*

ORDERS OF THE BASIDIOMYCETES

Basidia borne on a hymenium which is soon exposed; the hymenium spread over a smooth, gyrose or wrinkled surface, or over gills, teeth, and the internal surface of tubes .... Order **Agaricales.**
(Hymenomycetes)

Basidia borne within a container (peridium) .... Order **Lycoperdales.**
(Gasteromycetes)

Families of the Agaricales

Basidia transversely to longitudinally divided into separate chambers, or rounded-club-shaped and divided above .... Family **Tremellaceae.**

Basidia undivided

Hymenium spread over simple fleshy clubs or branches........ Family **Clavariaceae.**
(See *Physalacria,* p. 208 and *Sparassis,* p. 209)

Hymenium smooth or m e r e l y wrinkled .... Family **Thelephoraceae.**

Hymenium spread over teeth or spines .... Family **Hydnaceae.**

Hymenium lining the inside of tubes .... Family **Polyporaceae.**

Hymenium spread over gills...... Family **Agaricaceae.**
(See *Physalacria,* pp. 208, 286)

Family **Tremellaceae** (Gelatinous fungi)

Basidia transversely septate, elongate or fusoid .... Genus *Auricularia* (figures 20m, 53b)

Basidia longitudinally divided into four separate chambers.

Fruit-body spathulate .... Genus *Gyrocephalus* (figure 53c)

Fruit-body more or less globose; spores cylindrical, s o m e w h a t curved .... Genus *Exidia* (figure 20i)

Fruit-body cerebriform or frondose; spores round to elliptical....... Genus *Tremella* (figures 5, 6)

Fruit-body dimidiate, attached laterally; furnished with teeth on the underside, as in *Hydnum*... Genus *Tremellodon*.
Fruit-body branched, as in some Clavarias .... Genus *Tremellodendron*.
Basidia rounded-club-shaped, divided above.
Fruit-body globose-gyrose .... Genus *Dacryomyces* (figure 20k)
Fruit-body irregularly cup-shaped, spathulate or top-shaped........ Genus *Guepinia*.
Fruit-body clavate to branched.... Genus *Calocera*.

Family **Clavariaceae** (Club fungi)

Fruit-body a little bladder supported on a small stem, usually growing in dense tufts...................... Genus *Physalacria* (figures 54c, d)
(This genus belongs in the Agaricaceae. The "bladder" is a dilated cap with the upper side sterile and the lower—folded, gill-like,—bearing the hymenium [Krieger, '23])

Fruit-body diminutive in size, simple or only slightly branched
Fruit-body simple and very small, stem comparatively stout, sometimes arising from sclerotia...... Genus *Pistillaria*.
Fruit-body more or less branched
Fruit-body slightly branched, stem flaccid................... Genus *Typhula*.
Fruit-body slender, t u f t e d-branched, elastic-tough........ Genus *Pterula*.
Fruit-body usually quite large, though some small
Fruit-body fleshy and fragile, club-shaped, tufted, or much branched; tips and hymenial surface not tomentose .... Genus *Clavaria* (figures 54a, b, 76, 77, 78)
(See *Tremellodendron*, in the *Tremellaceae*)

Fruit-body very tough and pliable; tips and hymenial surface tomentose .... Genus *Lachnocladium*
(Burt places this genus in the Thelephoraceae)

Family **Thelephoraceae**

Fruit-body resupinate (to pileate), spread over the substratum (wood) in one or several closely adhering layers
 Fruit-body in one layer
  Spores hyaline
   Cystidia present
    Cystidia usually awl-shaped. Genus *Peniophora.*
    Cystidia spinose, short-branched, sometimes blunt. Genus *Aleurodiscus.*
    Cystidia absent............... Genus *Corticium.*
   Spores dark
    Cystidia present.............. Genus *Coniophorella.*
    Cystidia absent.............. Genus *Coniophora.*
  Fruit body in several layers
    With hyaline or dark cystidia.... Genus *Hymenochaete.*
    Cystidia absent................. Genus *Stereum.*
Fruit-body usually erect, either funnel- or cup-shaped, cylindric or club-shaped, frequently stipitate, leathery, or membranous
 Fruit-body leathery, resupinate, lacerate-lobed, dimidiate, or semi-pileate; spores spinose......... Genus *Thelephora* (figure 21)

 Fruit-body semi-fleshy, funnel-shaped, sometimes turbinate, stipitate; hymenium wrinkled; spores smooth .... Genus *Craterellus* (figures 53a, 86, plate 17)
 (Compare *Cantharellus,* in the Agaricaceae)

Fruit-body large, more or less globular, composed of a great number of semi-tough, spathulate-foliate, sometimes crisped, clavarioid branches.. Genus *Sparassis* (figure 123)
(On the systematic position of this genus, see Cotton, '12. See also *Lachnocladium,* under Family Clavariaceae [p. 208])

Family **Hydnaceae** (Hedgehog, or teeth fungi)

Fruit-body absent
 Teeth arising directly from the substratum (rotting wood)......... Genus *Mucronella.*

Fruit-body present
  Fruit-body resupinate (see also *Gloeothele, Grammothele,* and *Irpex* below) or semi-detached; with granular warts, crests, or teeth
    With granular warts
      Wart tips generally finely divided .... Genus *Odontia.*
      Wart tips undivided........... Genus *Grandinia.*
    With crests
      Edges of crests incised; fruit-body membranous.......... Genus *Lopharia.*
      Edges of crests not incised; fruit-body fleshy-waxy....... Genus *Phlebia.*
    With distinct teeth
      Cystidia present
        Cystidia simple; fruit-body cork-like .... Genus *Hydnochaete.*
        Cystidia stellate; fruit-body floccose-membranous ...... Genus *Asterodon.*
      Cystidia absent; fruit-body waxy, with blunt, stout teeth Genus *Radulum.*
  Fruit-body generally mushroom-like (i. e., with distinct cap and stem), sometimes coraloid (See *Lachnocladium,* in the Clavariaceae), imbricate, dimidiate, or crustose, fleshy, woody, or leathery; t e e t h distinctly formed, reticulate-poroid, or semi-lamellate
    Teeth distinctly formed, fruit-body mushroom-like, coraloid, or imbricate................. Genus *Hydnum* (plates 18, 19)
                           (See *Tremellodon,* in the Tremellaceae. The genus *Hydnum* has been split up into a number of genera by some authors. See Banker, '02, '06, '12, '12a, '13a–c.)
    Teeth reticulate-poroid; fruit-body crustose
      Gloeocystidia present.......... Genus *Gloeothele.*
      Gloeocystidia absent.......... Genus *Grammothele.*

Teeth semi-lamellate
  Margins of teeth spiny-serrate. Genus *Echinodontium.*
  Margins of teeth not spiny-
    serrate
    Fruit-body leathery, generally
      crustose to dimidiate...... Genus *Irpex.*
    Fruit-body   pileate-stipitate,
      generally fleshy.......... Genus *Sistotrema.*

Family **Polyporaceae** (Tube fungi)

(This family has been divided into a great number of genera. See Murrill, '07, '10, '14a, b, c.)

Fruit-body thin, almost mycelioid or
  membranous, resupinate on the substratum (rotting wood); tubes
  wart-like, separate............... *Poria.*
Fruit-body more or less fleshy, putrescent.
  Flesh coarsely and radiately fibrous
    and mottled with red streaks;
    hymenium papillate .... Genus *Fistulina* (figure 87)
  Flesh of even, uniform texture.
    Cap surface divided into coarse,
      blackish, strobiliform, e r e c t
      scales .... Genus *Strobilomyces* (figures 55c, 125)
    Cap smooth, viscid, pruinose or
      tomentose.
      Tubes not readily separable
        from the cap nor from each
        other, gill-like, radiating.... Genus *Boletinus* (figures 55a, b)
      Tubes readily separating from
        the cap and from each other. Genus *Boletus* (figures 55d, e, plates 7, 8, 9, 10)
Fruit-body tough, corky, or woody,
  persistent (except in *Merulius*)
  Hymenium at first covered with a
    membrane .... Genus *Cryptoporus* (figure 56d)
  Hymenium exposed from the first
    Hymenium gill-like
      "Gills" arranged concentrically. Genus *Cyclomyces* (figure 56a)

"Gills" arranged radiately, interconnected, forming large hexagonal or labyrinthiform pores

"Gills" forming hexagonal pores .... Genus *Favolus* (see *Hexagona* below)

"Gills" forming a labyrinthiform structure .... Genus *Daedalea* (figures 43, 56e)

Hymenium composed of small, roundish, hexagonal or gyrose tubes

Tubes in stratified layers..... Genus *Fomes* (figures 41, 56c)

Tubes in a single layer

Tubes not unequally sunk into the substance of the fruit-body

Fruit-body thick, toughfleshy, stalked or sessile. Genus *Polyporus* (figures 42, 115, 116, 117, 118)

Fruit-body thin, coriaceous or membranous, stalked, dimidiate or sub-resupinate .... Genus *Polystictus* (figure 44)

Tubes often unequally sunk into the substance of the fruit-body.

Fruit-body tough.

Tubes subrotund .... Genus *Trametes* (figure 56b)

Tubes hexagonal .... Genus *Hexagona* (see *Favolus* above)

Fruit-body of a soft consistency, tubes reticulate, gyrose .... Genus *Merulius*.

Family **Agaricaceae** (Gill mushrooms)

(Underwood and Earle, 1897; with modifications by the author.

Copyright, The National Geographic Society. By special permission from the National Geographic Magazine)

Before using this key the reader should familiarize himself with the structural parts of gill mushrooms as presented on p. 226. A spore-print is also necessary (see p. 68).

1. Plants fleshy, soon decaying..... 2 (See *Mycena* [10]; and *Physalacria,* in the Clavariaceae)

   Plants tough, leathery or woody, reviving or persistent......... 13

2. Juice milky, white or colored.... *Lactarius* (figures 97, 98, 99; some species of *Mycena* exude a milky juice [10])

   Juice usually wanting, watery when present 3

3. Stem central or nearly so....... 4

   Stem excentric, lateral, or wanting (sometimes central in certain species of *Pleurotus*).... 12

4. Spores white (greenish or reddish in certain species of *Lepiota* [6]; dirty-pinkish-buff in some species of *Tricholoma* [8]; more or less yellow to almost cinnamon-color in certain species of *Russula* [9]; pale yellow in a *Cantharellus* [11] 5

   Spores rosy or salmon-colored (see 4, spores white).......... 16

   Spores yellowish-brown or rusty-brown 19

   Spores dark-brown or purplish-brown 24

   Spores black or nearly so....... 27

5. Volva and ring present......... *Amanita* (figures 37 D, E, F, G) (See *Lentinus* [13])

   Volva present; ring wanting..... *Amanitopsis*

   Volva wanting; ring present (certain species of *Lepiota* [6] have volva-like remains at the base of the stem; and *Armillaria* species sometimes have a volva-like, secondary ring).......... 6

   Volva and ring wanting (traces of a ring on the stem or on the margin of the caps of some species of *Tricholoma* [=genus *Cortinellus*] and *Hygrophorus* [8] 7

6. Gills free or even remote from the stem (lightly attached in species of the section Granulosae of *Lepiota*) ; ring often movable; cap usually scaly or granular (sometimes densely so), occasionally smooth and even viscid .... *Lepiota* (plates 24, 25)

Gills united with the stem; cap smooth, finely tufted-scaly, or with the cuticle torn into appressed patches .... *Armillaria* (figure 69)

7. Gills thin, their edges acute..... 8

Gills in the form of shallow folds, their edges obtuse............ 11

8. Gills decurrent on the stem (sinuate in some species of *Laccaria*)

Stem fleshy .... *Clitocybe* (and in species of the sections Camarophyllus and Limacium of *Hygrophorus* [9]; some species of *Clitocybe* have *Tricholoma*-like [8], sinuate gills. Figure 57d, plate 12)

Stem with a cartilaginous rind. *Omphalia* (figures 57h, 109)

Gills adnexed, adnate, or rarely sinuate, not decurrent.

Stem with a cartilaginous rind. *Collybia* (figures 81, 82)

Stem fleshy; cap often bright-colored 9

Gills sinuate.

Stem fleshy .... *Tricholoma* (and *Laccaria*. See *Clitocybe* above. Figure 57f. Some species with buff-colored, separable gills [*Lepista*] recall *Paxillus* [21])

Stem with a cartilaginous rind. 10

9. Plants rigid, the gills usually brittle .... *Russula* (plate 31)

Plants with wax-like gills....... *Hygrophorus* (figures 92, 93, plate 20)

10. Cap thin-fleshed, more or less striate .... *Mycena* (figure 108)

(A genus, *Eomycenella*, with a membranous cap that bears but few gills, has been described)

Cap very thin, without a pellicle.. *Hiatula.*
11. Gills decurrent; plants terrestrial. *Cantharellus* (figure 75, plate 11)
(One species, *Cantharellus floccosus,* forms mycorrhizae on the roots of a fir, in Japan. *Craterellus,* a genus of the Thelephoraceae, has shallow folds or wrinkles, no distinct gills.)

Gills adnate; plants parasitic on other agarics .... *Nyctalis.*
12. Spores white (lilac or flesh-colored in some species)...... *Pleurotus* (figures 2f, 114)
Spores rosy or salmon-colored... *Claudopus.*
Spores yellowish-brown .... *Crepidotus.*
13. Gills normally serrate on their edges; stem central, excentric, or attached to the side of the cap, lateral .... *Lentinus* (figure 57e)
(Some species of *Lentinus* with entire gills scarcely can be distinguished from *Panus* [15], while some of the more fleshy species of the latter genus are apt to be taken for species of *Pleurotus* [12]. Some aberrant Lentini simulate *Amanita.*)

Gills with edges entire.
Stem central 14
Stem excentric, lateral, or wanting 15
14. Gills simple.
Cap firm and dry............ *Marasmius* (figures 105, 106)
Cap somewhat gelatinous...... *Heliomyces.*
Gills branched .... *Xerotus.*
15. Gills simple; plant leathery...... *Panus.*
Gills deeply divided along their edges; surface of cap finely shaggy .... *Schizophyllum* (figure 20f)
Gills longitudinally channeled or crisped along their edges; surface of cap smooth........... *Trogia.*

Gills more or less cross-connected,
at least at the base; plant corky. *Lenzites.*
Gills with so many cross-connec-
tions that the whole of the
hymenial surface appears por-
ous or labyrinthiform......... *Daedalea* (figures 43, 56e)

16. Volva and ring present.......... *Metraria.*
(Australian genus)
Volva present; ring wanting..... *Volvaria* (plate 32)
Volva wanting; ring present..... *Annularia* (=*Chamaeota*)
Volva and ring wanting......... 17

17. Gills free from the stem........ *Pluteus*
Gills adnate or sinuate.
Stem fleshy .... *Entoloma.*
Stem with a cartilaginous rind. 18
Gills decurrent on the stem.
Stem fleshy .... *Clitopilus* (figures 57d, 80,
plate 13)
Stem with a cartilaginous rind. *Eccilia* (figure 57h)

18. Cap finely scaly; margin incurved. *Leptonia.*
Cap conic to bell-shaped, with a
central nipple; margin straight. *Nolanea.*

19. Volva and ring present.......... *Rozites* (*Pholiota caperata*
belongs here. See plate
27)
Volva present; ring wanting.... *Locellina*
Volva wanting; ring present.
Ring usually plainly evident and
membranous .... *Pholiota* (figures 112, 113)
Ring cobweb-like, filamentous,
or very evanescent......... 20
Volva and ring wanting......... 21

20. Gills variously attached, but not
truly decurrent; ring cobweb-
like; plants terrestrial........ *Cortinarius* (figure 57b,
plate 16)
Gills adnate to decurrent; ring
fibrillose; plants mostly upon
old wood .... *Flammula.*
Gills narrowly attached to the
stem; becoming free and moist;
plants delicate; mostly on ma-
nure or well-manured ground.. *Bolbitius.*

21. Gills decurrent or broadly adnate
(easily separated from the
cap in *Paxillus*)
Stem fleshy .... *Paxillus* (figure 57i)
(See *Tricholoma* [8])
Stem with a cartilaginous rind. *Tubaria.*

Gills not decurrent.
 Stem fleshy 22
 Stem with a cartilaginous rind. 23
22. Cap fibrillose or silky........... *Inocybe* (figure 65a)
 Cap smooth and viscid.......... *Hebeloma* (figure 89)
23. Margin at first incurved........ *Naucoria.*
 Margin at first straight.
 Cap viscid; gills free......... *Pluteolus.*
 Cap not viscid; gills attached.. *Galera.*
24. Veil rather conspicuous, remaining on the stem as a ring (in *Psalliota* sometimes double and forming a pseudo-volva; in *Clarkeinda* [=*Chitonia*] a volva alone is present).............. 25
 Veil slight, remaining on the stem or often only on the margin of the cap, sometimes disappearing entirely in old specimens; gills adnate or sinuate.. *Hypholoma* (figures 57k, 94, 95, plates 21, 22)

 Veil inconspicuous or wanting.
 Gills free .... *Pilosace.*
 Gills decurrent .... *Deconica.*
 Gills adnate or sinuate........ 26
25. Gills free from the stem........ *Psalliota* (figures 37a, b, c, 119–122, plates 29, 30)

 Gills united with the stem....... *Stropharia.*
26. Margin of the cap incurved when young .... *Psilocybe.*
 Margin of the cap always straight. *Psathyra.*
27. Stem dilated above into a disk which bears the radiating gills. *Montagnites* (figure 57a) (This genus properly belongs among the Lycoperdales, sub-family Podaxae, p. 220)

 Cap of the normal form........ 28
28. Cap leathery or horny.......... *Anthracophyllum.*
 Cap fleshy, membranous or deliquescent 29
29. Gills deliquescent, melting into an inky fluid .... *Coprinus* (figures 83–85, plates 14, 15)

 Gills not deliquescent.
 Ring present .... *Anellaria.*
 Ring wanting entirely, or very slight.
 (Cobweb-like and glutinous in *Gomphidius*) 30

30. Gills decurrent .... *Gomphidius* (figure 57c)
    Gills not decurrent.............. 31
31. Cap striate .... *Psathyrella.*
    Cap not striate .... *Panaeolus* (figures 35, 57g)
    (ring rather pronounced=
    Chalymotta)

Families of the Lycoperdales (Stomach fungi)

Fruit-body growing underground or
slightly exposed.................. Family **Hymenogastraceae.**
(Genus *Rhizopogon,* figure
58d)

Fruit-body growing above ground.
    Spores developed in an ill-smelling,
    slimy liquid (gleba)........... Family **Phallaceae.**
    Spores developed as a dry powder.· Family **Lycoperdaceae.**
    Spores developed within one or
    more tiny, viscid, or dry and hard,
    peridioles which may or may not
    be attached to the wall of the
    enveloping peridium .... Family **Nidulariaceae.**

Family Phallaceae

(All but *Phallogaster* at first enclosed in a volva)

Gleba borne on the outside of a cap-
    like structure or on the naked
    apex of the stem.
    Gleba-bearing structure cap-like,
    borne on the end of a stem.
        Stem with a more or less pro-
        nounced net-like veil.......... Genus *Dictyophora* (figures
        58e, 59b)

        Stem without a veil............. Genus *Ithyphallus* (figure
        59c)

    Gleba borne on the naked apex of
    the stem .... Genus *Mutinus* (figure 59a)
Gleba borne on the inside of a hollow,
    perforated, free-lobed, or col-
    umnar structure which may be
    with or without a stem.
    Gleba-bearing structure, hollow, per-
    forated.

Structure borne on a stem; openings small and polygonal...... Genus *Simblum* (figure 58c)

(As to the gleba structure, the genus *Colus* (figure 58* c) occupies an intermediate position, between *Simblum* and *Laternea,* the openings being simbloid above, and elongate below. Seaver, '31; Sumstine, '16.)

Structure sessile; openings large, irregularly angular or elongated .... Genus *Clathrus* (figure 59e)

Gleba-bearing structure divided into connivent or spreading, armlike structures, or into irregular lobes.
Lobes the ends of a flaring tube.. Genus *Anthurus* (figure 58* a)

Lobes on the end of a distinct, columnar stem............... Genus *Lysurus* (figure 58a)

Lobes irregularly shaped, developed by the breaking open of the sessile or somewhat stipitate, pear-shaped fruit-body.... Genus *Phallogaster* (figure 59d)

Gleba-bearing structure columnar.. Genus *Laternea* (figure 58* b)

Family Lycoperdaceae

Distinct stem (columella) present within; gleba gill-like, contorted, divided into irregular spaces, or uniform in structure................. Sub-family **Podaxae.**

Columella indistinct or absent
Gleba without peridioles
Peridia elevated on a long or short stem (short stems sometimes numerous, as in *Myriostoma*); outer peridium inconspicuous and disappearing, breaking away in flakes or splitting and becoming star-shaped .... Sub-family **Geastrae.**

Peridia sessile or with a sterile base which may or may not be cellular; outer peridium spiny or warty, or thin and forming mere discolored patches on the inner one .... Sub-family **Lycoperdae.**

Gleba composed of cell-like spaces which may appear as distinct, spore-filled, large or small, peridioles, or as small areas circumscribed by white lines........... Sub-family **S c l e r o d e r-matae.**

Sub-family **Podaxae**

Gleba gill-like, contorted........... G e n u s *Gyrophragmium* (figure 60a) (*Montagnites,* with distinct gills, and yet with dry, powdery spores, is here placed in the Agaricaceae)

Gleba not gill-like, more or less divided into irregular spaces by separating trama-membranes, or of uniform structure.
Gleba with separating trama-membranes.
Fruit-body club-shaped .... Genus *Cauloglossum* (figure 60d)

Fruit-body roundish to conic, more or less mushroom-shaped. Genus *Secotium* (figure 60c)

Gleba with mere strands of hyphae of the trama, uniform in structure .... Genus *Podaxón* (also given as *Podaxis*) (figure 60b)

Sub-family **Geastrae**

Both peridia on a distinct stem.
Outer peridium inconspicuous, disappearing.
Peridium remaining attached to the stem; apical mouth distinct. Genus *Tylostoma* (figures 61b, 63a)

Peridium becoming detached from the stem; mouth absent....... Genus *Queletia* (figure 62c)

Both peridia persistent, outer one
falling away in thick pieces, inner
one thin but tough; mouth bright-
colored, raised and variously
formed .... Genus *Calostoma* (=*Mitremyces*) (figures 58f, 63d)

Inner peridium alone more or less
elevated on one or more narrow
stems; outer peridium splitting
and becoming star-shaped.
Inner peridium with but one stem
and one apical mouth........... Genus *Geaster* (figures 3h,
22, 62e, 63b)

Inner peridium with many stems and
mouths, the mouths scattered over
the upper surface.............. Genus *Myriostoma* (figure 62d)

Sub-family Lycoperdae (Puff-balls [Lloyd, '02])

Outer peridium thin (=cortex, mostly
peeling off). Inner peridium firm
or papery. Mature plant loosened
from place of growth.
Capillitium of separate threads, with
slender pointed branches. Inner
peridium papery................ Genus *Bovista* (figures
63c, e)

Capillitium of separate threads bearing spiny points. Inner peridium
thick, firm, cork-like........... Genus *Mycenastrum* (figure 63f)

Capillitium threads broken into
short fragments with blunt ends.
Inner peridium with a basal, in-
stead of an apical, mouth........ Genus *Catastoma* (figure
62b)

Outer peridium thin (=cortex, mostly
disappearing). Inner peridium
usually flaccid. Plants normally
remaining attached to place of
growth.
Capillitium of separate threads with
slender, pointed branches........ Genus *Bovistella*
Capillitium of long threads more or
less broken into fragments.
Peridium opening by a definite,
apical mouth.................. Genus *Lycoperdon* (figures
61a, 102–104)

Peridium irregularly ruptured.   Genus *Calvatia* (figures 3d, 71–74) (For a careful study of the peridia of *Lycoperdon* and *Calvatia,* see Swartz, '33)

Sub-family Sclerodermatae

Gleba uniform, peridioles indistinct..   Genus *Scleroderma* (figure 62a)

Gleba with numerous, distinct peridioles.

Peridioles large, dark-colored......   Genus *Polysaccum* (figures 58b, 63g)

Peridioles very small, granular, grayish ....   Genus *Arachnion.*

Family Nidulariaceae (Bird's-nest fungi; fairy-purses)

Peridium containing one viscid peridiole which is forcibly thrown off
by the sudden turning-inside-out
of half of the peridium..........   Genus *Sphaerobolus* (figure 61c)

Peridium containing many dry and
hard peridioles.
Peridioles attached to the inner wall
of the peridium.
Peridium composed of three
layers; spores mixed with fila-
ments ....   Genus *Cyathus* (=*Cyathia*)
(figures 2g, 61d)

Peridium composed of one homogeneous layer; spores not mixed
with filaments ....   Genus *Crucibulum.*
Peridioles not attached to the inner
wall of the peridium.
Peridium thick, opening by a
regular, definite mouth........   Genus *Nidula.*
Peridium thin, rupturing irregu-
larly ....   Genus *Granularia.*

PROBABLE KINSHIP AND ANCESTRY OF THE FUNGI (PHYLOGENY)

Mushrooms have a pedigree more ancient than those of "our best families." Their beginnings go back to the time when the vegetation of the seas (the algae, or sea-weeds) made its first attempt to leave the waters to try life on land; in other words, to a period when man was only potentially, not actually, existent. Even today certain lowly groups, the Phycomycetes, or algal fungi, bear distinct evidences of relationship to the seaweeds. Their hyphae are non-septate, permitting of the free circulation of the plant's juices, and their spores are often provided with flagellae or little, motile whips, by means of which they propel themselves in the fluids inhabited by the plants to which they belong. In the higher or true fungi (those under consideration in these pages), living as they do on dry land, changes took place as they adapted themselves to the conditions of a new life. With few exceptions, the hyphae that compose their bodies are septate, that is, those fine, hollow threads, instead of remaining hose-like, became divided into short chambers, each chamber separated from the adjoining ones by partitioning walls or septa. The spores, too, underwent a change; their motile whips disappeared. Not having to swim about any longer, but depending instead upon "the winds that blow", these appendages were dropped.

The question as to the exact mode of descent is still unanswered. It is generally conceded that the red seaweeds were the ancestors of most of our present day fungi, though other algal groups may also have given rise to some (Atkinson, '09, '15; Bessey, '13; Dodge, B. O., '14).

The larger, basidia-bearing fungi unquestionably show lines of kinship (phylae) among themselves. Beginning with the very lowly Hyphomycetes (*Tomentella*), in which, in the place of a distinct fruit-body, there is a mere loosely-woven tomentum and hymenial layer, the ascent is gradual through more and more complex forms (genera) until we get the variously figured, hymenial structures of *Psalliota, Boletus, Polyporus,* and *Hydnum,* borne upon well-developed fruit-bodies of diverse shapes. The genealogical tree of basidia-bearing fungi, adapted from Underwood (1899), will illustrate the main lines of relationship and the development from simple to complex structures (figure 64). (See also Gäumann, '28.)

Beginning with the simply constructed *Tomentella* (before mentioned), we ascend to find in *Corticium* (figure 2b) a flat hymenium spread out upon the substratum (branches, twigs, etc.). In *Thelephora* (figure 21) the tough fruit-body becomes erect and more or less branched. From here three main stems arise, one leading to the gill mushrooms, typified here by the genus *Psalliota* (=*Agaricus*) (plates 29, 30), another to the tube-bearing fungi (Polyporaceae [*Polyporus*, figures 115–118, *Strobilomyces*, figure 125, *Boletus*, plates 7–10]), and the third to the teeth-bearing kinds, *Hydnum* (plates 18, 19). *Psalliota* leads to the puffballs (*Lycoperdon*, figures 102–104) by way of *Gyrophragmium* (figure 60a) and *Secotium* (figure 60c); to *Podaxon* (figure 60b) through *Coprinus* (plates 14, 15) and *Montagnites* (figure 57a); and also to *Boletus* (*Gomphidius*, figure 57c, *Paxillus*, figure 57i, *Boletinus*, figures 55a, b), already approached through *Polyporus* and *Hydnum*. A series of genera (*Lentinus*, figure 57e, *Lenzites*, *Daedalea*, figures 43, 56e), also connects the gill and tube-bearing kinds. The disposition of these genera, as well as that of the others (*Sparassis*, figure 123, *Lachnocladium*, *Craterellus*, figure 53a, plate 17, *Cantharellus*, plate 11, *Merulius*, *Grandinia*, *Radulum*, and *Irpex*), will prove instructive to the inquiring student, who, having identified a mushroom by means of the key (p.), wishes to know the position the plant occupies with relation to others, i. e., from the phylogenetic standpoint.

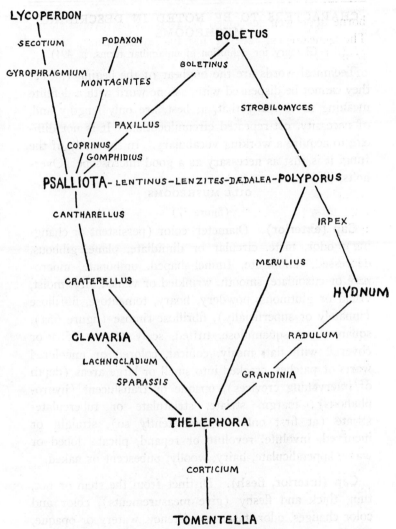

Figure 64 Diagram showing the relationship of the principal genera of the Basidiomycetes. See p. 224. Adapted from Underwood (1899)

CHARACTERS TO BE NOTED IN DESCRIBING MUSHROOMS

(See Glossary for definition of unfamiliar terms, p. 494)

Technical words are the bugbear of the beginner. Yet they cannot be dispensed with, as one word with a definite meaning saves many that, at best, are only lengthy and, of necessity, oft-repeated circumlocution. It is not difficult to acquire a working vocabulary. In the study of the fungi it is just as necessary as a good microscope (Overholts, '29).

GILL MUSHROOMS

(figure 57)

Cap (exterior). Diameter, color (persistent or changing), odor, taste, circular or dimidiate, plane, gibbous, depressed, umbilicate, funnel-shaped, umbonate, mucronate or cuspidate, smooth, wrinkled or veined, dry, moist, viscid or glutinous, powdery, hoary, tomentose, fibrillose (innately or superficially), fibrillose-rimose (figure 65a), squamose or squamulose, tufted, scaly (figure 65b) or covered with flat, mealy, conical, colored or uncolored warts or patches, cracked into small or large areas (depth of intervening crevices), opaque or translucent (hygrophanous); margin striate, striatulate or tuberculate-striate (at first only, or persistently so), straight or incurved, involute, revolute or repand, plicate, lobed or wavy, appendiculate, hairy, woolly, pubescent or naked.

Cap (interior, flesh). Distinct from the stem or not, thin, thick and fleshy (give measurements), color and color changes, odor, taste, consistency, watery or opaque, exuding a watery, milky, colored, uncolored, or color-changing juice or not.

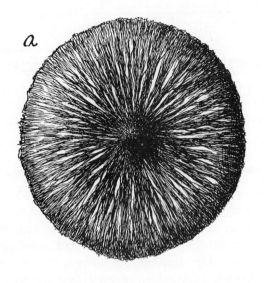

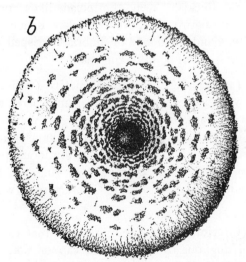

Figure 65   a, Top of the cap of a species
of *Inocybe* of the Rimosae section, showing
the fibrillose-rimose character.   b, Top of the
cap of the Parasol Mushroom, *Lepiota procera,* showing the breaking up of the cuticle
into more or less concentric scales

[227]

Gills. Narrow or broad (give measurements), separable from the underside of the cap or not, distant, close or moderately distant, branching (regularly or irregularly), veined (on their sides or deep down between adjoining gills), equal in length or unequal (inner ends of short ones with rounded outline, or more or less abruptly terminating), straight or crisped, color when young and after spores have matured, consistency (waxy, fleshy, dry and friable, or deliquescent), free or remote from stem, if attached, state whether adnexed, adnate, emarginate, uncinate-emarginate, decurrent, seceding from stem or remaining attached, exuding a watery, milky, colored, uncolored, or color-changing juice or not; edges rounded and thickish, keen (knifeblade-like), or longitudinally split (figure 20f), even, undulate, dentate, crenulate, serrate, glandular-dotted or fimbriate, crisped, colored like the sides, or of a different color.

Stem (exterior). Length, diameter (variation of diameter, whether equal, or enlarged anywhere, whether bulbous at the base, and whether rooting or not), smooth, fibrillose, mealy, warty, fleshy or cartilaginous (snapping, like crisp celery stalks), dry, moist or glutinous, provided with a ring or not (for characters of ring, see below), provided with a volva or not (for characters of volva, see below).

Stem (interior). Flesh merging into that of cap, or distinct, lifting out of a socket in cap or not, fibrous, fleshy, solid, stuffed or hollow, colored, uncolored, or changing color, exuding a watery, milky, colored, uncolored, or color-changing juice or not.

Ring. Present or not, large or small, movable or not, high up on stem, median or low, cobwebby, fibrillose, membranous or glutinous, colored or not, single or double; under side smooth, floccose or stellately split; upper side smooth or marked with longitudinal, gill-like ridges, or merely finely striate; edge entire, incised, clawlike, fibrillose, thin or thickened, lobed, colored, or uncolored.

Volva (figure 39). Present or absent, large or small, colored, or uncolored, membranous or not; free limb present or not, if present, whether entire, incised, or divided into lobes (state number of lobes), lobes appressed to stem or standing free; if free limb is absent, describe the bulb at base of stem, whether longitudinally split or margined (keenly, or rounded into one or two rolls); if volva is not membranous, state whether it is scaly, powdery (state color of powder), or divided into projecting eminences (pinecone-like); state also whether there is a secondary volva present down deep within the regular one.

Mycelium (figure 19). Whether in sheets, coarse, stringy, feathery, cobwebby, colored, or uncolored (if distinctively colored, an attempt should be made to learn whether it forms mycorrhizas on the roots of nearby trees or other higher plants, as color enables one to follow the course of strands in the soil).

Sclerotia. A search should always be made to ascertain whether the fungus grows from one of these bodies (see p. 80).

Mode of growth. Solitary, scattered, gregarious, cespitose, or forming circles or arcs of circles (see Fairy-rings, p. 44).

Spores. Color, especially as deposited on white or black paper (see p. 68), measurements (preferably given in microns [see Glossary], that is, in micromillimeters), shape (whether round, ovate, elliptical, fusiform, kidney-, lemon- or pip-shaped, cuneate, stellate or elongate, apiculate or not, germ-pore evident or not); exospore (whether smooth, reticulate in part or all over, echinulate, verrucose, or dull or sharp spinose, spines long or short); whether unicellular or septate, and guttulate, granular, or homogeneous within. (Figure 24.) (Gilbert, '27; Crawshay, '30.)

Cystidia. Present or absent, shape, with or without prongs, protuberances, or incrustations on terminal end (figure 20c); whether limited in their occurrence to the gill-edges, or whether amphigenous.

Crystals. Present or not, shape.

Habitat (see p. 50). Whether in woods, in swamps, or in the open; state nearby trees, etc., whether on wood or not.

Locality. Give state, county, or name of nearby city.

BOLETI
(figures 20g, 70, plates 7-10)

The terminology used to describe gill-mushrooms is also applicable to the species of *Boletus, Boletinus,* and *Strobilomyces,* except that a few additional observations must be made on the tubes, whether they are (as a mass) easily separable from the underside of the cap, whether some of their dissepiments show a radiating, gill-like arrangement, whether there are present granular exudations (on stems as well as on tubes), whether their mouths are stuffed, red (or otherwise colored), and whether the dissepiments exhibit a gyrose arrangement.

TEETH FUNGI
(figures 2a, 20h, plates 18, 19)

As with the gill mushrooms and Boleti, the terms used in describing these will also do for the present group. The color of the teeth, whether uniform all over the surface, or whether different on tip and base, should be observed. Also whether terete or flattened, whether the tips are simple or divided. In the *erinaceus-caput ursi-coralloides* group, the conformation of the fruit-body is important, whether it is a simple, solid body, or whether it is more or less divided into branches. The disposition of the teeth on the branches should be determined, whether confined to one side (lower) only, or whether they cover them entirely. Many species are resupinate. (See under Tremellineae, p. 232.)

CLAVARIAS
(figures 54a, b, 76–78, plate 1)

The fruit-body should be described with regard to its shape and the degree and manner of branching (whether irregular, or regularly dichotomous), whether the tips are blunt, cup-shaped, or variously incised and fimbriate; whether the plant is rigid or flaccid, whether solid or hollow. Of special significance is the color of the spore deposit. Ascertain habitat. (See under Tremellineae, p. 232.)

THELEPHORES
(figures 2b, 21, 53a, 123, plate 17)

The shape of the fruit-body must be noted, whether funnel-shaped, spathulate, or flat and spread out over the substratum. Of great importance are the microscopic characters (metuloids, setae, etc.). (Overholts, '29.)

STOMACH FUNGI
(puffballs, earthstars, stinkhorns, etc., figures 58–63, 71–74, 102–104)

In the puff-balls the ornamentation of the exterior, the manner of dehiscence of the peridia, and the color of the ripe spore mass are determinative. In *Mycenastrum corium,* the capillitium (microscopic threads present in the spore mass) is curiously ornamented with thorn-like spines. In *Geaster* (figure 62e), the structure of the mouth and the hygroscopic or non-hygroscopic nature of the rays distinguish the main groups. *Myriostoma* has a number of mouths. In the stinkhorns, the shape of the spore-bearing surface, and the presence or absence of the veil, are generically noteworthy.

TREMELLINEAE
(or gelatinous fungi, including *Auricularia* and *Calocera* of related families, figures 5, 6, 20i, k, m, 53b, c)

The shape of the fruit-body is generically distinctive, whether auricular (*Auricularia,* figure 53b), spathulate (*Gyrocephalus,* figure 53c), Clavaria-like (*Calocera*), or much folded or lobed (*Tremella*). *Tremellodon* has Hydnum-like teeth.

ASCOMYCETES
(Figures 46–52)

The shape and color of the fruit-body must be observed. Further noteworthy features are brought out in the key (p. 203) and in the descriptions of the few species included.

DESCRIPTIONS OF GENERA AND SPECIES
The descriptions of the genera and species, and the accompanying illustrations (both colored and uncolored), are presented in alphabetic order. For the convenience of

those readers unfamiliar with the use of twelfths of an
inch, a small ruler, so divided, has been included. It will
be found following the colored plates.

Genus AMANITA (Pers.) Quél. Spores white.

The beginner will do well to impress upon his mind
the botanical features of this genus in which are contained
the plants that are the usual cause of death due to mushroom poisoning.

The spores are white, the gills free or only slightly
attached, there is a ring and a volva (death-cup), the
latter being either distinctly membranous or bag-like,
scaly, or formed of crumbling particles that soon disappear. In some species the base is a mere bulb which
may have a somewhat pronounced margin, or it may
be rounded, and divided into one or two encircling rolls.

Unfortunately, both ring and volva are more or less
evanescent in some species. Also, in plucking an *Amanita*
from the place of growth, the telltale volva is apt to be
left in the ground. Compare the next genus, *Amanitopsis*.

CAESAR'S MUSHROOM (Edible); PLATE 2, FIGS. 66 a, b

Amanita caesarea (Scop.) Pers.

Cap 4–6 in. broad, hemispheric, then expanded, somewhat umbonate, smooth, bright-red or orange, fading to
yellow, widely and *distinctly long-striate on the margin,*
flesh whitish, yellow or orange immediately under the
surface, taste mild and pleasant. **Gills** free, *bright-yellow
(on their sides as well as on their edges).* **Stem** 5–8 in.
long, 4–8 lines or more thick, equal or slightly tapering
upward, flocculose, stuffed with cottony fibrils or hollow,
yellowish, saffron-colored in places. **Ring** near the top

Figure 66 Caesar's Mushroom, *Amanita caesarea*, lauded in prose and verse by ancient Roman writers, grows in forests. *a*, Three young specimens just emerging from their volvas. *b*, Fully grown plant. See also plate 4

of the stem, yellow, with darker, saffron-colored hues, flaccid. **Volva**, a *distinct large, loose, ovate, white, bag,* containing a short, secondary, white volva within, as in *Amanitopsis vaginata.* **Spores** white, elliptic, 7.6–10 μ. long (figure 24d).

In thin woods, seemingly preferring Pine woods and sandy soil. Occasionally in Beech woods. It sometimes forms "fairy-rings". July to September. It is to be deplored that this stately and gorgeously colored agaric is not more abundant. So highly was it prized by the ancient Romans, that one of their writers referred to it as "the food of the gods". Pliny gives a good description of it. Those who wish to try its edible qualities should first familiarize themselves with most of the species of the genus *Amanita,* especially with the characters of the deadly *A. muscaria.* To aid in distinguishing the two plants, the essential characters may be briefly contrasted as follows:

Amanita caesarea (Edible)	Amanita muscaria (Deadly)
Cap subumbonate, almost never with adhering patches of the volva; *margin distinctly marked with long striations.*	**Cap** never subumbonate, covered with whitish warts, unless the rain has washed them off; margin *only slightly striate.*
Gills *unmistakably bright yellow, on their sides as well as on their edges.*	**Gills** white or faintly creamy.
Stem and **Ring** yellow.	**Stem** and **Ring** white or only faintly yellow (creamy).
Volva, *a distinct, white, egg-like bag.*	**Volva** *broken up into scales which form more or less distinct rings on the basal portion of the stem.*

A recently described, southern relative of *Amanita caesarea, A. arkansana* Rosen, is a heavier, more robust plant, with gills that are occasionally *white*. (Rosen, '26.)

CRENULATE AMANITA (Edible)
Amanita crenulata Pk.

Cap 1–2 in. or more broad, thin, broadly ovate, whitish or grayish, sometimes tinged with yellow, becoming convex or nearly plane and somewhat striate on the margin, adorned with a few thin, whitish, floccose warts, or with whitish, flocculent patches. **Gills** close, reaching the stem, and sometimes forming decurrent lines upon it, *floccose-crenulate on their edges,* the short ones truncate at the inner extremity, white. **Stem** 1–2 in. or more long, 3–4 lines or more thick, equal, bulbous, floccose-mealy above, stuffed or hollow, white. **Ring** slight, evanescent, usually wanting in mature plants. **Volva** very slight, quickly disappearing from the bulb at the base of the stem and remaining as slight, floccose warts or patches on the surface of the cap. **Spores** broadly elliptic or subglobose, usually containing a single, large nucleus, 7.5–10 μ long and nearly as broad (figure 24e).

On low ground under trees. September. It is said to be of excellent flavor, but those who wish to eat it should realize, of course, that they are browsing in a dangerous field, the genus *Amanita. A. russuloides* Pk. is similar, but the cap is a clearer yellow, the margin is long and distinctly tuberculate-striate, and the spores are very different (see figure 24f).

FROST'S AMANITA
Amanita frostiana Pk.

Cap 1–2 in. broad, convex or expanded, bright orange or yellow, only slightly viscid, adorned with yellowish scales or warty patches, sometimes nearly or quite smooth, *striate on the margin*. **Gills** free, white or slightly tinged with yellow, close, broadest toward the front. **Stem** 2–3 in. long, between 2–3 lines thick, white or yellow, *stuffed,* bulbous at the base, the *bulb slightly margined above by a collar-like ring,* some of the remains of the volva. **Ring** high above on stem, slight, evanescent. **Volva** floccose-membranous, adhering to the bulb of the stem as just described, sometimes forming concentric circles as in *Amanita muscaria,* but these are not so well defined. **Spores** globose, 7.5–10 μ in diameter.

In dense, especially mixed or Hemlock, woods. June to October. Grows solitary or a few scattered. The constantly smaller size and the globose spores distinguish this species from *Amanita muscaria. Amanita flavoconia* Atk. differs in the powdery, chrome-yellow volva, non-striate margin of the cap, and in the oval spores. According to Ford and Sherrick, it contains no deadly poisons; which does not mean, however, that one should promptly proceed to eat it. Amanitas should be tested as to their edibility with the utmost caution.

FLY MUSHROOM (Deadly); PLATES 1, 3. FIGS. 36, 38, 67

Amanita muscaria (L.) Pers.

Cap 3–8 in. broad, at first ovate or hemispheric, then broadly convex or nearly plane, slightly viscid when young and moist, white, yellow, or yellow with the center orange-red (the entire surface bright-scarlet-red in the European form), *rough with numerous whitish or yellowish warts,* rarely smooth, *narrowly and slightly striate on the margin,* flesh white, yellowish under the pellicle when the surface is yellow. **Gills** white or slightly tinged

Photo by C. E. Cummings. Courtesy Buffalo Society of Natural Sciences

Figure 67 Fly Mushroom, *Amanita muscaria* (young and mature specimens), in its natural place of growth. The danger signals (warts on the caps and concentric, scaly rings at the bases of the stems) are plainly visible

with creamy-yellow (never bright-yellow), reaching the stem but free, or with a short line on the stem, crowded, broadest near the margin of the cap, the short ones ending rather abruptly. **Stem** 4–8 in. long, ½–1 in. thick, equal or slightly tapering upward, stuffed with webby fibrils or hollow, whitish or pale-creamy, *the lower portion, down to the ovate-bulbous base, covered with prominent, encircling scales* (remains of the volva. **Ring** whitish or pale creamy-white, large, membranous, fairly persistent, high up on the stem. **Volva** as described above. **Spores** broadly ovate, white, obliquely apiculate, 7.6–10 x 6.3–7.6 µ (figure 24c).

In thin, open woods (deciduous or coniferous), and in bushy pastures. June to October or even into November. Grows gregariously, sometimes forming "fairy-rings" As in the case of *Gyromitra esculenta,* this species, though known to be deadly, is eaten without ill effects by some people. Some authorities claim that the poison resides in the removable pellicle of the cap (see figure 36). With certain tribes of northeastern Siberia, a decoction, made from this plant, takes the place of alcohol. On special, festive occasions (weddings and the like), the entire population of a village indulges in an *Amanita* debauch. Individuals intoxicated from drinking the liquid act as if they were insane, and, running amuck with drawn knives and false courage, endanger the lives of their fellows. It is said that the "berserker rage" of the ancient Teutons was induced by partaking too freely of this juice. *Amanita frostiana* is smaller and has brighter, yellow warts on the cap. Rain sometimes washes off the warts of *Amanita muscaria.* The European scarlet form (plate 1) has been found in Oregon and Colorado by Kauffman. For the symptoms of poisoning by *Amanita muscaria,* and treatment, see p. 142.

PANTHER AMANITA (Deadly) Plate 4

Amanita pantherina (DC.) Fr.

Cap 4 in. or more broad, commonly olivaceous-umber
when young, fleshy, convex, then flattened or somewhat
depressed, with a viscid pellicle, which is at first thick and
olivaceous-fuscous, then thinned out, almost disappearing
and livid, the center only remaining fuscous, adorned with
small, equal, white, regularly arranged, moderately persistent warts, *margin conspicuously striate,* sometimes
tuberculately so, flesh wholly white, never yellow beneath
the cuticle.   **Gills** free, reaching the stem, broader in
front, shining white.   **Stem** 3–4 in. or more long, 6 lines
or more thick, equal or tapering upward, slightly firm and
sometimes squamulose below, *the large, basal bulb margined by two roundish, encircling rims (peronate),* at first
stuffed, then hollow, with cobwebby fibrils within.   **Ring**
large, white, grooved on the thickened edge, oblique,
almost invariably low down, near the middle of the stem.
Volva evanescent, appearing as warts on the cap, and as
rims on the basal bulb of the stem. (**Spores** elongate-
ovate, 10–12 μ long.   Quélet and Bataille.)

In woods and pastures.   Autumn.   The plant represented shows the cap paler than in the typical, European
form, but the color is recognizable as a pale tint of olivaceous-umber.   The margin, it will be noted, is tuberculate-striate.   *Amanita spissa* (Fr.) Quél., similarly
colored (though more smoky), has the margin of the cap
even, the stem solid, and the basal bulb not marginate, but
globose, depressed (turnip-shaped), and somewhat rooting,
with the ring high up on the stem.   *Amanita cothurnata*
Atk. looks much like *A. pantherina,* but the plant is much
smaller, has a white cap (rarely citron-yellow or tawny-

olive in the center), and globose spores. *Amanita velatipes* Atk. is undoubtedly a mere form of *A. pantherina*
in which the ring is formed by a ripping upward of the
outer layer of the stem. *A. pantherinoides* Murr. is a
poisonous, Pacific coast species. For an account of the
poisonous properties of *A. pantherina,* see p. 143.

POISON AMANITA (Deadly)

Amanita phalloides (Fr.) Quél.

Cap 2–5 in. broad, at first ovate or subcampanulate,
then expanded, slightly viscid when young and moist,
smooth or rarely adorned with a few fragments of the
volva, whitish, greenish, yellowish-brown or blackish-
brown, *margin even, not at all striate.* **Gills** white, rather
broad, rounded behind and free, or adnexed by a line.
Stem 4–8 in. long, 3–6 lines thick, equal or slightly tapering upward, smooth or slightly floccose, white or with
pale tints of the cap-color, stuffed or hollow, *bulbous at
the base,* the ruptured, membranous volva either appressed
loosely to the stem or merely forming a narrow margin
to the bulb. **Spores** spheric-ovate, 9–12 (with apiculus)
x 8–9 μ (Kauffman). **Ring** high up on the stem, membranous, pendulous, white or with pale tints of the cap-
color. **Volva** as described above.

In deciduous or coniferous woods or their borders,
rarely in the open (lawns, etc.). July to September.
Scattered or gregarious in its mode of growth. The cap
of the true *Amanita phalloides* should be green (unquestionably green), as that form was the first to be definitely
described. To the writer's knowledge it does not occur
in the United States. As the species is known here, the
cap is usually some shade of brown or grayish-brown,

with the margin paler. Many descriptions include forms that have been set up as independent species. *Amanita brunnescens* Atk. is one of them. The writer's figure of *Amanita phalloides* in the National Geographic Magazine ('20, plate 16) represents that species, according to Kauffman (in a letter to the writer). Atkinson's species is distinguished by the peculiar, longitudinal splitting of the always naked and broad margin of the bulb at the base of the stem, and by the reddish-brown stains assumed by the stem when much handled. This species is sometimes pale or even white all over (var. *pallida*. Krieger, '27), and except for the characteristic bulb, and color changes, one would not readily take it to be associated with *Amanita brunnescens*. (Here it must be borne in mind that *Amanita rubescens* also changes color, but to a dull-red, not to brown.) Plants with a permanently circumscissile bulb-margin and with tomentose-floccose patches on the cap are *Amanita mappa* (Batsch) Quél. Fr. (figure 39b), and if, in addition, the cap be colored a clear citron-yellow, the var. *citrina* (figure 24b). *Amanita crassivolvata* (Krieger, '27), also a member of this great assemblage formerly designated by the all-embracing name, *Amanita phalloides,* has a *brown-black,* even-margined cap, *adnate gills, and a thick-lobed, chunky volva.* The pure shimmering white forms are very apt to be either *Amanita verna,* or *A. virosa.* For an account of the symptoms produced by *Amanita phalloides* and its allies, see p. 137.

see p. 137.

BLUSHER (Edible)

Amanita rubescens Pers.

Cap 3–5 in. broad, at first ovate, then broadly convex or nearly plane, *warty,* slightly viscid when young and

Painting by Louis C. C. Krieger

Plate 1 Mushrooms in their natural habitat. The species shown are: *Clavaria stricta, Boletus versipellis, Cantharellus cibarius,* and *Amanita muscaria,* scarlet form

EDIBLE
Compare with Plate 3

Plate 2 Caesar's Mushroom, *Amanita caesarea*

Painting by Louis C. C. Krieger

Plate 3   Fly Mushroom, *Amanita muscaria*

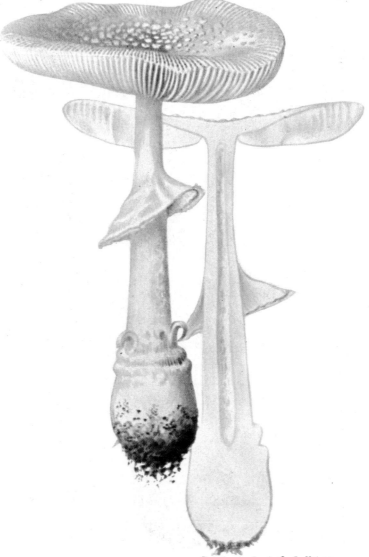

Plate 4 Panther Amanita, *Amanita pantherina*

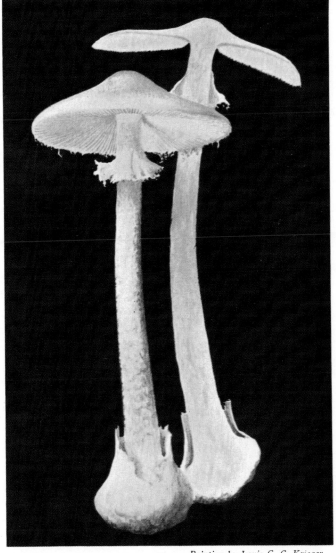

Painting by Louis C. C. Krieger

Plate 5 Destroying Angel, *Amanita virosa*

Painting by Louis C. C. Krieger

Plate 6 Sheathed Amanitopsis, *Amanitopsis vaginata var. fulva,*
and *Amanitopsis vaginata var. plumbea*

Plate 7 Edible Boletus, *Boletus edulis*

Painting by Louis C. C. Krieger

Plate 8   Bitter Boletus, *Boletus felleus*

Plate 9   Granulated Boletus, *Boletus granulatus*

Plate 10   Rough-stemmed Boletus, *Boletus scaber*

Painting by Louis C. C. Krieger

Plate 11   Orange Chantrelle, *Cantharellus aurantiacus* and Chantrelle, *Cantharellus cibarius*

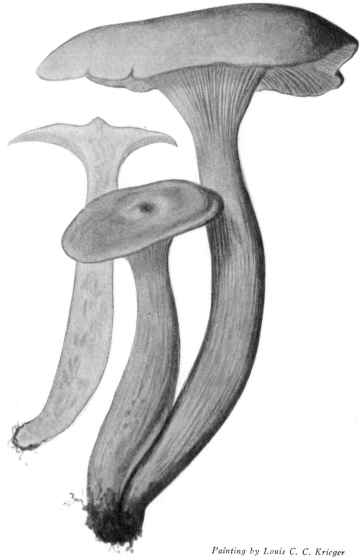

Painting by Louis C. C. Krieger

Plate 12   Jack-o'-lantern or False Chantrelle, *Clitocybe illudens*

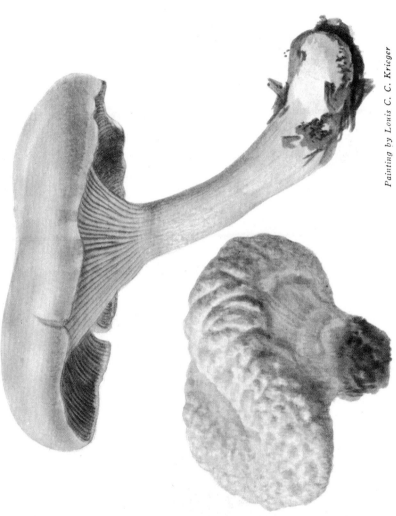

Plate 13 Abortive Clitopilus, *Clitopilus abortivus*, and its abortive form

EDIBLE

Plate 14   Ink Coprinus, *Coprinus atramentarius*

Plate 15   Shaggy-mane, *Coprinus comatus*

Painting by Louis C. C. Krieger

Plate 16   Bracelet Cortinarius, *Cortinarius armillatus*

Plate 17   Cornucopia Craterellus, *Craterellus cornucopioides*

Plate 18. Bear's-head Hydnum, *Hydnum caput-ursi*, as one encounters it in the woods.

Painting by Louis C. C. Krieger

Plate 19 Finnish Hydnum, *Hydnum fennicum*, and Spreading
Hydnum, *Hydnum repandum*

Plate 20   Russula Hygrophorus, *Hygrophorus russula*

Painting by Louis C. C. Krieger

Plate 21   Uncertain Hypholoma, *Hypholoma incertum*

Painting by Louis C. C. Krieger

Plate 22 Perplexing Hypholoma, *Hypholoma perplexum*

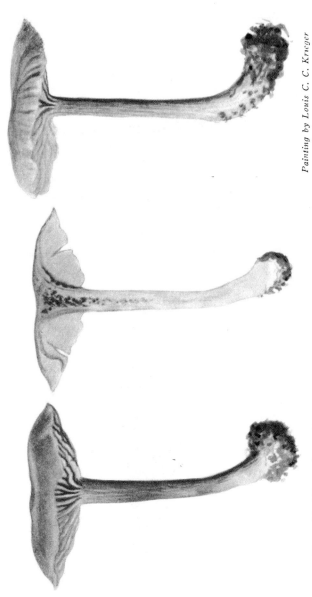

Painting by Louis C. C. Kreger

Plate 23   Waxy Laccaria, *Laccaria laccata,* and Amethyst Laccaria, *Laccaria amethystina*

Painting by Louis C. C. Krieger

Plate 24 American Lepiota, *Lepiota americana*

Painting by Louis C. C. Krieger

Plate 25   Parasol Mushroom, *Lepiota procera*

Painting by Louis C. C. Krieger

Plate 26 Thick-stemmed Morel, *Morchella crassipes*

Painting by Louis C. C. Krieger

Plate 27   Wrinkled Pholiota or Gypsy, *Pholiota caperata*

Painting by Louis C. C. Krieger
Plate 28   Sulphurous or Chicken Mushroom, *Polyporus sulphureus*

Painting by Louis C. C. Krieger

Plate 29 Horse Mushroom, *Psalliota arvensis*, and Meadow Mushroom,
Psalliota campestris

Painting by Louis C. C. Krieger

Plate 30　Reddish Psalliota, *Psalliota subrufescens*

Painting by Louis C. C. Krieger

Plate 31 Fetid Russula, *Russula foetens,* and Encrusted Russula, *Russula crustosa*

EDIBLE

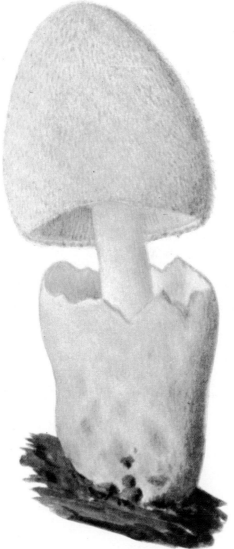

Plate 32 Silky Volvaria, *Volvaria bombycina*

moist, even or sub-striate on the margin, whitish, reddish-brown or brown. **Gills** white, reaching to the stem toward which they are narrowed. **Stem** 4–6 in. long, 4–6 lines thick, equal or slightly tapering upward, squamulose, stuffed or hollow, thickened or bulbous at the base, slightly striate at the top, white or pallid, after some time *the flesh becomes reddish where wounded.* **Volva** *breaking up (friable) into wart-like crumbs,* most of which adorn the surface of the cap, only a few being left on the bulb of the stem. **Spores** white, elliptic, 7.6–9 x 5–6.3 μ.

In thin and dense woods. July to September. This is a perfectly safe *Amanita* to eat, a statement the writer bases on personal experience. The flavor is most delicate and enjoyable. The cap eaten was quickly fried in hot butter and sprinkled with salt and pepper. *Amanita flavorubescens* Atk. is much like the "Blusher", but the margin of the cap and the ring exhibit yellow hues. The reddening is sometimes slow to develop, and frequently specimens are found that refuse to present this convenient mark of identification. Not infrequently young, undeveloped specimens look as if someone had applied a whitewash brush to them. This whitening effect, accompanied by a complete stoppage of development, is due to *Hypomyces inaequalis* Pk. (=*H. hyalinus*). See remarks under *Amanita phalloides.*

SPRING AMANITA (Deadly) Fig. 68

Amanita verna (Bull.) Quél.

Cap 2–4½ in. broad, convex to flattened, *without an umbo,* glabrous, pure white, viscid when moist, margin even. **Gills** white, crowded, subventricose, not broad, free or adnexed by a line. **Stem** 3–8 in. long, 4–7 lines

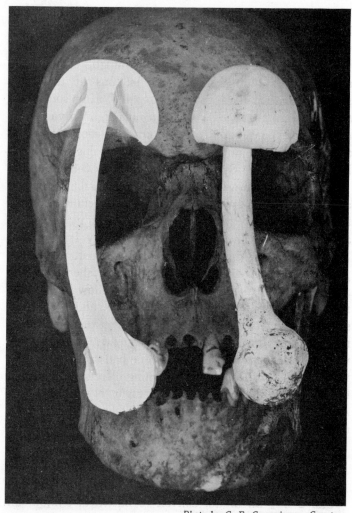

Photo by C. E. Cummings. Courtesy
Buffalo Society of Natural Sciences

Figure 68 Spring Amanita, *Amanita verna*. Note how closely
the "free limb" of the volva hugs the stem

thick, white, glabrous or floccose, stuffed or hollow. **Ring** ample, attached high up on the stem, white, *usually persistent and pendant.* **Volva** membranous, thick below, *thinning out toward the upper part which is closely applied to the stem.* **Spores** white, globose or almost so, about 8 μ in diameter, apiculate (figure 24a).

In deciduous or coniferous woods, sometimes in clearings, rarely on lawns (near trees, or where trees have recently stood). According to the specific name, it should occur in spring, but it is usually found later, from July until well into autumn.

It is commonly small, growing solitary or scattered in groups. *Amanita bisporigera* Atk. looks exactly like *A. verna,* except that it is less robust, and the basidia bear only two spores each. (On the taxonomic value of the bisporigerous character in the genus *Mycena,* see Smith, A. H., '34.) *Amanita virosa* is a very close relative. In typical forms, it is separable by its more conic (almost subumbonate) cap and by its often tattered ring, shreds of which are generally found hanging suspended from the margin of the cap and from the gill-edges. White forms of *Amanita mappa* have a large, marginate bulb, with every trace of the volva obliterated (figure 39b). For an account of the poisonous properties, etc., of this species, see p. 137.

DESTROYING ANGEL (Deadly) Plate 5, Figs. 37D, E, F, G

Amanita virosa (Fr.) Quél.

Very much like *Amanita verna,* but differing in the elevated, almost umbonate, center of the cap, in the ragged margin of the cap and gill-edges, in the tattered ring, and in the free condition of the limb of the volva.

It is usually much larger and more substantial than that species. For an account of the poisonous properties, etc., of this species, see p. 137.

see p. 137.

Genus AMANITOPSIS Roze. Spores white.

True members of this genus lack the ring, but in other respects (manner of gill attachment, presence of volva) they resemble Amanitas. Some of the latter often lose their rings, or have poorly developed ones, in which cases one is frequently in a quandary as to just where to place a specimen systematically. The spores of *Amanitopsis* species are white. *Volvaria,* with pink spores, has the same structural features. *Amanitopsis volvata* is regarded with suspicion, as it is deadly poisonous to small rodents.

STRANGULATED AMANITOPSIS (Edible)
Amanitopsis strangulata (Fr.) Karst.

Cap 1½–4 in. broad, fleshy but rather thin, fragile, at first ovate, then broadly convex or subcampanulate, finally nearly plane, grayish-brown or mouse-color, nearly always *adorned with soft, woolly, grayish warts,* slightly viscid when moist, deeply and distinctly striate and pale on the margin. **Gills** close, free, broader toward the outer extremity, white or whitish. **Stem** 3–5 in. long, 3–6 lines thick, equal or slightly tapering upward, stuffed or hollow, white or whitish, and *floccose with grayish squamules.* **Volva** *usually torn into two or three, collar-like structures that encircle, and seem to constrict (strangle), the lower part of the stem.* **Spores** white, globose, 10–12.7 μ.

In or near the borders of woods. July and later. Grows singly or in groups. It differs from the gray variety of *Amanitopsis vaginata* (var. *plumbea*) in having remains of the volva on the cap, and in the fragmentary character of its volva. *Amanitopsis farinosa* (Schw.) Atk., another grayish species, has a pulverulent volva, the powdery fragments of which adhere to the surface of the cap and to the base of the stem.

SHEATHED AMANITOPSIS (Edible) PLATE 6

Amanitopsis vaginata (Bull.) Karst.

Cap 2–4 in. broad, rather thin and fragile, at first ovate or subcampanulate, then convex or nearly plane, sometimes with a more or less developed, blunt umbo, *smooth,* rarely adorned with a few fragments of the volva, slightly viscid when young or moist, *deeply and distinctly striate on the thin margin,* almost sulcate, very variable in color (see the color varieties described below). **Gills** free, white or whitish. **Stem** rather slender, 4–7 in. long, 2–4 lines thick, equal or slightly tapering upward, stuffed or hollow, fragile, nearly smooth or minutely mealy-squamulose, not bulbous. **Volva** whitish, elongated, flabby, sheathing the base of the stem. A short, second volva present within, as in *Amanita caesarea.* **Spores** white, globose, shining, 7.6–10 μ in diameter.

Woods and copses, sometimes on much decayed wood. June to October. Several color varieties have received separate names. Var. *fulva* (the commonest form), tawny; var. *badia* (figure 24n), very dark-brown, almost black in the center (rare and found only in swampy ground of mountainous regions); var. *plumbea* (*Amanita livida* Pers. and *Amanita spadicea* Pers.), gray, lead-colored (*A. farinosa* [Schw.], also gray, has the cap covered with a gray powder), and var. *alba* (*A. nivalis* [Grev.]), white in all its parts, and of northern distribu-

tion. There is even an arctic (Greenland) variety which
has been published as *Amanitopsis hyperborea* Karst. As
an esculent, the sheathed *Amanitopsis* is of mediocre
quality. Cows enjoy it.

VOLVATE AMANITOPSIS (Poisonous)

Amanitopsis volvata (Pk.) Sacc.

Cap 2–3 in. broad, convex, then nearly plane, white or
whitish, sometimes brownish in the center, *hairy or
floccose-scaly, the margin slightly (sometimes indistinctly)
striate.* **Gills** close, free, white at first, when dry colored
a dull cinnamon-brown except on the more or less floccose
edges, which remain white. **Stem** 2–3 in. long, 3–4 lines
thick, equal or slightly tapering upward, whitish, minutely
floccose-scaly, stuffed. **Volva** *large, firm, brown, cup-
shaped, persistent.* **Spores** white, elliptic, 10 x 7.6 μ.

In woods and open places. July and August. Sometimes the cap retains patches of the volva, and not infrequently the upper part of this envelope is poised on
the center of the cap, forming a kind of hood (calyptrate).
It is said to be identical with *Amanitopsis agglutinata*
(Berk. and Curt.) Sacc. There is no record of a human
poisoning case, but it is fatal to rabbits and guinea pigs.

Genus ARMILLARIA (Fr.) Quél. Spores white.

This genus, as Professor Kauffman ('22) has recently
indicated, is a kind of dumping-ground for a variety of
plants for which no better place in the system of classification could be found. The gills may be sinuately
attached (as in *Tricholoma*), or decurrent (as in *Clitocybe*), and the more or less evident ring may be single
or double. The spores are white and there is no trace of
a volva, unless the lowermost of the double rings

(present in some species) may be so regarded. The genus is a safe one from the viewpoint of edibility, though the flesh of the plants is apt to be hard, or acrid.

BOOTED ARMILLARIA (Edible)

Armillaria caligata Vitt.-Bres.

Cap 2–4 in. broad, firm, convex, then expanded and depressed in the center, *covered with adpressed, torn, reddish-brown or dark-brown, patchy scales,* white or brownish-white between the scales, margin white, incurved, appendiculate with remains of the white veil, flesh white, firm, odor none, taste somewhat bitter. **Gills** white, crowded, of medium breadth, sinuate-adnate to slightly decurrent. **Stem** stout, 1½–3 in. long, 9–14 lines thick, equal, attenuated below, white or mealy above the ring, *breaking up below it into somewhat concentrically arranged, reddish-brown scales.* **Ring** membranous, torn, turned upward and flaring, white inside, with remnants of red-brown scales on the outside. **Spores** smooth, white in mass, ovate-globose to short-elliptic, 6–7.5 x 5 μ.

Ground in woods. Autumn. Singly or in twos. Not rare.

HONEY MUSHROOM; OAK FUNGUS (Edible) FIG. 69

Armillaria mellea (Vahl) Quél.

Cap 1–6 in. broad, fleshy, rather thin, except on the disk, at first hemispheric or subconic-subumbonate, then convex or nearly plane, *adorned with numerous, dark, hairy, evanescent squamules,* especially in the center, pale-yellowish, dingy-yellowish (honey-color), or reddish-brown, mostly striate on the margin, flesh whitish, taste unpleasant. **Gills** subdistant, emarginate, adnate or de-

Figure 69   Honey Mushroom, *Armillaria mellea*, the "white plague" of trees

current, whitish or pallid, often with rufescent spots when old. **Stem** 1–6 in. long, 3–10 lines thick, equal or slightly thickened at the tomentose base, stuffed or hollow when old, sometimes floccose squamose, externally fibrous, pallid or brownish. **Ring** thin, webby, or well developed, white, with a thick, split, greenish-yellow or olivaceous margin, sometimes much torn and disappearing. **Spores** white, 7.6–10 x 5–6.3 μ.

On the ground and on decaying wood of a great variety of trees, in woods, orchards and cleared lands. Late summer and autumn. Solitary, gregarious, or in clusters, sometimes of many individuals. The hairy squamules of the cap are very fine and easily brushed away, or washed off by heavy rains. In coloring, the plant varies extremely. The cap may be almost white, dirty-yellow, or reddish-brown. The stem, equally variable, may be pinkish-white above, and livid-brown or olivaceous-brown (with a distinct luster) below. Sometimes specimens, or entire clusters, are found in which there is no trace of a ring (see *Clitocybe monadelpha*). The tomentum at the base may be greenish-yellow or olivaceous. If the bark of the tree on which the plants are growing be removed, blackish cords, the so-called rhizomorphs, or "shoestrings", will usually be found. Not infrequently whitish, irregularly shaped, subglobose bodies are seen near perfectly normal clusters. These are abnormalities produced by the fungus. *Clitopilus abortivus* develops similar monostrosities (see figure 80, plate 13). The abnormal form is also edible. The rather persistently acrid taste of *A. mellea* is lost if the caps be parboiled before the final preparation. According to an Italian authority, his countrymen preserve the caps in vinegar, salt and oil, for use in winter.

Since it is one of the commonest and most abundant of mushrooms, it ought to be used as an esculent. It is one of the worst tree diseases. For an account of its activities as a tree destroyer, see p. 155.

see p. 155.

Genus BOLETINUS Kalchbr.

This genus agrees with *Boletus,* except that the tubes are not readily detachable from the under surface of the cap, and the tube walls (dissepiments) show a radiating, gill-like arrangement. As in *Boletus,* a ring may or may not be present. One species (*B. spectabilis*) has a double ring, the outer one tomentose, the inner one more or less glutinous. There are no poisonous species, so far as is known.

HOLLOW-STEMMED BOLETINUS (Edible) Fig. 55b

Boletinus cavipes (Opat.) Kalchbr.

Cap 1½–4 in. broad, broadly *convex-obtuse to subumbonate,* rather tough, flexible, soft, fibrillose-squamulose, tawny-brown, sometimes tinged with reddish or purplish (when wet), flesh yellowish. **Tubes** slightly decurrent, at first pale-yellow, then darker and tinged with green, becoming dingy-ochraceous with age, the tube walls showing a radiate arrangement. **Stem** 1½–3 in. long, 3–6 lines thick, equal or slightly tapering upward, somewhat fibrillose or floccose, *hollow,* tawny-brown or yellowish-brown, yellowish at the top and marked by the decurrent dissepiments of the tubes, white within. **Veil** *white or whitish,* partly adhering to the margin of the cap, slight and soon disappearing. **Spores** 7.6–10 x 4 μ.

Swamps and damp mossy ground, under or near Tamarack trees. Late summer and autumn. To be sought in the mountainous regions where it is sometimes plentiful. Var. *aureus* Roll., which is like the typical form in all respects except in the yellow coloring of cap and stem, seems to be common in Idaho, where it reaches rather large dimensions (information from J. R. Weir). The mycelial envelope of the base of the stem in *Boletinus cavipes* is white as contrasted with the salmon-pink of that of *B. pictus*.

PAINTED BOLETINUS (Edible)

Boletinus pictus Pk.

Cap 2–4 in. broad, convex or nearly plane, at first covered with a dark, *carmine-red, fibrillose tomentum, soon spotted with red, fibrillose, appressed scales,* flesh yellowish, mottled with dull-red. **Tubes** tenacious, adnate, radiating, pale yellow, becoming darker or ochraceous with age, their mouths rather large, angular, compound. **Stem** 1½–3 in. long, 3–6 lines thick, cylindric, a little thicker at the base than at the top, *solid,* yellow and glabrous above the ring, clothed and colored like the cap below it. **Ring** slight, evanescent, fibrillose, webby, sometimes appendiculate on the margin of the cap. **Spores** ochraceous, 9–11.4 x 4–5 μ.

In woods and mossy swamps, mostly under Pine trees. July to September. A conspicuously beautiful plant, because of the carmine-colored scales that adorn the cap. *Boletinus cavipes* has a rusty-brown or yellowish tomentum on the cap, and a hollow stem. *Boletinus spectabilis* has two rings, the outer tomentose, the inner glutinous. *Boletinus paluster* Pk., colored like *B. pictus,* is a much smaller plant, the breadth of the cap, in fully expanded specimens, rarely exceeding an inch and three-quarters. Sometimes old specimens of *B. pictus* are found with the cap a dull-yellow and entirely devoid of the characteristic red scales, and with dirty-grayish remains of the ring on the margin of the cap, a condition of the species which Peck described under the name, *B. appendiculatus*. The mycelial envelope at the base of the stem is salmon-pink, not white, as in *B. cavipes*.

SHOWY BOLETINUS (Edible)

Boletinus spectabilis Pk.

Cap 2–5 in. broad, at first hemispheric and covered by a reddish, tomentose veil, becoming broadly convex or nearly plane and scaly by the breaking up of the tomentum, the actual surface visible between *the large, more or less polygonal, scales* being bright-red and viscid, merging into yellow toward the margin, flesh pale-yellow, taste slightly disagreeable. **Tubes** adnate, pale-yellow when young, becoming dingy-ochraceous with age, their mouths at first small, then larger and angular, obscurely radiating. **Stem** 2–5 in. long, 4–6 lines or more thick, cylindric, equal or nearly so, solid, red below the ring, yellow above and within. **Ring** *double, the outer one (a continuation of the covering of the cap) tomentose, the inner one red and glutinous-membranous, collapsing on the former and leaving a dark, purplish-brown, tumid, encircling mass on the stem.* **Spores** purplish-brown, 12.7–15.2 x 6.3–7.6 μ.

In swamps and wet places, under or near Tamarack trees, especially in the mountainous regions of the State. July to October. The woolly scales on the cap, pale at first, finally become immersed in the moisture of the cap, appearing then as dark blotches, not unlike those one sees on the caps of old specimens of *Pholiota adiposa*. The disagreeable flavor disappears in cooking.

Genus BOLETUS (Dill.) Fr.

This genus comprises a great number of species. The tubes are more or less readily detachable from the under surface of the cap and from each other, and the walls do not show a radiate arrangement, as in *Boletinus*. The tube mouths of one group of species (and one or two exceptional species in other groups) are colored some shade of orange-red, red, or deep-maroon. *Boletus luridus* and *B. alveolatus* are members of this group. In some, the spore color is significant. In *B. felleus* it is reddish, while in *B. castaneus* it is creamy-white. In the rest it is some shade of brown. Some species have a ring, while others lack this membrane. Certain central-stemmed *Polyporus* species (see *P. ovinus*) resemble Boleti, but they are readily recognized by the toughness of their substance. *Boletus luridus, B. miniato-olivaceus,* and other species that turn blue, stand under suspicion, but, for the most part, the genus is a safe one for the budding mycophagist. See also *Fistulina*.

RELATED BOLETUS (Edible)

Boletus affinis Pk.

Cap 2–4 in. broad, convex to nearly plane or even repand, sub-glabrous, reddish-brown or chestnut-color, fading to tawny or dingy-ochraceous with age, flesh white, sometimes slowly becoming yellowish. **Tubes** plane or convex, adnate or slightly depressed around the stem, at first white and stuffed, then glaucous-yellow or sub-ochraceous, *changing to rusty-ochraceous where wounded.* **Stem** 1½–3 in. long, 4–8 lines thick, subequal, even, glabrous, sometimes obscurely reticulated above, colored like or paler than the pileus. **Spores** *rusty-ochraceous,* 9–12.7 x 4–5 μ.

In thin woods or in bushy places, especially along the borders of old wood roads. July and August. Var. *maculosus* Pk. differs simply in having a few yellowish spots scattered over the cap. *Boletus nobilis* Pk. appears to be a luxuriant form of this species, from which it differs in its larger size, the paler color of cap and stem, and in its larger spores.

ALVEOLATE BOLETUS (Edible)

Boletus alveolatus Berk. and Curt.

Cap 3–6 in. broad, convex, glabrous, shining, *bright-crimson* or maroon-color, sometimes paler and varied with patches of yellow, flesh firm, white, changing to blue where wounded. **Tubes** *adnate, subdecurrent,* yellow with maroon-colored mouths, *the surface of the tube layer uneven with irregular, alveolar depressions.* **Stem** 3–4 in. long, 9 lines thick, *very rough with the margins of rather coarse, subreticular depressions,* the reticulations bright-red above and with yellow stains. **Spores** yellowish brown, 12.7–15.2 x 4–5 μ.

In damp woods. Summer and autumn. It is not very common and is peculiar to North America. *Boletus frostii* Russell is scarcely different. Two species, also found only in North America, and similarly noted for the very coarse, rough, lacerated reticulations on their stems (group Laceripedes), differ from *Boletus alveolatus* in the duller red or yellow coloring of the stem, and in the yellow or yellowish-green of the tube-mouths. They are, *B. russellii* Frost (stem with red reticulations) and *B. betula* Schw. (stem with yellow reticulations), the former northern in its distribution, the latter southern. A further definite means of distinguishing between the two species is to be found in the spores, *B. russellii* having them longitudinally striate, *B. betula,* papillate. (See Overholts, '34, p. 509.)

TWO-COLORED BOLETUS (Edible)

Boletus bicolor Pk.

Cap 2–4 in. broad, convex, glabrous or merely pruinose-tomentose, *dark-red,* firm, becoming soft, paler and sometimes spotted or stained with yellow when old, flesh yellow, not at all or but slightly and slowly changing to blue where wounded. **Tubes** nearly plane, adnate, *bright-yellow,* becoming ochraceous, slowly changing to blue where wounded, their mouths small, angular or subrotund. **Stem** 1–3 in. long, 4–6 lines thick, subequal, firm, solid, *red, generally yellow at the top.* **Spores** pale ochraceous-brown, 10–12.7 x 4–5 μ.

Woods and open places. Summer and autumn. The color in this plant, as it ages, is sometimes very deceptive. When young, both cap and stem are of a rich and deep carmine-red, with a curious, rusty color added to the cap. Later on, yellow tints begin to appear on the cap, and, not infrequently, old specimens occur in which every trace of red has disappeared, only a dull-yellow tint remaining. Even the surface-structure undergoes changes. Continuous and pruinose-tomentose at first, it soon shows small cracks, which at length may become so conspicuous and deep as to form chunky scales, almost as coarse as those on the cap of *Hydnum fennicum* (plate 19), but red on their exterior, not brown.

Boletus castaneus (Bull.) Fr.

Cap 1½–3 in. broad, convex, nearly plane or depressed, sometimes repand with age, firm, brittle, even, dry, *minutely velvety-tomentose, cinnamon or reddish-brown,* flesh white, unchangeable. **Tubes** free, short, small, *white, becoming creamy-yellow.* **Stem** 1–2 ½ in. long, 3–5 lines thick, brittle, equal or tapering upward, sometimes constricted, even, stuffed or *hollow, clothed and colored like the cap.* **Spores** cream-colored, 10–12.7 x 6.3–7.6 μ.

Woods and open places. During the summer months. Rather common. A related, pale, dirty-cream-colored species, *Boletus subalbellus* Murrill, has been described from the South. *Boletus cyanescens* (Bull.) Fr., a larger, grayish-yellow, white-tubed species that turns dark-blue instantly on being touched or broken, is also related. Like *B. castaneus* it is hollow-stemmed, and of a brittle consistency. It prefers to grow by roadsides in woods, on sandy embankments.

Boletus chrysenteron (Bull.) Fr.

Cap 1–3 in. broad, convex or plane, soft, floccose-squamulose, often rimose-areolate, brown or brick-red, flesh *yellow, red beneath the cuticle,* often slightly changing to blue where wounded. **Tubes** subadnate, greenish-yellow, *changing to blue where wounded,* then to greenish, their mouths rather large, angular, unequal. **Stem** 1–3 in. long, 3–6 lines thick, subequal, rigid, fibrous-striate, red or pale-yellow. **Spores** pale-brown, fusiform, 11.5–12.7 x 4–5 μ.

Woods and mossy banks. July to September. Extraordinarily variable, especially in color. The cap, for instance, may be yellowish-brown, reddish-brown, brick-red, tawny, olivaceous, or even carmine-red (*B. sanguineus* With.). In one form the flesh is whitish tinged with red (var. *albocarneus* Pk.). The tubes in some specimens are strongly depressed around the stem, with the dissepiments decurrent in descending lines. It is often difficult to decide whether one should refer a plant to this species or to the closely allied, and perhaps even more variable, *Boletus subtomentosus* L. Ordinarily the color of the flesh exposed between the areolae of the cracked cuticle of the cap suffices, this being red in typical *Boletus chrysenteron,* and yellow in *B. subtomentosus.* The latter species, when typical, has large, clear-yellow tubes that do not change to blue or green. *Boletus auriporus* Pk., a species likely to be taken for *B. subtomentosus,* has a viscid stem in wet weather and *permanently golden-yellow tubes.* Not even in dried specimens is the slightest change of color noticeable. *Boletus chrysenteron* is very susceptible to the attack of a beautiful, golden-yellow species of *Hypomyces, H. chrysospermum* Tul. Sometimes a white species of this parasitic genus covers every part of the plant. Indeed, during a very wet season, it is often impossible to secure specimens free from these parasites. Two varieties, with caps not much over an inch in diameter, are noteworthy. Var. *deformatus* Pk., with very irregularly formed cap and stem, grows almost hidden in the earth of sloping embankments, and var. *sphagnorum* Pk., with the thin margin of the cap extending slightly beyond the tube layer, and with white flesh (compare var. *albocarneus,* above), in sphagnum moss. Compare *Paxillus rhodoxanthus.*

CLINTON'S BOLETUS (Edible)
Boletus clintonianus Pk.

Cap 2–5 in. broad, convex, very viscid or glutinous, glabrous, golden-yellow, reddish-yellow or chestnut-color, flesh pale-yellow or whitish, taste mild. **Tubes** adnate, their mouths small, angular or subrotund, pale-yellow when young, ochraceous when mature, changing to brown or purplish-brown where bruised. **Stem** 2–5 in. long, 4–9 lines thick, equal or slightly thickened at the base, solid, yellow above the ring, colored like the cap below. **Ring** thick, persistent, white or whitish. **Spores** brownish-ochraceous, 10–11.4 x 4–5 μ.

In woods and in open places, generally under or near Tamarack trees. It is especially fond of damp, mossy places. July to September. The apex of the stem is sometimes slightly reticulated by the decurrent tube walls. From *Boletus elegans* Schum., of Europe, it differs in its generally darker color, in its persistent, non-fugacious ring, and in its stem, which is not at all dotted, either above or below the ring.

EDIBLE BOLETUS OR CÈPE (Edible) PLATE 7
Boletus edulis (Bull.) Fr.

Cap 4–6 in. broad, convex or nearly plane, *glabrous, moist*, at first compact, then soft, variable in color, grayish-red, brownish-red or tawny-brown, *paler on the gently lobed and slightly overlapping margin*, flesh white or yellowish, reddish beneath the cuticle. **Tubes** convex, depressed around the stem, nearly free, long, minute, at first stuffed, then round, *white, then creamy-yellow, finally greenish*. **Stem** 2–6 in. long, 6–18 lines thick, straight or flexuous, subequal or bulbous, stout, whitish, pallid or brownish, *more or less adorned* (*always above*) *with a raised network of whitish lines* (*reticulated*). **Spores** oblong-fusiform, 12.7–15.2 x 4–5 μ.

In groves, woods and their borders, sometimes in open waste places. July and August. This most desirable of all Boleti is unfortunately not very common. The writer has, on occasions, found it growing in troops in Pine woods, the specimens (cap and stem) being colored a dull-red, and corresponding with var. *pinetis,* of some recent, European authors. The more familiar form, shown in the plate, occurs in Oak woods, and is doubtless the var. *quercetis* of the same authors. Peck's var. *clavipes* has the everywhere-reticulated stem tapering upward from a much enlarged base. *Boletus nobilis* Pk., referred to *B. edulis* by one author, seems more akin to *B. affinis* (p. 255.)

SELECT BOLETUS (Edible)
Boletus eximius Pk.

Cap 3–10 in. broad, at first very compact, subglobose or hemispheric, subpruinose, *purplish-brown or chocolate-color,* sometimes with a faint tinge of lilac, becoming convex, soft, smoky-red or pale-chestnut, flesh grayish- or reddish-white. **Tubes** at first concave or nearly plane, stuffed, *colored nearly like the cap,* becoming paler with age and depressed around the stem, their mouths minute, rotund. **Stem** stout, generally short, 2–4 in. long, 6–12 lines thick, equal or tapering upward, abruptly narrowed at the base, *minutely furfuraceous,* colored like, or a little paler than the cap, *purplish-gray within.* **Spores** sub-ferruginous, 11.5–15.2 x 5–6.3 μ.

Woods and their borders. Summer and autumn. A very unique and well marked species, utterly unlike any other, either here or in Europe. It occurs occasionally, sometimes in clusters.

BITTER BOLETUS (Unwholesome) PLATE 8

Boletus felleus (Bull.) Fr.

Cap 3–8 in. broad, convex or nearly plane, firm, becoming soft, *glabrous,* even, variable in color, pink or purplish when young, then pale-yellowish, grayish-brown, yellowish-brown, reddish-brown or chestnut, flesh white, often changing to flesh-color where wounded, *taste bitter*. **Tubes** adnate, long, convex, depressed around the stem, their *mouths angular,* white, becoming tinged with flesh-color, changing to a deeper tint when wounded. **Stem** short or long, 2–4 in. long, 6–12 lines thick, equal or tapering upward, sometimes bulbous or enlarged at the base, subglabrous, generally reticulated above, colored like or a little paler than the cap. **Spores** flesh-colored, oblong-fusiform, 12.7–17.8 x 4–5 μ.

Woods and open places, on or about much decayed stumps and prostrate trunks of Hemlock, or in soil largely composed of decayed wood and other vegetable matter. July to September. The bitter taste is sometimes slow to assert itself, especially in young specimens. Several, mild-tasting species are difficult to distinguish from the Bitter Boletus. *Boletus indecisus* Pk., one of them, has subrotund, flesh-colored tube-mouths that change to brownish when injured, a furfuraceous stem reticulated above, and darker-colored, brownish-flesh-colored spores. *Boletus alutarius* Fr. also has flesh-colored tubes that change to brown, but the stem is never reticulated, but merely rugulose above, the rounded ridges being dotted with small, yellow-brown granules (scrupose). *Boletus gracilis* Pk. (figure 24t), which also comes in for consideration in this series of closely related species, has subrotund tube-mouths and a very slender, furfuraceous

stem marked with thin, elevated, longitudinal, anastomosing lines. The diameter of the stem rarely exceeds four
lines. Usually it is even thinner. *B. felleus* Bull. var.
obesus Pk. has a large, convex cap and a thick, very
bulbous stem coarsely reticulated nearly or quite to the
base.

GRANULATED BOLETUS (Edible) PLATE 9

Boletus granulatus L.

Cap 1½–3 in. broad, thick, convex or nearly plane,
very viscid or glutinous when moist, variable in color,
*pinkish-gray, reddish-brown, yellowish, tawny-ferru-
ginous or brownish,* sometimes with obscure, blotchy
squamules immersed in the gluten, flesh white or tinged
with yellow. **Tubes** nearly plane, adnate, *small,* at first
whitish or very pale-yellow, becoming dingy-ochraceous,
glandular dotted. **Stem** rather short, 1–2 in. long, 4–6
lines thick, subequal, without a ring, whitish or pallid,
sometimes yellowish, *glandular dotted.* **Spores** *ochraceous-ferruginous,* subfusiform, 7.6–9 x 4 μ.

Woods, especially of Pine, and in open places. July to
October. Very common and edible, but the slimy pellicle
of the cap should be removed. Peck has described three,
closely related species of *Boletus granulatus* which some
authors are inclined to view as mere variants: *B. albus,
B. brevipes,* and *B. punctipes.* The first differs in having
both cap and stem white; the second has a more glutinous,
darker cap, and a shorter stem almost completely devoid
of glandular dots, and the last has a rhubarb-yellow,
upward-attenuated, clavate stem, and tubes that are dark-
brownish when young. *Boletus rubropunctatus* Raddi
would seem to be an early name for *Boletus boudieri*

Quél., the south European representative of the white form of *B. granulatus* (*B. albus*). The latter sometimes occurs very large (var. **giganteus,** var. nov.; see painting by Mrs. E. B. Blackford, in the Herbarium of the University of Michigan).

LARCH BOLETUS (Edible)
Boletus laricinus Berk.

Cap about 2½–3 in. broad, fleshy, broadly convex or nearly plane, covered with a viscid, dirty-yellowish or brownish gluten, sometimes squamose with brown or blackish (easily removed) scales, *dingy-white or grayish-white,* flesh white or whitish, and soft. **Tubes** short, adnate or slightly decurrent, whitish when young, becoming darker and brown (Sepia-brown) with age, their mouths large, angular, subdivided into smaller mouths (subcompound), extending downward on the stem to the ring and forming a low network there. **Stem** short, 1½–2 in. long ¼–½ in. thick, solid, grayish or brownish, and *scrobiculate below.* **Ring** slight. **Spores** brown, oblong, 10–12.7 x 4–5 μ.

Always under or near larches. Autumn. *Boletus elbensis* Pk., which is also found under or near larches (tamarack trees) in the Adirondack mountains, differs in the pinkish, grayish-brown color of the innately fibrillose cap (the fibrils sometimes forming patches), and in the absence, from the stem, of the low network above the ring and of the scrobiculations below. *Boletus laricinus* has somewhat the habit of a *Boletinus. Boletinus grisellus* Pk. has been referred to as a synonym, but the spores differ in their measurements.

LURID BOLETUS (Unwholesome)

Boletus luridus Schaeff. (not of Fries!)

Cap globose to convex, then expanded, dirty-olivaceous-yellow, glabrous, flesh yellowish, becoming bluish. **Tubes** short, yellow, becoming greenish, their mouths angular, vermilion. **Stem** terete, thick, dirty-yellow above, red and thicker below, everywhere covered with plainly visible reticulations, the very base black and supplied with mycelial strands. (Description based on the original description and plate of Schaeffer.)

Kallenbach ('26) has pointed out that Fries' (1874) description of *Boletus luridus* is a mixture of the original descriptions of *B. luridus* Schaeff. and *B. miniatoporus* Secr. (=*B. erythropus* Fr.). Killerman ('22), who at the present time is collecting and critically studying the fleshy fungi of the region around Regensburg, Germany (where Schaeffer made his collections), asserts that the true *B. luridus* of Schaeffer still grows there. A *Boletus,* to be the plant of Schaeffer, must have a conspicuously reticulated stem. A plant that has not such a stem cannot be referred to Schaeffer's description and colored plate (1762). Plants dotted with red squamules are likely to be *Boletus miniatoporus*. Peck (1889), following Fries, presents the same mixture. The dimensions of *B. luridus* Schaeff., as given by Kallenbach, are: cap rarely more than 8 in. broad; stem, up to 6 in. long, ¾–2¾ in. thick. The spores are described as olive to brownish-olive (when deposited), elliptic to elliptic-fusiform, guttulate, and measuring (on the average) 11–15 x 6–7 µ. For an account of its poisonous properties, see p. 143.

Boletus firmus Frost, a species recently studied by the writer in Canada, resembles Kallenbach's figure of *B.*

erythropus Pers., except that the cap is gray, while the stem is covered with a meshwork of reticulations so exceedingly fine that it is visible only under a hand-lens. It is pale-yellow and clearly marked under the glass.

Boletus luridus has a great number of closely allied varieties and forms.

Photo by Edwin J. Stein

Figure 70   Yellow-brown Boletus, *Boletus luteus,* an edible species

YELLOW-BROWN BOLETUS (Edible) Fig. 70

Boletus luteus L.

Cap 2–5 in. broad, gibbous or convex, sometimes nearly plane, viscid or glutinous when moist, virgate-spotted, yellowish-brown, flesh white or yellowish, margin sometimes with adhering remains of the ring. **Tubes** small, simple, adnate, at first pale-yellow, then dingy-ochraceous. **Stem** stout, rather short, 1–2 in. long, 5–8 lines thick, *rough with dots and yellowish above the ring,* brownish-white or yellowish below. **Ring** large, membranous, median, or low down on the stem and then appearing almost volva-like, sometimes much torn, and again with the margin flaring. **Spores** ochraceous-ferruginous, nearly fusiform, 7.6 x 3.8 μ.

In Pine woods. October. Specimens with the ring volva-like should have their spores carefully scrutinized, as it is just possible that one has found that rare western species, *Boletus sphaerosporus* Pk. Peck's *B. subluteus* is smaller and has a slender stem that is dotted both above and below the very slight, band-like ring. *Boletus luteus* is usually gregarious in its mode of growth, rarely subcespitose.

SENSITIVE BOLETUS (Unwholesome)

Boletus miniato-olivaceus Frost var. *sensibilis* Pk.

Cap 2–6 in. broad, red, pruinose-tomentose, becoming glabrous and ochraceous-red with age, *instantly changing to dark-blackish-blue when wounded or even lightly touched,* flesh yellow, also changing as above. **Tubes** bright-yellow tinged with green, becoming sordid-yellow, changing color like the cap when touched or wounded. **Stem** 3–4 in. long, 3–6 lines or more thick, lemon-yellow with red or rhubarb stains at the base, contracted at the top when young, also changing color like the other parts, utterly devoid of reticulations, clothed like the cap, but tomentum finer and punctate. **Spores** 10–12.7 x 4–5 μ.

Woods and their borders. Summer and autumn. Although entirely unlike *Boletus cyanescens,* every part of the plant similarly changes color to a dark inky-blue. So rapidly does the change take place, that one cannot remove a specimen from its place of growth without causing blotches, streaks, and stains of blue to appear. Sometimes it grows in clusters of a few individuals. On one occasion (at a meeting of the Boston Mycological Club, August 22, 1910), the writer saw a form of this variety in which every trace of red was absent from cap and stem, the whole plant being yellow, but with the instantaneous color change just as strongly evident. *Boletus pseudo-sulphureus* Kallenb. would, therefore, seem to be a yellow form of the American plant. Another characteristic feature of Peck's variety is its pronounced, garlic odor. The only colored figure published of the sensitive *Boletus* is to be found in Palmer's Mushrooms of America (1885, Pl. 7, figure 4), where it appears as *B. subtomentosus* L. Collins (1899), guided by this bit of misinformation, was made ill by the specimens he ate. The writer has amplified Peck's description from the type material at the New York State Museum, Albany. For an account of its poisonous properties, see p. 144.

ORNATE-STEMMED BOLETUS (Edible)

Boletus ornatipes Pk.

Cap 2–5 in. broad, convex, firm, dry, glabrous or very minutely tomentose, *grayish-brown or yellowish-brown,* flesh yellow or pale-yellow. **Tubes** adnate, plane or concave, rarely convex, mouths small or of medium size, *clear-yellow.* **Stem** 2–4 in. or more long, 4–6 lines or more thick, firm, subequal, distinctly and beautifully reticulated, yellow without and within. **Spores** ochraceous-brown, oblong, 11.4–14 x 4–5 μ (figure 24u).

Thin woods and open places. Midsummer and early autumn. This species is perhaps too close to *Boletus retipes* Berk. and Curt., which is said to differ in its tufted mode of growth, pulverulent cap, and paler, greenish-ochraceous spores. *Boletus griseus* Frost is also nearly related, but the tubes are white or whitish, the cap grayish or dark-gray, merging into brownish, while the stem is either entirely whitish or there are blotches of the tell-tale yellow. The flesh is whitish or grayish. In all three species the stem is covered with a conspicuous network that extends from the apex to the base.

ROUGH-STEMMED BOLETUS (Edible) PLATE 10
Boletus scaber Bull.

Cap 1–5 in. broad, commonly convex, *glabrous and viscid when moist,* sometimes minutely tomentose, subvelvety or even squamulose, at length rugulose or rivulose. **Tubes** generally long, free, leaving a deep, broad depression around the apex of the stem, convex (as a mass), white, then sordid, their mouths minute, rotund, flesh white or whitish, sometimes changing slightly to brown or pinkish (var. *mutabilis*). **Stem** 3–5 in. long, 3–8 lines thick, attenuated upwards, solid, *roughened with small, blackish-brown or reddish dots or fibrous scales.* **Spores** snuff-brown, oblong-fusiform, 14–17.8 x 4–6.3 μ.

Woods, swamps and open places. Summer and autumn.

Very common and very variable, especially in the coloration of the cap, which may be white (var. *niveus*), brick-red (var. *testaceus*), yellowish-tan-color (var. *alutaceus*), olivaceous (var. *olivaceus*), orange-red (var. *aurantiacus;* which is *Boletus versipellis* without the overlapping cap-margin), smoke-colored or grayish-smoke-colored (var. *fuligineus*), and brown or dark-brown (var. *fuscus;* which is close to *Boletus duriusculus* Schulz., figure 55d). Var. *areolatus* has the cap surface cracked into small, angular areas or scales. Occasionally a lemon-yellow-tubed plant is found that shows *scaber*-like, yellowish or brownish points on the stem, the cap being coarsely rugulose to rimose, and of a rich, olivaceous yellow-brown. This is *Boletus rugosiceps* Pk., or *B. luteo-scaber* Secr., which, in turn, has been referred to *B. rimosus* of Venturi by Kallenbach ('26). Var. *gracilipes* is small and very slender.

Boletus scaber is not as desirable an esculent as the celebrated *B. edulis,* for its flesh, though thick and usually white, is soft and soggy in specimens at all advanced in age, and the point of juncture between cap and stem is nearly always larva-infested.

SMALL YELLOWISH BOLETUS (Edible)
Boletus subluteus Pk.

Cap 1½–3 in. broad, convex or nearly plane, viscid or glutinous when moist, sometimes obscurely virgate-spotted, dingy-yellowish inclining to ferruginous-brown, flesh whitish, varying to dull-yellowish. **Tubes** plane or convex, adnate, small, subrotund, yellow, becoming ochraceous. **Stem** slender, 1½–3 in. long, 2–4 lines thick, equal, pallid or yellowish, *marked both above and below* *the ring with reddish or brownish, glandular dots.* **Ring** submembranous, *glutinous,* at first concealing the tubes, then *collapsing and forming a narrow, whitish or brownish band* on the upper part of the stem. **Spores** ochraceous-ferruginous, subfusiform, 7.6–10 x 4–5 μ.

Sandy soil in Pine woods or groves. September and October. The ring is never situated at the lower end of the stem, as is sometimes the case in *Boletus luteus.* Compare the description of the latter species (p. 267).

ORANGE-CAP BOLETUS (Edible) Plate 1, Fig. 55e

Boletus versipellis Fr.

Cap 2–6 in. or more broad, convex, *dry,* at first compact and minutely *tomentose,* then squamose or smooth, reddish or orange-red, *margin appendiculate with the inflexed remains of the membranous veil, flesh white or grayish.* **Tubes** at first concave or nearly plane, almost or quite free, minute, sordid-white, their mouths gray. **Stem** 3–5 in. or more long, 4–10 lines or more thick, equal or tapering upward, solid, whitish or pallid, *rugose, the intervening ridges surmounted by numerous, reddish or blackish points.* **Spores** oblong-fusiform, 14–17.8 x 4–6.3 μ.

Woods and open places, especially in sandy soil. August to October. Grows singly or scattered. Not as common as its congener, *Boletus scaber.* The writer has encountered huge specimens with caps almost a foot in diameter. When young it is useful as a second-best, edible mushroom. The overlapping margin of the cap is peculiar to it. Its exceeding hardness of tissue is equalled only by *Boletus duriusculus* Schulz., a closely related species with a dark, smoky-brown, finely rimose-areolate, cap (figure 55d). *Boletus scaber* var. *aurantiacus* differs only in lacking the appendiculate cap-margin.

GENUS BOVISTA Pers.

Bovistas are puffballs with thin, parchment-like, usually dark-colored, inner peridia. See the species descriptions for further details. For microscopic details, see figures 63c, e.

BALL BOVISTA (Edible)

Bovista pila Berk. and Curt.

Fruit-body 1½–3 in. in diameter, usually globose or somewhat plicate at the base. Cortex early broken into granules which disappear, exposing the smooth, shining, black or bronze-colored peridium which opens by an irregular, torn aperture. Spore-mass firm, compact, at first olivaceous, finally dark-purplish-brown. **Spores** globose, 4–5 μ in diameter, even, usually without a pedicel, or with a very short one. **Capillitium** threads much branched, with short, thick, rigid, tapering branches (figure 63c). Larger than *Bovista plumbea.*

LEAD-COLORED BOVISTA (Edible)

Bovista plumbea Pers.

Fruit-body 9–14 lines in diameter, globose or depressed-globose, at first smooth and white, breaking up into little, white granules as it dries, then shelling off and exposing the smooth, firm, parchment-like, lead-colored peridium which opens by a small, definite mouth. Spore mass compact, elastic, at first olivaceous, finally dark-purplish-brown. **Spores** subglobose or ovate, smooth, even, 5–6 μ long, with long pedicels (10–12 μ, figure 63e). **Capillitium** threads much branched, with slender, tapering branches.

Usually in old pastures. It is readily distinguished from *Bovista pila* by its lead-color, small size, and long-pedicellate spores.

Genus CALVATIA Fr.

Species belonging to this genus are usually quite large, one, *Calvatia gigantea,* occasionally growing to immense size. The ripe spores escape as a dark, more or less brown, powder through cracks in the inner peridium (outer peridium, the cortex, disappears early), not through a single, apical mouth, as in *Lycoperdon* (figures 3d, 61a). The beginner is advised to start with these puffballs in risking his life in the cause of mycophagy. But there is no risk, for they are all both safe and good to eat so long as the flesh is white, dry, and compact. (On the structure of the peridium of this genus, and of *Lycoperdon,* see Swartz, '34.)

ENGRAVED PUFFBALL (Edible) Fig. 71

Calvatia caelata (Bull.) Morg.

Peridium 4–8 in. broad, *narrowed below into a short, stout, stem-like base,* white, covered with a rather thick, mealy or floccose coating (which usually breaks up into warts, scales or areas, and which, when old, either wholly or partly disappears), obtuse, at length flattened or depressed above, the upper part finally rupturing and leaving a brownish, cup-shaped base with a lacerated margin. **Capillitium** and spores at first dingy greenish-yellow, becoming darker or umber-colored with age, the former distinct from the sterile base. **Spores** smooth, 4 μ in diameter.

Meadows, pastures, and other grassy places. Autumn.

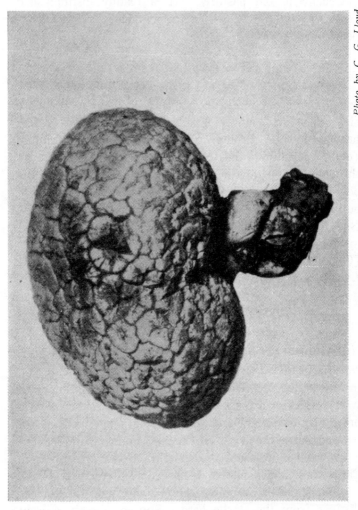

Figure 71 Engraved Puffball, *Calvatia caelata*; a puff-ball not to be despised

[274]

The smaller size, rougher surface, and distinct, stem-like base distinguish this species from *Calvatia gigantea*. The color of its ripe spore-mass separates it from *C. cyathiformis*.

SKULL-SHAPED PUFFBALL (Edible) Fig. 72

Calvatia craniiformis (Schw.) Fr.

Peridium very large, 3–6 in. in diameter, 4–5 in. high, obovate or top-shaped, depressed above, the base thick and stout. Cortex a smooth, continuous layer, very thin and fragile, easily peeling off, pallid or grayish, sometimes with a reddish tinge, often becoming plicate-areolate. Inner peridium thin, ochraceous to bright-brown, velvety, extremely fragile, after maturity the upper part breaking up into fragments and falling away. Subgleba (sterile base) occupying about one-half of the peridium, cup-shaped above and persistent for a long time. **Capillitium** and spore-mass greenish-yellow, then ochraceous or dirty-olivaceous, the threads very long, about as thick as the spores, branched. **Spores** globose, even, 3–3.5 µ in diameter, minutely pedicellate.

On ground in mixed woods. August to October. Occurs in scattered groups of many individuals.

CUP-SHAPED PUFFBALL (Edible) Fig. 73

Calvatia cyathiformis (Bosc) Morg.

Peridium 3–6 in. in diameter, globose or depressed-globose, smooth or minutely floccose or scaly, whitish, grayish-brown or pinkish-brown, soon cracking into irregular-shaped, darkish areas in the upper part, with paler chinks between, commonly with a short, thick, stem-like base, flesh white at first, then colored like the spores. **Capillitium** and spores purple-brown, this mass (the

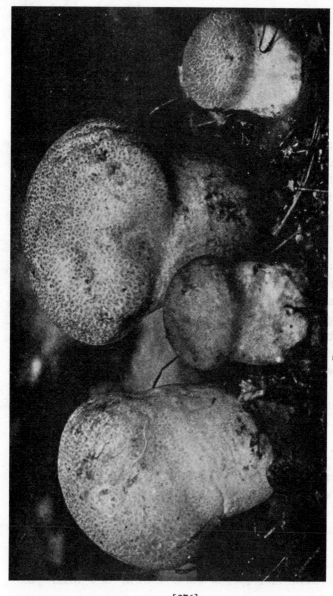

Figure 72 The Skull-shaped Puffball, *Calvatia craniiformis*, like the rest of the large puff-balls, is good to eat. Copyright, The National Geographic Society

gleba) and the upper part of the peridium falling away and disappearing when old, leaving a cup-shaped base with a ragged margin. **Spores** globose, rough, purple-brown, 5–6.3 μ in diameter.

In pastures, sometimes in cultivated ground. August and September. In hunting the Meadow Mushroom it

Reproduced by special permission from The National Geographic Magazine

Figure 73 The Cup-shaped Puffball, *Calvatia cyathiformis,* is usually found growing in company with the Meadow Mushroom (*Agaricus campestris*). Copyright The National Geographic Society

frequently happens that one does not find enough specimens to make a respectable meal. If, then, quantities of the Cup-shaped Puff-ball are available, these can be added to the few mushrooms, the latter giving the flavor, the former making bulk.

GIANT PUFFBALL (Edible) Figs. 3d, 74

Calvatia gigantea (Batsch) Fr.

Peridium 8–15 in. in diameter, but sometimes very much larger, globose or depressed-globose, sessile or nearly so, glabrous or slightly flocculose, white, whitish or slightly yellowish, becoming dingy with age, flesh white at first, then colored like the spores. **Capillitium** and spores greenish-yellow, then dingy-olivaceous. **Spores** globose, about 4 μ in diameter.

In grassy places. August and September. This is the largest species of the puffball family. One specimen is often enough for a very large family.

LONG-STEMMED PUFFBALL

Calvatia saccata (Vahl) Fr.

Peridium 2–4 in. high, 1–2 in. broad, depressed-globose or somewhat lenticular, supported by a long, stem-like base, furfuraceous, with minute, persistent, mealy or granular warts or spinules, often plicate beneath, white or creamy-white, at maturity becoming brown or olive-brown, somewhat shining and very thin or membranous, breaking up into irregular fragments which sometimes adhere to the capillitium for a considerable time, the stem-like base cylindric or narrowed downwards, sometimes thick, occasionally uneven with shallow depressions. **Capillitium** rather dense, somewhat persistent, the spore-mass dingy-olive or dingy-brown, sometimes verging toward purplish-brown. **Spores** rough, 4–5 μ in diameter.

Low, mossy grounds and bushy swamps, especially under alders. August to October. An attractive species.

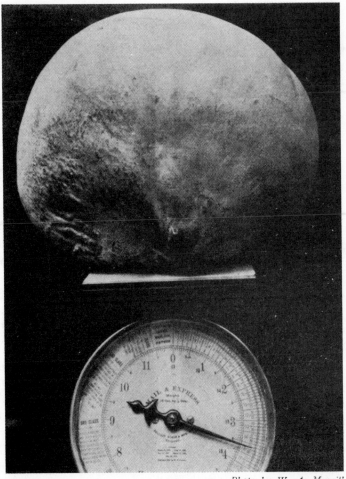

Photo by W. A. Murrill

Figure 74 A nice, solid, substantial Giant Puffball, *Calvatia gigantea,* "touching the scales" at more than three and a half pounds

Genus *CANTHARELLUS* (Adans.) Fr. Spores white to creamy.

Species belonging to this genus look somewhat like Clitocybes, but the anastomosing, dull-edged gills at once mark a true *Cantharellus*. The spores of some species show a creamy tint. *Cantharellus aurantiacus* is sometimes put down as deleterious. Compare *Craterellus*.

ORANGE CHANTRELLE. Plate 11
Cantharellus aurantiacus (Wulf.) Fr.

Cap 1–3 in. broad, fleshy, thick, soft, minutely tomentose, plane or slightly depressed, *yellowish-orange,* often tinged with smoky-brown, margin decurved or involute, flesh whitish or yellowish. **Gills** narrow, close, *regularly and repeatedly (dichotomously) forked,* decurrent, *bright-orange,* sometimes yellowish. **Stem** 1–2 in. long, 2–5 lines thick, equal or slightly tapering upward, solid, colored somewhat like the cap. **Spores** subelliptic, 6.3–7.6 x 4–4.6 μ.

On ground and much decayed wood, also in damp, mossy soil filled with vegetable mold. July to October and later. Common in hilly and mountainous districts. The plant is variable in color. Sometimes the cap fades to a dingy buff-red. The margin or the entire cap may be pale-yellow or even whitish, and a form with whitish gills has been found in a sphagnous marsh. In Europe it has been known to have a black stem, and wholly white specimens have also been found there. It is readily distinguished from *Cantharellus cibarius* by its very regular, dichotomously forked (usually orange), close gills.

CHANTRELLE (Edible) PLATES 1, 11. FIG. 2h

Cantharellus cibarius Fr.

Cap 1½–4 in. broad, fleshy, firm, convex, then expanded or slightly depressed, glabrous, *yellow,* the margin at first involute, then spreading, often wavy or irregular, flesh white within, odor fragrant, like ripe apricots. **Gills** narrow, thick, distant, decurrent, more or less *irregularly branched* or anastomosing, yellow, edges rounded. **Stem** 1½–3 in. long, 3–6 lines thick, firm, *solid,* glabrous, *yellow,* usually curved and tapering downwards. **Spores** white with a slight, yellowish or salmon tint (when deposited on white paper), subelliptic, 7.6–10 x 5–6.3 μ.

Preferably in the deep shade of hemlocks, but it also grows freely and plentifully in thin woods of deciduous trees. June to September. Common. The American plant lacks the delightful, fruity odor, but it is nevertheless eagerly sought by the mushroom hunter. Unless gently stewed over a slow fire for a long time, it is apt to be tough. In England, it is served up at festive dinners. In continental Europe, it has more than two hundred common names. The common German name is *Pfifferling.* The coloring resembles that of the hard fried yolk of an egg. The False Chantrelle, *Clitocybe illudens* (plate 12), is utterly different, being much larger and having simple, unbranched, keen-edged gills. *Craterellus cantharellus* (figure 53a), an edible species, is almost a double, but the hymenial surface is merely wrinkled, not provided with gills. *Cantharellus aurantiacus* has close, orange-colored gills that fork with the greatest regularity, dividing dichotomously. The Chantrelle grows either scattered or in arcs of circles, usually around trees, as if attempting to form "fairy-rings".

VERMILION CHANTRELLE (Edible)

Cantharellus cinnabarinus Schw.

Cap 8–18 lines broad, firm, convex or slightly depressed in the center, often irregular, with a wavy or lobed margin, glabrous, *vermilion-red,* flesh white, taste tardily acrid. **Gills** narrow, distant, branched, decurrent, *vermilion-red.* **Stem** 6–12 lines long, 1–3 lines broad, equal or tapering downward, glabrous, solid, or stuffed, *colored like the cap and gills.* **Spores** elliptic, 7.6–10 x 4–5 μ.

In thin woods and open places. July to September. Grows gregariously, sometimes occurring in great abundance. The acrid taste disappears in cooking. The decided, vermilion-red coloring of all its exterior parts readily distinguishes it from the other species of the genus.

SHAGGY CHANTRELLE (Edible)

Cantharellus floccosus Schw.

Cap 2–4 in. broad at the top and 3–6 in. long, elongate-funnel-form or trumpet-shaped, deeply excavated, firm, rather thin-fleshed, floccose-squamulose, yellowish to sub-ochraceous. **Gills** thick, narrow, close, repeatedly forked, branched or anastomosing, very decurrent, ochraceous-yellow. **Stem** short, glabrous or hairy, sometimes elongated and somewhat curved or flexuous. **Spores** ochraceous, elliptic, 12.7–15.2 x 7.6 μ, with an oblique apiculus at one end and usually uninucleate.

Among fallen leaves in woods. Reported to form mycorrhizas on the roots of Fir trees in Japan (Masui, '27). July to September. Grows scattered or in clusters of two or three individuals. Resembling a good-sized calabash pipe, it cannot readily be confounded with another species, unless it be with the equally safe *Craterel-*

lus cantharellus (figure 53a), but that plant has a merely wrinkled, hymenial surface, instead of true gills. The edible qualities of the Shaggy Chantrelle are said to be satisfactory.

FUNNEL-SHAPED CHANTRELLE (Edible)

Cantharellus infundibuliformis (Scop.) Fr.

Cap 1–2 in. broad, thin, broadly convex when young, becoming umbilicate or funnel-form with age, often perforated in the depth of the umbilicus, frequently lobed, wavy or irregular on the margin, hygrophanous, sooty-brown, brownish-yellow or dingy-yellow when moist, grayish, grayish-yellow or grayish-brown and slightly floccose or fibrillose when dry. **Gills** narrow, distant, decurrent, irregularly or dichotomously branched and venosely connected, yellowish or subcinereous, becoming lilac (pruinose) with age or in drying. **Stem** 1–4 in. long, 1½–2½ lines thick, glabrous, hollow, yellow, or yellowish. **Spores** broadly elliptic or subglobose, 9–11.4 x 7.6–9 μ.

In damp woods or mossy, shaded swamps. June to October. Grows gregariously or in tufts. Quite common and variable in color. The larger spores help in distinguishing between this species and *Cantharellus lutescens*.

YELLOWISH CHANTRELLE (Edible)

Cantharellus lutescens Fr.

Cap about 1 in. broad, thin, convex, becoming nearly plane and umbilicate, nearly regular, pale orange or yellow when moist, paler and slightly virgate when dry **Gills** narrow, distant, forked or branched, decurrent, pale-orange or yellow. **Stem** 1–2 in. long, about 2 lines thick, equal or slightly tapering upward, glabrous, hollow, pale-orange or yellow. **Spores** broadly elliptic, 10 x 7.6 μ.

In woods, and shaded places, growing among mosses, about old stumps, or in soil well filled with decomposed, vegetable matter. July and August. Sometimes grows in tufts. Rare. Somewhat variable in the color of the cap, the European form having that part colored a brownish-yellow. A wholly yellow form occurs at times. The cap of young plants is not always umbilicate, but becomes so with age. Sometimes the umbilicus opens into the cavity of the stem. It is regarded by some writers as a mere variety of *Cantharellus tubaeformis* Fr., from which it is distinguished by its more regular, convex and umbilicate cap and by its more regular stem, which is equal or slightly upward tapering, not compressed, irregular and tapering downwards, as in that species. It holds an intermediate position between *C. tubaeformis* and *C. infundibuliformis*.

SMALL CHANTRELLE (Edible)

Cantharellus minor Pk.

Cap 6–12 lines broad, fleshy, thin, convex, then expanded, often umbilicate or centrally depressed, glabrous, *yellow,* flesh pale-yellow. **Gills** narrow, distant, sparingly branched, yellow. **Stem** 1–1½ in. long, 1–2 lines thick, *slender,* subflexuous, subequal, smooth, appearing solid when young but *stuffed or hollow* later (especially in the upper part), yellow, with a whitish mycelium at the base. **Spores** subelliptic, 6.3–7.6 x 4–5 μ.

In thin woods and open places. June and July. Grows scattered or in tufts. Sometimes large areas are dotted with the cheerful yellow of the diminutive caps. It is colored like *Cantharellus cibarius,* from which it is dis-

tinguished by its smaller size, thin and frequently umbilicate cap, comparatively broader gills, more slender stem,
and by the smaller spores. In wet weather the cap appears
watery.

UMBONATE CHANTRELLE (Edible) Fig. 75

Cantharellus umbonatus (Gmel.) Fr. (Emended by Peck)

Cap 6–12 lines broad, thin, soft, at first convex, then
plane or centrally depressed, umbonate, papillate or even,

Photo by H. D. House

Figure 75 Umbonate Chantrelle, *Cantharellus umbonatus*

smooth or flocculose-silky, rarely minutely squamulose, bluish-gray, grayish-brown or blackish-gray, flesh white, often changing to red when wounded. **Gills** thin, straight, more or less decurrent, dichotomous, white, often changing to red when wounded. **Stem** 1–5 in. long, 2–4 lines thick, equal or slightly tapering upward, solid or stuffed, generally slightly silky, villose or white-tomentose at the base, whitish or tinged with the color of the cap. **Spores** white, oblong or subfusiform, 10–12.7 x 4–5 μ.

Damp, mossy ground in woods and open places. August to October. The variability of this species is expressed in the following varieties described by Peck. Var. *subcaeruleus:* cap bluish or bluish-gray, silky and shining. Var. *dichotomus:* cap even or the umbo reduced to a mere papilla, grayish-brown. Var. *brevior:* cap as in variety *dichotomus,* but the stem very short, about 1 in. long, equal and scarcely silky. When the plant grows among mosses the stem is often long, and the white tomentum so closely covers the surrounding mosses that it is difficult to pluck the plant entire without taking with it a good-sized tuft of moss.

Genus CLAVARIA (Vaill.) Fr.

The club or coral mushrooms scarcely need a formal description. A few are simple clubs (*C. pistillaris,* figure 77) ; others are more or less intricately branched (*C. stricta,* plate 1). Most species are cespitose tufts, and in one genus, *Physalacria* (figures 54c, d), small bladders surmount the ends of tiny stems. As a matter of fact, *Physalacria* is not a clavariaceous fungus at all, but belongs rather in the Agaricaceae. The radiately folded, gill-like hymenium is borne on one side of the "bladder" only, and originally faces earthwards. Later on, the "bladder", or cap, is erected by the contraction of the tissues of the stem, at the point where that part merges into the cap (Krieger, '23).

RED-TIPPED CLAVARIA (Edible) FIG. 76
Clavaria botrytis (Pers.) **Fr.**

Plant about the same size as *Clavaria flava*. **Stem** short, thick, fleshy, whitish, densely branched. **Branches** often somewhat rugose-wrinkled, repeatedly branched, whitish, yellowish or pinkish, *the thick, closely packed tips red*. **Spores** oblong-elliptic, 12.7–15.2 µ long.

In thin woods and open places. July to September. Not as common as *Clavaria flava*. It is eagerly sought by all who have once tasted its agreeably flavored flesh. Young specimens are compact and "meaty".

CRESTED CLAVARIA (Edible)
Clavaria cristata (Holmsk.) **Fr.**

Plant small, usually not more than 2 or 2½ in. high and broad. **Stem** rather slender, even, tenacious, stuffed, branched. **Branches** white or sometimes smoky-grayish or even dull-pinkish to yellowish, dilated above and acutely incised or crested, the end tips generally becoming brown or blackish-brown with age. **Spores** globose or broadly elliptic, white, 6.3–7.6 µ long.

In woods and open places, especially in cool, shaded, moist situations, on naked soil, or among mosses and sphagnum. Summer and autumn. Usually grows in groups, sometimes in lines. Rather plentiful in the hilly and mountainous districts of the State. *Clavaria cinerea,* a very closely allied species, has, when typical, merely toothed apices on the terminal branches. Also, it grows in more protected places, under fallen foliage, and in the shade of moist, rotting logs.

Photo by W. A. Murrill

Figure 76 Red-tipped Clavaria, *Clavaria botrytis,* a rather fleshy plant, is easily known by the pink or red coloring on the tips of the terminal branchlets

PALE YELLOW CLAVARIA (Edible)
Clavaria flava (Schaeff.) Fr.

Plant 2–5 in. high and nearly as broad. **Stem** short, thick, white, much branched. **Branches** terete, even, erect and close together (fastigiate), whitish or yellowish (pale flesh-color in the form *carnicolor* Kauffm.; under conifers), the tips divided into one to three blunt, pale-yellowish, tooth-like points. **Spores** oblong-elliptic, yellowish, 7.6–11.4 μ long.

In thin woods and open places. July to September. Common. Its white flesh is tender and well-flavored. In *Clavaria stricta* (Pers.) Fr. (plate 1), a tough, bitter-tasting plant, the branches are straighter and more strictly parallel with each other. *Clavaria aurea* (Schaeff.) Fr. and *C. formosa* (Pers.) Fr. are closely related and equally desirable species.

LARGE CLUB CLAVARIA (Edible) FIGS. 54b, 77
Clavaria pistillaris (L.) Fr.

Club simple, large, 2–6 in. long, 6–12 lines thick, usually enlarged at the top (especially good-sized specimens sometimes cracked there), obtuse or occasionally umbonate (var. *umbonata* Pk.), soft, fleshy, glabrous, even or nearly so, yellowish, ochraceous-buff or tan-color, solid or slightly spongy and white within, taste mild. **Spores** elliptic, 10–12.6 x 5–6 μ.

In woods. August to September. Scattered in its mode of growth.

CUP-BEARING CLAVARIA (Edible) FIG. 78
Clavaria pyxidata (Pers.) Fr.

Plant 1–4 in. high, pale yellow to dull ochraceous or tan-color, much branched, *each terminal branchlet ending*

Photo by C. E. Cummings.   Courtesy
Buffalo Society of Natural Sciences

Figure 77 Large Club Clavaria, *Clavaria pistillaris*,
and the Partridge Berry vine, have together "hit it off"
in "composing" a beautiful picture

in a small cup, the rims of the cups beset with small spines. Flesh white, firm. **Spores** white, elliptic, 4 x 3 μ. On rotting wood in forests. Autumn. Easily recognized by the curious, little cups at the ends of the youngest branches. When one examines the older branches it will be seen that they, too, end in cups from the margins of which the branches next above arise. Not rare.

CLOSE CLAVARIA PLATE 1

Clavaria stricta (Pers.) Fr.

Plant up to 4 in. high, pallid yellow, becoming fuscous when bruised. **Stem** distinct, thick, short, tough, with root-like strands of white mycelium at the base. **Branches** slender, erect and straight, parallel to each other, crowded. **Spores** ochraceous in mass, pip-shaped, almost smooth, average size 8–9 x 4 μ.

On rotten wood, stumps, or on the ground near logs. Because of its bitter taste it is not desirable.

GENUS CLITOCYBE (Fr.) Quél. Spores white.

Like *Clitopilus,* in the pink-spored group, the gills, in typical members of the genus, are strongly decurrent. If one encounters such a species as *Clitocybe multiceps,* however, it is often difficult to make up one's mind as to whether its gills are to be interpreted as being decurrent or sinuate. In the latter case one would naturally try to identify the plant in *Tricholoma.* Unfortunately for the beginner there are many such species which "sit on the fence" between two, or even more, genera. True Clitocybes have fleshy stems, while Omphalias, also decurrent-gilled and white-spored, have cartilaginous ones. See remarks under *Laccaria.* For deleterious species, see *Clitocybe illudens* and *C. sudorifica.*

Photo by W. A. Murrill

Figure 78   In the Cup-bearing Clavaria, *Clavaria pyxidata,* each branch ends in a cup, on the margin of which new branches arise.   Nature stopped with the small cups on the terminal branchlets but, as nothing is impossible with her, she could have kept up this process of division into infinity

ADIRONDACK CLITOCYBE (Edible)

Clitocybe adirondackensis (Pk.) Sacc.

Cap 1–2 in. broad, thin, convex or nearly plane and umbilicate, or centrally depressed and funnel-form, glabrous, moist, white or pale tan-color, flesh white. **Gills** thin, narrow, close, very decurrent, white. **Stem** 1½–3 in. long, 1–2 lines thick, nearly equal, glabrous, stuffed or hollow, colored like the cap, often with a white tomentum at the base. **Spores** subglobose or broadly elliptic, 4–5 x 3–4 µ.

In forests. July to October. Compare *Clitocybe infundibuliformis*. A very desirable esculent, the flavor resembling that of the common Meadow Mushroom. It is of frequent occurrence in the northern forests, though not limited to them.

CESPITOSE CLITOCYBE

Clitocybe caespitosa Pk.

Cap 1–1½ in. broad, thin, infundibuliform, often irregular, hygrophanous, grayish-brown when moist, cinereous or clay-color when dry. **Gills** narrow, close, decurrent, some of them branched, white. **Stem** ¾–1¼ in. long, $\frac{3}{16}$–¼ in. thick, equal or slightly tapering upward, stuffed or hollow, white. **Spores** subglobose or broadly ellipsoid, 3–4 µ long.

In woods (Catskill and Adirondack mountains). August and September. Commonly cespitose. Rare. It is remarkable for its irregular and deformed appearance. The center of the cap is sometimes perforate, and the stem is stout in proportion to the size of the cap. Few individuals compose a tuft.

CLUB-FOOTED CLITOCYBE (Edible)

Clitocybe clavipes (Pers.) Quél.

Cap 1–3 in. broad, very fleshy, convex or nearly plane, *obconic,* obtuse or with a small umbo, soft, grayish-brown, sooty-brown, sometimes darker in the center than on the margin, flesh white, taste mild. **Gills** rather broad, sub-distant, decurrent, white or cream-colored. **Stem** ½–2½ in. long, ¼–½ in. thick at the top, ⅝–1 in. at the base, *tapering upward from a thickened or sub-bulbous base,* solid, elastic, soft and spongy within, glabrous or slightly fibrillose, colored like or a little paler than the cap. **Spores** ellipsoid, 6–8 x 4–5 µ.

In woods. July to October. It grows solitary or in troops, rarely in clusters. *Clitocybe media* Pk. resembles it, but the stem of that species is equal or nearly so, and the cap is thinner. *Clitocybe nebularis* (Batsch) Quél. has closer gills, a firmer stem, smaller spores (4–5 x 2–3 µ), and is a much larger and rarer plant.

CUP-SHAPED CLITOCYBE

Clitocybe cyathiformis (Fr.) Sacc.

Cap about 1½ in. broad, fleshy but thin, centrally depressed or infundibuliform, hygrophanous, glabrous or nearly so, even on the margin or occasionally striate when old, blackish-brown or grayish-brown when moist, paler when dry, flesh colored like the surface, separable into two horizontal layers. **Gills** distant, adnate or decurrent, united behind, dingy or grayish-brown. **Stem** about 2 in. long, equal or slightly tapering upward stuffed or hollow, fibrillose, obscurely reticulated by the fibrils, colored like the cap. **Spores** ellipsoid, 8–9 x 4–5 µ.

Decaying wood on the ground, in woods and open places. August and September. Common. Peck states that his *Clitocybe pocula* is referable to this species.

JACK-O'-LANTERN OR FALSE CHANTRELLE (Unwholesome)
PLATE 12

Clitocybe illudens (Schw.) Sacc.

Cap 2½ x 4¾ in. broad, convex or nearly plane, sometimes centrally depressed, obtuse or umbonate, glabrous or obscurely virgate, often irregular, saffron-yellow or orange-yellow, flesh white or yellowish, odor strong, taste disagreeable. **Gills** close, decurrent, narrowed toward each end, colored like the cap. **Stem** 2½–7 in. long, often attenuated toward the base, sometimes excentric, firm, glabrous, solid, stuffed or rarely hollow, colored like the cap or sometimes brownish below. **Spores** globose, 4–5 μ in diameter (figure 24g).

Woods and open places, often about old Chestnut and other stumps. July to October. Usually found growing in dense clusters. Its gaudy coloring, large size, and luminescent properties (when placed in the dark) make it an attractive species. As food it is worthless for it causes nausea and vomiting (see p. 146). Boiling in salt water for half an hour is said to render it comparatively harmless. It is said to be identical with *Pleurotus olearius* (DC.) Quél., a species that grows on Olive trees in southern Europe. Whether *Clitocybe illudens* grows on these trees in California is not known. Inoculation experiments might prove to be enlightening.

FUNNEL-SHAPED CLITOCYBE (Edible)

Clitocybe infundibuliformis (Schaeff.) Quél.

Cap 1½–2¾ in. broad, at first convex and slightly umbonate, becoming infundibuliform, thin and minutely silky on the margin, dry, reddish or pale tan-color, fading with age, flesh white. **Gills** thin, moderately close, decurrent, white or whitish. **Stem** 2–2¾ in. long, ¼–⅜ in. thick, generally tapering upward, spongy or stuffed, soft, elastic, colored like the cap or rarely whitish. **Spores** 5–6 x 3–4 μ.

Among fallen leaves in woods. July and August. Grows singly, scattered or in tufts. Common. The var. *membranacea* Fr. has a thinner, non-umbonate cap, and a slenderer, equal stem (compare *C. adirondackensis*). *Clitocybe catina* (Fr.) Sacc., which resembles *C. infundibuliformis*, is easily distinguished by its white color.

UNITED CLITOCYBE (Edible) Fig. 79

Clitocybe monadelpha (Morg.) Sacc.

Cap 1–2¾ in. broad, fleshy, convex, sometimes becoming centrally depressed, squamulose in the center, pale-brown, reddish-brown or honey-color. **Gills** moderately close, distinctly decurrent, pallid or flesh-colored. **Stem** 2¼–4 in. long, ³⁄₁₆–¼ in. thick, flexuous, fibrous, solid, often becoming hollow with age and twisted and tapering at the base, brown, pale-brown or tinged with flesh-color. **Spores** broadly ellipsoid or slightly irregular, 7–9 x 5–6 μ.

Woods and open places. September. The cap is sometimes dingy-yellow or yellowish-brown. The plant has the color of some forms of *Armillaria mellea*, the exannulate variety of which is perhaps identical. It has been made a synonym of *Clitocybe tabescens* (Scop.) Bres. by some authors.

Photo by *W. A. Murrill*

Figure 79 United Clitocybe, *Clitocybe monadelpha*

MANY-CAPPED CLITOCYBE (Edible)

Clitocybe multiceps Pk.

Cap 1–2¾ in. broad, fleshy, firm, convex, moist in wet weather, very variable in color, whitish, grayish, yellowish-gray or grayish-brown, sometimes slightly silky and brownish in the center, often irregular from mutual pressure, flesh white, taste oily, slightly disagreeable. **Gills** close, adnate to sinuate, or slightly decurrent, white or whitish. **Stem** 2–4 in. long, ¼–½ in. thick, equal or slightly thickened at the base, firm, glabrous, solid or stuffed, slightly pruinose at the top, white or whitish. **Spores** globose, 5–8 μ in diameter.

Open ground or in grassy places. June to October. This common species is found in tufts of few or many individuals. When the gills are occasionally sinuate on one side of the stem, one is likely to look in *Tricholoma*. In var. *tricholoma* Pk. nearly all the gills are sinuate. The taste varies as does also opinion with regard to its edibility. Parboiling may get rid of the objectionable, oily flavor. It is regarded highly by some. *Clitocybe multiformis* Pk., a rare species that grows in low, damp places in woods, has a much thinner cap, and ellipsoid spores.

SWEET-SCENTED CLITOCYBE (Edible)

Clitocybe odora (Bull.) Sacc.

Cap 1½–2¾ in. broad, fleshy, tough, convex, becoming plane or nearly so, obtuse or subumbonate, even, glabrous, regular or sometimes wavy on the margin, moist in wet weather, green or dingy-green, fading with age or in drying, flesh whitish, odor pleasant, like anise. **Gills** thin, close, adnate or slightly decurrent, white or whitish. **Stem** 1–2 in. long, $\frac{3}{16}$–$\frac{5}{16}$ in. thick, equal or slightly thickened at the base, solid, stuffed or hollow, elastic, glabrous, whitish or greenish. **Spores** 6–8 x 4–5 μ.

In woods and bushy places. Summer. Grows scattered or somewhat gregariously. The above description applies to the species as it occurs in New York. The original description describes the gills as "not close" and as becoming pallid, no mention being made of the occasional solidity of the stem. *Clitocybe virens* (Scop.) Sacc. and *C. viridis* (With.) Sacc. are identical. Var. *anisaria* Pk. differs in having the cap adorned with innate fibrils and in the more or less striate margin. *Clitocybe connexa* (Pk.) Sacc., with a similar, sweet odor, has the green (or bluish-green) color limited to the margin of the cap.

SUDORIFIC CLITOCYBE (Unwholesome)

Clitocybe sudorifica Pk.

Cap ¾–1½ in. broad, fleshy but thin, broadly convex or nearly plane, often becoming slightly depressed in the center or umbilicate, irregular, splitting or lobed on the thin, spreading margin, glabrous, watery-white when moist, whitish or grayish-white when dry, flesh watery when moist, white when dry, taste mild, odor none. **Gills** thin, narrow, close, adnate or slightly decurrent, whitish. **Stem** ⅜–1 ⅛ in. long, 1–2 lines thick, equal or sometimes narrowed at the base, glabrous or merely pruinose, stuffed, with a white, soft or spongy center, or hollow when old, often curved or somewhat flexuous, white or whitish. **Spores** subglobose, 4–5 x 3–4 μ.

Lawns or grassy places. September to November. Gregarious in its mode of growth. Sometimes an obscure zone is present on the margin of the cap. When eaten it causes profuse perspiration (see p. 146). This peculiar property and the differently shaped spores constitute about the only distinguishing features between *Clitocybe sudorifica* and *C. dealbata* (Sow.) Gill., to which the former was at first attached as a variety. The spores of *C. dealbata* are ellipsoid and measure 4–5 x 2–2.5 μ. A very irregularly grown variety of the latter (var. *deformata* Pk.) is apt to come up in beds of the cultivated Meadow Mushroom. *Clitocybe corda* Schulzer, a species described from Hungary, seems to be identical with *C. sudorifica* (Szemere, '32).

Genus CLITOPILUS (Fr.) Quél. Spores rosy.

Like *Clitocybe,* except that the spores are rosy. *Eccilia,* also decurrent-gilled and rosy-spored, has a cartilaginous stem as compared with the fleshy one of *Clitopilus.*

ABORTIVE CLITOPILUS (Edible) Plate 13. Fig. 80

Clitopilus abortivus (Berk. and Curt.) Sacc.

Cap 2–4 in. broad, fleshy, firm, convex or nearly plane, regular or irregular, dry, *clothed with a minute, silky tomentum,* becoming smooth with age, gray or grayish-brown, flesh white, taste and odor somewhat farinaceous. **Gills** thin, close, slightly or deeply decurrent, at first whitish or pale-gray, then flesh-colored. **Stem** 1½–3 in. long, 3–6 lines thick, nearly equal, solid, minutely flocculose, sometimes fibrous-striate, colored like or paler than the cap. **Spores** irregular, 7.6–10 x 6.3 μ.

Ground and old prostrate trunks of trees in woods and open places. August and September. Gregarious, scattered or cespitose. Frequently specimens fail to develop properly, producing irregularly shaped, somewhat globose and nodulose, whitish masses (see the plate), similar to

Photo by C. E. Cummings. Courtesy
Buffalo Society of Natural Sciences

Figure 80 Abortive Clitopilus, *Clitopilus abortivus*, and its abortive form (the cluster of rounded, white bodies in the foreground). Both are good to eat. See also plate 15

those sometimes formed by *Armillaria mellea.* The flavor is not especially agreeable, but no doubt exists as to the edibility of the plant.

SWEETBREAD MUSHROOM (Edible)

Clitopilus orcella (Bull.) Fr.

Cap fleshy, *soft,* plane or slightly depressed, often irregular, even when young, *slightly silky, somewhat viscid when moist,* white or yellowish-white, flesh white, taste and odor farinaceous. **Gills** deeply decurrent, *close,* whitish, then flesh-colored. **Stem** short, solid, flocculose, often excentric, thickened above, white. **Spores** reddish, elliptic, 10 x 5 μ.

In pastures and open places. July and August. Generally a little smaller than *Clitopilus prunulus,* softer and more irregular, but very closely allied. Its flavor is delicate. Sometimes it forms "fairy-rings".

PLUM CLITOPILUS (Edible)

Clitopilus prunulus (Scop.) Quél.

Cap 1½–3 in. broad, fleshy, *compact,* at first convex and regular, then repand, *dry, pruinate,* white or grayish-white, flesh white, unchangeable, with a pleasant, farinaceous odor. **Gills** deeply decurrent, subdistant, flesh-colored. **Stem** ½ in. long, 3–4 lines thick, solid, naked, striate, white. **Spores** reddish, subelliptic, pointed at each end, 10–11.5 x 5–6.3 μ.

In open, thin woods. July and August. Solitary or a few individuals scattered in a place. One of the best of edible mushrooms. Compare *Clitopilus orcella.*

Genus COLLYBIA (Fr.) Quél. Spores white.

Collybia is *Tricholoma* with a cartilaginous stem, and *Mycena* with the margin of the cap inrolled. The spores are white. The genus offers no highly desirable species for the table. See remarks under *Marasmius*.

TUFTED COLLYBIA (Edible)
Collybia acervata (Fr.) Karst.

Cap 1–2 in. broad, fleshy but thin, convex or nearly plane, obtuse, glabrous, hygrophanous, pale tan-color or dingy pinkish-red, and commonly striatulate on the margin when moist, paler or whitish when dry. **Gills** narrow, close, adnexed or free, whitish or tinged with flesh-color. **Stem** 2–3 in. long, about 1 line thick, slender, rigid but fragile, hollow, glabrous, reddish, reddish-brown or brown, often whitish at the top, especially when young, commonly with a white, mycelioid tomentum at the base. **Spores** elliptic, 6 x 3–4 µ.

Decaying wood and ground among fallen leaves in woods. August and September. Grows cespitosely. The European plant is given as larger.

YELLOWISH WHITE COLLYBIA (Edible)
Collybia albiflavida (Pk.) Kauffm.

Cap 2–3 in. or more broad, fleshy, convex, becoming plane or slightly depressed, glabrous, even, *white, sometimes tinged with yellow,* the margin at first involute, flesh white. **Gills** narrow, crowded, thin, marginate, white. **Stem** 3–4 in. long, 3–4 lines thick, equal, solid, cartilaginous, rigid, fibrillose-striate, *somewhat bulbous,* whitish. **Spores** elliptic, 7.6–9 x 4–5 µ.

Woods and fields. August. This species was originally described as a *Tricholoma,* but the cartilaginous stem indicates its proper place, in *Collybia.* Sometimes the cap is slightly and broadly umbonate, and in very wet weather it is moist. The gill edges, being uneven, cause characteristic depressions to appear, as one views the gills as a whole, by oblique lighting. Kauffman has found a smaller form with an almost smoky-brown cap. It grows in low wet or swampy places.

BUTTERY COLLYBIA
Collybia butyracea (Bull.) Quél.

Cap 1½–3 in. broad, fleshy, thin, convex, then expanded, umbonate, smooth, reddish-brown, becoming paler with age, *moist in wet weather, buttery to the touch,* flesh dingy or whitish when moist, white when dry. **Gills** thin, crowded, *crenulate,* adnexed or almost free, white. **Stem** 1½–3 in. long, 2–3 lines thick at the top, tapering from the much thicker, lower half, glabrous, *striate,* reddish or reddish brown, usually with a white tomentum on the thickened base, white within and stuffed or hollow, easily compressible like the rubber bulb of an atomizer. **Spores** elliptic, 6–7.6 x 3–4 μ.

Woods in hilly and mountainous regions, especially under or near coniferous trees. June to October. Not rare and closely related to *Collybia dryophila* from which the umbonate cap, crenulate edges of the gills, and the more distinctly striate and upward-tapering stem will separate it.

OAK-LOVING COLLYBIA (Edible)
Collybia dryophila (Bull.) Quél.

Cap 1–2 in. broad, thin, convex or nearly plane, sometimes with the margin elevated, irregular, obtuse, glabrous, varying in color, commonly some shade of bay-red or tan-color, flesh white. **Gills** narrow, crowded, adnexed or almost free, white or whitish, rarely yellowish. **Stem** 1–2 in. long, 1–2 lines thick, equal or sometimes thickened at the base, cartilaginous, glabrous, hollow, yellowish or rufescent, commonly similar in color to the cap. **Spores** 6–7.6 x 3–4 μ.

Woods, groves and open places, on the ground among decaying leaves, or on decaying wood. It is especially fond of Pine groves. June to October. One of the commonest and at the same time one of the most variable of species. Usually gregarious, but sometimes growing in tufts. The cap varies in color from whitish or yellowish to dark-bay or almost chestnut-color. The plant is sometimes attacked by an *Exobasidium* (*E. mycetophilum* [Pk.] Burt), and its gills give rise, occasionally, to minute, supernumerary caps. Compare *Collybia butyracea*.

FAMILY COLLYBIA (Edible)

Collybia familia (Pk.) Sacc.

Cap 6–12 lines broad, thin, rather fragile, convex or hemispheric, glabrous, somewhat hygrophanous, whitish, yellowish-gray or brownish, sometimes darker or brown on the disk, margin often striatulate when moist. **Gills** narrow, close, rounded at the inner extremity and almost free, white. **Stem** 2–4 in. long, about 1 line thick, slender, glabrous or (under a lens) minutely pruinose-pubescent, hollow, white or whitish, commonly with a white, mycelioid villosity at the base. **Spores** globose, 4–5 μ broad.

Much decayed wood and prostrate trunks of Hemlock trees in woods. August and September. Grows densely cespitose. The plants are apt to assume darker colors in drying, and the margin of the cap becomes strongly involute.

BROAD-GILLED COLLYBIA (Edible)

Collybia platyphylla (Pers.) Quél.

Cap 3–5 in. broad, thin, fragile, convex, innately fibrillose, grayish-brown or blackish-brown, flesh white. **Gills** *broad,* subdistant, commonly deeply emarginate, adnexed, white. **Stem** 3–5 in. long, ½ in. or more thick, stout, equal, fibrillose-striate, stuffed or hollow, white or pallid, sometimes with branching, root-like strands of white mycelium at the base. **Spores** subglobose or broadly elliptic, 7.6–10 x 6–7.6 μ.

In thin woods or open places, about stumps and old, prostrate trunks, or on much-decayed wood. From spring to autumn. Distorted and irregular forms are sometimes found, and the cap frequently exhibits small, white holes or fissures where very active, little insects (spring-tails) have made their escape. The interior of the stem in young, insect-free specimens is solid-fibrous. The gills are often transversely striate and split. Var. *repens* (figure 81) has the root-like strands at the base of the stem extending horizontally, or very nearly so. It is not a particularly desirable species from the standpoint of edibility.

ROOTING COLLYBIA (Edible) FIG. 82

Collybia radicata (Relh.) Fr.

Cap 1–4 in. broad, thin, convex or nearly plane, glabrous, generally radiately rugose or wrinkled, sometimes umbonate, viscid when moist, grayish-brown or smoky-brown, flesh white. **Gills** broad, subdistant, white or slightly yellowish, adnexed. **Stem** 2–8 in. long above

Figure 81 Broad-gilled Collybia, *Collybia platyphylla* var. *repens,* a common representative of the genus

*Photo by C. E. Cummings. Courtesy
Buffalo Society of Natural Sciences*

Figure 82   Rooting Collybia, *Collybia radicata,* so named because
of the long tap-root which extends deep into the ground

the surface of the ground, 2–3 (rarely 4) lines thick, firm, glabrous, generally tapering upward, stuffed, whitish or colored like or a little paler than the cap, ending below in a long, root-like prolongation, which penetrates the earth deeply (to a depth of 8 or 10 in.). **Spores** elliptic, with a slight, oblique apiculus at one end, 15–17.8 x 10–12.7 μ (white, becoming yellowish with age).

In woods or recent clearings. June to October. Grows singly or sparsely scattered and is quite common, more so than its close relative, *Collybia longipes* (Bull.), which may be known by the dense, velvety, brown covering on cap and stem. The root-like prolongation of the stem is usually oblique. Several varieties of *Collybia radicata* have been recognized, namely, var. *furfuracea,* in which the stem is minutely scurfy, and var. *pusilla,* a small form with the cap about one inch broad. Occasionally specimens present themselves in which both cap and stem are white. The flesh is somewhat tough, but agreeable in flavor.

VELVET-FOOTED COLLYBIA (Edible)

Collybia velutipes (Curt.) Quél.

Cap 1–2¼ in. broad, rather thin, convex or nearly plane, obtuse, glabrous, *viscid,* reddish-yellow or tawny. **Gills** broad, subdistant, rounded behind, slightly adnexed, white or tinged with yellow. **Stem** 1–4 in. long, 1–3 lines thick, firm, externally cartilaginous, stuffed or hollow, brown or tawny-brown, *velvety-hairy when mature.* **Spores** narrowly elliptic, 7.6–9 x 4 μ.

On dead trunks of trees, either standing or prostrate, or on old stumps and decaying wood. Throughout the year, even in midwinter, if the weather is mild. Usually grows in dense clusters, and, due to pressure, the caps are often misshapen. The flesh is quite tender but rather insipid to the taste. The caps should be peeled to get rid of adhering dirt, leaves, etc. A variety (*spongiosa*) has been described from Alaska.

Genus COPRINUS (Pers.) Fr. Spores black or blackish

A child can learn to recognize Ink-caps. One and all have gills that deliquesce, that is, during the period of spore ripening, the substance of the gills is dissolved by a process known as autodigestion. Beginning at the marginal portion of the cap, the gills continue to "liquefy" until the stem is reached.

INK COPRINUS (Edible) PLATE 14

Coprinus atramentarius (Bull.) Fr.

Cap 1–3 in. in diameter, at first ovate, becoming expanded, glabrous and *with a grayish bloom that is readily rubbed off,* exposing the brown surface underneath, a few, obscure, spot-like scales in the center of typical specimens, margin coarsely and *longitudinally furrowed and irregularly notched and lobed.* **Gills** crowded, at first white (and flocculose on the edge), then black. **Stem** 2–4 in. or more long, 2–4 lines thick, glabrous and white above the indistinct, basal ring, light-brownish and provided with small, upward-pointing squamules below, hollow. **Spores** elliptic, black, 7.6–10 µ long.

In rich soil, in gardens, waste places, or in woods (var. *silvestris* Pk., small, and lacking the spot-like scales on the cap). Late summer and autumn. Usually in dense clusters. It is not as tender as *Coprinus comatus. Coprinus soboliferus* Fr. is a heavier, coarser plant, with a scalier, paler cap, a flattened, depressed disk, and with a substantial stem, many of which arise from a common, tuberous base. *C. dunarum* Stoll, which inhabits sand-dunes in the Baltic region, is related.

SHAGGY-MANE (Edible) PLATE 15 FIGS. 2d, 83
Coprinus comatus (Muell.) S. F. Gray

Cap 1½–3 in. or more long (before expansion), at first oblong or cylindric, becoming campanulate or expanded and splitting on the margin, adorned with scattered, yellowish, fibrillose or fluffy scales, between the scales whitish. **Gills** very crowded, white, then tinged with grayish-red or pink, finally black and dripping an inky fluid. **Stem** 3–6 in. long, 3–9 lines thick, *hollow, with a delicate, white cord suspended in the cavity,* smooth or slightly fibrillose, white or whitish, at first with a slight movable ring which generally rests on the base or vanishes entirely. **Spores** elliptic, black, 12.7–17.8 μ long.

In rich, loose earth by roadsides, in pastures, waste places or dumping grounds. On one occasion the writer found it growing luxuriantly and in dense clusters among weeds to which, for their destruction, saltpeter had been applied. In autumn, until quite late. Occasionally it appears earlier. It is a very fragile plant and must be handled with care in the process of removing the scales. Before liquefaction begins, noticeable in the change of color, it makes a very desirable addition to the breakfast toast. It is one of the few species recognizably described by the Roman naturalist, Pliny. *Coprinus sterquilinus* Fr. (figure 85), a small plant, much resembles the Shaggy Mane.

Figure 83 The Shaggy-mane, *Coprinus comatus,*
in perfect condition for treatment in the kitchen

GLISTENING COPRINUS (Edible) FIGS. 3c, 84

Coprinus micaceus (Bull.) Fr.

Cap 1–2 in. broad, thin, at first ovate, then campanulate or expanded, striate, sometimes *glistening with shining particles when young,* buff-yellow or tawny-yellow. **Gills** crowded, whitish, then tinged with pinkish- or purplish-brown, finally black. **Stem** 1–3 in. long, $\frac{1}{8}$–$\frac{3}{16}$ in. thick, slender, fragile, hollow, white. **Spores** elliptic, brown, 6.3–7.6 μ long.

Photo by C. E. Cummings. Courtesy Buffalo Society of Natural Sciences

Figure 84 Glistening Coprinus, *Coprinus micaceus.* The April rains cause this little ink-cap to appear in just such a place as is here shown, near the base of trees

Photo by C. E. Cummings.   Courtesy Buffalo Society of Natural Sciences

Figure 85   *Coprinus sterquilinus.* Near *C. comatus*, but smaller, and the white covering of the cap cracks differently forming easily-removed, white scales. The margin of the cap is beautifully marked with forked striations

On grassy ground, usually from covered-up stumps, or at the base of old trees. May to November. Sometimes grows in dense clusters. Because of its abundance everywhere, throughout the growing season, it ought to be utilized. In tenderness and delicacy it is not inferior to *Coprinus comatus*. It should not be confounded with species of *Panaeolus* (figure 35). Panaeoli, too, have black gills, but they do not deliquesce, and their sides are distinctly mottled.

Genus CORTINARIUS Fr. Spores ferruginous.

This genus comprises such a perfectly astounding number of species that not much can be done in the matter of identification unless one uses the recently published Kauffman monograph (Kauffman, '32). Only a few, well-marked species are described here. All are characterized by the peculiar, cobwebby veil which may be viscid or dry. The gills show a marked change in color, from youth to maturity, due to the ripening of the spores. The spores are usually of a ferruginous tint. Cortinarii are inclined to have a woody flavor and are therefore not much sought as edible species. Compare *Pholiota*.

BRACELET CORTINARIUS (Edible) PLATE 16

Cortinarius armillatus Fr.

Cap up to 5 in. broad, convex-campanulate to expanded, broadly umbonate or gibbous, reddish-tawny verging toward brick-red, smooth, then innately fibrillose-squamulose, margin at first incurved, flesh dingy-pallid, rather spongy. **Gills** adnate to sinuate-uncinate, distant, pallid cinnamon-color, then dark-ferruginous to almost bay-brown. **Stem** up to 6 in. long, about ¾ in. thick, bulbous to elongate-bulbous at the base, whitish, brownish with age, *with several, irregularly encircling, red bands,* solid within. **Cortina** reddish-white, slight, evident mainly because of the ferruginous spores which fall upon it. **Spores** elliptic, minutely verrucose, 10–12 x 5–6.5 μ (Kauffman).

Solitary or gregarious on the débris of coniferous forests, usually in late summer and autumn. *Cortinarius haematochelis* Fr. differs only in its more ochraceous coloring and in having but one encircling band on the stem.

CINNAMON CORTINARIUS (Edible)

Cortinarius cinnamomeus (L.) Fr.

Cap usually 1–2 in. broad, thin, convex, obtuse or umbonate, dry, finely silky-fibrillose, at least when young, cinnamon-brown, brownish-ochraceous or tawny-brown, flesh yellowish, odor often like that of radishes. **Gills** thin, close, adnate, yellow when young, cinnamon-color when spores mature. **Stem** 1–3 in. long, ¼ in. or less thick, equal, often flexuous, fibrillose or silky, yellowish or colored like the cap, or a little paler, stuffed or hollow. **Ring** cobwebby, scarcely evident. **Spores** elliptic, cinnamon-color, 7.6 μ long.

In woods, or their borders, under trees or in mossy swamps. During the summer and autumn months. Very common and extremely variable. Var. *semisanguineus* has the gills colored a rich blood-red. It is also quite common.

SMEARED CORTINARIUS (Edible)

Cortinarius collinitus (Sow.) Fr.

Cap 1½–3 in. broad, yellow to golden or tawny-yellow, convex, obtuse, glabrous, *glutinous when moist,* shining when dry. **Gills** rather broad, dingy-bluish-white or grayish clay-color when young, cinnamon-color as the spores ripen, edges minutely uneven. **Stem** 2–4 in. long, ¼–½ in. thick, cylindric, solid, viscid or *glutinous when moist,* transversely cracking when dry, whitish, violaceous, or paler than the cap. **Spores** subelliptic, cinnamon-color, 12.7–15.2 µ long. **Ring** glutinous, usually evident as the termination of the similarly-constituted covering of the lower stem.

In thin woods, copses, and partly-cleared lands. August to September. Not as rare as *Cortinarius violaceus. Cortinarius mucifluus* Fr., another glutinous species, differs in the duller coloring of cap and stem, in the striate margin of the former, and in the stuffed interior of the latter. The stem is not at all violaceous.

CORRUGATED CORTINARIUS (Edible)
Cortinarius corrugatus Pk.

Cap 2–4 in. broad, fleshy, broadly campanulate or very convex, viscid when moist, *coarsely and radiately to reticulately corrugated,* bright-yellow, reddish-yellow, tawny or ochraceous, flesh white. **Gills** close, pallid when young, becoming tawny with age, slightly narrowed toward the stem, transversely wrinkled on their sides, and usually minutely uneven and eroded on their edges. **Stem** 3–5 in. long, 3–8 lines thick, equal, hollow, smooth but sometimes sprinkled above with minute, yellowish particles and adorned below with a few fibrils, pallid or yellowish, bulbous, the bulb viscid and usually colored like the cap. **Volva** glutinous, evident in young plants before the stem lengthens. **Spores** broadly elliptic, rough, 11.4–14 x 7.6–10 µ.

In woods and bushy places. June to September. Gregarious and quite common. It is undoubtedly related to *Pholiota caperata* (=*Rozites caperata,* see plate 27), as is shown by the corrugations of the cap, the transversely wrinkled gills (the edges of which are commonly eroded), the long, equal stem with traces of a volva, and the similarly shaped, rough spores with approximate measurements (see further remarks under *Pholiota caperata*). A variety in which the cap is adorned with darker-colored spots or scales bears the name, var. *subsquamosus* Pk. In all other respects it is like the typical form.

VIOLET CORTINARIUS (Edible)

Cortinarius violaceus (L.) Fr.

Cap 2–4 in. broad, convex, becoming nearly plane, dry, *adorned with numerous, persistent, hairy tufts or scales,* dark violet, flesh more or less violet. **Gills** rather thick, distant, rounded or deeply notched at the inner extremity, colored like the cap in the young plant, brownish-cinnamon in the mature plant. **Stem** 3–5 in. long, about ½ in. thick, thicker below and there swollen into a bulb, solid, fibrous, colored like the cap. **Ring** a cobwebby, rusty-ochraceous band above on the stem, made visible by the spores which it catches. **Spores** subelliptic, brownish-cinnamon, 12.7 μ long.

Among fallen leaves in the woods of hilly and mountainous districts. July and August. Grows solitary or scattered. It must be extraordinarily rare as the writer has collected it but once and that over thirty years ago. The two violaceous or bluish species, *Cortinarius albo-violaceus* (Pers.) Fr. and *C. cyanites* Fr., respectively, are readily distinguished, the former by its pale coloring, the latter by the blood-red flesh of the stem which, when pressed, exudes a juice of that color. Curiously, *C. cyanites,* an American species (Krieger, '25), is not included in Kauffman's monograph (Kauffman, '32). Specimens, from New England, are preserved in the herbarium of the Boston Mycological Club. *Cortinarius violaceus* is said to equal in flavor the common Meadow Mushroom.

Genus CRATERELLUS Fr.

If the reader will imagine a small trumpet made of mushroom tissue, he will have a good conception of what Craterelli look like. Their hymenial surface is merely wrinkled, not provided with gills, as in *Cantharellus*.

CHANTRELLE CRATERELLUS (Edible) Fig. 53a

Craterellus cantharellus (Schw.) Fr.

Cap 1–3 in. broad, fleshy, firm, convex, often becoming centrally depressed or infundibuliform, glabrous, yellow or pinkish-yellow, flesh white. **Hymenium** nearly even, slightly wrinkled, yellow running into salmon or orange. **Stem** 1–3 in. long, 3–5 lines thick, glabrous, solid, yellow. **Spores** subelliptic, yellowish to pale-salmon (when deposited on white paper), 7.6–10 x 5–6.3 μ.

In copses or in thin woods. August and September. This plant resembles the True Chantrelle (*Cantharellus cibarius,* plate 11) so closely that only the absence of gills enables one to decide whether the specimen in hand is the chantrelle Craterellus. To complicate matters, Peck has described a plant that stands intermediate between the *Cantharellus* and the *Craterellus, Craterellus cantharellus* var. *intermedius,* which has such pronounced wrinkles that they are very apt to be interpreted as gills. It is often

Figure 86 Because of its somber coloring, the Cornucopia Craterellus, *Craterellus cornucopioides* (also shown in color, plate 19), is not readily detected

tufted in its mode of growth. The flesh is somewhat tough but no less well-flavored than that of its double. Compare also *Cantharellus floccosus.*

CORNUCOPIA CRATERELLUS; HORN OF PLENTY (Edible)
PLATE 17, FIG. 86

Craterellus cornucopioides (L.) Fr.

Cap 1–2½ in. broad at the flaring top, 2–4 in. long, thin, flexible, tubiform, hollow to the base, blackish-brown, sometimes roughened with a few, obscure, fibrous tufts or scales. **Hymenium** even or somewhat rugose-wrinkled, paler than the upper surface of the cap, varying from ashy-gray to pinkish-brown or dark smoky-brown. **Stem** very short, almost wanting. **Spores** elliptical, whitish, 12.7–17.8 µ long.

In woods and shaded places, especially in old wood roads, on naked soil, or on shaded banks, but sometimes among mosses and fallen leaves. July to September. Found gregariously or in tufts. Because of its "protective coloring" it is not readily discovered when growing among dead leaves. It is praised very highly by Cooke, an English mushroom authority, who states that a friend thought nothing of walking six or eight miles to procure a dish of this *Craterellus.*

GENUS ENTOLOMA (Fr.) Quél. Spores rosy.

Entoloma is like *Tricholoma* but with rosy spores. The pink of the gills is unchangeable, a character which will enable one to distinguish the species from young specimens of the Meadow Mushroom (*Psalliota*). No edible species of any consequence are offered by the genus. The single species here described is known to be distinctly poisonous. Compare *Hebeloma.*

SINUATE ENTOLOMA (Poisonous)

Entoloma sinuatum (Bull.) Quél.

Cap 2–3 in. or more broad, fleshy, convex, becoming expanded or centrally depressed, glabrous, moist, even, yellowish-white, margin spreading or *wavy,* flesh white. **Gills** slightly adnexed, very broad, close, pallid, becoming pinkish or rufescent. **Stem** 3–5 in. long, 5–6 lines thick, stout, equal, firm, *solid,* fibrillose, becoming glabrous, white. **Spores** subglobose, angular, 7.6–10 µ in diameter.

In mixed woods. July to October. Grows gregariously. The odor is said to be strong and pleasant, not unlike that of burnt sugar. It is stated to be very poisonous, producing headache, vertigo, stomach pains, and vomiting. *Entoloma lividum* (Bull.) Sacc., a close relative and equally poisonous, is described as having a hollow stem. See p. 145 for a poisoning case by *Entoloma sinuatum.*

Genus FISTULINA (Bull.) Fr.

The generic characters are indicated in the description of *Fistulina hepatica,* the Beefsteak Mushroom. The tubes are distinct and free from each other, as in *Boletus.*

BEEFSTEAK MUSHROOM (Edible) Fig. 87

Fistulina hepatica (Huds.) Fr.

Cap 2–6 in. broad, with or without a short, lateral stem, fleshy, juicy, soft, dark-red, skin roughened with minute papillae and usually movable on a gelatinous layer underneath (like the skin on the back of the open hand), flesh red, variegated with brighter streaks, taste slightly acid. **Tubes** at first like small papillae but soon lengthening and becoming cylindrical, yellowish or slightly

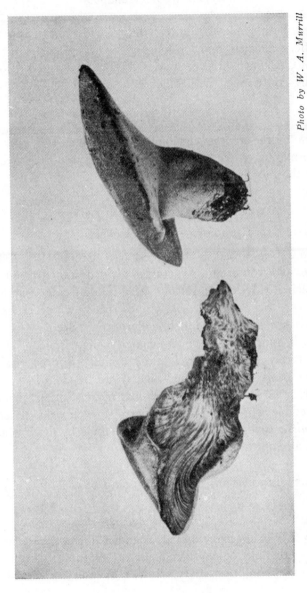

Photo by W. A. Murrill

Figure 87 The Beefsteak Mushroom, *Fistulina hepatica*. The mottled, striated appearance of the cut flesh is shown in the figure on the left

tinged with pink, becoming dingy with age. **Spores** elliptic, yellowish, 5–6.3 μ long.

On Chestnut and Oak stumps. July and August. Not readily confounded with other polypores.

Genus GYROMITRA Fr.

The more or less convoluted, brain-like, *not pitted,* conformation of the cap at once sets the Gyromitras apart from the morels (*Morchella*).

BROWN GYROMITRA (Edible) Fig. 88

Gyromitra brunnea Underw.

Cap 2–4 in. broad in the widest part, irregularly lobed, plicate and contorted, sometimes divided into areas by interlacing ridges, the various parts closely adhering to the stem, rich chocolate-brown, or paler where leaves covered the surface, whitish underneath. **Stem** ¾–1½ in. thick, more or less enlarged and spongy, solid at the base, rarely slightly fluted, clear white. **Spores** oval, hyaline, somewhat roughened-tuberculate, 28–30 x 14 μ.

In rich woods, mostly in beech-leaf mold. Spring. Said to be edible, but as it is a *Gyromitra,* the remarks under *Gyromitra esculenta* should be borne in mind by those who would attempt to eat it.

"EDIBLE" GYROMITRA; LOREL (the LORCHEL of the Germans); FALSE MOREL (Deadly), Fig. 50a

Gyromitra esculenta (Pers.) Fr.

Cap 2–3 in. or more broad, rounded, lobed, irregular, gyrose-convolute, glabrous, bay-red. **Stem** 2–2½ in. long, stout, slightly scurfy, stuffed or hollow, whitish,

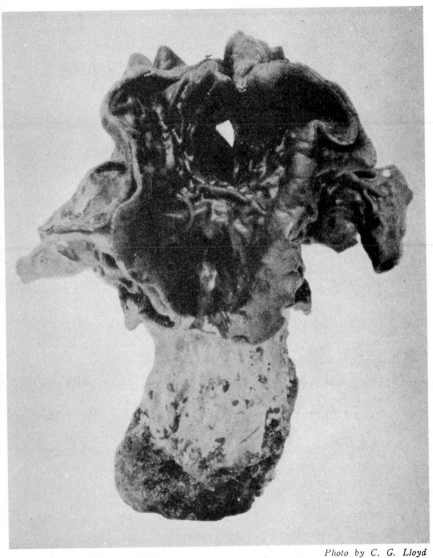

Figure 88 Brown Gyromitra, *Gyromitra brunnea.* Under suspicion along with the other *Gyromitra, G. esculenta*

[325]

often irregular. **Spores** elliptical, binucleate, yellowish, 20–23 μ long.

In wet ravines or in springy places in the vicinity of Pine groves or Pine trees. It is fond of sandy soil. In May and June. The brain-like convolutions and the chestnut-red coloring of the cap sharply differentiate this species from any morel. Huge specimens are sometimes found. It is known to be deadly poisonous, and yet it is consumed by many people, both here and abroad, without the slightest trace of serious consequences. Dr. Rudolf Ruedemann, of the New York State Museum, assures the writer that he has eaten it for the past thirty years, consuming even the tasty juice which, according to authorities, is the purveyor of the water-soluble and deadly helvellic acid. Against this stands the plant's record as the slayer of one hundred and sixty people. It would seem that either we are dealing with two distinct forms of a species, one edible, the other deadly, or such consumers as survive are possessed of a natural insensitivity to the poison (See Dearness, '11). For an account of the poisonous properties of this *Gyromitra,* see p. 144.

Genus HEBELOMA (Fr.) Quél. Spores yellowish clay-colored

As in *Inocybe,* the spores in species of this genus are never ferruginous (as in *Cortinarius,* for example), but rather alutaceous to dirty-yellow or brownish. The cap is more or less viscid, not fibrillose-scaly as in *Inocybe,* and the margin is at first incurved. A membranous ring, such as one finds in *Pholiota,* is lacking, only a few scant, fibrillose traces remaining on the margin of the young caps of some species. As to gill-attachment (more or less emarginate) the genus corresponds to *Tricholoma* and

Entoloma. The genus offers no edible species of value. One, *H. crustuliniforme,* is even regarded with suspicion.

COLVIN'S HEBELOMA. Fig. 89

Hebeloma colvini (Pk.) Sacc.

Cap 1–3 in. broad, fleshy, convex or nearly plane, sometimes gibbous or broadly umbonate, rarely centrally depressed, glabrous, grayish or alutaceous, with an ochraceous tint. **Gills** close, broad, sinuate, adnexed, whitish, becoming brownish-ochraceous. **Stem** 1–3¼ in. long, 1–3 lines thick, equal, flexuous, silky fibrillose, stuffed or hollow above, solid toward the base, whitish. **Spores** subelliptic, 10–12 x 5–6 μ.

Sandy soil in open places. October. The mycelium binds the sand into a globose mass which adheres to the base of the stem, as in *Laccaria trullisata.*

Genus HELVELLA (L.) Fr.

Cap more or less inflated, deflexed or concave, or sinuously lobed, attached by its center to a stem which may be more or less lacunose. **Hymenium** on upper surface of cap, the lower one sterile and pruinose. The substance of the plants is waxy-membranaceous.

CRISPED HELVELLA (Edible) Fig. 50d

Helvella crispa (Scop.) Fr.

Cap about 1½–2 in. broad, deflexed, lobed or variously contorted, *white or whitish.* **Stem** 2–2 ¾ in. long, 3–6 lines or more thick, equal or slightly swollen at the base, *ribbed and deeply and interruptedly grooved,* white or whitish. **Spores** elliptic, 17.8–23 μ long.

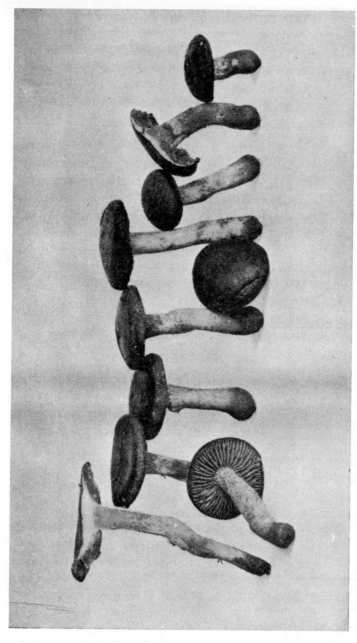

Figure 89 Colvin's Hebeloma, *Hebeloma colvini*, a sand-inhabiting mushroom

[328]

In woods. August and September. The flavor is said to be similar to that of morels. Compare *Helvella lacunosa.*

ELASTIC HELVELLA Fig. 50c
Helvella elastica (Bull.) Fr.

Cap under 1 in. broad, free, even, inflated, at length acutely 2–3 lobed. **Stem** slender, 3–4 in. long, often irregularly lacunose, attenuated upwards, pruinose, elastic, pellucid, stuffed when young, becoming hollow. **Spores** 20 x 10–11 μ.

On the ground in moist places in shady woods. Summer and autumn.

LACUNOSE HELVELLA (Edible)
Helvella lacunosa (Afz.) Fr.

Cap inflated, lobed, *grayish-black;* lobes deflexed, adnate, later becoming free. **Stem** fistulose, ribbed and grooved (costate-lacunose). **Spores** elliptic, 18 x 10 μ.

In woods, especially on burnt-over ground. Spring and autumn. Very much like *Helvella crispa,* but the cap is more regularly lobed (2–4 lobes), scarcely torn, and the color is blackish. It is also of smaller stature.

Genus HYDNUM (L.) Fr.

This teeth-bearing genus has in recent years been split up into a number of distinct genera. In the present, short treatment the species described are either stipitate or more or less branching. One species, *Hydnum septentrionale,* grows somewhat like *Polyporus sulphureus,* that is, in an imbricated fashion.

BEAR'S-HEAD HYDNUM (Edible) PLATE 18. FIG. 90

Hydnum caput-ursi Fr.

Fleshy, forming roundish or elongated masses from 2–6 in. thick and high (sometimes greatly exceeding these dimensions), tuberculiform, immarginate, pendulous, lateral or erect, white, becoming more or less yellowish with age, the surface of the tubercle everywhere giving rise to short branches or tuberculiform projections which are clothed with still smaller branchlets, and with subulate, deflexed teeth or spines that measure from 4–12 lines in length. **Spores** globose or subglobose, 5–6 μ broad.

On dead or decaying wood of deciduous trees, especially of Beech and Birch. In summer and autumn. Both in size and shape this fungus sometimes bears a striking resemblance to the heart of an ox. The spines are longer than in *Hydnum coralloides,* and shorter than in *H. erinaceus.* A short-spined form bears the name, var. *brevispineum* Pk.

CORAL HYDNUM (Edible)

Hydnum coralloides Scop.

Plant 2–4 in. or more broad and high, pure white, sometimes becoming yellowish with age. **Branches** numerous, spreading, dense, angular or flattened, bearing the numerous, crowded, awl-shaped teeth (2–5 lines long) along the lower side. **Spores** white, globose to subovate, uninucleate, 5.5–7 μ wide.

On prostrate trunks of trees of various kinds, but especially on Beech. August to October. When first encountered, this startlingly beautiful *Hydnum,* its pure whiteness seen in contrast with the dark colors of some fallen, moss-covered monarch of the forest, will

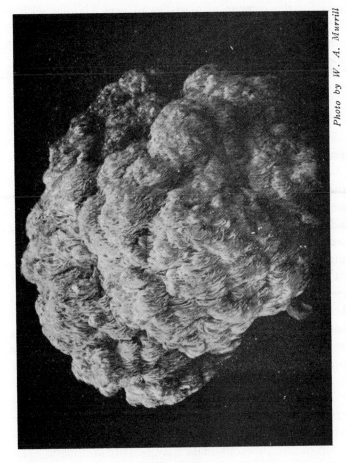

Figure 90 The Bear's-Head Hydnum, *Hydnum caput-ursi*

cause even the most callous to stop in wonder and admiration. It seems almost sacrilegious to recommend it as food for the camper who wishes to vary his diet with a taste of mushrooms. Let him turn to the more humble kinds to satisfy his craving for something to eat, and reserve this glorious *Hydnum* for a feast of the eye.

HEDGEHOG MUSHROOM (Edible)

Hydnum erinaceus Bull.

Fleshy, forming a more or less tuberous, whitish to creamy-white, roundish or somewhat heart-shaped mass (2–4 in. long, 1¼–4¾ in. wide, ¾–1½ in. thick), narrowed behind to a comparatively small point of attachment, projecting usually horizontally from the substratum and terminating outwardly in long, pendent teeth that measure 9–14 lines in length. **Spores** globose to subovate, 4.5–5 x 5–6 μ.

On living Oak, Locust or Beech, also at times on dead trees. May to November. Occasionally much larger than above stated. The species is so extremely variable in shape that, as Banker ('02–'14), our chief authority on the Hydnums, says, one might make a species of every specimen found. The tuberous base may be stipitate or not, it may point upward or downward, it may be more or less branched (suggesting an approach to *H. caput-ursi*), or it may be irregularly perforate at the base of the teeth or throughout, due to coalescing branches. The substance of the tuberous mass may be soft or tough. The teeth may vary in length from 2½ to 14 lines, they may be straight, curved or flexuous, terete or flattened. The upper surface of the tuberous mass may be sparsely fibrillose or spiny, or it may be densely invested with long, contorted, fertile fibrils or teeth, suggesting the head of Medusa with its covering of wriggling snakes for hair (hence the name for such forms, *H. caput-medusae* Bull.). It is eaten in certain European countries, but as it readily turns sour, it should be consumed only when young and perfectly fresh.

FINNISH HYDNUM PLATE 19
Hydnum fennicum Karst.

Cap 2–8 in. broad, convex, subumbilicate, slightly uneven to strongly lobed and undulating, surface dark-brown to *reddish-* or even purplish-brown, darker on the thick scales, scales (arranged more or less concentrically and in radiating lines) becoming smaller toward the margin, flesh fibrous, brittle, light-brown, taste bitter. **Teeth** *slender, 1½–2 lines long, less than ¼ of a line thick,* terete, acute, dark-umber at base to whitish at the tips, minute teeth scattered among those of regular length, scatteringly decurrent on the stem. **Stem** 1½–3½ in. long, 3–12 lines or more thick, central or nearly so, somewhat flexuous, usually strongly inclined, attenuate to the base, colored like the cap, becoming very dark at the base, solid, *flesh blue at the base.* **Spores** brown, subglobose, tuberculate, 6–7 μ wide.

On ground in mixed woods. August to October. Very much like *Hydnum imbricatum L.,* from which it differs in its finer teeth, reddish color, and in the bluish base of the stem.

SPREADING HYDNUM (Edible) PLATE 19. FIGS. 2a, 20h
Hydnum repandum L.

Cap 1–4 in. broad, fragile, convex or nearly plane, often irregular, nearly smooth, variable in color from pale-buff or rusty-yellow to pale-red or even Sienna-red, margin usually wavy or lobed, flesh dry, white, sometimes changing color slightly. **Teeth** whitish to cream-colored, coarse, straight, terete, pointed at the tip or somewhat flattened and incised. **Stem** 1–3 in. long, 6–8 lines thick, stout or slender, whitish or paler than the cap, solid, often excentric. **Spores** globose, yellowish, 7.6 µ broad.

In woods and open places, either on naked soil or among grass or fallen leaves. July to October. Singly or in clusters. A reddish variety, var. *rufescens* Schaeff., is smaller, thinner and more regular, with the stem mostly central. Var. *umbilicatum* Pk. is large and stout and has a deeply umbilicate cap, the surface of which sometimes cracks into thick scales (Banker, '04). *Hydnum repandum* is said to be as good as oysters, which, however, would not be a recommendation to individuals afflicted with *ostreophobia*. It should be stewed slowly in a closed vessel.

NORTHERN HYDNUM Figs. 40, 91

Hydnum septentrionale Fr.

Fruit-body consisting of many horizontal, imbricate, subdimidiate, convex to depressed, white caps which grow, densely crowded, from a vertical disk; surface of caps uneven, subrugose, floccose-pubescent, azonate; margin incurved to repand, obtuse; flesh tough, fibrous, moist, obscurely zonate, white. **Teeth** long, terete to subangular, crowded, milk-white, becoming buff to reddish in drying. **Spores** smooth, oblong, hyaline, 5–7 x 3–3.5 µ.

On trunks of dead or dying sugar maples, Hickory, and other deciduous trees, emerging from knots. Autumn. A large, conspicuous plant of northern distribution. *Hydnum pulcherrimum* Berk. and Curt., a more southern species, differs mainly in its smaller spores (4.5–5 x 2–2.5 µ).

Genus HYGROPHORUS Fr.   Spores white.

The waxy consistency of the gills is the most prominent feature of the species of this genus. Bright colors are present in some species, while others, often less brightly colored, might be taken for Clitocybes were it not for the wax-like gills, and the more or less evident, glutinous, to somewhat floccose, veil.

Photo by W. A. Murrill

Figure 91   *Hydnum septentrionale.* For a picture showing the effect of this fungus on a hickory tree, see fig. 40

CHANTRELLE HYGROPHORUS (Edible) Fig. 92

Hygrophorus cantharellus (Schw.) Fr.

Cap ½–1 in. broad, thin, convex, often umbilicate, sub-glabrous or minutely squamulose, orange, red, or yellow. **Gills** rather broad, distant, arcuate, decurrent, whitish or yellowish, sometimes tinged red. **Stem** 1–3 in. long, about 1 line thick, slender, fragile, glabrous, stuffed or hollow, orange, red, or yellow. **Spores** elliptic, 10 x 6 μ.

Photo by W. A. Murrill

Figure 92 Chantrelle Hygrophorus, *Hygrophorus cantharellus*

On naked, damp soil, among fallen leaves, under the shelter of tall ferns or among mosses in swamps and wet places, in woods and open places. July to October. It is a variable species, as the following varieties indicate. Var. *roseus:* margin very wavy or lobed, the lobes often crowded or overlapping, suggesting a double rose; var. *flavipes:* cap red or orange, stem yellow; var. *flaviceps:* cap yellow, stem yellow, red, or orange; and var. *flava:* cap and stem pale-yellow. The Chantrelle *Hygrophorus* is closely related to *Hygrophorus miniatus,* from which it differs in its decurrent gills and in its usually longer and more fragile stem. When eaten raw it is apt to have a disagreeable flavor that disappears in cooking.

SULPHUR-COLORED HYGROPHORUS (Edible)
Hygrophorus chlorophanus Fr.

Cap 10–20 lines broad, thin and fragile, convex, becoming nearly plane, often irregular, with the margin split or lobed, glabrous, viscid, striate on the margin, yellow, sometimes tinged with red in the center. **Gills** rather broad, subdistant, thin, ventricose, emarginate, adnexed, pale yellow. **Stem** 1½–3 in. long, about 2 lines thick, equal or nearly so, glabrous, viscid when moist, shining when dry, hollow, yellow. **Spores** elliptic, 7.6 x 5 μ.

In damp or mossy places in woods. July to September. *Hygrophorus ceraceus* (Wulf.) Fr., which resembles this species, has adnate to subdecurrent, sub-triangular, nonemarginate gills. *Hygrophorus nitidus* Berk. and Curt. has gills like *H. ceraceus,* but the color of the cap soon changes from yellow to white. A European variety of *H. chlorophanus* is said to have white gills.

CONIC HYGROPHORUS (Poisonous)
Hygrophorus conicus (Scop.) Fr.

Cap conic at first, at length expanded (then up to 2¼ in. broad), *acute or subacute in the center,* fragile, glabrous or fibrillose, slightly viscid when moist, shining when dry, often lobed and split on the margin, *red, scarlet, orange, or yellow, soon showing signs of blackening, flesh thin, white, blackening.* **Gills** thin, rather close, ventricose, narrowed behind, almost free, commonly yellowish. **Stems** ¼ in. long, 1–3 lines thick, equal, fibrously striate, hollow, *yellow, then blackening.* **Spores** broadly elliptic, 10–12.7 x 6–7.6 μ.

Woods and in mossy or grassy places. Quite common. In drying, the whole plant turns black. A species, described by Peck under the name, *Hygrophorus cuspidatus,* is more slender, has longer and comparatively narrower spores, and a strongly cuspidate (instead of merely acute) apex of the cap. The plant also blackens more or less. *Hygrophorus immutabilis* Pk., a related species, differs in its less regularly and acutely conical, greenish-brown to yellowish-brown cap, in its paler or whitish gills, and in not changing to black. *Hygrophorus ruber* Pk. is even more closely related, especially as to coloring, but the stem is red and there is no change to black. *Hygrophorus conicus* has been the cause of at least four deaths in China (see p. 146).

IVORY HYGROPHORUS (Edible) Fig. 93

Hygrophorus eburneus (Bull.) Fr.

Cap 1–2 in. broad, convex or nearly plane, viscid when moist, slightly pubescent on the margin when young, *white,* flesh white, taste mild. **Gills** distant, decurrent, *white.* **Stem** 1½–3 in. long, 2–4 lines thick, equal or narrowed at the base, straight or flexuous, *stuffed or hollow,* viscid, *white, with white points or squamules at the top.* **Spores** subelliptic, 6–7.6 x 5–6 μ.

Photo by W. A. Murrill

Figure 93 A mushroom of ivory whiteness, with beautifully arched, wax-like gills, is very apt to be the above, *Hygrophorus eburneus*, called Ivory Hygrophorus

In woods and open places. September and October. Sometimes grows cespitosely. Among other characters, its hollow stem distinguishes it from *Hygrophorus virgineus,* another white species. The viscidity of the stem makes it difficult to pluck from its place of growth. The two varieties of *Hygrophorus laurae* are placed by Kauffman under *H. eburneus.* Compare the white variety of *H. pratensis.*

YELLOW-DISKED HYGROPHORUS (Edible)

Hygrophorus flavodiscus Frost and Pk.

Cap 1–3 in. broad, fleshy, convex or nearly plane, glabrous, very viscid or glutinous, white, pale-yellow or reddish-yellow in the center, flesh white. **Gills** adnate or decurrent, subdistant, white, sometimes tinged with a slight, flesh-colored tint, the interspaces sometimes venose. **Stem** 1–3 in. long, 3–6 lines thick, subequal, solid, very viscid or glutinous, white at the top, white or yellowish elsewhere. **Spores** elliptic, white, 6.3–7.6 x 4–5 μ.

In Pine woods. Late autumn. Much like *Hygrophorus fuligineus,* except in coloring. The two species are sometimes found growing in the same woods. The gluten on the lower part of the stem ends abruptly, leaving the upper part dry.

SMOKY HYGROPHORUS (Edible)

Hygrophorus fuligineus Frost and Pk.

Cap 1–4 in. broad, convex or nearly plane, glabrous, very viscid or glutinous, grayish-brown or fuliginous, the disk often darker or almost black. **Gills** subdistant, adnate or decurrent, white. **Stem** 2–4 in. long, 4–8 lines thick, solid, viscid or glutinous, white or whitish. **Spores** elliptic, 7.6–9 x 5 μ.

In Pine woods or woods of Pine and Hemlock intermixed. October to November. The gluten on the cap is sometimes so copious that it flows over the margin, connecting, in young specimens, with that on the stem and forming a beautiful, translucent veil. After the removal of the gluten-bearing pellicle of the cap, the clean, white flesh is exposed. Members of the Boston Mycological Club refer to it as the "sweetbread mushroom", but this name had already been applied to *Clitopilus orcella*. It grows singly or in tufts. The flesh is tender and of excellent flavor. *Hygrophorus flavodiscus* should be compared.

LAURA'S HYGROPHORUS (Edible)

Hygrophorus laurae Morg.

Cap 2–4 in. broad, fleshy, convex, umbonate, becoming expanded and depressed, more or less irregular, glutinous, white, with a reddish or brownish tinge, especially in the center, flesh white. **Gills** unequal, adnate or decurrent, distant, white. **Stem** 2–4 in. long, 3–6 lines thick, more or less curved or crooked, often tapering downward, solid, yellowish white, the apex scabrous with scaly points. **Spores** elliptic, apiculate, 7.6 x 5 μ.

Woods and open places. August and September. Single, gregarious, or cespitose. *Hygrophorus rubropunctus* Pk., a rare species, is distinguished by the tomentose, glutinous, orange-yellow to straw-colored, ringed stem, and by the reddish, glandular dots at the top of the stem. Several varieties of *Hygrophorus laurae* have been detected. Var. *unicolor* Pk. has the cap wholly white or only faintly tinged with yellow. Both cap and gills become darker-colored with age or in drying, characteristics which this variety shares with the typical form, but not with the other variety. Var. *decipiens* Pk. has a thin, white cap, with a dingy yellow or smoky brown spot in the center. Gills subdistant. Stem long, slender, white. Color changes in gills slight. Grows cespitosely in the borders of woods. September. The varieties are placed by Kauffman under *Hygrophorus eburneus*.

VERMILION HYGROPHORUS (Edible)

Hygrophorus miniatus (Scop.) Schroet.

Cap 1½–2 in. broad, thin, fragile, at first convex, becoming nearly plane, bright red or vermilion, sometimes fading to paler or orange shades, glabrous or minutely squamulose, often umbilicate. **Gills** distant, adnate, sometimes emarginate or even slightly decurrent, yellow, often tinged with red. **Stem** slender, 1–2 in. long, 1–2 lines thick, glabrous, colored like the cap or paler, solid when young, wholly or partly hollow later. **Spores** elliptic, white, 7.6 µ long.

In woods, swamps, and old fields in soil (either wet or dry), among mosses or fallen leaves, or on naked earth. In clearings, where fire has run, it often occurs in great profusion with caps measuring up to 3 in. in diameter. June to September. Grows singly, in groups, or in clusters. It is very variable and its beautiful colors soon fade. The following varieties are worthy of note. Var. *subluteus* Pk. (=var. *lutescens* Pk.) : cap yellow or reddish yellow; gills and stem yellow. Var. *congelatus* Pk. (=*Hygrophorus congelatus* Pk.) : cap small, convex, dingy red, glabrous; gills submarginate, red. Var.

sphagnophilus Pk.: cap subconic or broadly convex, sometimes centrally depressed, glabrous, red or orange; stem colored like or a little paler than the cap, white or yellow at the base. Growing among peat mosses in bogs. More fragile than the typical form. Compare *Hygrophorus cantharellus*. The substance of *H. miniatus* is tender and of agreeable flavor.

MEADOW HYGROPHORUS; BUFF CAP (Edible)

Hygrophorus pratensis (Pers.) Fr.

Cap 1–2 in. broad, compact, convex-turbinate or nearly flat, glabrous, buff or yellowish, more or less reddish or tawny, sometimes almost white, the margin thin, flesh whitish, mild. **Gills** thick, distant, decurrent, whitish or yellowish, the interspaces venose. **Stem** short, 1–2 in. long, ¼–½ in. thick, glabrous, white or whitish, sometimes yellowish. **Spores** broadly elliptic, whitish, 6–7 μ long.

In old pastures and clearings, or in thin woods; often in old, abandoned fields partly overgrown with brakes and bushes. July to September. Authorities are agreed as to its edibility. It is said to have a delicate flavor. Sometimes color varieties are found. Var. *albus* is entirely white (compare *H. virgineus* and *H. eburneus*); var. *cinereus* is either wholly gray or with the stem whitish, while var. *pallidus* has every part colored ochraceous white.

BLUSHING HYGROPHORUS (Edible)

Hygrophorus pudorinus Fr.

Cap 2–4 in. broad, fleshy, firm, convex, becoming nearly plane, glabrous, viscid when moist, pinkish buff or pale flesh-color, flesh white, taste mild. **Gills** distant, adnate or decurrent, white. **Stem** 2–5 in. long, 6–10 lines thick, equal or pointed at the base, solid, white or whitish, with white points at the top. **Spores** elliptic, 7.6–10 x 4–5 μ.

Commonly under Spruce or Balsam Fir trees. September. Gregarious or cespitose. One of the very best of edible mushrooms. *Hygrophorus russula,* perhaps just as fine, is colored a dull carmine-pink, and the center of the cap bears numerous, dark carmine-red, squamulose dots. *Hygrophorus proximus* Krieger has close gills. *Hygrophorus pudorinus* varies much in size and, within limits, in color. The stem may be colored like the cap.

RED HYGROPHORUS (Edible)

Hygrophorus puniceus Fr.

Cap 1–3 in. broad, thin, fragile, conic or campanulate, becoming expanded and often wavy or lobed, glabrous, viscid, bright red, paler when old. **Gills** broad, thick, distant, yellow, often reddish, narrowly attached. **Stem** 2–3 in. long, 4–6 lines thick, equal or somewhat ventricose, hollow, yellow, or red and yellow, *usually white at the base.* **Spores** elliptic, 7.6–10 x 5 μ.

In damp or mossy places both in woods and open grounds. July to September. The bright red coloring is apt to fade to yellow in old plants. When in its full glory, it must be carefully separated from the following species. From *Hygrophorus coccineus* (Schaeff.) Fr. the narrowly attached gills and the white stem-base serve as distinguishing features, and *Hygrophorus miniatus* has a dry, umbilicate, minutely tomentose to scaly cap, and a cylindric stem.

RUSSULA HYGROPHORUS (Edible) PLATE 20

Hygrophorus russula (Fr.) Kauffm.

Cap 3–5 in. broad, fleshy, convex, becoming plane or centrally depressed, obtuse, viscid, *dotted with dark red, granular squamules* in the center, *dull carmine-pink or darker,* the margin usually paler, involute and minutely downy in the young plant, flesh white, sometimes tinged with red, taste mild. **Gills** subdistant, rounded behind or subdecurrent, white, often becoming spotted with red when mature. **Stem** 1–3½ in. long, 6–12 lines thick, solid, firm, equal, sometimes twisted, whitish or rose-red, finely striate below, squamulose at the top, and just below the gills ornamented with an encircling, raised, pinkish line. **Spores** elliptic, 7 x 4 μ.

In mixed, frondose woods. September and October. Solitary or cespitose, generally under a dense mat of leaves, which the plants lift up into mounds. Owing to the viscidity of the caps, all kinds of forest débris adheres to the surface. But once the skin is removed, a perfectly clean, white, appetizing flesh appears. See remarks under *Hygrophorus pudorinus.*

SHOWY HYGROPHORUS (Edible)

Hygrophorus speciosus Pk.

Cap 1–2 in. broad, broadly convex, often with a small, central umbo, glabrous, very viscid or glutinous when moist, yellow, usually bright red or scarlet in the center, flesh white, yellow under the thin, separable pellicle. **Gills** distant, decurrent, white or slightly tinged with yellow. **Stem** 2–4 in. long, 2–4 lines thick, nearly equal, solid, viscid, slightly fibrillose, whitish or yellowish. **Spores** elliptic, 7.6 x 5 μ.

Under or near Tamarack trees. September to October.
This is closely related to *Hygrophorus aureus* (Arrh.)
Fr. of Europe which differs mainly in possessing a ring.
Hygrophorus coloratus Pk. has a floccose ring and a persistently red or red-orange cap and is apparently the
American representative of *H. aureus*. *Hygrophorus
laricinus* Pk., another species that occurs under Tama-
racks, is smaller, has a reddish, tawny-red or grayish-red
cap, and a hollow stem.

WHITE HYGROPHORUS (Edible)

Hygrophorus virgineus (Wulf.) Fr.

Cap 1–3 in. broad, fleshy, convex, often becoming plane
or centrally depressed, sometimes irregular or wavy on
the thin margin, moist, *white,* flesh white, taste mild.
Gills thick, distant, decurrent, *white.* **Stem** 1–2 in. long,
3–5 lines thick, firm, smooth, solid, equal or tapering
downward, *white.* **Spores,** elliptic, 6.3–7.6 x 5 μ.

In grassy ground, pastures, and in meadows, where it
is often hidden from view by tall grass. July to October.
Its flesh is not very tender, but it is good eating nevertheless. See under *Hygrophorus pratensis* and *H. eburneus*.

GENUS HYPHOLOMA (Fr.) Quél. Spores purple-brown.

Close to *Psalliota* and *Stropharia*. From the former
(a free-gilled genus), the sinuate, sinuate-adnate or
adnexed (to seceding!) gills separate it, while the
latter has the gills adnate to subdecurrent. Cap not
usually viscid. Ring generally slight and fugacious,
silky-fibrillose or woolly, often merely appendiculate on
the margin of the cap. *Psilocybe* resembles *Hypholoma,*
but the ring, when at all present in youth, soon disappears.

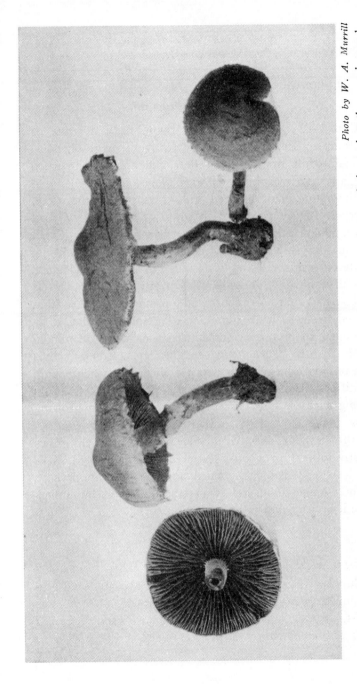

Figure 94 *Hypholoma boughtoni*. Very close to *H. lacrymabundum* and *H. velutinum*, but the cap is much given to cracking, the resulting chinks being usually more evident than in the specimens shown

UNCERTAIN HYPHOLOMA (Edible) PLATE 21. FIG. 95

Hypholoma incertum Pk.

Cap 1–2½ in. broad, thin, fragile, at first ovate or subcampanulate, then broadly convex, hygrophanous, whitish, often tinged with yellow, commonly white when dry, the thin margin often wavy, lobed or irregular and in the young plant adorned with fragments of the white, floccose, fugacious veil, flesh white. **Gills** thin, narrow, close, adnate, at first whitish, then purplish-brown. **Stem** 1–3 in. long, 1–3 lines thick, equal, hollow, easily splitting, white or whitish. **Ring** fugacious, usually appendiculate, as stated above. **Spores** elliptic, 7.6 x 5 μ.

In lawns, gardens, copses and pastures, usually from buried wood (dead roots, etc.). Summer and early autumn. In groups or sometimes in clusters. Common. Very close to *Hypholoma candolleanum* (Fr.) which is said to have adnexed gills that are violaceous when young. It differs from *Hypholoma appendiculatum* (Bull.) in having a paler, and more even, dry cap, and in growing in a grouped fashion, rather than in dense clusters. Kauffman adds a variety, var. *silvestris,* which grows mostly solitary in woods, scattered among decayed sticks and leaves. It is long-stemmed, and its spores are perhaps slightly longer and slightly variable in shape, but otherwise it is very similar to the typical form.

WEEPING HYPHOLOMA

Hypholoma lacrymabundum (Fr.) Quél.

Cap 1½–4 in, broad, convex to campanulate, obtuse to expanded, *whitish to buff,* then brownish-ochraceous, moist, all except the sometimes rugulose center *covered with scattered, rather large, appressed, brownish, hairy*

Photo by W. A. Murrill

Figure 95 Uncertain Hypholoma, *Hypholoma incertum.* If the reader will "keep an eye" on his lawn, he will without doubt encounter this plant. It usually marks the spot where a tree once stood

scales, paler on the margin, the latter at first incurved and appendiculate with the thickish, white-floccose veil, flesh white, firm. **Gills** adnate-seceding, narrow, crowded, at first whitish, at length purplish-brown, edges white-flocculose, *rarely beaded with droplets of moisture.* **Stem** 2½–5 in. long, 2½–5 lines thick, equal, hollow, striate above, fibrillose or somewhat scaly below, becoming glabrous, *whitish,* then sordid, base sometimes stained yellowish when bruised, with a white mycelium at the base. **Ring** fugacious, generally retained by the margin of the cap, as described above. **Spores** 6–7.5 x 3–4 μ, elliptic, slightly curved, *smooth,* dark brownish-purple under the microscope.

At or about the base of trees, in Beech, Maple and Birch woods; also in coniferous regions. August to September. Densely cespitose. Not common. There are several more or less closely allied species. *Hypholoma aggregatum* Pk. is, in Kauffman's opinion, only a smaller form. *Hypholoma velutinum* (Fr.), more frequent than *H. lacrymabundum,* has a darker and more tawny cap, and, most important, spores that are larger (9–12 x 7 μ) and tuberculate. The gills are more certain to be beaded with droplets of moisture. *Hypholoma rigidipes* Pk. is smaller, grows gregariously, has a more slender, rigid stem, and apiculate spores. *Hypholoma boughtoni* Pk. (figure 94) usually has the cap cracked into large areas; in *H. rugocephalum* Atk. it is glabrous and rugulosely wrinkled. *Hypholoma pyrotrichum* Fr. has reddish scales. The description of *H. lacrymabundum* is based on that given by Kauffman ('18).

PERPLEXING HYPHOLOMA (Edible) Plate 22

Hypholoma perplexum Pk.

Cap 1–3 in. broad, convex or nearly plane, glabrous, sometimes broadly and slightly umbonate, reddish or brownish-red, fading to yellow on the margin, flesh white or whitish, not bitter. **Gills** thin, close, slightly rounded at the inner extremity, at first pale-yellow, then tinged with green, finally purplish-brown. **Stem** 2–3 in. long, 2–4 lines thick, nearly equal, firm, hollow, slightly fibrillose, whitish or yellowish above, ferruginous, reddish or reddish-brown below. **Veil** evanescent, usually present only on the margin of the cap as a white, silky projection. **Spores** elliptic, purplish-brown, 7.6 x 4 μ.

On or about old stumps or prostrate trunks of trees, in woods or open places. In autumn, continuing until the first frosts. Usually grows in dense clusters, though sometimes singly. Very common: It differs from *Hypholoma sublateritium* (Schaeff.), its almost indistinguishable relative, in its usually smaller size, more slender, hollow stem, in the yellow, greenish and purplish tints of the gills, and in the absence of a bitter flavor. *Hypholoma fasciculare* (Huds.), a species reputed to be deleterious, has a light-yellow cap, and light-yellow flesh. These, and other species more or less closely related to *Hypholoma perplexum,* may be differentiated by the following key, prepared by Professor Peck.

```
Taste bitter ...........................................  1
Taste mild or not clearly bitter.......................  3
1 Stem solid or stuffed, flesh whitish, gills whitish, then
    sooty-olive ...................................sublateritium
1 Stem hollow, flesh yellow...............................  2
    2 Cap yellow or tinged with tawny, stem yellow, gills
        yellow, becoming greenish...................fasciculare
    2 Cap brick-red, stem ferruginous, gills green, be-
        coming olive ...............................elaeodes
```

3 Cap red or brick-red, with a yellow margin, gills yellow,
then greenish, finally purplish-brown.............*perplexum*
3 Cap yellow, or slightly tawny on the disk only.............. 4
4 Gills gray, becoming purplish-brown.............*capnoides*
4 Gills yellow, becoming gray, neither greenish nor
purplish ....*epixanthum*

With a previous soaking in acidulated water (for about twenty minutes) and a little spicing, this common and abundant species can be turned to good account at a time when most mushrooms have disappeared.

Genus HYPOMYCES (Fr.) Tul.

The species of this genus are mostly parasites on other fungi (*Lactarius, Boletus,* etc.) and consist of small, more or less flask-shaped bodies (perithecia, figure 20r) immersed in a thin layer (the subiculum) which covers the substance of the host, only the elongated mouths showing on the surface. The asci and their spores are contained within the perithecia.

RED HYPOMYCES (Edible) Fig. 46a

Hypomyces lactifluorum (Schw.) Tul.

Specimens of *Boletus chrysenteron* and *Amanita rubescens* are sometimes found with species of *Hypomyces* growing upon them. The former is converted into a bright lemon-yellow (or white) object that bears no resemblance to a *Boletus,* while the latter is made to look like a thick stalk, surmounted by a knob, the whole painted a glistening white. If one searches further for such monstrosities, due to the attack of parasites, one will in all probability be rewarded by the finding of a very bright-orange or vermillion-colored object, which is neither an agaric nor a *Boletus.* In shape and size it recalls some of the larger, funnel-shaped species of *Lactarius* (*L. piperatus,* for example, figure 98), but there is not the slightest trace of gills, merely a somewhat wrinkled surface where they normally should appear. On closer examination with a hand-lens, this surface will be seen to be covered with minute and innumerable, red dots, the mouths of tiny perithecia imbedded in a thin layer (the subiculum) produced by the parasite. Under this layer is the substance of the host, just as good to eat as that of unattacked plants, except that it is harder, dryer, and more crisp. A little seasoning is necessary to make it palatable.

GENUS INOCYBE (Fr.) Quél.   Spores yellowish clay-colored.

Very close to *Hebeloma* from which (in the mature stage) it is distinguishable by the innately silky, fibrillose or fibrillose-scaly (not viscid) cap (figure 65a). The spores, more or less alutaceous and dull-colored (as in *Hebeloma*), may be smooth or rough, characters that must be observed if one wishes to have any success in the classification of the rather numerous, and often closely akin species. In very young specimens, the margin of the cap is frequently seen to be connected with the stem by a more or less evanescent, fibrillose veil. The species are for the most part of small or medium size and offer no special attractions to mushroom hungry individuals. Two species (the only ones here described) are on the black list, *Inocybe infelix* and *I. infida* (see p. 145).

UNFORTUNATE INOCYBE (Poisonous)

Inocybe infelix Pk.

Cap ⅝–1 in. broad, campanulate, broadly convex or nearly plane, subumbonate, floccosely squamulose, grayish-brown or umber, flesh whitish. **Gills** close, adnexed, ventricose, broad, whitish, becoming brownish-ferruginous. **Stem** ¾–2 in. long, 1–2 lines thick, equal, solid, silky-fibrillose, pallid or whitish above, generally brownish toward the base, pruinose at the top. **Spores** oblong, even, 10–15 x 5–6 μ.

Naked, sterile soil, or among mosses. May to August. Ford ('11) found in this species of insignificant size a poison that resists heating and drying. The poison is a powerful narcotic.

UNTRUSTWORTHY INOCYBE (Unwholesome)

Inocybe infida (Pk.) Earle.

Cap ⅝–1 in. broad, firm, campanulate or expanded, subumbonate, slightly squamulose on the disk, often split on the margin, whitish, the umbo or center often reddish-brown. **Gills** close, narrow, adnexed, pallid, becoming somewhat cinnamon-colored. **Stem** 1¼–2 in. long, 1–2 lines thick, equal or a little enlarged at the base, furfuraceous at the top, hollow, white. **Spores** subglobose, nodulose, 8–10 x 6–8 μ.

Mossy ground in low woods. September. This species is known to have caused a slight, temporary illness in some members of a family who had cooked and eaten specimens of this tiny plant.

GENUS LACCARIA Berk. and Br. (emended). Spores white.

Cap convex, becoming umbilicate or depressed, flesh thin or thick. Gills broadly adnate, sometimes with a decurrent tooth, becoming mealy with the copious, globose, subglobose or oblong-cylindric, minutely warted (verruculose) or smooth, white spores. Stem central, externally fibrous, veil not evident.

The species of this genus were formerly included in *Clitocybe,* but the rather thick, subdistant, more or less adnate gills (that with age become powdered with the white spores) separate the two genera unmistakably. One species, *Laccaria trullisata,* although possessing every external mark of a *Laccaria,* differs from the other members of the genus in having oblong or cylindric, smooth spores.

AMETHYST LACCARIA (Edible) PLATE 23

Laccaria amethystina (Bolt.) Pk.

Cap ½–1 in. broad, thin, broadly convex, umbilicate or centrally depressed, hygrophanous, brown or violaceous-brown when moist, grayish when dry, unpolished. **Gills** subdistant, adnate or decurrent, violaceous, color more persistent than in the cap. **Stem** 1–2 in. long, 1–2 lines thick, slender, equal, flexuous, hollow, colored like or paler than the cap. **Spores** globose, verruculose, 8–10 µ in diameter.

Damp ground in shaded places. July and August. Solitary or gregarious in its mode of growth and not as common as *Laccaria laccata,* to which it was formerly attached as a variety. The dimensions of the cap sometimes exceed those given.

WAXY LACCARIA (Edible) PLATE 23

Laccaria laccata (Scop.) Berk. and Br.

Cap ⅝–2 in. broad, fleshy, rather thin, convex or nearly plane, sometimes umbilicate or centrally depressed, hygrophanous, glabrous, furfuraceous or minutely squamulose, pale-red, buff-red or flesh-red when moist, pale-ochraceous, grayish or buff when dry, margin even. **Gills** rather broad, thick, subdistant, adnate or decurrent, flesh-color or pale flesh-color. **Stem** 1–3 in. long, 1–3 lines thick, nearly or quite equal, fibrous. firm, straight or flexuous, stuffed, colored like the cap. **Spores** globose, verruculose, 8–10 µ in diameter.

Woods, groves, swamps, mossy places and pastures in wet, dry or sandy soil, and even in sphagnum. May to October. This extremely common and variable species at first perplexes the beginner. A European authority (Barla, 1888) devotes an entire, quarto plate to the different guises the plant assumes.

Peck describes two varieties, var. *pallidifolia*, in which the gills are very pale and barely tinged with flesh-color, and var. *decurrens*, with distinctly decurrent or arcuate-decurrent gills. Lacking flavor and inclining to be tough, it is at best a good bulk maker with more desirable but rarer kinds.

PURPLISH-OCHER LACCARIA (Edible)

Laccaria ochropurpurea (Berk). Pk.

Cap 2–4 in. broad, fleshy, firm, subhemispheric or convex with decurved margin, becoming plane or slightly depressed in the center, hygrophanous, purplish-brown when moist, grayish or pale-alutaceous when dry, unpolished. **Gills** thick, distant, broad, adnate or decurrent, purplish. **Stem** 1¼–3½ in. or more long, ¼–½ in. or more thick, equal or sometimes thicker in the middle, sometimes at each end, fibrous, solid, colored like or paler than the cap. **Spores** globose, verruculose, 8–10 µ in diameter.

Open, grassy or bushy places. July to September. Solitary or rarely gregarious. Common. This species, the largest in the genus, is often misshapen. The cap is apt to show deep cracks, the margin splits, and the coarse, thick gills are often much torn. When young, the latter are colored a beautiful, deep violet. A curious feature is the coldness of the plant, even in the hottest weather. This phenomenon may be due to the rapid evaporation of the water from the loosely-compacted tissues of the plant. On the other hand, *Boletus aereus* Bull. has been described as a heat-producing plant.

STRIATULATE LACCARIA
Laccaria striatula Pk.

Cap ½–¾ in. broad, *very thin,* submembranaceous, convex or nearly plane, glabrous, hygrophanous, buff-red and *striatulate when moist,* grayish or pale-buff when dry. **Gills** broad, distant, adnate, pale flesh-color. **Stem** ⅝–1⅛ in. long, ½–1 line thick, equal, fibrous, *hollow,* colored like the cap. **Spores** globose or subglobose, verruculose, 11–13 μ in diameter.

In wet or damp places. June to September. Grows gregariously. It was formerly appended to *Laccaria laccata* as a variety, but its larger spores alone would seem to entitle it to specific rank.

TWISTED LACCARIA
Laccaria tortilis (Bolt.) Pat.

Cap $\frac{3}{16}$–⅜ in. broad, membranaceous, convex, plane or centrally depressed, deflexed and sometimes torn on the margin, obscurely striate, irregular, subferruginous. **Gills** thick, subdistant, adnate, flesh-color. **Stem** $\frac{5}{16}$–½ in. long, ½–1 line thick, equal or slightly thickened at the base, stuffed or hollow, *twisted,* fragile, colored like the cap. **Spores** globose, echinulate, 12–16 μ in diameter.

Damp places in woods or by roadsides. **August.** Closely gregarious or cespitose. Rare. This, the smallest species of the genus, is easily recognized by its diminutive size and irregular shape. The spores are larger and more sharply verruculose than in *Laccaria striatula.* **Var.** *gracilis* Pk. has a more regular cap, a longer stem, and a less cespitose mode of growth.

SANDY LACCARIA. Fig. 96

Laccaria trullisata (Ellis) Pk.

Cap 1–2 in. broad, fleshy, convex or plane, becoming depressed in the center, innately fibrous, squamose or squamulose, smoother in the center, thin on the margin, reddish flesh-color. **Gills** unequal, subdistant, thick, adnate or with a decurrent tooth, at first purplish-violet, then brick-red and pruinose or white-pulverulent. **Stem** 1–3 in. long, ¼–⅜ in. and more thick, stuffed, fibrillose, colored like the cap, *the enlarged, more or less deeply radicating and clavately thickened, base covered by a mass of mycelium and adhering sand.* **Spores** oblong or cylindric, *even,* granular within, 15–20 x 8–9 μ.

In sandy soil. September and October. Solitary or sparsely gregarious. The fresh mycelium is violet-colored. The characteristic marks are the large, sand-plastered bulb of the stem, and the oblong or cylindric, smooth spores. It is not uncommon in its habitat.

Genus LACTARIUS Fr. Spores white or yellowish.

Usually plants of conspicuous size, fleshy, the flesh (and gills) exuding a colored, uncolored, color-changing, or watery-milky juice. The trama is composed of vesiculose tissue (see figure 20o). Closely related to *Russula.*

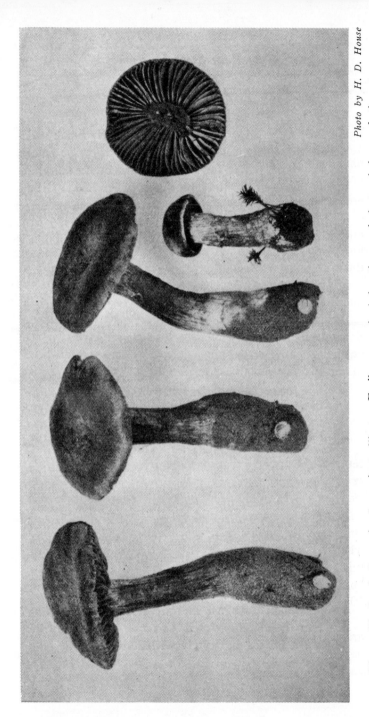

Photo by *H. D. House*

Figure 96 Sandy Laccaria, *Laccaria trullisata*. Easily recognized by the sand-plastered base of the stem

CELANDINE LACTARIUS (Edible)
Lactarius chelidonium Pk.

Cap 2–3 in. broad, convex, becoming nearly plane and umbilicate or centrally depressed, grayish-yellow or pale-tawny, sometimes with a few, narrow zones on the margin, assuming bluish-green tints or stains when old. **Gills** narrow, close, adnate or slightly decurrent, grayish-yellow, *milk saffron-color,* scanty, mild. **Stem** short, 1–1½ in. long, 4–6 lines thick, nearly equal, hollow, colored like the cap, sometimes spotted or stained with bluish-green in old specimens. **Spores** yellowish, globose, 7.6 µ in diameter.

In light, sandy soil under or near Pine trees. July to September. The saffron-colored milk serves to distinguish it from *Lactarius deliciosus*. The edible qualities of the two species are about equal.

CORRUGATED LACTARIUS (Edible)
Lactarius corrugis Pk.

Cap 3–5 in. broad, firm, convex, then nearly plane or centrally depressed, *rugose-reticulated, covered with a velvety pruinosity or pubescence, dark-reddish-brown or chestnut-color,* fading with age to tawny-brown, taste mild, milk copious, white. **Gills** close, dark cream-color or sub-cinnamon, *becoming paler when old,* sordid or brownish where bruised or wounded. **Stem** 3–5 in. long, 6–12 lines thick, equal, solid, glabrous or merely pruinose, paler than, but similar in color, to the cap. **Spores** subglobose, 10–12.7 µ.

In thin woods. August and September. It is separable from the closely related *Lactarius volemus* by its darker colors and its intricately wrinkled cap. The gills

Photo by C. E. Cummings. Courtesy Buffalo Society of Natural Sciences

Figure 97 *Lactarius hygrophoroides*, a very near relative of *L. corrugis*. Notice the droplets of white milk exuding from the injured gills

bear numerous, spine-like or acicular cystidia or spicules, 40–50 μ long. They are so numerous on and near the edges of the gills that they give them a pubescent appearance. *Lactarius hygrophoroides* Berk. and Curt. has distant gills, but its general appearance (figure 97) will convey some idea of *Lactarius corrugis*. The coloring of the two plants is somewhat similar.

DECEPTIVE LACTARIUS (Edible)

Lactarius deceptivus Pk.

Cap 3–6 in. broad, fleshy, compact, convex-umbilicate, becoming expanded and centrally depressed or almost infundibuliform, glabrous or slightly tomentose except on the margin, white or whitish, often with dingy-yellowish or rusty stains, *the margin at first involute and clothed with a dense, but soft, white, cottony tomentum which conceals the young gills,* becoming expanded and more or less fibrillose, flesh and milk white, taste acrid. **Gills** rather broad, subdistant, adnate or slightly decurrent, some of them forked, white or yellowish. **Stem** 1–3 in. long, 8–15 lines thick, equal or tapering downward, solid, white. **Spores** white, subglobose, 9–12.7 μ broad.

Woods and open spaces. July to September. This species is closely related to *Lactarius piperatus* (Scop.) Fr. (figure 98) and *L. vellereus* Fr. Its taste is very hot and peppery when raw, but fried in butter it makes an acceptable dish in which no trace of acridity is noticeable. Being bulky and rather plentiful, it helps to fill the basket when one is out after edible species.

DELICIOUS LACTARIUS (Edible)

Lactarius deliciosus (L.) Fr.

Cap 2–5 in. broad, at first convex and subumbilicate, then nearly plane or subinfundibuliform, *yellowish-orange* *or grayish-orange* varied by brighter spots and zones, fading to grayish-yellow when old or dry, *milk orange-colored.* **Gills** close, *orange-colored* with paler reflec-

Photo by C. E. Cummings. Courtesy
Buffalo Society of Natural Sciences

Figure 98 *Lactarius piperatus,* here represented, is very closely related to *L. deceptivus,* described on page 362. The latter has the margin covered with cottony flocci; in the former, the margin is naked, even in young specimens. Note the deposit of the white spore-rain on the dead leaves, etc., under and around the plant

tions, less clear orange and often greenish-stained with age. **Stem** 2–4 in. long, 4–8 lines thick, nearly equal, stuffed or hollow, often spotted, colored like the cap, sometimes hairy at the base. **Spores** subglobose, 7.6–10 μ.

In mossy places in deciduous or coniferous woods. July to September. Wounds often turn green. It is the commonest species of the group with colored milk, and very desirable for the table. Like all milk-mushrooms, it is especially appetizing when baked in a closed vessel. Compare the closely related *Lactarius chelidonium*.

INDIGO LACTARIUS
Lactarius indigo (Schw.) Fr.

Cap 2–5 in. broad, at first umbilicate, with the margin involute, then depressed or infundibuliform, *indigo-blue with a silvery-gray luster,* zonate, especially on the margin, sometimes spotted, becoming paler and less distinctly zonate with age or in drying, milk *dark-blue.* **Gills** close, *indigo-blue,* becoming yellowish and sometimes greenish with age. **Stem** short, 1–2 in. long, 6–10 lines thick, nearly equal, hollow, *colored like the cap, often spotted with blue.* **Spores** subglobose, 7.6–9 μ long.

Dry places, especially under or near Pine trees. July to September. This uniquely colored plant is not rare but it is seldom found in abundance.

SWEETISH LACTARIUS (Edible) Fig. 99
Lactarius subdulcis (Bull.) Fr.

Cap ½–2 in. broad, thin, convex, then plane or sub-infundibuliform, with or without a small umbo or papilla, glabrous, even, zoneless, moist or dry, tawny-red, cinna-mon-red or brownish-red, margin sometimes wavy or

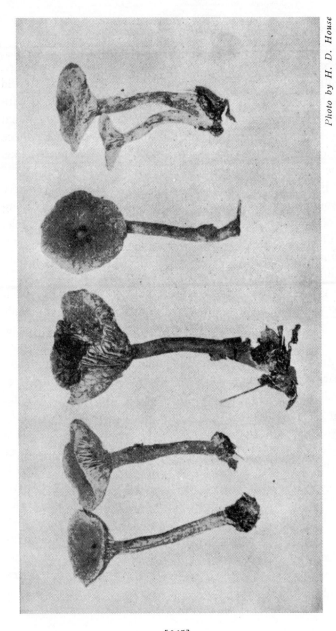

Figure 99 Sweetish Lactarius, *Lactarius subdulcis*, so common that one meets it in almost any woodland

[365]

flexuous, flesh whitish, pinkish or reddish-gray, *odorless,* milk white, taste mild or tardily and slightly acrid. **Gills** rather narrow, thin, close, whitish, sometimes tinged with red. **Stem** slender, 1–2½ in. long, 1–3 lines thick, equal or slightly tapering upward, glabrous, sometimes villose at the base, stuffed or hollow, paler than, or colored like, the cap. **Spores** white, globose, 7.6–9 µ in diameter.

Fields, copses, woods, swamps and wet places, on bare ground, among mosses or fallen leaves, also on decaying wood. July to October. Very common and variable. Gillet has described the following varieties. Var. *cinnamomeus:* cap cinnamon-red, somewhat shining; stem stuffed, then hollow, elastic, and furnished with a whitish or grayish tomentum or strigose villosity at the base, when growing among moss in swamps. Var. *rufus:* cap dull-chestnut-red, becoming concave; stem spongy; taste mild. Var. *badius:* cap bay-red, shining as if varnished, with an obtuse center and an inflexed, elegantly crenulate margin; stem very glabrous, hollow. The first and second varieties have been found in New York State. *Lactarius camphoratus* (Bull.) Fr. is much like *L. subdulcis,* except that it smells of dried melilot. *Lactarius rufus* (Scop.) Fr., a species given as poisonous by most writers, resembles both, but it is a much larger plant with a dark-red cap, a sometimes pruinose, similarly colored stem, and a very acrid taste. *Lactarius paludinellus* Pk., on the other hand, is much smaller, has a dingy-brownish cap that grows paler, and a striatulate margin. *Lactarius rimosellus* Pk. has the cap surface cracked into fine areolae. Occasionally *Lactarius subdulcis* produces supernumerary caps.

PURPLISH LACTARIUS (Edible)

Lactarius subpurpureus Pk.

Cap 2–3 in. broad, convex, becoming nearly plane or subinfundibuliform, glabrous, slightly viscid when moist, somewhat zonate, purplish-red with a grayish luster, assuming greenish stains where wounded or when old, flesh paler than the surface, milk *dark-red,* slightly acrid. **Gills** close, adnate or decurrent, purplish-red, becoming tinged with dull-yellow or stained with greenish hues when old. **Stem** 1½–3 in. long, 3–5 lines thick, equal or slightly tapering upward, hollow, glabrous or sometimes hairy at the base, adorned with a few round or oval, depressed, red spots. **Spores** subglobose, rough, 9–10 µ broad.

In woods and swamps among mosses and fallen leaves. July to October. Related to *Lactarius deliciosus,* but with dark-red, instead of orange, milk. The slightly acrid taste disappears in cooking.

ORANGE-BROWN LACTARIUS (Edible)

Lactarius volemus Fr.

Cap 2–5 in. broad, firm, convex, nearly plane or centrally depressed, rarely infundibuliform, sometimes with a small umbo, generally even, *glabrous,* dry, *golden-tawny or brownish-orange,* sometimes darker in the center, often becoming rimose-areolate, flesh firm, brittle, white or yellowish, milk *copious, white, mild.* **Gills** *close,* adnate or subdecurrent, white or yellowish, becoming sordid or brownish where bruised or wounded. **Stem** 1–4 in. long, 4–10 lines thick, subequal, firm, solid, glabrous or merely pruinose, colored like the cap, sometimes a little paler. **Spores** globose, white, 9–11.5 µ.

Thin woods and open places. July to September. In drying it smells of rotting fish. Var. *subrugosus* Pk. has the margin of the cap rugose-reticulate. Compare *Lactarius corrugis*. *L. volemus,* when baked, *en casserole,* with a few strips of bacon, makes an unforgettable delicacy.

Genus LENTINUS Fr. White-spored.

Texture tough, becoming almost wood-like when old and dry. The gill-edges are serrate, often coarsely so. The stem, when present, is lateral or excentric. *Panus,* which also has a tough substance, has even-edged gills, and *Schizophyllum,* of similar consistency, has the gill-edges divided longitudinally (see figure 20f). Compare *Pleurotus.*

SCALY LENTINUS. Fig. 57e

Lentinus lepideus Fr.

Cap 2–4 in. broad, fleshy, compact, tough, hard when dry, convex or nearly plane, sometimes slightly depressed in the center or umbonate, often irregular, the cuticle cracking and forming brownish, spot-like scales, white or pale-ochraceous, flesh tough, white. **Gills** subdistant, broad, sinuate-decurrent, transversely lacerate and dentate-serrate on their edges, white. **Stem** short, 1–2½ in. long, 3–6 lines thick, central or excentric, white or whitish, hard, solid, often pointed at the base, more or less adorned with recurved scales, sometimes furnished, when young, with an imperfect, evanescent ring, and, occasionally, with a few basal scales which simulate a volva. **Spores** elliptic, 10–12.7 x 5–6 μ.

On wood of coniferous trees, often causing the decay of fence posts, bridge timbers, and railroad ties. May to October. Very common. Its destructive effect on rail-

road ties has earned for it the name, "train-wrecker".
Lentinus spretus Pk. is a more slender plant with a thinner cap, smaller scales, more decurrent, nonsinuate gills,
and smaller spores (oblong, 7.6–10 x 4–5 μ). *Lentinus
tigrinus* (Bull.) Fr. is smaller than either, has a
thinner, umbilicate cap spotted with innate, hairy, blackish
scales, close gills, and still smaller spores (5–7.6 x 2.5–
4 μ). Sometimes specimens of *Lentinus lepideus* are
found in which the gills are obliterated or overrun by
a mass of mycelium. A special name, *Lentodium
squamulosum* Morg., was applied to this abnormal
condition.

GENUS' LEOTIA Pers. Fig. 100

Leotia lubrica (Scop.) Pers. is one of the commonest
representatives of the Geoglossaceae. It is usually found
growing in rich humus, or in sandy soil. In very wet
situations the plants are so viscid that it is quite diffcult
to keep a hold on them. The color is an ochraceous
yellow, tinged with olive green. Further description is
scarcely necessary.

GENUS LEPIOTA (Fr.) Quél. Spores white, rarely reddish or
greenish.

In this genus the spores are usually white, the gills free
(except in a group of species, the Granulosae, recently
transferred to *Armillaria* by Kauffman, '22), the stem
provided with a ring but devoid of a volva (except in
L. acutesquamosa [Weinm.] and *L. rhacodes,* in which
indications of at least the remains of this tissue are
observable). Excepting *Lepiota morgani,* and a few of
the smaller species (notably *L. helveola* Bres. and *L.
clypeolaria*), the genus is a safe one for the mushroom
eater.

AMERICAN LEPIOTA (Edible) Plate 24

Lepiota americana Pk.

Cap 1–4 in. broad, at first ovate, then convex or expanded, umbonate, squamose, white, the umbo and scales reddish or reddish-brown, margin generally marked

Photo by C. E. Cummings. Courtesy Buffalo Society of Natural Sciences

Figure 100 Slippery as an eel, it is almost impossible to get a good hold on specimens of *Leotia lubrica*, when one wishes to pluck them from their place of growth in dank woods.

with short, radiating lines or striations, especially in older plants. **Gills** close, free, white, more or less interconnected near the stem. **Stem** 3–5 in. long, 2–5 lines thick, white at first but soon assuming a brownish-vinous-red tint, somewhat thickened at or a little above the base, hollow. **Ring** membranous, small, thin except on the border where it is slightly thickened, evanescent. **Spores** subelliptic, uninucleate, 7.6–10 x 5–7.6 μ.

In grassy ground or on old stumps, also under hedges. July to October. *Easily known by the brownish-vinous-red color assumed by the plant in aging, and by the stem, which is shaped like an athlete's Indian club. Lepiota badhami* (Berk. and Br.) Sacc., of Europe, has a non-striate cap-margin, and the enlargement of the stem is confined to the base. The two species are very closely related, if not actually identical.

ONION-STEMMED LEPIOTA (Edible) Fig. 101

Lepiota cepaestipes (Sow.) Quél.

Cap ¾–3 in. broad, thin, fleshy in the center, ovate or obtusely conic, becoming campanulate or expanded, broadly umbonate, soon squamulose except in the center, dry, plicate-striate on the thin margin, white, the umbo and squamules brownish, flesh white, taste mild. **Gills** thin, narrow, close, free, white. **Stem** 1½–4¾ in. long, 2–3 lines thick above, slender, enlarged toward the base, slightly mealy, pruinose or glabrous, stuffed or hollow, white. **Ring** slight, evanescent. **Spores** white, 7.6–10 x 5–7.6 μ.

In rich soil, tan bark, sawdust, or decomposing vegetable matter, also in greenhouses and conservatories. June to September. Grows cespitosely. A lemon-yellow variety (var. *lutea*) sometimes occurs in cellars.

Photo by C. E. Cummings. Courtesy Buffalo Society of Natural Sciences

Figure 101 Onion-stemmed Lepiota, *Lepiota cepaestipes*, a species with a mealy covering. Normally it is glistening white, but a lemon-colored variety also occurs

SHIELD LEPIOTA

Lepiota clypeolaria (Bull.) Quél.

Cap 1–2½ in. broad, thin, soft, convex or subcampanulate, becoming nearly plane, obtuse or umbonate, squamose, whitish or yellowish, the center or umbo smooth, yellowish or brownish, margin often appendiculate with fragments of the ring, flesh white. **Gills** thin, close, free, white. **Stem** slender, 1½–3 in. long, 1½–3 lines thick, equal or slightly tapering upward, hollow, fragile, pallid, adorned with soft, loose, white or yellowish, floccose scales or filaments. **Ring** indefinite, consisting of soft, white, shaggy, projecting, cobwebby flocci on the upper part of the stem. **Spores** oblong or subfusiform, 12.7–20.3 x 6–7.6 μ (figure 24s).

In woods, especially in hilly and mountainous regions. July to October. Generally solitary or only a few in a place. *Lepiota metulaespora* Berk. and Br. is kept distinct by some writers on account of the striate margin of the cap.

MORGAN'S LEPIOTA (Unwholesome)

Lepiota morgani Pk.

Cap 4–8 in. broad, globose, then convex and finally flat, cuticle *creamy-buff* to pale-amber, soon breaking up into irregular scales or patches, somewhat after the fashion of *Lepiota procera*, flesh thick, firm, white. **Gills** free (remote), close, rather broad, ventricose, *white at first but soon changing to dull-green,* finally sordid. **Stem** 4–8 in. long, 5–9 lines thick, tapering upward from the club-shaped base, *hard, firm, glabrous,* whitish or grayish-white to pale-umber, stuffed with fibrils. **Ring** *large, thick,* movable. **Spores** (in mass) *at first bright-green, fading to dull-green, eventually sordid,* subelliptic, 9–12 x 6–8 μ (figure 24i).

In meadows, pastures, and in open woods. Gregarious, often forming huge "fairy-rings". This rather poisonous relative of the edible *Lepiota procera* grows mostly in the western and southern states. Recently, however, it has been reported from Canada. Compare *L. procera*.

SMOOTH LEPIOTA (Edible)

Lepiota naucinoides Pk.

Cap 2–4 in broad, convex to flattened-hemispheric, smooth or slightly mealy-granular in the center, white or smoky-white. **Gills** free, *white, slowly changing with age to a dirty-pinkish-brown or smoky-brown*. **Stem** 2–3 in. long, ¼–½ in. thick, colored like the cap, equal or slightly thicker in the middle and usually with a small, smooth bulb below, smooth, glabrous, colored like the cap, hollow or stuffed with webby or cottony fibrils in young plants. **Ring** narrow, white, slightly thickened on the margin, sometimes movable and frequently disappearing. **Spores** subelliptic, uniguttulate, *with a very faint suggestion of pink*, 7.6–10 μ long.

Grassy grounds, in lawns, by roadsides, rarely in cultivated fields or in thin woods. August to November. Scattered or gregarious. *Lepiota naucina* (Fr.) Sacc., of Europe (and Australia), differs in its spheric spores. *Lepiota schulzeri* (Kalchb.) Sacc., a closely related species with nauseating properties (as the writer can testify from personal experience), has a more obtuse cap that rests upon a rather weak, oblique stem with a pronounced, laterally bent bulb. The specimens eaten were found on an open lot among weeds, in Cambridge, Massachusetts. Five persons were affected by this mushroom which was collected for *Lepiota naucinoides*. Dearness ('11) mentions a similar case of poisoning due to *"Lepiota nau-cinoides."* Perhaps, in that case, too, the offender was *L. schulzeri.* Miss Wakefield's *L. nauseosa,* also rosy-gilled, seems to fit into this group of closely akin species. A very unusual form of *Lepiota naucinoides* sometimes occurs in which the surface of the cap is broken into rather large, thick scales. This form is known as var. *squamosa* Pk. Recently, the. author was favored with some very large, squamose specimens that appeared to fit in nowhere except under *L. naucinoides.* The plants were received from Doctor F. E. Daigneau, of Austin, Minnesota. The varietal name, **ponderosa,** would seem appropriate.

PARASOL MUSHROOM (Edible) PLATE 25. FIG. 65b

Lepiota procera (Scop.) S. F. Gray

Cap 3–6 in. broad, fleshy, ovate, then campanulate and expanded, *umbonate, covered with a rufous- to umber-colored cuticle which soon tears into scattered, loosely-attached scales* except on the umbo where it remains intact, between the scales the whitish-rufescent, radiately fibrillose surface is visible, flesh thick, soft, white. **Gills** broad, close, *white to slightly pinkish,* slightly narrower toward the stem from which they are separated to such a degree that a deep channel is formed. **Stem** tall, 6–10 in. or more long, about ½ in. thick, slightly attenuated upward from the bulbous base, colored like the cap but paler, *the cortex cracking to form minute, darkish scales,* the interstices whitish, hollow or cottony to webby-stuffed, *set into a socket in the cap.* **Ring** thick, soft, white, fluffy above, tougher and colored like the cap on the lower margin, soon movable on the stem like a bracelet. **Spores** ovate-elliptic, apiculate, 14–18 x 9–11 μ, with one or more oily guttulae (figure 24h).

In meadows, pastures, open woods, and by roadsides. July to September. Usually grows singly or scattered, sometimes in clusters of a few individuals. Not infrequently paler specimens occur, and in some the umbo is much reduced in size or almost entirely lacking. The latter are apt to be taken for *Lepiota rhacodes* which never has an umbo, but which is at once distinguishable by its perfectly smooth, thicker, white stem, by its huge ring, and by the smaller spores. *Lepiota morgani* Pk., a deleterious species, infrequent in the north Atlantic states, is so much like *L. procera* in general appearance that close attention must be paid to certain details in order to differentiate between the two. Morgan's Lepiota is a *much heavier plant, paler colored (creamy-buff scales on the cap, rather than brown ones), with a perfectly smooth, non-scaly stem and dull-green gills. L. procera* is one of the finest of all edible mushrooms!

RAGGED LEPIOTA (Edible)

Lepiota rhacodes (Vitt.) Quél.

Cap 4–6 in. broad, fleshy, globose, then convex and expanded or slightly depressed, *never umbonate,* the bay-brown, thick, smooth cuticle soon cracking and separating everywhere but on the broad, central, flat disk into large, irregularly shaped scales, the white, shaggy, fibrillose-tomentose, subcuticular surface showing between the scales, flesh very thick, soft, *white, changing immediately to saffron-red when cut or broken.* **Gills** broad, close, whitish or pinkish, tapering inward, remote from the apex of the stem. **Stem** thick, stout, 4–8 in. long, tapering upward from the very thick, obscurely margined bulb of the base, fistulose, fibrous-stuffed, smooth and glabrous, whitish, quickly changing to dirty grayish-saffron-red when handled. **Spores** elliptic-ovate, 10–12 x 6–8 μ.

In rich soil in fields and woods, also indoors, in riding stables, growing in the spent tan-bark covering the floor. Solitary or in dense clusters. Compare *Lepiota procera*. It is the equal of that species in edibility. Since it responds readily to pure culture methods of propagation it ought, in time, to rival *Psalliota campestris* as a market mushroom. It is a very large plant and grows luxuriantly in spent tan-bark. When in the button stage, the cap is inclosed in a pseudo-volva, the remains of which cause the obsoletely margined appearance on the base of the stems of specimens not too far advanced in age. Farlow and Burt (Farlow, '29) describe and figure *L. brunnea,* a new species which differs from *L. rhacodes* mainly in the much browner color of the cap and stem, in the striate stem, and in the smaller, truncate spores. The latter are shown in figure 24, at k.

GENUS LYCOPERDON Tourn.

Puffballs that open by a single, apical mouth. Usually of small size, as compared with the large Calvatias.

GEM-STUDDED PUFFBALL (Edible) FIGS. 61a, 102

Lycoperdon gemmatum Batsch.

Peridium 10–18 lines in diameter, globose or depressed-globose, generally narrowed below into a stem-like base, subumbonate, whitish or cinereous, often tinged with yellow, pinkish, or brown. *Warts generally unequal, the larger mostly gemmate or papilla-like, pointed at the apex,* *scattered among smaller, granular and more persistent ones,* at length falling off and leaving the surface areolate-dotted, or reticulate with a network of fine, dotted lines. **Capillitium** and spores greenish-yellow, then dingy-olive

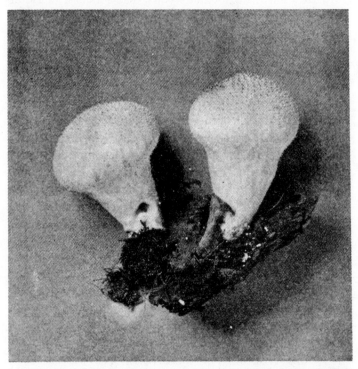

Photo by H. D. House

Figure 102 *Lycoperdon gemmatum,* the Gem-studded Puffball (see also fig. 61a), is not very large and its interior soon becomes soggy; hence it is not much sought as an esculent

or brown, columella present. **Spores** smooth or very minutely rough, 4–4.6 μ in diameter.

Ground and decaying wood in woods and fields. July

to October. Very common. Scattered, cespitose, or even densely cespitose. The stem varies much in length and sometimes it is entirely wanting. In some instances it is elongated nearly as much as in *Calvatia saccata.* It may be cylindric or tapering downward, nearly equal to the peridium in diameter or very much narrower. The warts, too, vary from almost hairy to coarsely papillose. The following varieties have been recognized. Var. *hirtum:* peridium top-shaped (turbinate), subsessile, hairy, with soft, slender warts which generally become blackish. Var. *papillatum:* peridium subrotund, sessile, papillose, furfuraceous-pulverulent. Var. *excipuliforme* (=*L. excipuliforme* Scop.): peridium subrotund, warts scattered and subspinulose. Stem elongated and subplicate at the base. Tufts two feet in diameter sometimes occur. Owing to its small size, the flesh soon changes color and is then no longer edible. Flavor not pleasant.

PEAR-SHAPED PUFFBALL (Edible) FIGS. 103, 104

Lycoperdon pyriforme Schaeff.

Peridium 6–15 lines broad, 10–20 lines high, obovate, pear- to top-shaped, sessile or with a short, stem-like base, radicating with white, branching and creeping, root-like fibers, subumbonate, covered with very minute, subpersistent, nearly uniform warts and scales, often with a few slender, scattered, deciduous spinules intermingled, pallid, dingy, whitish or brownish. **Capillitium** and spores greenish-yellow, then dingy-olivaceous, columella present. **Spores** smooth, 4 μ in diameter.

Decaying wood and ground in woods and cleared lands. July to October. Very common. Generally cespitose, forming (like *L. gemmatum*) large patches of hundreds

*Photo by C. E. Cummings. Courtesy
Buffalo Society of Natural Sciences*

Figure 103 The Pear-shaped Puffball, *Lycoperdon pyriforme,* is small, but as it sometimes occurs in great numbers (see picture on opposite
page), it may fill a good-sized basket

Figure 104 The Pear-shaped Puffball, *Lycoperdon piriforme,* shown covering an old, mossy tree base. The fruit-bodies are strung together on long, white, mycelial cords. See picture on opposite page

of individuals on old, prostrate, mossy logs, the individuals strung together on the intricately branching, coarse, mycelial strands. During wet weather the peridium frequently cracks into areas, a character properly belonging to plants of the genus *Calvatia*. In one form the peridium is abruptly narrowed into a small, distinctly scaly, stem. In another it is very pale in color and almost smooth, the warts being scarcely visible to the naked eye. Excellent when the flesh is white and hard.

PINKISH-BROWN PUFFBALL (Unwholesome)

Lycoperdon subincarnatum Pk.

Peridium 6–12 lines broad, globose, rarely either depressed or obovate, sessile, with but little cellular tissue at the base, covered with minute, nearly uniform, pyramidal or subspinulose, at length deciduous, warts, pinkish-brown, the denuded peridium whitish or cinereous, *minutely reticulate-pitted*. **Capillitium** and spores greenish-yellow, then dingy-olivaceous, columella present. **Spores** minutely rough, 4–4.6 μ in diameter.

On prostrate trunks, old stumps, etc., in woods, not on the ground, nor in clearings. August to October. Common. Gregarious or cespitose, occasionally in dense patches, the individuals attached to creeping, white, root-like fibers. The little pits or depressions, left on the peridium by the deciduous warts, are smaller and deeper than those of *Lycoperdon gemmatum,* and are not surrounded by dotted lines. The plant should not be eaten, as prolonged diarrhea is likely to be the result.

WRIGHT'S PUFFBALL (Edible)

Lycoperdon wrightii Berk. and Curt.

Peridium ½–2 in. in diameter, globose, depressed-globose or lentiform, generally sessile, white or whitish, echinate with deciduous, sometimes crowded, stellate spines or pyramidal warts, smooth or minutely velvety when denuded. **Capillitium** and spores dingy-olive, columella present. **Spores** smooth, 4 μ in diameter.

In pastures and grassy places (lawns, etc.), also in cultivated grounds and stubble fields. July to October. Very common. Generally grows gregariously but sometimes it forms tufts of several individuals closely crowded together. The under surface is occasionally plicate as in *Calvatia saccata*. When the denuded surface of the peridium is velvety, it is usually of a darker color than when smooth, being subcinnamon, reddish-brown or dark-brown. Three varieties exist. Var. *typicum* (=*L. wrightii* Berk. and Curt.) : small, 6–9 lines broad, globose, minutely echinate, the warts quickly falling off and leaving the peridium smooth. Var. *separans* (= *L. separans* Pk.) : larger, 10–24 lines broad, subglobose or lentiform, echinate with coarse, substellate spines or pyramidal warts, which at length fall off leaving the peridium smooth or velvety. The warts or spines are crowded at their thickened bases and slightly attached to each other so that they come off at maturity in flakes or patches. Var. *atropunctum*: also larger than var. *typicum,* 10–15 lines broad, subglobose, pure white, warts or coarse spines brown or blackish at the tips.

GENUS MARASMIUS Fr. Spores white.

Marasmius species are very apt to be taken for Collybias, but they are readily distinguished by the substance of their caps, which is somewhat tough and persistent in drying, and revives on the application of moisture. In Collybias it is fleshy, and putrescent with age. *Marasmius oreades,* the Fairy-ring Mushroom, is a well-known member of the genus. For the most part the species are small, and unimportant from the standpoint of edibility.

BLACK-STEMMED MARASMIUS
Marasmius androsaceus (L.) Fr.

Cap 1½–6 lines broad, membranous, convex, subumbilicate, glabrous, fuscous or often with a pinkish tint, sometimes nearly white, margin striate. **Gills** simple, distinct, subdistant, adnate, whitish. **Stem** ¾–2 in. long, ¼ line thick, horny, contorted and sulcate when dry, hollow, black, glabrous. **Spores** ovoid-ellipsoid or oblong, 6–9 x 3 μ.

On dead needles in Pine woods. Summer and autumn. Very common. Peck differentiates between a pale form, on Spruce needles, and a dark-capped one, on Pine needles. Another species, *Marasmius melanopus* Morg., which seems to grow only on the leaves of deciduous trees, has purplish-gray gills, a non-striate cap, and smaller spores.

FAIRY-RING MUSHROOM; SCOTCH BONNETS (Edible) Fig. 105
Marasmius oreades (Bolt.) Fr.

Cap 1¼–2 in. broad, fleshy, tough, convex, plane or subumbonate, white to pale-tan or pale-reddish, glabrous, margin at first involute, smooth, even, sometimes reflexed in age or in dried plants, flesh somewhat tough, thick at the disk, whitish, taste pleasant, odor fragrant. **Gills** thickish, white, yellowish when dry, broad, *distant,* free. **Stem** 1½–2 in. long, $\frac{2}{16}$–$\frac{3}{16}$ in. thick, pallid, solid, corticate, *with a whitish, villose, interwoven cuticle, appearing nearly smooth or slightly villose-pubescent.* **Spores** 7–9 x 4–5 μ.

Lawns and grassy places where it is usually found growing in circles (see Fairy-rings, p. 44). Common. Its habitat, its pale-tan-color, the broad umbo, together with the curious, whitish, appressed down that clothes

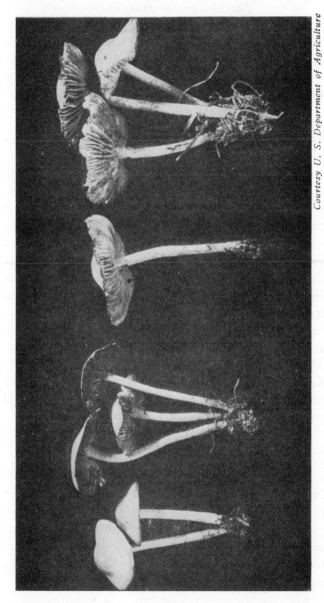

Courtesy U. S. Department of Agriculture

Figure 105 The familiar Fairy-ring Mushroom, *Marasmius oreades*, common on lawns, golf links and other grassy places

its stem, are distinguishing characteristics. Sometimes, when growing in deep grass, the stem is very much longer than indicated. Prussic acid, in minute quantity, has been found in the tissues of this perfectly harmless species.

LITTLE WHEEL MARASMIUS. Fig. 106
Marasmius rotula (Scop.) Fr.

Cap 1½–5 lines broad, membranous, convex, umbilicate, gregarious or subcespitose, dull-whitish, often light-brown in dried plants, disk sometimes darker, margin plicate. **Gills** few, broad, distant, whitish, *joined behind into a free collar which encircles the stem.* **Stem** ¾–2 in. long, less than ½ line thick, fistulose, horny, smooth, shining, blackish-brown, inserted into the substratum, or arising from rhizomorphic strands, occasionally capless. **Spores** 6–8 x 3–4 μ.

On dead leaves, wood and bark in woods, sometimes in great numbers. Summer and autumn. Even though common, it is always a pleasure to encounter this delicately wrought, little agaric. *Marasmius capillaris* Morg., except for its smaller size, brownish cap (with white center), and larger spores, is much like *M. rotula.*

GARLIC MARASMIUS (Edible)
Marasmius scorodonius Fr.

Cap ½–¾ in. broad, soft, fleshy, soon expanded, at first even and rufous, soon becoming rugulose, crisped and white, *flesh smelling strongly of garlic.* **Gills** adnate, crisped, white. **Stem** 1–1¾ in. long, ½–1 line thick, firm, horny, hollow, equal or enlarged above, red or reddish-brown, glabrous, shining. **Spores** 6–8 x 3–4 μ.

Photo by C. E. Cummings. Courtesy Buffalo Society of Natural Sciences

Figure 106 Little Wheel Marasmius, *Marasmius rotula*. Its gills are wrought with the skill of an expert mechanician. It is at its best just after heavy rains. In dry weather the plants shrink so as to become almost invisible

On decaying twigs, needles, etc., in woods. Common. Summer and autumn. Peck compares the odor to that of skunk cabbage. In the author's opinion the plant smells of garlic. Sometimes, as one enters a forest, the odor is so strong that one notices it before the plants are espied. *Marasmius alliatus* (Schaeff.) Schroet. is an earlier name for the same species. *Marasmius calopus* (Pers.) Fr. is very near it, differing mainly in the absence of the odor.

DRY MARASMIUS
Marasmius siccus (Schw.) Fr.

Cap ¼–⅝ in. broad, membranous, convex or campanulate, dry, glabrous, ochraceous, sometimes pink, rarely gray in dry plants, *margin conspicuously radiate-sulcate*. **Gills** somewhat free, narrowed behind, few, distant, broad, white. **Stem** 1–2 in. long, ½–1 line thick, slender, not capillary, tough, hollow, blackish-brown, glabrous, shining. **Spores** 12–15 x 6–7 μ.

On dead leaves in woods. Summer and autumn. Grows solitary or in troops. Very common and variable. The smaller *Marasmius pulcherripes* Pk. has a red or purplish-red cap and a stem that is clear-red at the top. It may be a mere form of *M. siccus*.

GENUS MORCHELLA (Dill.) Pers.

The species of *Morchella* have rather large, pitted caps. All are edible when in fresh condition. Compare remarks under *Gyromitra*.

NARROW-CAPPED MOREL (Edible)
Morchella angusticeps Pk.

Plant commonly 2–3 in. high, with the cap generally less than an inch broad in its widest part, but sometimes much larger specimens occur. The species differs from *Morchella conica* in its generally smaller size, more pointed cap and comparatively thicker stem. Usually the cap is scarcely thicker than the stem, even at its base, which is its thickest part. It is long and narrow and sometimes curved. Sometimes the stem tapers downwards.

Habitat and time of appearance the same as for *Morchella esculenta.*

TWO-SPORED MOREL (Edible) Fig. 107

Morchella bispora Sor.

In external appearance this morel is very similar to *Morchella hybrida,* but if the under side of the cap be examined, it will be found that whereas the latter species has this part only half free from the stem, the former has it entirely free or almost so, only the inner, upper portion being continuous with the stem. In the genus *Verpa* a similar condition is seen, but the caps in members of that genus are smooth or merely wrinkled, not ridged and pitted as in this and all other morels. Another feature which at once distinguishes it from its congeners is the presence of only two spores in each ascus, eight being the usual number. The stem is hollow in the American plant, not stuffed, as called for by the descriptions of European specimens. Perhaps our plants are stuffed when young. It is one of the rarest species.

CONIC MOREL (Edible)

Morchella conica Pers.

Plant commonly 3–5 in. high, with the cap 1½–2 in. thick in its broadest part, and distinctly broader than the stem. The longitudinal ridges on its surface run more

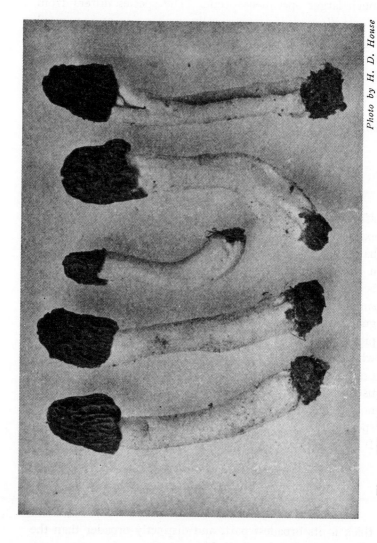

Figure 107 Two-spored Morel, *Morchella bispora*. Differs from the regular Morels in having but two spores in each ascus

regularly from top to base than in *Morchella esculenta*. They are connected by short, transverse ridges which are so far apart from each other, or so incomplete, that the resulting pits or depressions are generally longer than broad, and sometimes rather irregular. The color in the young plant is a beautiful buff-yellow or very pale-ochraceous, but it becomes darker with age.

Habitat and time of appearance the same as for *Morchella esculenta*.

THICK-STEMMED MOREL (Edible) Plate 26

Morchella crassipes (Vent.) Pers.

Cap large, somewhat conic, brown, adnate at the base; ribs irregularly undulating, thick; pits large, variable in form, deep, the bottom cellulose-plicate. **Stem** large, tall, thickened at the base, grooved (lacunose), glabrous, somewhat flesh-colored. **Spores** elliptic, yellowish, 24 x 12 μ.

On the ground. Spring. Sometimes the plants attain a height of one foot.

DELICIOUS MOREL (Edible)

Morchella deliciosa Fr.

Plant varies from 1½–3 in. high. It is easily known by its cap, which is cylindrical or nearly so. Sometimes it is slightly narrowed toward the top and occasionally curved, as in *Morchella angusticeps,* but because of its long, narrow shape and almost constantly blunt apex it is separable from that species. It is usually two or three times as long as it is broad, and generally longer than the stem. Specimens also occur in which the cap is slightly narrower in the middle than it is above or below.

The pits on its surface are rather narrow and mostly longer than broad. The stem is often short.

In grassy places. Time of occurrence the same as for the other morels. Authorities agree in pronouncing this species especially agreeable to the taste.

TRUE MOREL (Edible) FIG. 50b

Morchella esculenta (L.) Pers.

Plant commonly 2–4 in. high, stem ½ in. or more thick. The cap is generally a little longer than broad, sometimes nearly globose and slightly narrowed toward the top. The pits or depressions in its surface are rather broader and more rounded than in the other species, thereby giving the surface the appearance of a honeycomb. **Cap** variable in color, ochraceous to olivaceous-gray. Stem pale, whitish.

In old apple orchards, under elms, and on burnt-over, wooded ground; in sandy, gravelly, or clayey soils. Early in spring or, rarely, late in autumn. One of the most sought-after of all mushrooms and, unlike *Gyromitra,* perfectly safe to eat. It is said to be parasitic on sunflower roots (Roze, 1882).

HYBRID MOREL (Edible)

Morchella hybrida (Sow.) Pers.

Plants 2–4 in. high. **Cap** conic, the lower half free from the stem, rarely more than 1 or 1½ in. in length, usually much shorter than the stem. The pits on the surface are longer than broad. Deformed specimens occur in which the cap is hemispheric and very blunt or obtuse at the apex, while in others it is abruptly narrowed above and pointed. The flavor is said to be less agreeable than that of *Morchella esculenta*. *Morchella semilibera* DC. is another name for the plant. It is rather rare.

GENUS MYCENA (Fr.) Quél. White-spored.

Mycena is close to *Collybia* from which it differs in the straight margin of the cap. The species are of small or medium size, symmetrical, and often beautifully colored. The presence or absence of cystidia should be carefully noted, as well as the number of spores borne on a basidium (see Smith, A. H., '34a.). The stems of some species exude a juice.

BLEEDING MYCENA. Fig. 108

Mycena haematopus (Pers.) Quél.

Cap ¾–1½ in. broad, reddish, disk darker, obtuse-campanulate, *margin denticulate*. **Gills** adnate, whitish to flesh-color or violaceous, edges concolorous. **Stem** 2–4 in. long, ⅛–³⁄₁₆ in. thick, reddish, white-pulverulent, *containing a dusky-red juice*. **Spores** white, broadly elliptic, 10 x 6 μ.

Grows cespitosely on fallen tree trunks, especially of Birch. Autumn.

GENUS NAUCORIA (Fr.) Quél. Spores ocher-brown to rusty-brown.

This genus corresponds to *Psilocybe* and *Collybia*. There is no veil except in extremely young specimens. The cap is incurved at first, and the stem subcartilaginous, hollow or stuffed. Pholiotas with fugacious rings are apt to be sought in *Naucoria*. The spores are smooth.

Photo by C. E. Cummings. Courtesy Buffalo Society of Natural Sciences

Figure 108   When the stems of this lovely little *Mycena* (*M. haematopus*) are broken, a dark red juice gushes forth in droplets. This characteristic, along with the notched margin of the cap, at once marks this none too common species.

HEMISPHERIC NAUCORIA

Naucoria semiorbicularis (Bull.) Quél.

Cap ½–1½ in. broad, persistently hemispheric until well into maturity, glabrous, somewhat viscid, brownish-yellow, becoming ochraceous and somewhat wrinkled or even rimose with age, odor cucumber-like. **Gills** adnate to somewhat sinuate, sometimes seceding, close, pallid, slowly becoming rusty-brown, as the spores ripen. **Stem** up to 2½ in. long, about ⅛ in. thick, equal, to somewhat thickened at the base, somewhat rigid and tough, ochraceous to paler, smooth, *stuffed with a removable, white pith within.* **Spores** elliptic-ovate, 12–13.2 x 7.5–8.8 μ (figure 24r). Very common on lawns and other grassy places, from early spring to autumn.

Genus OMPHALIA (Fr.) Quél. White-spored.

Omphalia is close to *Clitocybe,* from which it differs in its cartilaginous stem and in its umbilicate cap. The plants are usually small.

BELL OMPHALIA. Fig. 109

Omphalia campanella (Batsch) Quél.

Cap less than ½ in. broad, convex, umbilicate, hygrophanous, rusty-yellow, striate. **Gills** yellow, arcuate, connected by veins. **Stem** ¾–1¼ in. long, thin, horny, bay-brown, base narrowed, tawny-strigose. **Spores** white, elliptic, 8–9 x 3–4 μ.

On fallen trunks of conifers, in dense cespitose masses. August and September.

Genus OTIDEA Pers. Fig. 110.

Much like *Peziza* except for the elongate, rabbit-ear-like shape of the fruit-bodies which are bright yellow to

Photo by C. E. Cummings. Courtesy Buffalo Society of Natural Sciences

Figure 109 Old mossy, fallen tree trunks are often covered with literally thousands of these little, rusty-red agarics. They are known as *Omphalia campanella*

Photo by C. E. Cummings. Courtesy Buffalo Society of Natural Sciences

Figure 110 Looking down on a cluster formed by a species of *Otidea* (*O. leporina*), a genus in which the fruit body is shaped somewhat like a rabbit's ear

yellow-brown, and occur in woods, growing on the ground.
Because of their inconspicuous coloring they are easily
overlooked. The species figured is *Otidea leporina* Fckl.

Genus PANAEOLUS Fr.   Spores black.

Species belonging to this genus are discussed on p. 147.

Genus PANUS Fr.   Spores white.

The fruit-bodies of plants belonging to this genus are
somewhat tough (almost coriaceous), like those of the
Lentini, but the gill-edges are entire, not serrate or lacerate. The stem may be centrally attached, lateral and short,
or entirely wanting. The consistency of the fruit-bodies
of *Pleurotus* species is more fleshy.

ASTRINGENT PANUS (Unwholesome)

Panus stipticus (Bull.) Fr.

Cap ½–1¼ in. broad, pale-cinnamon, becoming paler
and whitish, somewhat kidney-shaped (subreniform),
convex, depressed and abruptly narrowed behind, surface
breaking up into furfuraceous scales. **Gills** crowded,
cinnamon-colored, *ending abruptly behind on a distinct
line, beautifully veined deep down between the individual
gills.* **Stem** short, lateral, solid, compressed, pruinose,
paler than the gills. **Spores** narrowly oblong, smooth,
white, minute, 4–5 x 2 μ.

Common throughout the growing season of mushrooms,
on old stumps, logs, branches, etc. The taste is very
astringent. A luminescent form occurs in this country
(*P. stipticus* forma *luminescens*).

GᴇɴᴜS PAXILLUS Fr.   Spores more or less ochraceous

In *Paxillus,* the gills are usually decurrent, forked, and anastomosing on the stem, and separable from the under surface of the cap.   Some species of *Tricholoma* (*T. nudum,* for example) also exhibit the last mentioned character, but their spores, though not white (as they should be in any good *Tricholoma*) are not so distinctly ochraceous as in true Paxilli.   The genus name, *Lepista,* has been proposed for such aberrant Tricholomata.   *Paxillus* forms a stepping stone from the gill mushrooms to the Boleti.   Compare *Paxillus rhodoxanthus* with *Boletus chrysenteron.*

INROLLED PAXILLUS (Edible) Fɪɢ. 57i

Paxillus involutus (Batsch) Fr.

Cap 2–4 in. broad, compact, convex at first, soon expanded and centrally depressed, nearly glabrous, grayish-buff or ochraceous-brown or yellowish-ferruginous, *the margin rather persistently involute and, when young, covered with a grayish tomentum that exhibits fine, radiating markings* (the imprints of the gill edges), flesh not clear white, but tinged with gray.   **Gills** close, decurrent, *branched, and reticulately connected behind,* the interspaces bridged by veins, whitish, then dull yellowish or subferruginous, changing to reddish-brown where cut or bruised.   **Stem** 1–3 in. long, 3–6 lines thick, central or excentric, solid, glabrous, colored like the cap, sometimes with a few darker spots.   **Spores** ferruginous, elliptic, 7.6–10 µ long.

In mixed woods either on the ground or on decayed wood, a favorite place being on mossy, rocky embankments by roadsides.   It also occurs in cool Hemlock or Spruce forests and along the borders of marshes.   August to

November. Not highly regarded as an edible species, except in Russia. *P. atrotomentosus* Fr., a large, heavy plant, has the thick stem covered with a dense, blackish-brown tomentum.

RED-AND-YELLOW PAXILLUS (Edible)

Paxillus rhodoxanthus Schw.

Cap 1½–3½ in. broad, firm, convex, obtuse, expanded or depressed, somewhat top-shaped, reddish-rusty-brown, chestnut-brown or pale-cinnamon, minutely tomentose, becoming smooth, dry, frequently cracked into fine areolae, flesh thick in the center, pallid, tinged with yellow. **Gills** *bright-yellow,* close to sub-distant, thickish, broader toward the stem, arcuate-decurrent, rarely unattached to each other, *generally forking and inter-connected by veins, sometimes almost pore-like where they reach the stem.* **Stem** 1½–3 in. long, 2½–5 lines thick, equal or ventricose, solid, reddish-yellow, yellow at the base, dotted with small, reddish-brown scales. **Spores** yellowish in mass, elongate-oblong, almost fusiform, 9–12 x 3–4.5 μ.

Ground in woods or their borders. July to September. Gregarious or scattered. Viewed from above, the plant looks much like *Boletus chrysenteron.* Not until it is plucked, and the gills are seen, does one realize that it is an agaric, and not a *Boletus.*

Genus PEZIZA (Dill.) L. Fig 111.

The figure presents one of the commoner species of this genus, *Peziza badia* Pers. The colors are tan to dark-brown. Pezizas are to be sought in the springtime. The reader is referred to Dr. Seaver's monograph (Seaver, '28) for an exhaustive treatment of the genus *Peziza* and the other genera of the operculate Ascomycetes.

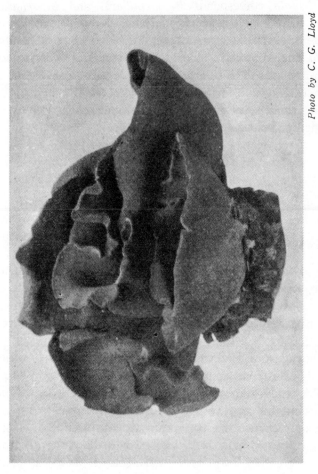

Photo by C. G. Lloyd

Figure 111 *Peziza badia.* Pezizas are simple, large cups, and, like the Morel, belong to those fungi which bear their spores in microscopic sacs

GENUS PHOLIOTA (Fr.) Quél. Spores ocher- or rusty-brown.

Pholiota corresponds to *Armillaria* and *Stropharia.*
The veil, though fugacious in some species, is usually a
more or less distinct membrane, not fibrillose as in *Flammula,* nor cobwebby, like the cortina of *Cortinarius.*
Compare also *Hebeloma. Pholiota* was considered a
rather safe genus from the mushroom eater's standpoint,
until a small species, *Pholiota autumnalis,* was found to
be deadly poisonous.

FAT PHOLIOTA (Edible)
Pholiota adiposa Fr.

Cap 2–4 in. broad, fleshy, firm, at first hemispheric or
subconic, then convex, very viscid or glutinous when
moist, squamose, yellow, flesh whitish. **Gills** close, adnate,
yellowish, becoming ferruginous with age. **Stem** 2–4 in.
long, 4–6 lines thick, equal or slightly thickened at the
base, squamose below the slight ring, solid or stuffed,
yellow, nearly white at the top, generally ferruginous at
the base. **Ring** very slight, floccose, radiating. **Spores**
elliptic, 7.6 x 5 μ.

On stumps or dead trunks of deciduous trees, in or near
woods ; also from wounds of living trees (Maple). September to November. Generally grows in tufts. The
scales on the cap are broad and may become erect or
reflexed. Sometimes their tips appear blackish. Most
frequently one finds them immersed in the gluten of the
cap where they form large, dark-colored blotches. The
flavor of the plant is agreeable and the substance is digestible and harmless. The closely related *Pholiota limonella*
Pk. is a smaller plant, with a thinner, more expanded cap
and with gills of the young plant whitish instead of

yellow. The color of the cap and stem is pale-yellow. Its habitat and mode of growth are the same as those of *Pholiota adiposa,* but the plant is rare.

AUTUMN PHOLIOTA (Deadly)

Pholiota autumnalis Pk.

Cap 6–16 lines broad, fleshy but thin, convex, hygrophanous, cinnamon-rufous and striatulate on the margin when moist, dingy-yellow when dry. **Gills** thin, close, slightly sinuate, adnate or slightly decurrent, yellowish, becoming subferruginous. **Stem** slender, 1–2 in. long, 1–2 lines thick, equal, hollow, fibrillose, colored like but paler than the cap, or sometimes brownish toward the base. **Spores** 7.6–10 x 5–6 μ.

On decaying wood in woods. September to November. Singly or cespitose. The ring is sometimes but slightly developed, and such specimens are liable to be mistakenly referred to the genus *Naucoria*. Small as it is, this plant caused the death of two children (Peck, '12). Extracts of this *Pholiota* are quite as poisonous as those obtained from *Amanita phalloides* (Ford and Clark, '14a).

WRINKLED PHOLIOTA; GYPSY (Edible) PLATE 27

Pholiota caperata (Pers.) Gill.

Cap 2–4 in. broad, fleshy, firm, thin toward the *radiately wrinkled margin,* ovate when young, becoming broadly campanulate or convex, obtuse, *glabrous except for the presence of a white pruinosity or of whitish flocci on and near the disk,* yellow, flesh white. **Gills** close, at first ascending and whitish, adnate, becoming brownish-ferruginous with age, *sides vertically wrinkled,* edges eroded. **Stem** 2–5 in. long, 6–10 lines thick, cylindric, equal, sometimes bulbous, glabrous or slightly flocculose, solid, white or whitish. **Ring** white, membranaceous, persistent, thick on the edge, usually turned upward.. **Volva** *slight, consisting of fine, upward-turned squamules near the base of the stem.* **Spores** brownish-ferruginous, subelliptic, rough with closely-placed, fine, dull, short points, 12.7–15.2 x 6.3–7.6 μ.

In woods, mossy swamps, and open places. July to September. Because of the presence of a volva-like structure at the base of the stem, a special genus, *Rozites,* was erected for it. It is fairly common and highly prized as an edible species.

HARDISH PHOLIOTA (Edible)

Pholiota duroides Pk.

Cap 1–2 in. broad, thin, convex, becoming nearly plane, glabrous or slightly rimose-squamose in the center, varying in color from creamy-white to ochraceous-buff either wholly or in the center only, flesh white, taste mild. **Gills** thin, close, narrow, adnexed, sometimes broadly sinuate and having a decurrent tooth, whitish, becoming brown or rusty-brown. **Stem** 1–2 in. long, 2–4 lines thick, equal or nearly so, stuffed or hollow, glabrous, whitish. **Ring** thick, cottony, white, often lacerated and evanescent. **Spores** broadly elliptic, 6–7 x 4–5 μ.

Rocky ground. August and September. Similar to *Pholiota dura* (Bolt.) Quél. from which its different colors, softer substance and smaller spores separate it. Its spores are also smaller (and browner) than those of *Pholiota praecox.*

EARLY PHOLIOTA (Edible)

Pholiota praecox (Pers.) Quél.

Cap 1–2 in. broad, convex or nearly plane, soft, nearly or quite glabrous, whitish, more or less tinged with yellow or tan-color. **Gills** close, adnexed, at first whitish to yellowish-gray, then brownish or rusty-brownish. **Stem** rather slender, 1½–3 in. long, 2–2½ lines thick, mealy or glabrous, stuffed or hollow, whitish. **Ring** small, evanescent, sometimes remaining as tattered fragments on the margin of the cap. **Spores** elliptic, rusty-brown, 10–12.7 x 6–7.6 μ.

Usually in grassy grounds, lawns and gardens. May to July. Several varieties have been noted. Var. *minor* Batt., a small plant having the cap only about one inch broad, and the remnants of the veil adherent to the margin of the cap. Var. *silvestris* Pk., with the center of the cap brownish or rusty-brown; grows in thin woods. *Pholiota temnophylla* (Pk.) Sacc. is distinguished by its dingy-yellow or ochraceous cap and by its very broad gills, which are obliquely truncate at their inner extremity. *Pholiota vermiflua* is larger and has a white, often areolate, cap, and appears later.

SHARP-SCALE PHOLIOTA (Edible) Figs. 112, 113

Pholiota squarrosoides Pk.

Cap 1–4 in. broad, fleshy, firm, whitish, subglobose when young, becoming convex, viscid when moist, adorned with terete, *erect, pointed, tawny scales* which are crowded in the center, scattered toward the margin, flesh white. **Gills** close, emarginate, whitish, becoming brownish-ferruginous with age. **Stem** 2–4 in. long, 3–5 lines thick, equal, firm, solid or stuffed, *rough with numerous,*

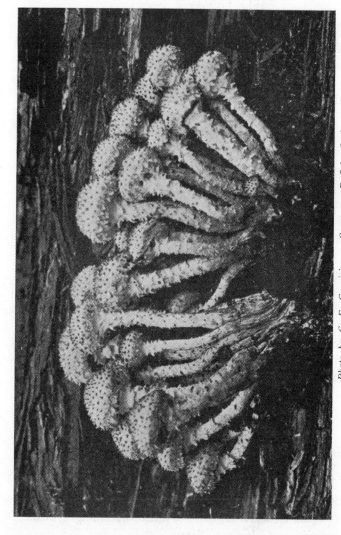

Photo by C. E. Cummings. Courtesy Buffalo Society of Natural Sciences

Figure 112 Sharp-scale Pholiota, *Pholiota squarrosoides*. A cluster of young specimens that will enliven the gloom of any forest. See picture on opposite page

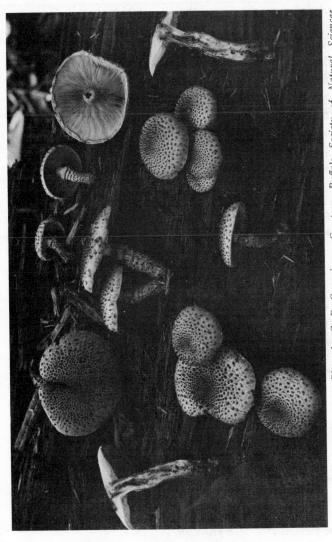

Photo by C. E. Cummings. Courtesy Buffalo Society of Natural Sciences

Figure 113 Sharp-scale Pholiota, *Pholiota squarrosoides*. Mature specimens. See picture on opposite page

recurved, tawny scales below the ring, white above. **Ring** floccose or lacerated. **Spores** minute, brownish-ferruginous, elliptic, 5 x 4 μ.

On dead or prostrate trunks or old stumps of Sugar Maple in woods. August and September. Singly or in dense tufts. Not uncommon. It is closely related to *Pholiota squarrosa* (Müll.), but is distinguished from it by its compact, papillose or almost spinose, erect, pointed scales, the viscid surface of its cap, its emarginate gills and its smaller, brownish-ferruginous spores. Var. *faginea* has the cap and scales smaller, and the latter more scattered. It grows on dead trunks of Beech. The caps of *P. squarrosoides* have a firm but excellently flavored flesh.

WORMY PHOLIOTA (Edible)

Pholiota vermiflua (Pk.) Sacc.

Cap 2–4 in. broad, convex or nearly plane, glabrous or sometimes floccose on the margin, *commonly rimose-areolate, especially in the center,* white, sometimes slightly tinged with yellow, flesh white. **Gills** close, adnexed, white, becoming ferruginous-brown, generally minutely eroded on their edges. **Stem** 2–3 in. long, 3–5 lines thick, equal, hollow, striate at the top, white. **Ring** white, more or less floccose on the lower surface, lacerated, often evanescent. **Spores** 12.7 x 7.6 μ.

Rich soil in grain fields, waste places, and about manure heaps. June to August. Its larger size, thicker flesh, stouter stem, whiter color, and the greater tendency of the surface of the cap to crack into areas, separate it from the related *Pholiota praecox.*

Genus PLEUROTUS (Fr.) Sacc. White-spored, with few exceptions.

Almost all Pleuroti grow on trees or on dead wood. Their stems, when present, are usually lateral, rarely central. *Panus* and *Schizophyllum* are distinguishable by their tough flesh. *Lentinus* by the tough flesh, together with the serrate edges of the gills. The larger Pleuroti are much sought for the table.

OYSTER MUSHROOM (Edible) Figs. 2f, 114
Pleurotus ostreatus (Jacq.) Quél.

Cap measurements as in *Pleurotus sapidus,* convex, soft, imbricated, glabrous, moist, whitish, grayish or brownish, flesh white. **Gills** broad, decurrent, anastomosing at the base, white or whitish. **Stem** (when present) generally shorter and more often lateral than in *Pleurotus sapidus,* firm, sometimes hairy at the base. **Spores** oblong, *white,* 7.6–10 µ long.

Habitat and time of occurrence the same as for *Pleurotus sapidus.* The white and smaller spores enable one to separate it from that species. Only young plants should be eaten, as older ones are inclined to be tough.

SAPID PLEUROTUS (Edible)
Pleurotus sapidus (Schulz.) Quél.

Cap 2–5 in. broad, convex or depressed, often irregular, glabrous, white, yellowish, ash-gray, dull lilac or even brownish, flesh white. **Gills** rather broad, subdistant, whitish, decurrent, often branched and interconnected where they run down on the stem, whitish or yellowish, sometimes presenting a tattered appearance. **Stems** generally short 1–2 in. long, 3–8 lines thick, tufted, two or

Photo by C. E. Cummings.   Courtesy
Buffalo   Society   of   Natural   Sciences

Figure 114   Oyster Mushroom, *Pleurotus ostreatus*

more growing from a common base, attached to the cap laterally or near the center (sometimes centrally attached), glabrous, solid and firm, white or whitish. **Spores** oblong, *pale-lilac,* 9–11.5 µ long.

In woods and open places, on decaying wood, on old stumps or prostrate trunks of trees, and occasionally on dead or dying trees still standing. Summer and autumn. It grows on a variety of deciduous trees such as Elm, Oak, Beech, Birch, Maple and Horse-chestnut. In Hungary it is not only eagerly sought growing wild, but cultivated on Elm trunks in gardens. Fried or stewed it makes a good dish. The lilac spores furnish a ready means of identification. The color should be ascertained from a deposit of the spores on white paper. *Pleurotus ostreatus* is closely related.

ELM PLEUROTUS (Edible)

Pleurotus ulmarius (Bull.) Quél.

Cap 3–5 in. broad, convex or nearly flat, firm, glabrous, white or centrally tinted with reddish-yellow or brownish, occasionally cracked into polygonal areas (var. *tessellatus* Bull.), flesh white. **Gills** rather broad, subdistant, rounded or notched at the inner extremity, adnexed, white or creamy-white. **Stem** 2–4 in. long, ½–¾ in. thick, firm, excentric (occasionally almost central), generally curved, white or whitish, sometimes a little downy or hairy at the base. **Spores** white, globose, 5–6.3 µ broad.

On standing Elm, Maple and Poplar trees, growing from dead places on the stumps of cut branches. September to November. When specimens grow from the top of a horizontal tree branch, the stems are central, and one is apt to search in the genus *Tricholoma* for a name. This not uncommon form is known as var. *verticalis.* A

European form has the entire stem covered with down or fine hairs. The Elm tree *Pleurotus* (as well as the other species of that genus here described) is held in high esteem by all mushroom-hungry Italians. It would seem that the plant might be "cultivated," after the manner employed by the Japanese with their "Shiitake," the cultivation consisting simply in stacking up a lot of Elm logs and sprinkling these occasionally with water containing the spores. One might even resort to inoculating the logs with the mycelium to insure prompt growth of the fungus.

Genus PLUTEUS (Fr.) Quél. Spores rosy.

A very distinct genus, with free gills, pink spores, and with a stem that lacks both ring and volva.

FAWN-COLORED PLUTEUS (Edible)

Pluteus cervinus (Schaeff.) Quél.

Cap 1½–4 in. broad, fleshy, very convex or campanulate, becoming broadly convex or nearly plane, glabrous or fibrillose, rarely squamulose in the center, variable in color, flesh white, taste disagreeable. **Gills** rather broad, close, rounded behind, free, white or whitish, becoming pink. **Stem** 2–6 in. long, 3–6 lines thick, equal or slightly tapering upward, solid, glabrous or slightly fibrillose. **Spores** pink, elliptic, 6.3–7.6 x 5–6.3 μ.

On decaying wood or other vegetable matter in woods or open places. May to October. The cystidia of this species are noteworthy, the ends of these bodies bearing from two to three prongs. The cap varies in color from white through yellowish and grayish to grayish-brown, and even to very dark-brown. The typical form is of a grayish-red or fawn, but specimens so colored are not known from New York State. Variety *albus* has both cap and stem white; variety *albipes* has only the stem white, the cap being grayish, yellowish or brown. The white-stemmed variety is sometimes found growing from sawdust in empty ice-houses. In view of the steadily decreasing supply of horse manure, used in the cultivation of the common Meadow Mushroom, this sawdust-inhabiting plant may help to prevent a possible dearth of cultivated, edible mushrooms. The disagreeable flavor of the fresh plant is destroyed in cooking.

Genus POLYPORUS Fr.

Polyporus, like *Hydnum,* and the old genus *Agaricus* of Fries, has been split up into a number of genera. As the name is used here, it comprises all polypores which, unlike the fleshy genera, *Boletinus, Boletus,* and *Strobilomyces,* are more or less fleshy-tough (becoming hard with age), and have a central, lateral stem, or none. The tube layer is simple, never stratified (as in *Fomes*), and the individual tubes do not enter the substance of the cap to different depths (as in *Trametes*). Such species as are sufficiently tender (mainly in youth) can be eaten, provided there are no other objections, such as acrid taste, etc. See also *Fistulina.*

FRONDOSE POLYPORUS; HEN OF THE WOODS (Edible)
FIG. 115

Polyporus frondosus (Dicks.) Fr.

Fruit-body composed of numerous rugose, lobed, fibrous-fleshy to leathery, smoky-gray caps which arise laterally attached from much-intergrown, white stems. **Pores** pure white, very small, round or very much torn. **Spores** subglobose to elliptic, smooth, hyaline (6 x 5 μ, punctate. Rea, '22).

From the base of living oaks. Autumn. Rather rare. Occasionally pure white forms occur. Fruit-body large, up to 16 in. in diameter. Caps ¾–2½ in. broad.

SHEEP POLYPORUS (Edible) FIG. 116
Polyporus ovinus (Schaeff.) Fr.

Cap 2–3 in. broad, compact but fragile, fleshy, variable in form, white, with a dull surface, smooth, but soon scaly cracked; flesh firm, white. **Pores** small, round, equal, white, then yellowish. **Stem** short, thick, 1–1½ in. long, generally central, dull white, unequal, sometimes bulbous. **Spores** subglobose, hyaline, smooth, guttulate, 3.5–4 μ.

In Pine woods. Rare. Autumn. The plant is apt to turn black in drying. *Polyporus confluens* (Alb. and Schw.) Fr. (when fresh and growing singly) looks somewhat like it, but it does not blacken; it reddens.

SCALY POLYPORUS (Edible) FIG. 117
Polyporus squamosus (Huds.) Fr.

Cap up to a foot or more broad, fan-shaped, flabelliform, tough-fleshy but pliant, ochraceous, covered with broad, appressed, dark scales; flesh white, thick, soft, becoming leathery. **Pores** thin, small, then large, angular and torn, white to pale yellowish. **Stem** thick, short, 1½ in. long, 1 in. thick, excentric or laterally attached to the cap or wanting, reticulated above from the descending pores, ochraceous, becoming black below and velvety. **Spores** broadly ovate, smooth, colorless, 5 x 12 μ.

Sometimes cespitose-imbricated and with longer stems. Grows on a variety of deciduous trees. It emits a strong odor. Said to be edible; perhaps, when very young.

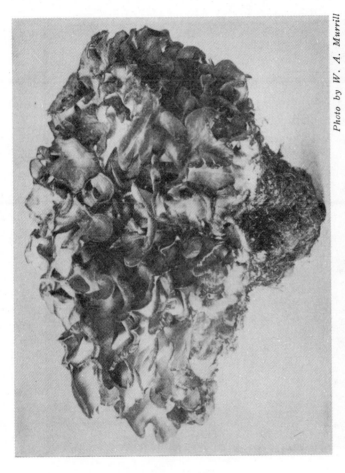

Photo by W. A. Murrill

Figure 115   Hen of the Woods, *Polyporus frondosus*, is a mass of laterally attached caps

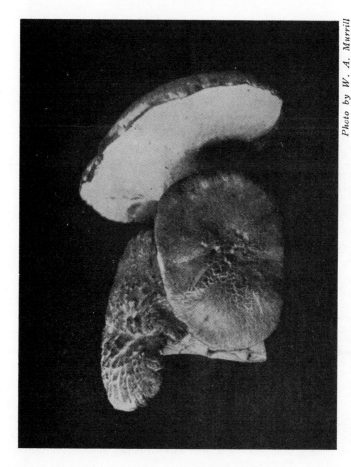

Photo by W. A. Murrill

Figure 116 Sheep Polyporus, *Polyporus ovinus*, is likely to be mistaken for a *Boletus*, but species of the latter genus are fleshy, whereas *Polyporus* species, with few exceptions, are either tough, corky, or even woody.

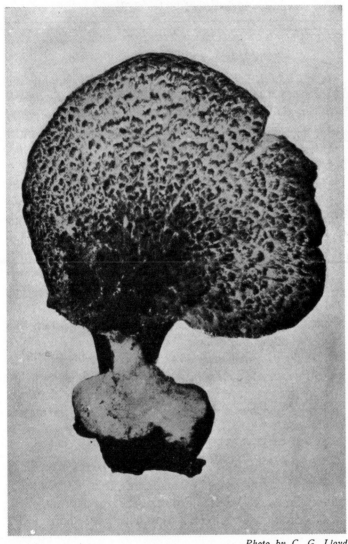

Figure 117 Top of the cap of the Scaly Polyporus, *Polyporus squamosus*. Usually several caps grow with their stems joined at the base

[417]

SULPHUROUS OR CHICKEN MUSHROOM (Edible) Plate 28. Fig. 42

Polyporus sulphureus (Bull.) Fr.

Caps up to 5 or 6 in. broad, closely overlapping each other (imbricated), somewhat irregular and wavy, uneven, reddish or orange-color when young and fresh, fading with age, flesh white, usually not more than ½ in. thick. **Tubes** minute, short, sulphur-yellow. **Spores** elliptic, white, 7.6 µ long.

In woods and in the open, from dead spots in the trunks of living trees of nearly all kinds, including fruit trees. June to September. This spectacularly colored polypore is not likely to escape the eye of the roaming and hungry mushroom hunter. Several varieties have been described. Var. *semialbinus* Pk. has white, imperfectly opened pores. This may be the same as the earlier described *Polyporus cincinnatus* Morg. Var. *overholtsii* Rosen ('27), from the South, has pinkish-salmon or salmon-buff caps and cream-colored tubes. Var. *glomeratus* Pk. has a multitude of small caps so closely and intimately united as to form a large mass in which their individuality is lost. The porous surface in this variety is partially developed in irregular holes or cavities in the surface of the mass.

UMBELLATE POLYPORUS (Edible) Fig. 118

Polyporus umbellatus Fr.

Fruit-body composed of numerous, thin, fleshy-fibrous, smoky-brown to white, fibrillose, more or less umbilicate and approximately circular caps which are more or less centrally attached to white, somewhat lengthened, separate stems united at the base to form a large clump. **Pores** small, unequal, white. **Stems** 2–3 in. or more long, 2–4 lines thick. **Spores** oblong, hyaline, 9–10 x 3–4 µ.

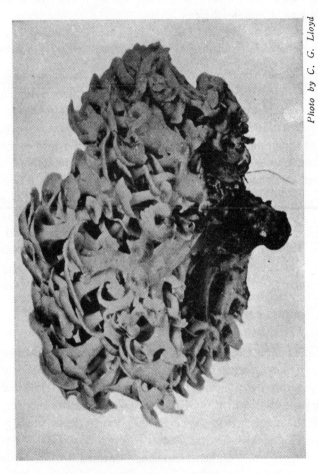

Photo by C. G. Lloyd

Figure 118 Umbellate Polyporus, *Polyporus umbellatus*. Each cap surmounts a little stem and the stems are joined together to form a large, fleshy base

[419]

At the base of oaks. Autumn. Rather infrequent. Fruit-bodies sometimes large, up to 8 in. or more in diameter. Caps 9–12 lines broad.

Genus PSALLIOTA Quél. (*Agaricus* of most writers) Spores purple-brown.

In this genus the spores are purple-brown, the gills free, there is a ring which may be single or double, when double the two are joined together, the lower one being either membranous and radiately split or divided into loose, floccose squamules. In *Psalliota rodmani,* the lower one is sometimes near the base of the stem, and it then appears to be a volva. No species has a true volva. The Meadow Mushroom is a member of this genus, and the other species are equally safe, except that poisonous Amanitas resemble in stature those that inhabit woodlands. The spore color is the determining feature when doubt exists. Compare *Stropharia, Hypholoma* and *Entoloma.*

ABRUPTLY BULBOUS MUSHROOM (Edible) FIG. 119
Psalliota abruptibulba (Pk.) Kauffm.

Cap 2–4 in. broad, ovate when young, becoming convex or nearly plane, rather thin and fragile, smooth or slightly silky, shining, white, usually becoming tinged with yellow in drying, flesh white. **Gills** narrow, close, thin, free, white or whitish when very young, soon pinkish, finally brown or blackish-brown. **Stem** 3–5 in. long, 3–6 lines thick, equal or slightly tapering upward, stuffed or hollow, terminating below in an abrupt, flattened bulb, white. **Ring** usually ample but variable, flabby, entire or torn, tomentose and yellowish on the lower surface, thin near the stem. **Spores** brown, elliptic, 6–7.6 x 4 μ.

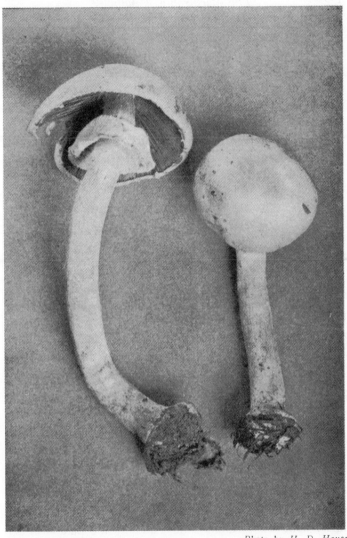

Photo by H. D. House

Figure 119   Abruptly Bulbous Mushroom, *Psalliota abruptibulba*.
This *Psalliota* is well named, as the abrupt bulb at the base of the
stem at once marks the plant

[421]

In thin woods or along their borders. July to September. Solitary, gregarious, or cespitose. Closely allied to *Psalliota silvicola* from which it differs in the abruptly flattened bulb at the base of the stem, and in the tomentose character of the lower surface of the ring. *Psalliota arvensis* is heavier in all its parts. The wooly layer on the under surface of the ring in the Abruptly Bulbous Psalliota sometimes separates into flakes of radiating patches, as in *P. arvensis*.

HORSE MUSHROOM (Edible) PLATE 29
Psalliota arvensis (Schaeff.) Quél.

Cap 3–5 in. or more broad, at first convex or conic-campanulate, then expanded, more or less appressedly fibrillose-squamulose, silky-shining, smooth, white, or yellowish on the disk, flesh white. **Gills** close, free, generally broader anteriorly, *at first whitish, then grayish-pink,* finally blackish-brown. **Stem** 2–5 in. long, 4–10 lines thick, equal or slightly thickened toward the base, white, staining yellowish, smooth, *hollow, or stuffed with a floccose pith.* **Ring** rather large, thick, *the lower or exterior, yellowish surface often cracked in a radiate manner.* **Spores** elliptic, purplish-brown, 6–7 x 4–5 μ (figure 24p).

Cultivated fields and pastures, but also on lawns and grassy places in woods. Summer and autumn. This species is at once distinguishable from the Meadow Mushroom, *Psalliota campestris,* by its large, thick ring (stellately split on its under side), and by the pale, whitish, young gills. Sometimes the cap attains gigantic proportions. It has a distinct, anise odor, and a sweetish taste. When old it is too tough to serve as food. Because of its excellent keeping qualities, this species (or one of its forms) has recently found its way into the mushroom trade. Its tough flesh and sweetish taste at once distinguish it from the true Meadow Mushroom.

MEADOW MUSHROOM (Edible) PLATE 29, FIGS. 2k, 120

Psalliota campestris (L.) Quél.

Cap 1½–4 in. or more broad, at first hemispheric or convex, then expanded, with decurved margin or nearly plane, smooth, silky-floccose or hairy-squamulose, white or brownish, the margin extending beyond the gills and often fringed and torn, flesh rather thick, firm, white. **Gills** free, close, ventricose, *at first a delicate pink or flesh-color,* then chocolate to blackish-brown, *subdeliquescent.* **Stem** 2–3 in. long, 4–8 lines thick, equal or slightly thickened toward the base, *stuffed,* white or whitish, nearly or quite smooth. **Ring** at or near the middle of the stem, more or less torn, sometimes delicate and evanescent. **Spores** elliptic, purplish-brown, 6.3–7.6 x 4–5 μ (figure 24o).

In fields, pastures, manured grounds, mushroom beds, etc., *never in woods.* Late summer and autumn, when growing in the open. This is the celebrated Meadow Mushroom that even the most timid do not hesitate to collect and eat. The clear-pink of the young gills, and the delicate veil distinguish this species from the other members of the genus *Psalliota.* How to distinguish it from the poisonous Amanitas has been told on p. 136. It is extremely variable, especially as to the scaliness of the cap.

Photo by W. A. Murrill

Figure 120 The well-known Meadow Mushroom, *Psalliota campestris*, brown, scaly variety

DIMINUTIVE PSALLIOTA (Edible)

Psalliota diminutiva (Pk.) Kauffm.

Cap 1–1½ in. broad, thin, fragile, at first convex, then plane or centrally depressed, sometimes slightly umbonate, whitish or pinkish-brown, faintly spotted with small, thin, silky, appressed, brownish scales, the disk brownish or reddish-brown. **Gills** close, thin, free, ventricose, dull-pink, then brownish-pink, becoming brown, blackish-brown, or black. **Stem** 1½–1¾ in. long, 1–2 lines thick, equal or slightly tapering upward, stuffed or hollow, smooth, whitish or pallid. **Ring** thin, persistent, white, slightly downy on the lower surface. **Spores** elliptic, purplish-brown, 5 x 3.8–4 μ.

In woods, among fallen leaves, on mossy ground, or in hollows at the base of old trees. Autumn. This small, fragile species resembles *Psalliota silvatica,* much reduced in size. Sometimes the whole surface of the cap is reddish.

BLEEDING MUSHROOM (Edible)

Psalliota haemorrhoidaria (Schulz.) Quél.

Cap 2–4 in. broad, fleshy, ovate or hemispheric, becoming broadly convex or nearly plane, fibrillose or squamose, brown with darker scales, flesh white or whitish, turning red where wounded, taste and odor agreeable. **Gills** rather broad, close, free, pink (rarely whitish when young), becoming brown. **Stem** 2–4 in long, 3–5 lines thick, equal or slightly tapering upward, sometimes bulbous, narrowly hollow, fibrillose, slightly squamulose toward the base, white, becoming darker with age. **Ring** membranaceous, persistent, silky and white or whitish, sometimes tinged with brown. **Spores** brown, elliptic, 6.3–7.6 x 4–5 μ.

In woods or bushy places, preferring damp soil rich in vegetable mold. August to October. Sometimes grows in clusters. It is easily recognized, when fresh, by the red color assumed by wounds of the flesh, either of the cap or stem. *Psalliota halophila* (Pk.) Kauffm. (=*P. maritima* Pk.) responds similarly when wounded, but that species has a solid stem, and grows by the sea. Var. *fumosa* Pk. has a shorter stem, and the cap is of a darker, smoky-brown color. It is sometimes abundant in low, damp ground on Long Island.

ALMOND MUSHROOM (Edible)

Psalliota micromegetha (Pk.) Kauffm.

Cap 1–3 in. broad, fleshy but thin, fragile, convex, becoming plane, sometimes slightly depressed in the center, dry, silky-fibrillose or fibrillose-squamulose, grayish-brown, darker (brown) in the center, often with yellowish or ferruginous stains, flesh white or whitish, not changing color where wounded, taste and odor of almonds. **Gills** thin, close, free, grayish, soon pinkish, finally brown. **Stem** 1–2 in. long, 3–5 lines thick, equal or slightly tapering upward, sometimes bulbous, stuffed or hollow, slightly fibrillose, white. **Ring** slight, often evanescent. **Spores** broadly elliptic or subglobose, 5 x 4 μ.

In sandy and clayey soil, and in tan yards, September to November. This is an uncommon species found in Massachusetts, Michigan and a few other states. It occurs singly or in clusters.

FLAT-CAPPED PSALLIOTA (Edible) FIGS. 121, 122

Psalliota placomyces (Pk.) Kauffm.

Cap 2–4 in. broad, fleshy but rather thin, at first convex or campanulate, then expanded and quite plane.

squamulose, whitish, *the disk and minute scales brown.*
Gills close, free, *white, then pinkish,* finally blackish-
brown. **Stem** 3–4½ in. long, 2–4 lines thick, smooth,
stuffed with a small pith, slightly tapering upward, *bulbous,* whitish, the bulb stained with yellow and *usually
giving rise to one or two mycelioid, white, root-like processes.* **Ring** large, thin, flabby. **Spores** elliptic, purplish-brown, 5–6.3 x 4–4.5 μ.

Under Hemlock trees. July. The flat cap, beautifully
decorated with numberless, minute, brown scales, the
bulbous stem, and the flabby ring mark this species.
Sometimes faint, radiating striae extend from the disk to
the margin of the cap. In damp weather the ring is
sometimes studded with drops of moisture of a dark color.
Compare *Psalliota silvatica* and *P. subrufescens.*

RODMAN'S PSALLIOTA (Edible)

Psalliota rodmani (Pk.) Kauffm.

Cap 2–4 in. broad, rather thick, firm, at first convex,
then nearly or quite plane, with decurved margin, smooth
or rarely rimose-squamose on the disk, white or whitish,
becoming yellowish or subochraceous on the disk, flesh
white, unchangeable. **Gills** close, *narrow,* rounded
behind, free, reaching nearly or quite to the stem, *at first
whitish, then pink or reddish-pink,* finally blackish-brown.
Stem short, 2–2½ in. long, 6–10 lines thick, subequal,
solid, whitish, smooth below the ring, often furfuraceous
or slightly mealy-squamulose above. **Ring** variable, generally rather thick, entire or torn, upper and lower margin projecting and *leaving a grooved band or collar on the
stem at or below the middle.* **Spores** purplish-brown,
almost globose, 5–6.3 x 4–5 μ. (figure 24 q).

Figure 121 Flat-capped Psalliota, *Psalliota placomyces*. Top view of caps showing the great number of fine, dark scales. In the center of the caps the cuticle remains intact. For a view of the underside of the caps, see picture on opposite page

Figure 122 Flat-capped Psalliota, Psalliota placomyces. A splendid collection showing the double ring, the lower one radiately split. For top view, see picture on opposite page

[429]

Grassy ground and paved gutters, generally where the soil is closely packed and hard. May to July. This species is intermediate between *Psalliota campestris* and *P. arvensis,* from both of which it may be distinguished by its narrow gills, solid stem and smaller, almost globose, spores. The cap has a tendency to crack into small areas or scales. The lower margin of the ring is in reality a sort of volva, the tissue of which, in young specimens, is continuous with the cuticle of the cap. In some specimens this lower portion of the ring is placed so low down on the stem as actually to suggest a true volva. The upper ring is sometimes impressed with radiating grooves, the result of intimate contact with the edges of the gills. Some Stropharias show similar impressions on their rings. It is closely related to *Psalliota bernardii* Quél. of Europe. Occasionally it grows in dense clusters. The flesh is rather tough. Except for that undesirable quality, it makes an excellent dish.

WOOD PSALLIOTA (Edible)

Psalliota silvatica (Schaeff.) Quél.

Cap 2–4 in. broad, thin, at first convex or campanulate, then expanded, *gibbous or subumbonate,* fibrillose or variegated with a few, thin, tawny, brownish or reddish-brown, *spot-like, appressed scales,* whitish, brownish or smoky-gray, the disk sometimes tinged with red or reddish-brown, flesh white or faintly reddish, odor strong. **Gills** thin, close, free, narrowed toward each end, reddish, then blackish-brown. **Stem** rather long, 3–4½ in. long, 4–6 lines thick, *equal or slightly tapering upward,* hollow, whitish, *not bulbous.* **Ring** simple, ample, white, somewhat striate above, flocculose below. **Spores** purplish-brown, 5–6.3 x 4–5 μ.

In woods. Summer and autumn. The absence of a bulb at the base of the stem distinguishes it from *Psalliota abruptibulba* and *P. placomyces*. In the latter the scales of the cap are much smaller and more numerous. *P. diminutiva,* a small species, resembles it somewhat.

SILVAN MUSHROOM (Edible)
Psalliota silvicola (Vitt.) Fr.

Cap 2–4 in. broad, convex or expanded, smooth or slightly silky, white, flesh white. **Gills** thin, close, rounded behind, free, pinkish when young, becoming darker with age, finally brown or blackish-brown. **Stem** long, 3–5 in. long, 3–6 lines thick, equal, smooth, stuffed or hollow, bulbous, white. **Ring** simple, lacking a tomentum on its under side. **Spores** elliptic, 7.6 x 4 μ.

In woods and groves. August to September. Mode of growth similar to that of *Psalliota abruptibulba* from which it is separated by its non-flattened bulb and by the simple, non-tomentose ring. It is not as common as that species.

REDDISH PSALLIOTA Plate 30
Psalliota subrufescens (Pk.) Kauffm.

Cap 2–4 in. broad, rather thin and fragile, at first deeply hemispheric, then convex and broadly expanded, often wavy or irregular, *silky fibrillose or minutely and obscurely squamulose,* varying in color from whitish or grayish to dull-reddish-brown, flesh white, unchangeable. **Gills** close, free, *at first white or yellowish-white,* then pinkish, finally blackish-brown. **Stem** 2–6 in. long, 4–8 lines thick, minutely floccose below the ring, hollow, white, somewhat thick or bulbous at the base. **Ring** membranous, white, externally flocculose. **Spores** elliptic, brown, 6–7 x 3.8–5 μ.

In leaf mold, also in greenhouses. August to October. Readily cultivated. Odor and taste of almonds. The mycelium is white and forms slender, branching, root-like strings. It differs from *Psalliota campestris* in the color of the young gills and in the large ring, flocculose on its under side. The squamules on the cap are much less apparent than those of *Psalliota placomyces* and *P. silvatica.* According to Farlow, the species is closely related, if not actually identical, with *Psalliota fabacea* (Berk.). *Psalliota amygdalina* M. A. Curtis is a synonym. Lange, the noted Danish agaricologist, says, that *P. subrufescens* is undoubtedly identical with *P. perrara* Schulz., of Europe.

Genus PSILOCYBE (Fr.) Sacc.

Spores more or less purplish-brown.

The species of this genus are, in many cases, rather difficult to separate from each other. Structurally, the genus corresponds to *Collybia, Naucoria,* and *Hebeloma.* The complete absence of a veil (except in a very young specimens of some species) separates it from *Hypholoma.*

HAYMAKER'S PSILOCYBE (Edible)

Psilocybe foenisecii (Pers.) Sacc.

Cap ½–1 in. broad, thin, campanulate or convex, obtuse, glabrous, hygrophanous, brown or reddish-brown when moist, paler when dry. **Gills** broad, ventricose, adnate, subdistant, brown. **Stem** 2–2¾ in. long, ¾–1 line thick, nearly straight, rigid, fragile, hollow, glabrous, pruinose at the top, pallid or rufescent. **Spores** brown, ovoid or unequally ellipsoid, obscurely and bluntly apiculate at one end, 12–16 x 8–10 µ.

Lawns and rich soil in grassy places. May to June. Gregarious. One of the commonest of mushrooms. Together with *Marasmius oreades* and *Galera tenera* it may be found in early summer on the lawns of any city park. The margin of the cap in fresh specimens is occasionally striatulate.

BAY-COLORED PSILOCYBE

Psilocybe spadicea (Fr.) Sacc.

Cap 1–2⅜ in. broad, fleshy, rigid, convex, becoming nearly plane, obtuse, scabrous, even, hygrophanous, bay or bay-brown when moist, pallid when dry. **Gills** close, rounded behind, adnexed, dry, whitish, becoming pinkish-brown. **Stem** 2–3¼ in. long, 2–3 lines thick, equal, rather tough, glabrous, hollow, even at the top, whitish. **Spores** brown, 8–9 x 4–5 μ.

Ground in woods, among fallen leaves, or on and about the base of trees. September. Commonly in tufts.

Genus RUSSULA (Pers.) Fr. Spores white or cream-color, in some species even yellow or ochraceous.

The dryness and brittleness of the flesh and gills are convenient ear-marks in the recognition of plants belonging in this difficult genus. (See Bataille, '07; Burlingham, '15; Crawshay, '30; Schaeffer, J., '33; Singer, '32.) As in *Lactarius,* the trama is composed of vesiculose tissue (see figure 20o), but no milk issues from the flesh or gills.

COMPACT RUSSULA (Edible)

Russula compacta Frost and Pk.

Cap 3–6 in. broad, fleshy, compact, broadly convex, sometimes umbilicate, becoming centrally depressed or even infundibuliform by the upcurving of the margin, dry or subviscid after heavy rain, unpolished, at first white or whitish, becoming rusty-ochraceous, flesh white, taste mild or sometimes slightly and tardily acrid, odor in drying strong and disagreeable. **Gills** rather close or sub-distant, adnate or slightly rounded behind, unequal, occasionally forked, white, becoming reddish-brown where wounded, and smoky-brown in drying. **Stem** short, stout, 1½–2½ in. long, 6–12 lines thick, equal or nearly so, solid, white, becoming stained with reddish-brown in handling or where wounded, and sometimes changing color like the cap. **Spores** globose or subglobose, 7.6–10 x 7.6 μ.

Ground in woods. July to September. *Russula magnifica* Pk., a related species, differs in its much larger size (cap up to 10 in. broad), in the rimose-squamose center of the cap in mature plants, in the slight, pinkish·tint of the gills, and in the strong alkaline taste and odor.

ENCRUSTED RUSSULA (Edible) PLATE 31

Russula crustosa Pk.

Cap 3–5 in. broad, convex, becoming nearly plane or centrally depressed, marked with small, appressed, areolate scales, except on the smooth, mostly depressed and sometimes subviscid, disk, *striate on the margin* when mature, color variable, straw-colored, pale-ochraceous, brownish-ochraceous, greenish or greenish-yellow, rarely brownish-purple, the center sometimes paler, sometimes darker than the margin, flesh white, also under the cuticle, *taste mild or slightly and tardily acrid*. **Gills** moderately close, narrowed toward the stem, some of them forked, some short, white. **Stem** short, stout, 1–2½ in. long, 6–12 lines thick, equal, stuffed or hollow, white. **Spores** subglobose, white, 7.6–10 x 6.3–7.6 µ.

Woods and open places. July and August. Common. The striate margin is a constant feature, at least when the plant is mature. *Russula cutifracta* Cke. has the flesh of the cap purplish under the cuticle, and *R. viridella* Pk. has a minutely squamulose or furfuraceous cap. Both species are extremely rare. Compare *Russula virescens*.

EMETIC RUSSULA (Unwholesome)

Russula emetica (Schaeff.) Pers.

Cap 2–3 in. broad, viscid, depressed, margin at length somewhat sulcate, cuticle separable, flesh white, red beneath the cuticle, *very acrid*. **Gills** persistently white, subdistant, free or adnexed, equal, edges not eroded. **Stem** white, softer within than on the surface, firm at first. **Spores** white, echinulate (7.5–10 µ, Kauffman).

The above description is from Burt, who describes specimens he thought clearly referable to this old species. He found them in a Sphagnum bog, growing scattered about in the Sphagnum, under small trees and bushes which thinly covered the marginal portions of the bog. Kauffman mentions that it has been found attached to Oak roots where it forms mycorrhizas, and adds that it grows quite constantly on the crumbling remains of wood or logs, where its white strings of mycelium are easily seen. When found growing thus, the gills were close. *Russula fragilis* (Pers.) Fr. is much like it, except that the gills are crowded and the cap is tinted pale rose-color which sometimes fades out to white. For an account of the poisonous properties of *Russula emetica,* see p. 143.

FETID RUSSULA Plate 31

Russula foetens (Pers.) Fr.

Cap 3–5 in. broad, fleshy, fragile, subglobose or convex, becoming plane or centrally depressed, viscid when moist, *widely tuberculate-sulcate or striate on the very thin margin,* yellowish or dingy-ochraceous, flesh pallid, taste acrid, *odor strong, amygdaline.* **Gills** rather close, adnexed, unequal, some of them forked, whitish, becoming yellowish with age, dingy where bruised, interspaces venose, *often studded with reddish drops of moisture when young.* **Stem** short, stout, 1½–2½ in. long, 6–12 lines thick, white or whitish, stuffed, becoming irregularly hollow. **Spores** white, subglobose, 7.6–10 μ long, nearly or quite as broad.

Woods and bushy places. July to September. Gregarious in habit and somewhat variable in color. Readily recognized by its peculiar, nauseatingly sweet odor, acrid taste, and widely tuberculate-sulcate or striate margin. *Russula foetentula* Pk., also with the odor of almonds, is smaller, has a more reddish-yellow cap, closer gills, and reddish-brown spots or stains at the base of the stem. *Russula pectinatoides* Pk., also smaller, has the cap colored grayish-brown.

MARY'S RUSSULA (Edible)

Russula mariae Pk.

Cap 1–3 in. broad, nearly hemispheric, becoming broadly convex, plane or centrally depressed, dry, *dark-crimson or purplish,* sometimes darker in the center than on the margin, *pruinose or minutely pulverulent,* rarely striate on the margin when old, flesh white, pinkish under the cuticle, taste mild or slightly and tardily acrid. **Gills** rather close, adnate, white, becoming yellowish with age, a few forked at the base. **Stem** 1–2 in. long, 3–5 lines thick, equal, solid or slightly spongy within, colored like or a little paler than the cap, usually white at each end, rarely entirely white. **Spores** pale yellow, globose, 7.6 μ broad.

In woods and in open places. July and August. Plainly marked by the dry, carmine-purplish, pruinose, or minutely granular, cap.

BLACKENING RUSSULA (Edible)

Russula nigricans (Bull.) Fr.

Cap 3–5 in. broad, fleshy, thick, firm, convex and umbilicate, with the margin incurved, becoming expanded and centrally depressed, slightly viscid when moist, *at first white, or white clouded with smoky-brown, then wholly brown or blackish, flesh white, slowly changing to reddish where cut or broken,* taste mild. **Gills** broad, subdistant, slightly rounded behind, adnexed, white, in young plants sometimes studded with drops of moisture. **Stem** short, 1–2½ in. long, ½–1 in. thick, solid, white. **Spores** white, globose or subglobose, 7.6–10 μ broad.

In woods and open places, on bare earth, or among fallen leaves. July to September. In drying, the whole plant usually becomes blackish. Occasionally specimens are found that are parasitized by another agaric of the genus *Nyctalis*. *Russula densifolia* (Secr.) Gill., which exhibits similar color changes, has very close, decurrent gills. *Russula adusta* Fr., a species belonging in this group, is smaller (cap 2–3 in. broad), with flesh that does not change color, though the exterior, at first white, slowly takes on a grayish or sooty cast. Despite the unattractive appearance of the Blackening Russula, it furnishes an acceptable addition to the mushroom menu.

VARIABLE RUSSULA (Edible)

Russula variata Banning and Pk.

Cap 2–4 in. broad, firm, convex, becoming centrally depressed or somewhat funnelform, viscid, even on the thin margin, *reddish-purple or brownish-purple, often variegated with green,* pea-green, sometimes varied with purple, flesh white, taste acrid or tardily acrid. **Gills** thin, *narrow,* close, *often forked,* tapering toward each end, adnate or slightly decurrent, white. **Stem** 1½–3 in. long, 5–8 lines thick, equal or nearly so, solid, sometimes cavernous (the cavities arranged one above the other), white. **Spores** white, subglobose, 7.6–10 x 7.6 μ.

In woods. July and August. The viscid pellicle is closely applied to the central portion of the cap, but separable on the margin. In drying it sometimes forms obscure spots. The acrid taste disappears in cooking and the flavor is then good. *Russula furcata* Fr. is very near this species, but the surface of the cap is umber-green (with no trace of red or purple) and "sprinkled with a slightly silky luster" (Stevenson, 1886).

GREEN RUSSULA (Edible)

Russula virescens (Schaeff.) Fr.

Cap 2–4 in. broad, fleshy, at first nearly globose, soon convex or nearly plane, often becoming centrally depressed, dry, adorned with small, flocculent patches or warts, *margin even,* green or grayish-green, flesh white, *taste mild and pleasant.* **Gills** moderately close, narrowed toward the stem, free or nearly so, a few of them forked, and a few shorter ones sometimes intermingled, white. **Stem** short, 1–2 in. long, 6–10 lines thick, firm, white, smooth, solid, or somewhat spongy within. **Spores** white, subglobose, 6–7.6 μ long.

Thin woods and in grassy, open places. July and August. The margin of the cap is usually even, but occasionally, in old specimens, it may be partly striate, as in *Russula crustosa*, a very similar plant. *Russula virescens* is of second-rate quality, depending upon the proper seasoning for flavor. Not as common as *Russula crustosa*.

Genus SPARASSIS Fr.

Fruit-body fleshy-tough, composed of many erect, flattened or crisped, more or less confluent branches which arise from a common base. The genus has been transferred from the Clavariaceae to the Thelephoraceae (see Cotton, '12).

SPATHULATE SPARASSIS (Edible) Fig. 123

Sparassis spathulata (Schw.) **Fr.**

Fruit-body 4–5 in. high, 5–6 in. broad, tough, moist, whitish to creamy yellow. **Branches** numerous, thin, flattened, grown together below, dilated above and spathulate or fan-shaped, often folded and wavy (like the ruffs seen in old Dutch portraits), or curved, rarely with a few indistinct, nearly concolorous, transverse zones near the broad, entire apices. **Spores** subglobose or broadly elliptic, 5–6 x 4–5 μ.

The above is the description of *Sparassis herbstii* Pk., which has been referred to Schweinitz's species. The material described by that writer was evidently old, discolored (reddish), and scrappy. Grows in summer or autumn, under oaks.

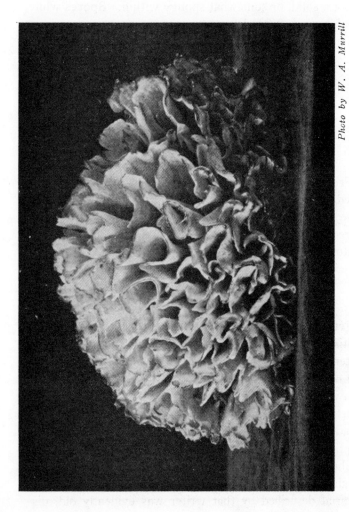

Photo by W. A. Murrill

Figure 123 Spathulate Sparassis, *Sparassis spathulata*, (=*Sparassis herbstii*) is the name of this fungus which looks not unlike the ruffs worn by seventeenth century cavaliers

GENUS SPATHULARIA Pers. Figs. 47a, 124

In northern pine forests the searcher after fungi will encounter plants which he will trace to the genus *Spathularia*. The pale-yellowish fruit-bodies of the species figured, *Spathularia clavata* (Schaeff.) Sacc., grow in groups on pine needle beds. Sometimes they are so disposed as to form arcs of circles, or complete circles, "fairy-rings." The species figured, our common one, is at once recognizable by its hollow, smooth (or farinose) stem, and by its pallid or yellowish mycelium. The other species (we have only two), *Spathularia velutipes* Cke. and Farlow, has a dark, bay-brown, solid, minutely velvety stem, and an orange-colored mycelium.

GENUS STROBILOMYCES Berk. (Emended).

This genus, as proposed by Berkeley, is based on the very common *Boletus strobilaceus* Scop., a species with a very dark, scaly cap, angular-mouthed, grayish-white tubes, and dark, verrucose, more or less globose, spores. But other species, with long-elliptic, smooth or longitudinally striate (!) spores have been referred to this genus, notably one from Australia (*Strobilomyces pallescens* Cke. and Massee), and another from Annam (*Strobilomyces annamiticus* Pat.). It is therefore necessary, if these species are to be retained in *Strobilomyces,* to emend Berkeley's original description by adding, that the spores may also be smooth or longitudinally striate, and elliptic. *Strobilomyces coccineus* (Plum.—Fr.) Sacc. (=*Boletus ananas* Curt.) also belongs here. Indeed, it may prove to be identical with the plants from Australia and Annam.

Figure 124 *Spathularia clavata*. It is always a pleasure to
encounter colonies of this charming ascomycete. The fruit-bodies
are of a pale, ochraceous yellow tint when fresh. The stem may
be darker

CONE-LIKE BOLETUS (Edible) Figs. 55c, 125

Strobilomyces strobilaceus (Scop.) Berk.

Cap usually 2–4 in. broad, fleshy, firm, subglobose, hemispheric or convex, dry, covered with a dense, thick, shaggy coat of black or blackish-brown tomentum which separates into prominent tufts or scales, with intervening chinks or spaces of a pale-gray or smoky-white color, flesh whitish changing to reddish on exposure to the air, then to blackish. **Tubes** rather long, depressed around the stem, plane or convex in mass, whitish when young and fresh, becoming red where wounded and then blackish, also becoming blackish or blackish-brown with age, mouths angular. **Stem** 2–5 in. long, 4–8 lines thick, equal or tapering upward, solid, often sulcate at the top, covered with a tomentum similar to that of the cap. **Spores** blackish-brown, globose or nearly so, rough, 10–12.7 μ in diameter.

In woods or their borders. July to September. Grows scattered, a few in a place. It is often difficult to discern, as its dark, mottled coloring renders it inconspicuous amid the bewildering lights and shadows that play upon the dead leaves covering the forest floor. It is highly prized by Bohemian people. Occasionally specimens are found that give off a pronounced, musky-camphorous odor (*Strob. camphoratus* Schwalb). *Strob. floccopus* (or *floccosus*) is a state of *Strob. strobilaceus* with a more or less pronounced ring.

Genus STROPHARIA (Fr.) Sacc. Spores purple-brown to violaceous.

The species of this genus are very close to *Psalliota,* but the gills are usually more or less adnate and even sub-

Figure 125   Cone-like Boletus, *Strobilomyces strobilaceus*.   The Unkempt Mushroom would be a suitable common name for this plant because of the cap, which reminds one of "Struwelpeter," a tousled-headed character well known in German children's nurseries

decurrent, never free, except by tearing away from the stem. The cap is viscid in a large number of species; when not so, such species are difficult to distinguish from Hypholomata of the *lacrymabundum-velutinum* group. The ring, though fugacious in some species, is generally more membranaceous and persistent than in *Hypholoma*.

DOUBLE GILLED STROPHARIA (Edible)

Stropharia bilamellata Pk.

Cap up to 3¼ in. broad, fleshy, convex, becoming nearly plane in large plants, even, obtuse, glabrous, whitish or yellowish, flesh white, odor like that of radishes. **Gills** thin, close, adnate, purplish-brown in the mature plant. **Stem** stout, about 2¾ in. long, about 5 lines thick, nearly equal or tapering upward, white, solid, sometimes hollow in large plants. **Ring** thick, white, with narrow, white, radiating, rough-edged, gill-like ridges on the upper surface which sometimes extend upwards and appear to connect with the gills above. **Spores** elliptic, 10–12.7 x 5–7.6 μ.

In cultivated fields. Summer and autumn. Very close to *Stropharia coronilla* (Bull.) Sacc. which has similar ridges on the upper surface of a narrower ring, but which differs in its ochraceous-tawny cap, stuffed, downward-tapering stem, and in its smaller spores (10 x 5 μ) There are cystidia on the gills, whereas *Stropharia bilamellata* lacks these bodies.

HEMISPHERIC STROPHARIA

Stropharia semiglobata (Batsch) Sacc.

Cap ⅜–1½ in. broad, hemispheric, obtuse, smooth, viscid, light-citron-yellow. **Gills** very broad, broadly adnate, close to subdistant, olive-gray to purplish-brown clouded with black. **Stem** 2–5 in. long, 2–4 lines thick, almost cylindric, straight, rigid, whitish, becoming yellowish, the apex paler, nearly equal, hollow. **Veil** narrow, terminating a thin, glutinous covering on the lower part of the stem. **Spores** brownish-purple, elliptic (15–18 x 9–10 μ. Kauffman).

On horse droppings and in grassy places, from early spring until the first frosts. *Stropharia stercoraria* (Fr.) Sacc. is so close as to be almost inseparable. Its spores are larger than those of *Stropharia semiglobata* (15–21 x 8–12 μ. Kauffman). It seems to be restricted to growing on dung, and the hollow of the stem is stuffed with a separable, fibrous pith.

GENUS TRICHOLOMA (Fr.) Quél. Spores white, except in a few species such as *Tricholoma nudum, T. personatum,* and *T. panaeolum* (Fr.) Quél., which species constitute a special group in *Tricholoma,* the *Lepista* group, with dirty flesh-colored spores.

Tricholoma corresponds to *Entoloma,* as to structural features, but the spores are white. Some species have traces of a veil (genus *Cortinellus* of some authors), and one is apt to turn to *Armillaria* in identifying them. Compare also *Hebeloma.*

EQUESTRIAN TRICHOLOMA (Edible)

Tricholoma equestre (L.) Quél.

Cap 3–5 in. broad, fleshy, compact, convex, becoming expanded, obtuse, pale yellowish, more or less tinged with reddish, disk and *central scales* often darker, margin naked, often flexuous, flesh white tinged with yellow. **Gills** rounded behind, close, nearly free, *sulphur-yellow.* **Stem** 1–2 in. long, 6–10 lines thick, stout, solid, pale-yellow or *white, white within.* **Spores** 6.3–7.6 x 4–5 μ.

Pine woods, especially in sandy soil. September to November. The cap is sometimes greenish and the stem may be sulphur-yellow exteriorly. The cap may lack the scales. The taste, mildly farinaceous at first, soon becomes unpleasant. *Tricholoma sulphureum* (Bull.), an undesirable plant, has the stem yellow within. Var. *pinastreti* Alb. and Schw. is a slender form with a thin, even cap, thinner, and more narrow gills, and with a more slender stem.

IMBRICATED TRICHOLOMA (Edible)

Tricholoma imbricatum Fr.

Cap 2–4 in. broad, fleshy, *compact,* convex or nearly plane, obtuse, dry, innately squamulose, fibrillose toward the margin, brown or reddish-brown, the margin thin, at first slightly *inflexed and pubescent, then naked,* flesh firm, thick, white. **Gills** slightly emarginate, almost adnate, rather close, white when young, becoming reddish or spotted with dull-red. **Stem** 2–3 in. long, 4–10 lines thick, *solid,* firm, nearly equal, fibrillose, white and mealy or pulverulent at the top, elsewhere colored like the cap. **Spores** 6.3 x 4–5 μ.

Under or near coniferous trees. September and October. *Tricholoma vaccinum* (Schaeff.) Quél., a related species, has the stem stuffed or hollow. Both are somewhat gregarious in their mode of growth and are partial to groves or thickets of young Spruce trees.

NAKED TRICHOLOMA (Edible)

Tricholoma nudum (Bull.) Fr.

Cap 1–3 in. broad, thin, broadly convex, nearly plane or slightly depressed in the center, obtuse, the thin, *naked* *margin* incurved when young, pale violaceous or lavender, fading with age and the escape of moisture to a pale, grayish-brown, often slightly tinged with reddish or yellowish hues, flesh of the young plant tinged with the color of the cap, becoming white with age, taste mild. **Gills** thin, narrow, close, slightly sinuate, adnate or decurrent, colored like the cap when young, becoming whitish with age. **Stem** 1–2 in. long, 2–4 lines thick, firm, *equal,* fibrous, *stuffed or hollow,* colored like the cap. **Spores** pale flesh-color in mass, elliptic 6–7.6 x 3–4 *μ.*

In flower beds (also in coniferous and deciduous woods, rarely in pastures [Rea, '22]). October. Grows singly or in clusters. Rather rare. An excellent species for the table. In France successful efforts have been made to cultivate the plant (Costantin and Matruchot, '01). *Tricholoma personatum,* a similarly colored species, has a solid stem and a villose-pruinose margin of the cap. Also, it is a more robust plant.

MASKED TRICHOLOMA (Edible)

Tricholoma personatum (Fr.) Quél.

Cap 2–5 in. broad, compact, becoming soft, thick, convex or plane, obtuse, regular, moist, glabrous, variable in color, generally pallid or cinereous tinged with violet or lilac, *margin at first involute and villose-pruinose,* flesh whitish. **Gills** broad, crowded, rounded behind, free, *violaceous, becoming sordid-whitish or fuscous.* **Stem** 1–3 in. long, ½–1 in. thick, generally thick, subbulbous, *solid,* fibrillose or villose-pruinose, whitish or colored like the cap. **Spores** *sordid-white,* subelliptical, 7.6–8.9 x 4–5 *μ.*

Woods and open places. September and October.

Common, and variable in color. The cap is occasionally whitish or grayish. The gills separate from the flesh of the cap, as in the genus *Paxillus*. It grows singly or in troops, rarely in tufts. Compare *Tricholoma nudum,* another species with violaceous coloring. Two forms occur, one in which the stem is decidedly bulbous, and another of smaller dimensions. The flesh is tender and well-flavored. *T. personatum* simulates certain Cortinarii (*Cortinarius alboviolaceus,* for example), but a spore-deposit at once settles the question. Cortinarii have ferruginous spores!

CENTRAL TRICHOLOMA (Edible)

Tricholoma portentosum (Fr.) Quél. var. *centrale* Pk.

Cap 1–3 in. broad, convex, sometimes slightly umbonate, viscid, virgate with innate, blackish fibrils, sooty-brown in the center, pale-yellow or greenish-yellow elsewhere, flesh white, taste mild. **Gills** moderately broad and close, emarginate, white or yellowish. **Stem** 1½–3 in. long, 3–5 lines thick, equal, solid, white. **Spores** broadly elliptic, 7.6 x 5 μ.

In thin (coniferous) woods. Autumn. Gregarious. The true *Tricholoma portentosum* has the cap colored a uniform sooty-brown. *Tricholoma sejunctum* (in the sense of Gillet, *not of* Fries) resembles var. *centrale,* but the cap lacks the innate, streaky, black fibrils. *Tricholoma saponaceum,* also similar, takes on reddish, salmon-colored stains.

VARIEGATED TRICHOLOMA

Tricholoma rutilans (Schaeff.) Quél.

Cap 2–4 in. broad, fleshy, campanulate, becoming plane, dry, at first *covered with a dark-red or purplish tomentum,* then somewhat squamulose, the margin thin, at first involute, flesh yellow. **Gills** crowded, rounded, *yellow, thickened, and villose on their edges.* **Stem** 2–4 in. long, 5–8 lines thick, somewhat hollow, nearly equal or slightly thickened or bulbous at the base, pale-yellow, variegated with red or purplish, floccose squamules. **Spores** 6.3–7.6 x 6.3 μ.

On or about Pine stumps, rarely on Hemlock trunks. July to November. Somewhat variable in size and color. Caps of old specimens sometimes become yellowish and variegated with purplish or reddish stains. The villosity on the edges of the gills is not always equally developed. *Tricholoma variegatum* (Scop.) is probably only a small form of this species with the edges of the gills nearly naked.

EARTH-COLORED TRICHOLOMA (Edible)

Tricholoma terreum (Schaeff.) Quél.

Cap 1–3 in. broad, fleshy, thin, soft, convex-campanulate or nearly plane, obtuse or umbonate, *innately fibrillose or floccose-squamose,* cinereous, fuscous, grayish-brown or mouse-color, flesh white or whitish. **Gills** adnexed, subdistant, more or less eroded on the edge, *white, becoming cinereous.* **Stem** 1–2 in. long, 2–4 lines thick, equal, varying from solid to stuffed or hollow, fibrillose, white or whitish. **Spores** broadly elliptical, 6–7 x 4–5 μ.

In woods. September to November. Gregarious or cespitose. It is an extremely variable plant. Var. *fragrans* Pk. is generally a little larger, and the cap is innately fibrillose and obtuse. Smaller forms occur with rather regular, slightly umbonate, or even papillate, floccose-squamulose caps. These grow in Pine woods. Another form, or subspecies (*T. argyraceum* [Bull.]), has the cap and gills white. *Tricholoma atrosquamosum* (Chev.), which should also be considered, has a whitish or cinereous, umbonate cap adorned with minute, black scales. *Tricholoma orirubens* (Quél.), a possible subspecies, has gills with rosy-red edges. Kauffman finds a plant in Michigan which he refers to *Tricholoma terreum*. It occurs in grassy, frondose woods and has minute, nucleated, narrow spores that measure 5-6 x 3 μ.

CHANGING TRICHOLOMA (Edible)
Tricholoma transmutans Pk.

Cap 2–4 in. broad, convex, *nearly glabrous,* viscid when moist, brownish, reddish-brown or tawny-red, usually paler on the margin, flesh white, taste and odor farinaceous. **Gills** narrow, close, sometimes branched, whitish or pale-yellowish, becoming dingy or reddish-spotted when old. **Stem** 3–4 in. long, 3–6 lines thick, equal or slightly tapering upward, *glabrous* or slightly silky-fibrillose, stuffed or hollow, whitish, often marked with reddish stains or becoming reddish-brown toward the base, white within. **Spores** subglobose, 5 μ broad.

In woods. August to September. Often cespitose. Both cap and stem, as well as the gills, are apt to assume darker hues with age or in drying.

Genus URNULA Fr. Figs. 51c, 126

New York State has but one of the two species known, namely, *Urnula craterium* (Schw.) Fr. It is to be looked for in deciduous woods where it grows on rotten, buried, or partly buried, branches. The figures convey an idea of the shape. The color of the exterior is carbonaceous black. *Urnula geaster* Pk., the other species, has been

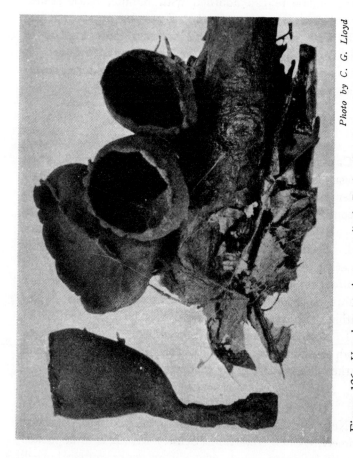

Photo by C. G. Lloyd

Figure 126 *Urnula craterium*, a stalked, *Peziza*-like fungus. It is blackish and of unattractive appearance

reported only from Texas. Its fruit-body soon shows fissures at the apex that finally extend downward, almost to the middle of the entire length. The exterior is colored brownish.

Genus VOLVARIA (Fr.) Quél. Spores rosy.

Corresponds to *Amanitopsis* of the white-spored genera. As in that genus, the gills are free, there is no ring, the stem is volvate, but the spores are some shade of pink or red. Compare *Pluteus*.

SILKY VOLVARIA (Edible) PLATE 32
Volvaria bombycina (Schaeff.) Quél.

Cap up to 8 in. broad, ovate-globose, then campanulate to convex-expanded, *white, covered with fine, silky, fibrillose squamules.* **Gills** free to remote, broad (especially toward the middle), very close, white, then rosy. **Stem** up to 8 in. long, ⅜–¾ in. thick, attenuated upwards from the somewhat enlarged base, often curved, glabrous, solid. **Volva** large, thick, loose, sometimes incised, whitish, mottled with brownish tints. **Spores** elliptic-ovate, pink, 6–8 x 4–5.5 μ.

Usually solitary, growing from wounds in the bark of a variety of deciduous trees, but commonly on Maple.

NAMES OF THE PRINCIPAL AUTHORS OF FUNGUS SPECIES

Adans.=M. Adanson (French)
Afz.=A. Afzelius (Swedish)
A. & S.=J. B. de Albertini (German) and L. D. de Schweinitz (American)
Atk.=G. F. Atkinson (American)
Badh.=C. D. Badham (English)
Barl.=J. H. J. B. Barla (French)
Bat.=F. Bataille (French)
Batsch=A. J. G. C. Batsch (German)
Batt.=A. J. A. Battarra (Italian)
Berk.=M. J. Berkeley (English)
Berk. & Br.=M. J. Berkeley and C. E. Broome (both English)
Berk. & Curt.=M. J. Berkeley (English) and M. A. Curtis (American)
Berk. & Rav.=M. J. Berkeley (English) and H. W. Ravenel (American)
Bolt.=J. Bolton (English)
Bonord.=H. F. Bonorden (German)
Boud.=E. Boudier (French)
Bres.=J. Bresadola (Italian)
Bull.=P. Bulliard (French)
Chev.=F. F. Chevalier (French)
Cke.=M. C. Cooke (English)
Curt. See Berkeley and Curtis
DC=A. P. de Candolle (Swiss)
Desv.=N. A. Desvaux (French)
Dicks.=J. Dickson (English)
Dill.=J. Dillenius (German)
Ell.=J. B. Ellis (American)
Ell. & Everh.=J. B. Ellis and B. M. Everhart (both American)
Fr.=E. M. Fries (Swedish)
Genev.=G. Genevier (French)
Gill.=C. C. Gillet (French)
Grev.=R. K. Greville (Scotch)
Henn.=P. Hennings (German)
Huds.=W. Hudson (English)
Jungh.=F. W. Junghuhn (Dutch)
Kalchbr.=C. Kalchbrenner (Hungarian)
Kallenb.=F. Kallenbach (German)
Karst.=P. A. Karsten (Finnish)
Kauffm.=C. H. Kauffman (American)
Krombh.=J. V. Krombholz (Austrian)
Lasch=W. G. Lasch (German)
Lév.=J. H. Léveillé (French)
L. or Linn.=C. v. Linnaeus (Swedish)

Lloyd=C. G. Lloyd (American)
Mass.=G. Massee (English)
Mich.=P. A. Micheli (Italian)
Mont.=C. Montagne (French)
Morg.=A. P. Morgan (American)
Müll.=O. F. Müller (Danish)
Nees=C. G. D. Nees v. Esenbeck (German)
Opat.=W. Opatowski (German ?)
Pat.=N. Patouillard (French)
Paul.=J. J. Paulet (French)
Pk. or Peck=C. H. Peck (American)
Pers.=C. H. Persoon (Dutch)
Quél.=L. Quélet (French)
Quél. & Bat.=L. Quélet and F. Bataille (both French)
Rab. or Rabenh.=L. Rabenhorst (German)
Relh.=R. Relhan (English)
Rich. & Roze=C. Richon and E. Roze (both French)
Roll.=L. Rolland (French)
Roq.=J. Roques (French)
Rostk.=J. F. Rostkovius (German)
Roze. See Richon and Roze
Sacc.=P. A. Saccardo (Italian)
Schaeff.=J. C. Schaeffer (German)
Schroet.=J. Schroeter (German)
Schulz.=S. Schulzer v. Mueggenburg (Austrian)
Schw.=L. D. de Schweinitz (American)
Scop.=J. A. Scopoli (Austrian)
Secr.=L. Secretan (Swiss)
Sor.=Sorokin (Russian)
Sow.=J. Sowerby (English)
Thax.=R. Thaxter (American)
Trog=J. G. Trog (German)
Tul.=L. R. and C. Tulasne (French)
Vahl=M. Vahl (Danish)
Vent.=J. Venturi (Italian); also E. P. Ventenat (French)
Vitt.=C. Vittadini (Italian)
Viv.=D. Viviani (Italian)
Wulf.=F. X. v. Wulfen (Austrian)

BIBLIOGRAPHY

(This list of books and papers forms a background for actual references, both from the text and the "Alphabetic Index to the Literature for Identification of the Higher Fungi" [see p. 168]).

Allen, R. F., and Jolivette, H.D.M.

1914 A Study of the Light Reactions of *Pilobolus*. Wisc. Acad. Sci. Arts and Letters Trans., 17:533–598.

Ames, A.

1913 A Consideration of Structure in Relation to Genera of the Polyporaceae. Ann. Mycol., 11:211–253.

Anderson, P. J., and Ickis, M. G.

1921 Massachusetts Species of *Helvella*. Mycologia, 13:201–229.

Arnold, J. D.

1934 A Comparative Taxonomic Study of Forms of *Collybia tuberosa* Fr. and *Collybia cirrata* Fr. Papers Mich. Acad. Sci., 19:55–58, pl. 1.

Atkinson, G. F.

1900 Studies of American Fungi, Mushrooms, Edible, Foisonous, etc. 275p. Ithaca, N. Y.

1901 Studies of Some Shade Tree and Timber Destroying Fungi. Cornell Univ. Agr. Exp. Sta. Bul., 193:199–235.

1902 Three new Genera of the Higher Fungi [*Eomycenella*, etc.]. Bot. Gaz., 34:36–43.

1908 On the Identity of *Polyporus applanatus* of Europe and North America. Ann. Mycol., 6:179–191.

1909 Evolution of the Lower Fungi. Ann. Mycol., 7:441–472.

1915 Phylogeny and Relationship in the Ascomycetes. Ann. Mo. Bot. Gard., 2:315–376.

1918 The Genus *Galerula* [*Galera*] in North America. Amer. Philos. Soc. Proc., 57:357–374.

Bachman, F. M.

1909 Discomycetes in the Vicinity of Oxford, Ohio. Ohio State Acad. Sci. Proc., 5:18–70.

Banker, H. J.

1901 A Preliminary Contribution to a Knowledge of the *Hydnaceae*. Bul. Torrey Bot. Club, 28:199–222.

1902 A Historical Review of the Proposed Genera of the Hydnaceae. Torrey Bot. Club Bul., 29:436–448.

1904 Notes on the Variability of *Hypothele repanda* [=*Hydnum repandum*]. Torreya, 4:113–117.

Banker, H. J.

1906 A Contribution to a Revision of the North American Hydnaceae. Torrey Bot. Club Mem., 12:99–194.
1912 Type Studies in the Hydnaceae. I. The Genus *Manina*. Mycologia, 4:271–278.
1912a Type Studies in the Hydnaceae. II. The Genus *Steccherinum*. Mycologia, 4:309–318.
1913 Type Studies in the Hydnaceae. III. The Genus *Sarcodon*. Mycologia, 5:12–17.
1913a Type Studies in the Hydnaceae. IV. The Genus *Phellodon*. Mycologia, 5:62–66.
1913b Type Studies in the Hydnaceae. V. The Genus *Hydnellum*. Mycologia, 5:194–205.
1913c Type Studies in the Hydnaceae. VI. The Genera *Creolophus, Echinodontium, Gloiodon,* and *Hydnodon,* Mycologia, 5:293–298.
1914 Type Studies in the Hydnaceae. VII. The Genera *Asterodon* and *Hydnochaete.* Mycologia, 6:231–234.
1929 Notes on the Hydnaceae. Mycologia, 21:145–150.

Barla, J. B.

1859 Les champignons de la province de Nice et principalement les espèces comestibles, suspectes ou vénéneuses, dessinées d'après nature. 138p., 48 col. pl. Nice.
1888–1892 Flore mycologique illustrée. Les champignons des Alpes Maritimes. 80p., 64 col. pl. Nice.

Barnhart, J. H.

1916 Bibliography. In North American Flora, 9 (part 6):427–459.

Barrett, M. F.

1910 Three Common Species of *Auricularia.* Mycologia, 2:12–18.

Bataille, F.

1907 Flore monographique des Astérosporées, Lactaires et Russules. Mém. Soc. Doubs., 2, 100pp.
1908 Les bolets, classification et détermination des espèces. Bull. Soc. Hist. Nat. Doubs., No. 15, 30p.
1910 Flore analytique des Inocybes d'Europe, 27p. Besançon.
1910a Flore monographique des Hygrophores d'Europe. 65p. Besançon.
1911 Flore analytique des Morilles et Helvelles. 44p. Besançon.
1911a Flore monographique des Cortinaires d'Europe. Bul. Soc. Hist. Nat. Doubs., 8:6:1–112p.

Bataille, F.
1919 Flore monographique des Marasmes d'Europe. 38p. Besançon.
1921 Flore analytique et descriptive des Tuberoïdes de l'Europe et de l'Afrique du Nord. Bul. Soc. Myc. Fr., 27:155–207.
1923 Flore analytique et descriptive des Hyménogastracées d'Europe. Bul. Soc. Myc. Fr., 39:157–196.

Baxter, D. V.
1924 The Heart-rot of Black Ash Caused by *Polyporus hispidus*. Papers Mich. Acad. Sci., III:39–50. Illus.
1925 The Biology and Pathology of Some of the Hardwood Heart-rotting Fungi. Pt. I, Amer. Jour. Bot. XII: 522–552. Illus.; Pt. II, 1. c., 553–576. Illus.
1927 Some Porias from the Region of the Lake States. Papers. Mich. Acad. Sci., 6:67–76. Illus.
1929 Some Porias from the Region of the Lake States. II. Papers Mich. Acad. Sci., 9:39–45. Illus.
1932 Some Resupinate Polypores from the Region of the Great Lakes. III. Papers Mich. Acad. Sci., 15:191–228, pl. XVII–XXVI.
1932a Some Resupinate Polypores from the Region of the Great Lakes. IV. Papers Mich. Acad. Sci., 17:421–439. Illus.
1934 Some Resupinate Polypores from the Region of the Great Lakes. V. Papers Mich. Acad. Sci., 19:305–332. Illus.

Beardslee, H. C.
1908 The Amanitas of North Carolina. Elisha Mitchell Sci. Soc. Jour., 24:115–124.
1918 The Russulas of North Carolina. Elisha Mitchell Sci. Soc. Jour., 33:147–197.
1924 Notes on the Scaly Species of Hydnaceae. Mycologia, 16:255–258.

Beardslee, H. C., and Coker, W. C.
1924 The Mycenas of North Carolina. Elisha Mitchell Sci. Soc. Jour., 40:49–91.

Bell, G. S.
1933 List of the Larger Fungi, Toronto Region. Trans. Roy. Canad. Inst., 19:275–299.

Bergenthal, W.

1933   Untersuchungen zur Biologie der Wichtigsten Deutschen Arten der Gattung *Stereum*. Zentralbl. Bakt. Abt. II. 89:209–236. Illus.

Bessey, E. A.

1913   Some Suggestions as to the Phylogeny of the Ascomycetes. Myc. Centr., 3:149–153.

1920   Guide to the Literature for the Identification of Fungi— A Preliminary Outline for Students and Others. Mich. Acad. Sci. Ann. Rep., 21:287–316.

Bisby, G. R.

1923   The Literature on the Classification of the Hysteriales. Trans. Brit. Myc. Soc., 8:176–189.

Boudier, E.

1905–1910   Icones mycologicae, ou iconographie des champignons de France, principalement Discomycètes, avec texte descriptif. Fol., 3 vols. of 600 col. pl, 1 of text. Paris.

1907   Histoire et classification des Discomycètes d'Europe. 221p. Paris.

Boughton, F. S.

1917   Hymenomyceteae of Rochester, N. Y., and Vicinity. Rochester Acad. Sci. Proc., 5:100–119.

Bourdot, H., and Galzin, A.

1909–1923   Hyménomycètes de France. [Descriptions of and Keys to the Families, Genera, and Species of the Thelephoraceae and Clavariaceae, with a Treatment of *Merulius* added. In vols. 25–39 inclusive of Bul. Soc. Myc. Fr.]

Brébinaud, P.

1931   Les Verpa. Bul. Bimens. Soc. Linn. Lyon, 10:108–109.

Bresadola, J.

1927–1932   Iconographia Mycologica. 24 vols., 1200 col. pl. Mediolani. [In course of publication.]

1933   Funghi Mangerecci e Velenosi. 3 Ed. Trento.

Bucholtz, F.

1903   Zur Morphologie und Systematik der Fungi hypogaei. Ann. Myc., 1:152–174.

Buller, A. H. R.

1909   Researches on Fungi. 287p. London.

1914   The Fungus Lore of the Greeks and Romans. Brit. Mycol. Soc. Trans., 5:21–26.

Buller, A. H. R.

1920 The Red Squirrel of North America as a Mycophagist. Brit. Mycol. Soc. Trans., 6:355–362

1921 Upon the Ocellus Function of the Subsporangial Swelling of *Pilobolus*. Brit. Mycol. Soc. Trans., 7:61–64.

1922 Researches on Fungi. 492p. London.

1922a Slugs as Mycophagists. Brit. Mycol. Soc. Trans., 7:270–283.

1924 Researches on Fungi. 611p. London.

1931 Researches on Fungi, vol. 4. Further Observations on the Coprini together with some Investigations on Social Organization and Sex in the Hymenomycetes. London.

1933 Researches on Fungi, vol. 5. Hyphal Functions and Protoplasmic Streaming in the Higher Fungi, together with an Account of the Production and Liberation of Spores in *Sporobolomyces, Tilletia* and *Sphaerobolus*. London.

1934 Researches on Fungi, vol. 6. The Biology and Taxonomy of *Pilobolus,* the Production and Liberation of Spores in the Discomycetes and Pseudorhizae and Gemmifers as Organs of certain Hymenomycetes. London

Bulliard, P.

1809 Herbier de la France. Fol., 6 vols., 603 col. pl., with text. Paris.

Burlingham, G. S.

1907 Suggestions for the Study of the Lactariae. Torreya, 7:118–123.

1908 A Study of the Lactariae of the United States. Torrey Bot. Club Mem., 14:1–109.

1910 Agaricales. Fam. 7. Agaricaceae. Tribe 2. Lactarieae. North American Flora, 9:172–200.

1913 The Lactarieae of the Pacific Coast. Mycologia, 5:305–311.

1915 *Russula*. North America Flora, 9:201–236.

1917 Methods for Satisfactory Field Work in the Genus *Russula*. Mycologia, 9:243–247.

1918 A Preliminary Report on the Russulae of Long Island. Torrey Bot. Club Mem., 17:301–306.

1918a New Species of *Russula* from Massachusetts. Mycologia, 10:93–96.

1921 Some new Species of *Russula*. Mycologia, 13:129–134, illus.

1924 Notes on Species of *Russula*. Mycologia, 16:16–23, illus.

1932 Two new Species of *Lactaria*. Mycologia, 24:460–463, illus.

Burt, E. A.

1896 The Phalloideae of the United States. I. Development of the Receptaculum of *Clathrus columnatus* Bosc. Bot. Gaz., 22:273–292.

1896a The Phalloideae of the United States. II. Systematic Account. Bot. Gaz., 22:379–391.

1897 The Phalloideae of the United States. III. On the Physiology of the Receptaculum. Bot. Gaz., 24:73–92.

1898 On Collecting and Preparing Fleshy Fungi for the Herbarium. Bot. Gaz., 25:172–186.

1899 Key to the Genera of Basidiomycetes of Vermont, with References to Scattered Literature for Determination of the Species. Contrib. Bot. of Vermont, 6:1–18. Middlebury.

1899a A List of Vermont Helvelleae with Descriptive Notes. Rhodora 1:59–65. Also as Boston Mycol. Club Bul., No. 9.

1914 The Thelephoraceae of North America. I. [*Thelephora*] Missouri Bot. Gard. Ann., 1:185–228.

1914a The Thelephoraceae of North America. II. *Craterellus.* Missouri Bot. Gard. Ann., 1:327–350.

1915 The Thelephoraceae of North America. III. *Craterellus borealis* and *Cyphella.* Missouri Bot. Gard. Ann., 1:357–382.

1915a The Thelephoraceae of North America. IV. *Exobasidium.* Missouri Bot. Gard. Ann., 2:627–658.

1915b The Thelephoraceae of North America. V. *Tremellodendron, Eichleriella,* and *Sebacina.* Missouri Bot. Gard. Ann., 2:731–770.

1916 The Thelephoraceae of North America. VI. *Hypochnus.* Missouri Bot. Gard. Ann., 3:203–241.

1916a The Thelephoraceae of North America. VII. *Septobasidium.* Missouri Bot. Gard. Ann., 3:319–343.

1916b *Pistillaria.* Ann. Missouri Bot. Gard., 3:405–406.

1917 The Thelephoraceae of North America. VIII. *Coniophora.* Missouri Bot. Gard. Ann., 4:237–269.

1917a *Merulius* in North America. Missouri Bot. Gard. Ann., 4:305–362.

1918 The Thelephoraceae of North America. IX. *Aleurodiscus.* Missouri Bot. Gard. Ann., 5:177–203.

1918a The Thelephoraceae of North America. X. *Hymenochaete.* Missouri Bot. Gard. Ann., 5:301–370.

1919 *Merulius* in North America, Supplementary Note. Missouri Bot. Gard. Ann., 6:143–145.

1920 The Thelephoraceae of North America. XI. *Tulasnella, Veluticeps, Mycobonia, Epithele,* and *Lachnocladium.* Missouri Bot. Gard. Ann., 6:253–280.

1920a The Thelephoraceae of North America. XII. *Stereum.* Missouri Bot. Gard. Ann., 7:81–248.

Burt, E. A.

1921   Some North American Tremellaceae, Dacryomycetaceae and Auriculariaceae. Missouri Bot. Gard. Ann., 8:361–396.

1922   The North American Species of *Clavaria*, with Illustrations of Type Specimens. Missouri Bot. Gard. Ann., 9:1–78.

1924   The Thelephoraceae of North America. XIII. *Cladoderris, Hypolyssus, Cymatella, Skepperia, Cytidia, Solenia, Matruchotia, Microstroma, Protocoronospora,* and *Asterostroma.* Missouri Bot. Gard. Ann. 11:1–36.

1925   The Thelephoraceae of North America. XIV. *Peniophora.* Missouri Bot. Gard. Ann., 12:213–357.

1926   The Thelephoraceae of North America. XV. *Corticium.* Missouri Bot. Gard. Ann., 13:173–354.

1929   Classification of Species of *Corticium* by the Tissues of the Fructification. Proc. Int. Congr. Plant Sci., 1926, 2:1598–1602.

Cejp, K.

1931   Notes on Iowa Species of the Genus *Irpex*. Mycologia, 23:130–133, illus.

1931a Contribution to the Knowledge of the Hydnaceae and Phylacteriaceae. Univ. Iowa Studies Nat. Hist., 13:3–5, illus.

Charles, V. K.

1931   Some Common Mushrooms and How to Know Them. U. S. Dept. Agr. Circ. No. 143, 58p., 49 figs.

Charles, V. K. and Lambert, E. B.

1933   Plaster Molds Occurring in Beds of the Cultivated Mushroom. Jour. Agric. Res., 46:1089–1098, illus.

Child, M.

1929   Preliminary Studies in the Genus *Daldinia*. Ann Missouri Bot. Gard., 16:411–486. Illus.

1932   The Genus *Daldinia*. Ann. Missouri Bot. Gard., 19:429–480. Illus.

Clark, J. A.

1898   Reference List of Publications Relating to Edible and Poisonous Mushrooms. U. S. Dept. Agri., (Library) Bul., 20:1–16.

Clements, F. E.

1909   The Genera of Fungi. 227p. Minneapolis.

1910   Minnesota Mushrooms. Minnesota Bot. Studies, 4:1–169.

Clements, F. E., and Shear, C. L.

1931   The Genera of Fungi, 2nd Edition, 496p., 58 pl., New York.

Coker, W. C.
1917 The Amanitas of the Eastern United States. Elisha
Mitchell Sci. Soc. Jour., 33:1–88.
1919 The Lactarias of North Carolina. Elisha Mitchell Sci.
Soc. Jour., 34:1–61.
1919a The Hydnums of North Carolina. Elisha Mitchell Sci.
Soc. Jour., 34:163–197.
1919b *Craterellus, Cantharellus,* and Related Genera in North
Carolina; with a Key to the Genera of Gill Fungi.
Elisha Mitchell Sci. Soc. Jour., 35:24–48.
1920 Notes on the Lower Basidiomycetes of North Carolina.
Jour. Elisha Mitchell Sci. Soc., 35:113–182, 45 pl.
1921 Notes on the Thelephoraceae of North Carolina. Elisha
Mitchell Sci. Soc. Jour., 36:146–196.
1923 The Clavarias of the United States and Canada. 209p.
Chapel Hill, N. C.
1924 The Geasters of the United States and Canada. Elisha
Mitchell Sci. Soc. Jour., 39:170–224.
1928 The Chapel Hill Species of the Genus *Psalliota.* Jour.
Elisha Mitchell Sci. Soc., 43:243–256. Illus.

Coker, W. C., and Beardslee, H. C.
1921 The Collybias of North Carolina. Elisha Mitchell Sci.
Soc. Jour., 37:83–107.
1922 The Laccarias and Clitocybes of North Carolina. Elisha
Mitchell Sci. Soc. Jour., 38:98–126.
1923 The Gasteromycetes of North Carolina. Elisha Mitchell
Sci. Soc. Jour, 38:231–236.

Coker, W. C., and Couch, J. N.
1928 The Gasteromycetes of the Eastern United States and
Canada. 201p. Chapel Hill, N. C.

Collins, F. S.
1899 A Case of *Boletus* Poisoning. Rhodora, 1:21.

Cooke, M. C.
1881–1891 Illustrations of British Fungi. 8 vols. [About 1,100
col. pl.] London.
1892 Vegetable Wasps and Plant Worms. A Popular History
of Entomogenous Fungi, or Fungi Parasitic on
Insects. 354p. London.
[On the species of *Cordyceps.*]
1895 Introduction to the Study of Fungi. 360p. London.

Cooke, M. C., and Berkeley, M. J.
1875 Fungi: Their Nature, Influences, Uses, etc. 299p.
London.

Corner, E. J. H.
1934 An Evolutionary Study in Agarics: *Collybia apalosarca* and the Veils. Trans. Brit. Mycol. Soc., 19:39–88. Illus.

Costantin, J., and Matruchot, L.
1901 Sur la culture du champignon comestible dit "Pied Bleu" (*Tricholoma nudum*). Rev. Génér. de Bot., 13:449–476.

Cotton, A. D.
1912 On the Structure and Systematic Position of *Sparassis*. Brit. Mycol. Soc. Trans., 3:333–339.

Cotton, A. D., and Wakefield, E. M.
1919 A Revision of the British Clavariae. Brit. Mycol. Soc. Trans., 6:164–198.

Couch, J. N.
1929 A Monograph of *Septobasidium*. I. Jour. Elisha Mitchell Sci. Soc., 44:242–260. Illus.

Cram, W. E.
1924 The Red Squirrel. Jour. of Mammalogy, 5:37–41.

Crawshay, R.
1930 The Spore Ornamentation of the Russulas. London.

Cummings, C. E.
1933 Mushrooms and Toadstools. Nat. Hist. Mag., 33:41–53. Illus.

Cummins, G. B.
1930 Montana Discomycetes from the Flathead National Forest. Papers Michigan Acad. Sci., 11:105–115. Illus.

Daniels, E. A.
1899 Glossary for Students of the Fleshy Fungi. Boston Mycol. Club Bul., 10:1–20.
1901 *Coprinus*. Boston Mycol. Club Bul., 15–16. [Original publication not paged.]

Davidson, J. E.
1930 Notes on the Agaricaceae of Vancouver (B. C.), District I. Mycologia, 22:80–93.

Day, D. F.
1882 A Catalogue of the Native and Naturalized Plants of the City of Buffalo and its Vicinity. 215p. Buffalo. [Reprinted from Buffalo Soc. Nat. Sci. Bul., 4:65–152, 153–290. 1882–1883.]

Dearness, J.
1911 The Personal Factor in Mushroom Poisoning. Mycologia, 3:75–78.
1924 *Gyromitra* Poisoning. Mycologia, 16:199.

Denniston, H. R.
1905 The Russulas of Madison and Vicinity. Wisc. Acad. Sci. Arts and Letters Trans., 15:71–88.

Dodge, B. O.
1914 The Morphological Relationships of the Florideae and the Ascomycetes. Bul. Torrey Bot. Club, 41:157–202.

Dodge, C. W.
1929 The Higher Plectascales. Ann. Mycol., 27:145–184. Illus. [Includes the Trichocomaceae and Elaphomycetaceae.]
1931 *Alpova,* a new Genus of Rhizopogonaceae, with Further Notes on *Leucogaster* and *Arcangeliella.* Ann. Missouri Bot. Gard., 18:457–464, pl. 40.
1934 Contribución al Conocimiento de la Evolución de los Gasteromicetos. Rev. Sudamer. Bot., 1:18–20.

Douglas, B.
1917 Mushroom Poisoning. Torreya, 17:171–175, 209–221. [*Panaeolus* poisoning, together with a general discussion of mushroom intoxication.]

Duggar, B. M.
1905 The Principles of Mushroom Growing and Mushroom Spawn Making. U. S. Dept. Agr. Bur. Plant Industry Bul., 85:1–60.
1915 Mushroom Growing. 250p. New York.
1922 The Cultivation of Mushrooms. U. S. Dept. Agr. Farm. Bul., 204:1–24. New ed.

Durand, E. J.
1900 The Classification of the Fleshy Pezizineae, with Reference to the Structural Characters Illustrating the Bases of their Division into Families. Torrey Bot. Club Bul. 27:463–495.
1908 The Geoglossaceae of North America. Ann. Mycol., 6:387–477.
1921 New or Noteworthy Geoglossaceae. Mycologia, 13:184–187.

Earle, F. S.
1902 A Key to the North American Species of *Hypholoma.* Torreya, 2:22–23.

Earle, F. S.
1902a Keys to the North American Species of the Coprineae. Torreya, 2:37–40.
1902b A Key to the North American Genera and Species of the Hygrophoreae. Torreya, 2:53–54, 73–74.
1902c A Key to the North American Species of *Russula*. Torreya, 2:101–103, 117–119.
1902d A Key to the North American Species of *Lactarius*. Torreya, 2:139–141, 152–154.
1902e A Key to the North American Species of *Cortinarius*. Torreya, 2:169–172, 180–183.
1903 A Key to the North American Species of *Stropharia*. Torreya, 3:24–25.
1903a A Key to the North American Species of *Lentinus*. Torreya, 3:35–38, 58–60.
1903b A Key to the North American Species of *Panus*. Torreya, 3:86–87.
1903c A Key to the North American Species of *Pluteolus*. Torreya, 3:124–125.
1903d A Key to the North American Species of *Galera*. Torreya, 3:134–136.
1903e A Key to the North American Species of *Inocybe*. Torreya, 3:168–170, 183–184.
1909 The Genera of the North American Gill Fungi. N. Y. Bot. Gard. Bul., 5:373–451.

Ellis, J. B., and Everhart, B. M.
1887 Synopsis of the North American species of *Xylaria* and *Poronia*. Jour. of Mycology, 3:97, 109.
1888–1889 Synopsis of North American Species of *Hypoxylon* and *Nummularia*. Jour. Myc., 4:38–44, 66–70, 85–93, 109–113; ibid., 5:19–23. [Pyrenomycetes.]
1892 The North American Pyrenomycetes. A Contribution to Mycologic Botany with Original Illustrations by F. W. Anderson. 793p. Newfield, N. J.

Emmons, C. W.
1927 The Thelephoraceae of Iowa. Univ. Iowa Studies Nat. Hist., 12:49–89. Illus.

Engler, A., and Prantl, K.
1897–1900 Die natürlichen Pflanzenfamilien. 23 vols. Leipzig. [This work presents a survey of the entire plant kingdom, arranged by classes, orders, families and genera, with representative species described and in many cases illustrated. Fungi in the first two volumes, which appeared in 1897 and 1900, respectively.]
1928 Die natürlichen Pflanzenfamilien. 2nd Edition, 6:1–290. [Includes the Tremellales and Agaricales.]

Eyre, W. L. W.
1904 Mycology as an Instrument of Recreation. Brit. Mycol.
Soc. Trans., for 1903:49–53.

Fairman, C. E.
1893 Hymenomyceteae of Orleans County, N. Y. Rochester
Acad. Sci. Proc., 2:154–167.
1896 Puff Balls, Slime Moulds and Cup Fungi of Orleans
County, New York. Rochester Acad. Sci. Proc.,
3:206–220.

Falconer, W.
1897 How to Grow Mushrooms. U. S. Dept. Agr. Farm. Bul.,
53:1–20.
1910 Mushrooms: how to grow them. A Practical Treatise
on Mushroom Culture for Profit and Pleasure. 169p.
New York.

Farlow, W. G.
1888 A Supplemental List of Works on North American Fungi.
Library of Harvard University, Cambridge, Mass. 9p.
[For the original publication, see Farlow and Trelease, '87.]
1905 Bibliographical Index of North American Fungi. 1 (part
1):1–312. Washington.
[The only part published.]
1929 Icones Farlowianae; Illustrations of the Larger Fungi of
Eastern North America . . . with Descriptive Text
by Edward Angus Burt. 103 col. pl. with text. Cambridge, Mass. [Since the plates are not accredited to
the artists who painted them (vide, Fries' Icones, in
which classic work a different custom was followed),
the present author records here the numbers of such
as were painted by him. They are: Nos. 2, 13, 14, 16,
18, 19, 22, 27, 28, 36, 38, 45, 47, 50, 51, 53, 65, 68, 69,
81 (which is *Boletus pachypus,* not *B. speciosus,* as
stated by Dr. Burt), 90 (all figures except the one at
the lower right), 91, 92. The other plates are by
my esteemed colleague, Joseph Bridgham.]

Farlow, W. G., and Seymour, A. B.
1888–1891 A Provisional Host-index of the Fungi of the
United States. 3 pts. 219p. Cambridge, Mass. [see
Seymour, '29.]

Farlow, W. G., and Trelease, W.
1887 List of Works on North American Fungi, with the Exception of Schizomycetes, Published before 1887. Bibl.
Contrib. Libr., Harvard Univ., 2:No. 25, 36p.
[A Supplemental list, by Farlow, '88.]

Fink, B., and Richards, C. A.

1915 The Ascomycetes of Ohio. Ohio Biol. Surv. Bul., 5:1–70.

Fischer, E.

1890, 1893, 1900 Untersuchungen zur vergleichenden Entwick-lungsgeschichte und Systematik der Phalloideen. I. Neue Denks. Schweiz. Nat. Ges., 32:No. 1, 103 p.; II, ibid., 33:No. 1, 51p.; III, Verwandt-schaftsverhältnisse der Gasteromyceten, ibid., 36:No. 2, 84p.

1897 Ascomycetes, Tuberaceae and Hemiasceae. Rabh. Krypt. Fl., 5:1–131.

1897a Tuberineae, Plectascineae. In Engler and Prantl, Natürl. Pflanzenfam., 1:1:278–320.

1900 Phallineae, Hymenogastrineae, Lycoperdineae, Nidularii-neae, Plectobasidiineae (Sclerodermineae). In Engler and Prantl, Nat. Pflanzenfam, 1:2:277–346.

1908 Zur Morphologie der Hypogaeen. Bot. Zeit. 66:141–168.

1934 Zur Kenntniss der Fruchtkörperentwicklung von *Podaxis* [*Podaxon*]. Ber. Schweiz. Bot. Ges., 43:11–18. Illus.

Fisher, M. C.

1932 A Comparative Morphological Study of Certain Species of the Dacryomycetaceae. Proc. Iowa Acad. Sci., 38 (1931):115–125. Illus.

Flora Batava.

[More than 2,000 colored plates of the plants of the Netherlands. Still in press.]

Flora Danica.

1761–1871 Fol., 16 vols. 2,880 col. pl. Copenhagen.

Ford, W. W.

1909 The Distribution of Poisons in the Amanitas. Jour. of Pharmac. and Exper. Therap., 1:275–287.

1909a The Distribution of Poisons in Mushrooms. Science, N.S., 30:97–108.

1911 The Distribution of Haemolysins Agglutinins and Poisons in Fungi, Especially the Amanitas, the Entolomas, the *Lactarius* and the Inocybes. Jour. of Pharmac. and Exper. Therap., 2:285–318.

1923 A New Classification of Mycetismus (mushroom poison-ing). Ass'n. Amer. Physicians Trans., 38:225–229.

Ford, W. W., and Clark, E. D.

1914 Deadly Poisonous Fungi. N. Y. Bot. Gard. Jour., 15:159–168.

1914a A Consideration of the Properties of Poisonous Fungi. Mycologia, 6:167–191.

Forel, A.

1928 The Social World of the Ants Compared with that of Man. Vol. 2:1–445. New York.

Forster, E. J.

1888 Agarics of the United States.—Genus *Panus*. Jour. of Mycology, 4:21.

Frank, A. B.

1885 Über die auf Wurzel-symbiose beruhende Ernährung gewisser Bäume durch unterirdische Pilze. Ber. Deutsch. Bot. Ges., 3:128–145.

Freeman, E. M.

1905 Minnesota Plant Diseases. 432p. St. Paul.

Fries, E. M.

1867–1884 Icones selectae Hymenomycetum nondum delineatorum. Fol., 2 vols. 200 col pl., with text. Upsala and Stockholm.

1874 Hymenomycetes Europaei sive Epicriseos systematis mycologici. 755p. 2d ed. Upsala.

Galloway, B. T., and Woods, A. F.

1896 Diseases of Shade and Ornamental Trees. U. S. Dept. Agr. Yearbook, p. 237–254.

Gäumann, E. A.

1928 Comparative Morphology of Fungi. Translated and revised by C. W. Dodge, 701p., 406 figs.

Gibson, W. H.

1895 Our Edible Toadstools and Mushrooms and How to Distinguish Them. 337p. New York and London.

Gilbert, E. J.

1918 Le Genre *Amanita*. Étude morphologique des espèces et variétés; revision critique de la systematique.

1927 La spore des champignons supérieurs, 219p. Paris.

1931 Les bolets. Paris (Les livres du mycologue, t. III).

Gilbert, E. M.

1910 Studies on the Tremellineae of Wisconsin. Wisc. Acad. Sci. Arts and Letters Trans., 16:1137–1170.

Gilkey, H. M.

1916 A revision of the Tuberales of California. Univ. Calif. Publ. (Botany) 6:275–356.

Gillet, C. C.

1878 Les champignons qui croissent en France. 4 vols., one of text, 828p., and three of col. pl. [more than 700]. Paris.

Graham, V. O.

1926 Seasonal Occurrence of the Larger Fungi. Trans. Ill. Acad. Sci., 19:182–186.
1927 Ecology of Fungi in the Chicago Region. Bot. Gaz., 83:267–287.
1928 Communities of Mushrooms. Trans. Ill. Acad. Sci., 20: (1927) 72–76
1933 Mushrooms of the Chicago Region. Program of Activities, Chicago Acad. Sci., 4:43–63. Illus.

Gramberg, E.

1921 Pilze der Heimat. 2 vols. 136 pl., mostly colored, text, fig. 3d ed. Leipzig.

Greville, R. K.

1823–1828 Scottish Cryptogamic Flora etc. 6 vols. 360 col. pl., with text. Edinburgh.

Guba, E. F., and Young, P. A.

1924 Check List of Important References Dealing with the Taxonomy of Fungi. Trans. Amer. Micros. Soc., 43:17–67. [See also **Young, P. A.; Solheim, W. G.**]

Güssow, H. T., and Odell, W. S.

1927 Mushrooms and Toadstools. An account of the More Common Edible and Poisonous Fungi of Canada. Dominion Experimental Farms, Div. of Bot. 274p.

Gwynne-Vaughan, H.

1922 Fungi (Morphology). 232p., 196 figs. London.
1927 The Structure and Development of the Fungi. 384p., 285 figs.

Haddow, W. R.

1931 Studies in *Ganoderma*. Jour. Arnold Arbor, 12:25–46. Illus.

Hard, M. E.

1908 The Mushroom, Edible and Otherwise. Its Habitat and its Time of Growth. 609p. Kirkwood, Ohio.

Harkness, H. W.

1899 Californian Hypogaeous fungi. Proc. Calif. Acad. Sci., 3d ser., vol. 1 (8):241–292, 4 col. pl.

Harper, E. T.

1913 Species of *Pholiota* of the Region of the Great Lakes. Wisc. Acad. Sci. Arts and Letters Trans., 17:470–502.
1913a Species of *Pholiota* and *Stropharia* in the Region of the Great Lakes. Wisc. Acad. Sci. Arts and Letters Trans., 17:1011–1026.

Harper, E. T.

1914   Species of *Hypholoma* in the Region of the Great Lakes. Wisc. Acad. Sci. Arts and Letters Trans., 17:1142–1164.

1916   Additional Species of *Pholiota, Stropharia* and *Hypholoma* in the Region of the Great Lakes. Wisc. Acad. Sci. Arts and Letters Trans., 18:392–421.

1918   The *Clavaria fistulosa* Group. Mycologia, 10:53–57.

1922   Species of *Lentinus* in the Region of the Great Lakes. Wisc. Acad. Sci. Arts and Letters Trans., 20:365–385.

Harshberger, J. W.

1917   A Textbook of Mycology and Plant Pathology. 779p. Philadelphia.

Hatch, A. B., and Doak, K. D.

1933   Mycorrhizal and Other Features of the Root Systems of *Pinus.* Jour. Arnold Arb., 14:85–99. Illus., pl. 57–60.

Hatch, A. B., and Hatch, C. T.

1933   Some Hymenomycetes forming Mycorrhizae with *Pinus Strobus* L. Jour. Arnold Arbor., 14:324–334, pl. 68–71.

Hatt, R. T.

1929   The Red Squirrel: Its Life History and Habits, with Special Reference to the Adirondacks of New York and Harvard Forest. Roosevelt Wild Life Annals, vol. 2, No. 1. [Notes on species of fungi used as food, p. 103–109, figs. 48–51.]

Heald, F. D.

1926   Manual of Plant Diseases. 891p. New York.

Heim, R.

1931   Le genre *Inocybe.* Paris (Encyclopedie Mycologique I).

Hennings, P.

1900   Dacryomycetineae, Exobasidiineae, Hymenomycetineae. In Engler and Prantl, Nat. Pflanzenfam., 1:2:96–276. Illus.

Henry, L. K.

1932   Mycorrhizas of deciduous trees. Proc. Penn. Acad. Sci., 6:121–124. Illus.

Herbst, W.

1899   Fungal Flora of the Lehigh Valley, Pa. 229p. Allentown, Pa.

Hesse, R.

1891–1894   Die Hypogäen Deutschlands: Hymenogastrales, 1:149; Tuberales, 2:140.

Höhnel, F. v.
1913 Fragmente zur Mykologie. XIV. Mitteilung. Sitzungsber, der Math.-Naturw. Klasse der Kais. Akad. der
Wissensch. (Wien) 122:255–309.
1914 Fragmente zur Mykologie. XV. Mitteilung. Sitzungsber.
der Math.-Naturw. Klasse der Kais. Akad. der Wis-
sench. (Wien) 123:49–155.
[New system of classifying *Mycena* species proposed,
based on cystidia characters.]

Hollós, L.
1904 Gasteromycetes Hungariae. Die Gasteromyceten Ungarns.
210p., 31 pl., mostly colored. Leipzig.

Hone, D. S.
1904 Minnesota Helvellineae. Minnesota Bot. Studies, III. ser.,
part III, p. 309–321.
1906 Some Western Helvellineae. Postelsia, Yearbook Minn.
Seaside Sta., 1906:235–244.
1909 The Pezizales, Phacidiales and Tuberales of Minnesota.
Minn. Bot. Studies, 4:65–132.

House, H. D.
1914 Origin of the Volva Aperture in *Cryptoporus volvatus*
(Peck) Hubbard. Mycologia, 6:217–218.
1916 A Bibliography of the Botany of New York State.
N. Y. State Mus. Bul., 188:66–105.

Huber, H.
1934 Die Korallenpilze [*Clavaria*]. Zeitschr. Pilzk. 18 (n. s.
13) :34–36.

Hussey, T. J.
1847–1855 Illustrations of British Mycology, etc. 2 vols., 140
col. pl., with text. London.

Imai, S.
1933 Gloeostereeae S. Ito et Imai, a new Tribe of Thelephoraceae. Trans. Sapporo Nat. Hist. Soc., 13:9–11.
Illus.
1934 Studies on the Geoglossaceae of Japan. Trans. Sapporo
Nat. Hist. Soc., 13:179–184. Illus.

Jackson, B. D.
1881 Guide to the Literature of Botany, etc. 626p. London.
1916 A Glossary of Botanic Terms with their Derivation and
Accent. 427p. 3d ed. London.

Jenkins, W. A.
1934 The Development of *Cordyceps agariciformia*. Mycologia,
26:220–243. Illus.

Johannsen, O. A.
1909–1912 The Fungus Gnats of North America. Maine Agric. Exper. Sta., Bul. Nos. 172, 180, 196 and 200.

Johnson, M. M.
1929 The Gasteromycetae of Ohio: Puff-balls, Birds' Nest Fungi and Stinkhorns. Bul. Ohio Biol. Surv. 22 (vol. 4, No. 7) :273–352. Illus.

Johnstone, R. B.
1921 Audibility of the Spore Discharge in *Otidea leporina*. Brit. Mycol. Soc. Trans., 7 :86.

Kalchbrenner, K.
1873–1877 Icones selectae Hymenomycetum Hungariae per St. Schulzer et C. Kalchbrenner. Fol., 65p., 40 col. pl. Budapest.

Kallenbach, F.
1926–1934 Die Röhrlinge (Boletaceae). Die Pilze Mitteleuropas 1 (part 1–13) :1–94. 36 pl. Leipzig. [Further parts to appear.]

Kauffman, C. H.
1905 The Genus *Cortinarius*. Torrey Bot. Club. Bul. 32 :315–321.
1906 *Cortinarius* as a Mycorhiza-producing Fungus. Bot. Gaz., 42 :208–214.
1909 Unreported Michigan Fungi for 1908, with a Monograph of the Russulas of the State. 11th Rept. Michigan Acad. Sci., p. 55–91.
1918 The Agaricaceae of Michigan. Mich. Geol. and Biol. Surv., Publication 26, Biol. Ser. 5. Vol. 1, 924p.; vol. 2, 172 pl.
1921 Studies in the Genus *Inocybe*. N. Y. State Mus. Bul., 233–234 :43–60.
1922 The Genus *Armillaria* in the United States and its Relationships. Papers Michigan Acad. Sci. Arts and Letters, 2 :53–66.
1924 *Inocybe*. North American Flora, 10 :227–260.
1924a The Genus *Lepiota* in the United States. Papers Michigan Acad. Sci. Arts and Letters, 4 :311–344.
1925 The Genus *Gomphidius* in the United States. Mycologia, 17 :113–126.
1926 The Genera *Flammula* and *Paxillus* and the Status of the American Species. Amer. Jour. Bot., 13 :11–32.
1927 Cystidia in the Genus *Clavaria* and Some Undescribed Species. Papers Michigan Acad. Sci. Arts and Letters, 8 :141–151.

Kauffman, C. H.

1927a The Genus *Clitocybe* in the United States, with a Critical
Study of all the North Temperate Zone Species.
Papers Michigan Acad. Sci. Arts and Letters, 8:153–214.

1929 A Study of the Fungous Flora of the Lake Superior
Region of Michigan, with some new Species. Papers
Michigan Acad. Sci., 9:169–218. Illus.

1932 *Cortinarius.* N. Amer. Flora, 10 [pt. 5]:282–348.

Kavina, K., and Pilat, A.

1934 Atlas des Champignons de l'Europe. Praha. Vol. 1,
Amanita, by R. Veselý. 16 p., 8 pl.

Kelly, A. P.

1932 The Literature of Mycorrhizae. Abstracts of Seven Hundred Publications, etc., etc. Malvern, Pa. [Typewritten.]

Kienholz, J. R.

1934 A Poisonous *Boletus* from Oregon. Mycologia, 26:275–
276. [*Boletus eastwoodiae.*]

Killermann, S.

1922 Pilze aus Bayern. Kritische Studien besonders zu
M. Britzelmayr; Standortsangaben u. (kurze) Bestim-
mungstabellen. 1 Teil: Thelephoraceen, Hydnaceen,
Polyporaceen, Clavariaceen und Tremellaceen. Bayer.
Bot. Ges. (Regensburg), Denkschr., 15:1–128. [In
course of publication.]

1928 Eubasidii (Tremellineae, Hymenomycetineae). In Engler
and Prantl, Nat. Pflanzenfam., 2nd Edition, 6:99–283.
Illus.

1934 Die Gattungen *Typhula* und *Pistillaria.* Kritische Dar-
stellung und neue Arten. Zeitschr. f. Pilzk. 18 (n. s.
13):98–108. Illus.; ibid., 137–139. Illus.

Krieger, L. C. C.

1911 Note on the Reputed Poisonous Properties of *Coprinus
comatus.* Mycologia, 3:200–202.

1914 Observations on the Use of Ridgway's New Color-book.
The Color of the Spores of *Volvaria speciosa* Fr.
Mycologia, 6:29–31.

1920 Common Mushrooms of the United States. Nat. Geogr.
Mag., 37:387–439. 16 col. pl. and text figures.

1920a Field Key to the Genera of the Gill Mushrooms.
Baltimore.
[Chart with text.]

1922 A Sketch of the History of Mycological Illustration
(higher fungi). Mycologia, 14:311–331.

1923 Preliminary Note on the Position of the Hymenium in
Physalacria inflata (Schw.) Peck. Maryland Acad.
Sci. Bul., 3:7–8.

Krieger, L. C. C.
1924 Catalogue of the Mycological Library of Howard A. Kelly. 260p. Baltimore.
[Compiled by L. C. C. Krieger, and privately printed. About 10,000 titles of mycological books and papers listed.]
1925 *Cortinarius cyanites* in the United States. Rhodora, 27:153–156. Illus.
1926 Sketching Fleshy Fungi with the Aid of the Camera Lucida. Mycologia, 18:132–133.
1927 New or Otherwise Interesting Agaricaceae from the United States and Canada. Mycologia, 19:308–314.

Krombholz, J. V. v.
1831–1847 Naturgetreue Abbildungen und Beschreibungen der essbaren, schädlichen und verdächtigen Schwämme. 10 Hefte. Folio., 76 col. pl., with text. Prague.

Kühner, R.
1933 Études sur les genre *Marasmius*. Botaniste, 25:57–114. Illus.

Kupfer, E. N.
1902 Studies on *Urnula* and *Geopyxis*. Torrey Bot. Club Bul., 29:137–144.

Lagarde, J.
1906 Contribution à l'étude des Discomycètes charnus. Ann. Myc., 4:125–256.

Lambert, E. B.
1932 Mushroom Growing in the United States. U. S. Dept. Agric., Circ. 251, 34p. Illus.

Lange, J. E.
1914 Studies in the Agarics of Denmark. Part 1: General Introduction. The Genus *Mycena*. Dansk Bot. Ark. I, No. 5, p. 1–40.
1915 Studies in the Agarics of Denmark. Part 2: *Amanita*. *Lepiota*. *Coprinus*. Dansk Bot. Ark. II, No. 3, p. 1–53.
1917 Studies in the Agarics of Denmark. Part 3: *Pluteus*. *Collybia*. *Inocybe*. Dansk Bot. Ark. II, No. 7, p. 1–47.
1921 Studies in the Agarics of Denmark. Part 4: *Pholiota*. *Marasmius*. *Rhodophyllus*. Dansk Bot. Ark. II, No. 11, p. 1–46.
1923 Studies in the Agarics of Denmark. Part 5: Ecological Notes. The Hygrophorei. *Stropharia* and *Hypholoma*. Supplementary Notes to Parts I–III. Dansk Bot. Ark. IV, No. 4, p. 1–55.
1926 Studies in the Agarics of Denmark. Part 6: *Psalliota*. *Russula*. Dansk Bot. Ark. IV, No. 12, p. 1–52.

Lange, J. E.

1928 Studies in the Agarics of Denmark. Part 7: *Volvaria. Flammula. Lactarius.* Dansk Bot. Ark. V, No. 5, p. 1–41.

1930 Studies in the Agarics of Denmark, Part 8: *Omphalia, Pleurotus, Clitocybe.* Dansk Bot. Ark., 6 (5) :1–62, 2 pl. (1 col.).

1933 Studies in the Agarics of Denmark, Part 9: *Tricholoma, Lentinus, Panus, Nyctalis.* Dansk Bot. Ark. Vol. 8, No. 3, 43p., col., pl. [Lange has recently issued a prospectus of a comprehensive, illustrated [200 col. pl.] Agaric Flora of Denmark. This excellent work should be in the hands of all students.]

Laplanche, M. C. de

1894 Dictionnaire iconographique de champignons supérieurs (Hyménomycètes) qui croissent en Europe, Algérie et Tunisie suivi des tableaux de concordance de Barrellier, Batsch, Battarra etc. 542p. Paris.

Lindau, G.

1897 Pezizineae-Hysteriineae; Pyrenomycetineae-Laboulbenii-neae. In Engler and Prantl, Nat. Pflanzenfam., 1 :1 :278, 321–505. Illus.

1900 Auriculariales, Tremellineae, etc. In Engler and Prantl, Nat. Pflanzenfam., 1 :2 :82–96, 347–523. Illus.

1928 Die höheren Pilze, Basidiomycetes, etc. 3d Edition. Berlin.

Lindau, G., and Sydow, P.

1908–1918 Thesaurus litteraturae mycologicae et lichenologicae etc. 5 vols. Leipzig.

Linder, D. H.

1928 Concerning the Status of the Genus *Laternea.* Ann. Missouri Bot. Gard., 15 :109–112, pl. 20.

1933 The Genus *Schizophyllum.* I. Species of the Western Hemisphere. Amer. Jour. Bot., 20 :552–564. Illus.

Ling, L.

1933 Studies on the Genus *Poria* of China. I. Contr. Biol. Lab. Sci. Soc. China, Bot. Ser., 8 :222–232. Illus.

Lloyd, C. G.

1898 A Compilation of the Volvae of the United States. Cincinnati.
[In vol. 1 of this author's Mycological Writings.]

1902 The Genera of Gastromycetes. Cincinnati.
[In vol. 1 of this author's Mycological Writings.]

1902a The Geastrae. Cincinnati.
[In vol. 1 of this author's Mycological Writings.]

Lloyd, C. G.
1905   The Genus *Mitremyces* [=*Calostoma*]. Cincinnati.
       [In vol. 2 of this author's Mycological Writings.]
1906   The Nidulariaceae. Cincinnati.
       [In vol. 2 of this author's Mycological Writings.]
1906a The Tylostomeae. Cincinnati.
       [In vol. 2 of this author's Mycological Writings.]
1909   Synopsis of the Known Phalloids. Cincinnati.
       [In vol. 3 of this author's Mycological Writings.]
1910   Synopsis of the Sections Microporus, Tabacinus and
       Funales of the Genus *Polystictus*. Cincinnati.
       [In vol. 3 of this author's Mycological Writings.]
1910a Synopsis of the Genus *Hexagona*. Cincinnati.
       [In vol. 3 of this author's Mycological Writings.]
1911   Synopsis of the Section Ovinus of *Polyporus*. Cincinnati.
       [In vol. 3 of this author's Mycological Writings.]
1912   Synopsis of the Stipitate Polyporoids. Cincinnati.
       [In vol. 3 of this author's Mycological Writings.]
1913   Synopsis of the Genus *Cladoderris*. Cincinnati.
       [In vol. 4 of this author's Mycological Writings.]
1913a Synopsis of the Stipitate Stereums. Cincinnati.
       [In vol. 4 of this author's Mycological Writings.]
1915   Synopsis of the Genus *Fomes*. Cincinnati.
       [In vol. 4 of this author's Mycological Writings.]
1915a Synopsis of the Section Apus of the Genus *Polyporus*.
       Cincinnati.
       [In vol. 4 of this author's Mycological Writings.]
1916   The Geoglossaceae. Cincinnati.
       [In vol. 5 of this author's Mycological Writings.]
1917   The Genus *Radulum*. Cincinnati.
       [In vol. 5 of this author's Mycological Writings.]
1917a Synopsis of Some Genera of the Large Pyrenomycetes.
       Cincinnati.
       [In vol. 5 of this author's Mycological Writings.]
1919   The Large Pyrenomycetes (second paper). Cincinnati.
       [In vol. 5 of this author's Mycological Writings.]

Lohman, M. L.
1927   The Iowa Species of *Lycoperdon*. Univ. Iowa Studies
       Nat. Hist., 12:5–28. Illus.

Long, W. H.
1907   The Phalloideae of Texas. Jour. of Mycology,
       13:102–114.

Longnecker, W. M.
1927   The Geasters of Iowa. Univ. Iowa Studies Nat. Hist.,
       12:29–47. Illus.

Looney, A. M.
1933   A Morphological Study of Certain Species of *Tremella*.
       Univ. Iowa Stud. Nat. Hist., 15:17–33. Illus.

Lorenz, F.

1933 Beiträge zur Entwicklungsgeschichte von *Sphaerobolus*. Arch. Protistenk., 81:361–398. Illus.

Lowe, J. L.

1934 The Polyporaceae of New York (Pileate Species). Bul. New York State College of Forestry, Technical Publication No. 41, Syracuse University, 142 p., 2 pl.

1934a Notes on some Species of *Polyporus*. Papers Mich. Acad. Sci., 19:141–148. Illus.

Lyman, G. R.

1907 Culture Studies on Polymorphism of Hymenomycetes. Boston Soc. Nat. Hist. Proc., 33:125–209.

Macadam, R. K.

1889 North American Agarics (Genus *Russula*). Jour. of Mycology, 5:58, 135.

Maerz, A., and Paul, M. R.

1930 A Dictionary of Color. 207p., 7056 Colors on 56 pl. New York and London.

Maire, R.

1910 Les bases de la classification dans le genre *Russula*. Bul. Soc. Myc. Fr., 26:49–125.

Marshall, N. L.

1910–1913 The Mushroom Book. 170p. Garden City and New York. (Also an edition of 1901 [1st?] 167p.)

Martin, G W.

1927 Basidia and Spores of the Nidulariaceae. Mycologia, 19:239–247. Illus.

1931[?] Notes on Iowa Fungi, 1928. [The Iowa Species of *Mutinus*, etc.]. Proc. Iowa Acad. Sci., 36 (1929): 127–130. 1 plate.

1931a Notes on Iowa Fungi, 1929–1930. Univ. Iowa Studies Nat. Hist., 13:1–10. pl. 1.

Martin, G. W., and Fisher, M. C.

1933 The Genera of the Dacrymycetaceae. Univ. Iowa Stud. Nat. Hist., 15:8–13. Illus.

Martin, G. W., and Huber, E. E.

1927 Notes on the Tremellales of Iowa with Keys. Univ. Iowa Studies Nat. Hist., 12:91–104. Illus.

Mason, E.

1928 Note on the Presence of Mycorrhizae in the Roots of Salt Marsh Plants. New Phytol., 27:193–195. Illus.

Massee, G. E.

1887   Revision of *Polysaccum.* Grevillea, 16:27.

1887a A Monograph of the Genus *Lycoperdon* (Tournef.) Fr. Roy. Microsc. Soc. Jour., part 5, p. 701–727.

1888   Revision of *Polysaccum.* Grevillea, 16:76.

1888a A Monograph of the Genus *Calostoma,* Desv. (*Mitremyces,* Nees). Annals of Bot., 2:25–45.

1888b A Revision of the Genus *Bovista* (Dill.) Fr. Separate of 9p. from Jour. of Bot., for May.

1889   A Monograph of the British Gasteromycetes. Ann. Bot., 4:103, 4 pl.

1890   A Monograph of the Genus *Podaxis* Desv. [=*Podaxon* Fr.] Separate of 16p. from Jour. of Bot., for February and March.

1891   New or Imperfectly Known Gastromycetes. Grevillea, 19:94–98.

1892–1895 British Fungous Flora. 4 vol. London and New York.

1895   A Revision of the Genus *Cordyceps.* Annals of Bot., 9:1–14.

1896   A Revision of the Genus *Coprinus.* Annals of Bot., 38:123–184.

1897   A Monograph of the Geoglossaceae. Annals of Bot., 11:225–306.

1902   European Fungus Flora: Agaricaceae. 274p. London.

1904   A Monograph of the Genus *Inocybe,* Karsten. Annals of Bot., 18:459–504.

1909   The Structure and Affinities of the British Tuberaceae. Ann. Bot., 23:243–265.

1911   British Fungi, with a Chapter on Lichens. 551p. London.

Masui, K.

1927   A Study of the Ectotrophic Mycorrhizas of Woody Plants. Memoirs of the College of Sci., Kyôto Imperial Univ., Ser. B., Vol. 3, No. 2, p. 149–279. Kyôto.

McDougall, W. B.

1914   On the Mycorrhizas of Forest Trees. Amer. Jour. of Bot., 1:48.

1917   Some Edible and Poisonous Mushrooms. Illinois State Lab. Nat. Hist. Bul., 11:413–555.

1925   Mushrooms, a Handbook of Edible and Inedible Species. 151p. Boston and New York.

McIlvaine, C., and Macadam, R. K.

1900   Toadstools, Mushrooms, Fungi, Edible and Poisonous. One Thousand American Fungi etc. 704p. Indianapolis.

       [Also revised edition by C. F. Millspaugh, Indianapolis, 1912.]

McKenny, M.

1929 Mushrooms of Field and Wood. 193p., 3 col. pl., 50 text figs. New York.

Meinecke, E. P.

1914 Forest Tree Diseases Common in California and Nevada. A Manual for Field Use. Forest Service, U. S. Dept. Agr. 67p.

1930 Forest Tree Diseases and Their Control. Doc. Mat. Inter. Amer. Conf. Agr., For. and Animal Ind., 2:109–116.

Melin, E.

1930 Investigations of the Significance of Tree Mycorrhiza. Translated from the German by Paul W. Stickel. Ann Arbor, Mich.

Mendel, L. B.

1898 The Chemical Composition and Nutritive Value of Some Edible American Fungi. Amer. Jour. of Physiol., 1:225–238.

Metcalf, M. M.

1925 *Amanita muscaria* in Maine. Science, N. S., 61:567.

Michael, E.

1918–1919 Führer für Pilzfreunde. Edit. B, 3 vols., 346 col. fig. with descriptions. Zwickau.
[A new, revised edition has been published by R. Schulz.]

Migula, W.

1931 Kryptogamen-Flora, vol. XI, 1–2. Die Pilze. Berlin.

Miller, L. W.

1933 The Genera of Hydnaceae. Mycologia, 25:286–302.
1933a The Hydnaceae of Iowa. I. Mycologia, 25:356–368. Illus.
1934 The Hydnaceae of Iowa. II. The Genus *Odontia*. Mycologia, 26:13–32. Illus.
1934a The Hydnaceae of Iowa. III. The Genera *Radulum, Mucronella, Caldesiella* and *Gloiodon*. Mycologia, 26:212–219. Illus.

Mimura, S.

1933 The Relation between Forest-trees and their Mycorrhizae. Extracts Bul. Imp. For. Exp. Sta. Japan, 2 (1915–1930):51–52.

Moffatt, W. S.

1909 The Higher Fungi of the Chicago Region. Part I. The Hymenomycetes. Chicago Acad. Sci. Nat. Hist. Surv. Bul., 7 (part 1), 156p.

1923 The Higher Fungi of the Chicago Region. II. The Gastromycetes. Chicago Acad. of Sci. Nat. Hist. Surv. Bul., 7 (part 2), 24p.

Möller, A.

1893 Die Pilzgärten einiger südamerikanischer Ameisen (Botan. Mittheil. aus den Tropen von A. F. W. Schimper, Heft 6). 127p. Jena.

Morgan, A. P.

1885 North American Geasters. Jour. of Mycology, 1:7.

1885a On the Study of the Agaricini. Jour. of Mycology, 1:41.

1887 North American Agarics.—The Subgenus *Amanita*. Jour. of Mycology, 3:25.

1889 North American Fungi. The Gastromycetes. Cincinnati Soc. Nat. Hist. Jour., January, p. 141–149.

1889a North American Fungi. The Gastromycetes. Cincinnati Soc. Nat. Hist. Jour., April, p. 8–22.

1890 North American Fungi. The Gastromycetes. Cincinnati Soc. Nat. Hist. Jour., January, p. 163–172.

1891 North American Fungi. The Gastromycetes. Cincinnati Soc. Nat. Hist. Jour., April, p. 5–21.

1892 North American Fungi. The Gastromycetes. Cincinnati Soc. Nat. Hist. Jour, 14:141–148.

1902 Morchellae—The Morels. Jour. of Mycology, 8:49–50.

1902a The Discomycetes of the Miami Valley, Ohio. Jour. of Mycology, 8:179–192.

1906 North American Species of *Marasmius*. Jour. of Mycology, 11:201–212.

1906a North American Species of *Heliomyces*. Jour. of Mycology, 12:92–95.

1906b North American Species of *Lepiota*. Jour. of Mycology, 12:154–159, 195–203, 242–248.

1907 North American Species of *Lepiota*. Jour. of Mycology, 13:1–18.

1907a North American Species of Agaricaceae. The Melanosporae. Jour. of Mycology, 13:53–62, 143–153, 246–255.

1908 North American Species of Agaricaceae. The Melanosporae. Jour. of Mycology, 14:27–32, 64–75.

Morse, E. E.

1933 A Study of the Genus *Podaxis* [*Podaxon*]. Mycologia, 25:1–33. Illus.

Morse, E. E.

1934   The Whispering Fungus [*Elvela mitra* = *Helvella mitra*].
Nature Mag., 24:84. Illus.

Murrill, W. A.

1906   A Key to the Agaricaceae of Temperate North America.
Torreya, 5:213–214.

1907–1908   Polyporaceae (pars.) North American Flora, 9:1–72,
73–131.

1909   A New Poisonous Mushroom. Mycologia, 1:211–214.

1910   Agaricales. Fam. 6. Boletaceae. Fam. 7. Agaricaceae.
Tribe 1.   Chantereleae.   North American Flora,
9:133–172.

1913   The Amanitas of Eastern North America. Mycologia,
5:72–86.

1914   (Agaricales) Agaricaceae. North American Flora,
10:1–76.

1914a   American Boletes. 40p. New York.

1914b   Northern Polypores. 64p. New York.

1915   Luminescence in the Fungi. Mycologia, 7:131–133.

1915a   Agariceae. North American Flora, 9:237–296.

1915b   Southern Polypores. 66p. New York.

1915c   Western Polypores. 36p. New York.

1916   A Very Dangerous Mushroom. Mycologia, 8:186–187.

1916a   *Pleurotus, Omphalia, Mycena,* and *Collybia* Published in
North American Flora. Mycologia, 8:218–221.

1916b   Agaricaceae (pars.)   North American Flora, 9:297–426.

1917   (Agaricales) Agaricaceae. North American Flora,
10:77–226.

1917a   The Taxonomy of the Agaricaceae. Amer. Jour. Bot.,
4:315–326.

1919   Boleti from Connecticut. Mycologia, 11:321–322.

1922   Dark-spored Agarics. I. *Drosophila, Hypholoma,* and
Pilosace. Mycologia, 14:61–76.

1922a   Dark-spored Agarics. II. *Gomphidius* and *Stropharia.*
Mycologia, 14:121–142.

1922b   Dark-spored   Agarics.   III.   *Agaricus*   [=Psalliota].
Mycologia, 14:200–221.

1922c   Dark-spored   Agarics.   IV.   *Deconica, Atylospora*
[*Psathyra*] and *Psathyrella.* Mycologia, 14:258–278.

1923   Dark-spored   Agarics.   V.   [*Psilocybe.*]   Mycologia,
15:1–22.

1924   Lake Placid Fungi. Mycologia, 16:96—98.

Neuhoff, J. J.

1924   Zytologie und systematische Stellung der Auriculariaceen
und Tremellaceen. Bot. Arch., 8:250–297.

Neuman, J. J.

1914   The Polyporaceae of Wisconsin. Wisc. Geol. and Nat.
Hist. Surv. Bul., 33:1–206.

Offner, J.

1905 Les spores des champignons au point de vue médico-
légal. p. 375–422. Grenoble.

Overholts, L. O.

1911 The Known Polyporaceae of Ohio. The Ohio Naturalist, June, p. 353–373.

1914 The Polyporaceae of Ohio. Missouri Bot. Gard. Ann.,
1 :81–155.

1915 Comparative Studies in the Polyporaceae. Missouri Bot.
Gard. Ann., 2 :667–730.

1915a The Polyporaceae of the Middle-Western United States.
Washington Univ. Studies, III : 3–98.

1919 The Species of *Poria* Described by Peck. New York State
Mus. Bul., 205–206 :67–166.

1922 Diagnoses of American Porias. I. Mycologia, 14 :1–11.
Illus.

1923 Diagnoses of American Porias. II. Bul. Torrey Bot.
Club, 50 :245–253. Illus.

1923a The Species of *Poria* Described by Schweinitz. Mycologia,
15 :207–232. Illus.

1924 *Pholiota.* North American Flora, 10 :261–276.

1927 A Monograph of the Genus *Pholiota* in the United States.
Missouri Bot. Gard. Ann., 14 :87–210.

1929 Research Methods in the Taxonomy of the Hymenomycetes. Proc. Int. Congr. Plant Sci., 1926, 2 :1688–1712.
Illus.

1931 Diagnoses of American Porias. III. Some Additional
Species, with a Key to the Common Brown Species of
the United States and Canada. Mycologia, 23 :117–129.
Illus.

1932 *Hypodendrum [Pholiota].* N. Amer. Flora. 10 [pt. 5] :
277–281.

1933 The Polyporaceae of Pennsylvania. I. The Genus
Polyporus. Pennsylvania Agr. Exp. Sta. Bul. 298, 28
pp. Illus.

1934 Mycological Notes for 1933. Mycologia, 26 :502–515.
Illus.

Palmer, J. A.

1885 Mushrooms of America, Edible and Poisonous. 4p., 12
col. pl. Boston.

Parker, C. S.

1933 A Taxonomic Study of the Genus *Hypholoma* in North
America. Mycologia, 25 :160–212. Illus.

Patterson, F. W., and Charles, V. K.

1915 Mushrooms and Other Common Fungi. U. S. Dept. Agr. Bul., 175:1–64.

Peck, C. H.

1872 New York Fungi (Agarici). Grevillea, 1:2–4, 17–19.

1872a *Mycena.* N. Y. State Cab. Rept., 23:80–84. Bot. ed.

1872b *Leptonia.* N. Y. State Cab. Rept., 23:89. Bot. ed.

1872c *Naucoria.* N. Y. State Cab. Rept., 23:91–93. Bot. ed.

1872d *Panaeolus.* N. Y. State Cab. Rept., 23:100–102. Bot. ed.

1872e *Psathyrella.* N. Y. State Cab. Rept., 23:102–103. Bot. ed.

1872f *Coprinus.* N. Y. State Cab. Rept., 23:103–104. Bot. ed.

1872g *Cortinarius.* N. Y. State Cab. Rept., 23:105–112. Bot. ed.

1872h *Marasmius.* N. Y. State Cab. Rept., 23:124–126. Bot. ed.

1872i *Clavaria.* [New York species.] N. Y. State Mus. Rept., 24:104–105.

1879 New York Species of *Helvella.* [A key.] N. Y. State Mus. Rept., 31:59.

1879a New York Species of *Xylaria.* N. Y. State Mus. Rept., 31:60.

1879b United States Species of *Lycoperdon* [including *Calvatia*]. N. Y. State Mus. Rept., 32:58–72.

1880 New York Species of *Amanita* [and *Amanitopsis*]. N. Y. State Mus. Rept., 33:38–49.

1884 New York Species of *Lepiota.* N. Y. State Mus. Rept., 35:150–164.

1884a New York Species of *Psalliota* [=*Agaricus*]. N. Y. State Mus. Rept., 36:41–49.

1885 New York Species of *Lactarius.* N. Y. State Mus. Rept., 38:111–133.

1885a New York Species of *Pluteus.* N. Y. State Mus. Rept., 38:133–138.

1886 New York Species of *Pleurotus, Claudopus,* and *Crepidotus.* N. Y. State Mus. Rept., 39:58–73.

1887 New York Species of *Paxillus.* N. Y. State Mus. Bul., 1:29–33.

1887a New York Species of *Cantharellus.* N. Y. State Mus. Bul., 1:34–43.

1887b *Craterellus.* N. Y. State Mus. Bul., 1:44–48.

1887c New York Species of Viscid Boleti. N. Y. State Mus. Bul., 1:57–66.

1889 New York Species of *Clitopilus.* N. Y. State Mus. Rept., 42:39–46. Bot. ed.

1889a Boleti of the United States. N. Y. State Mus. Bul., 2:73–106.

1890 New York Species of *Armillaria.* N. Y. State Mus. Rept., 43:40–44.

1890a Synopsis of the United States Species of *Armillaria.* N. Y. State Mus. Rept., 43:44–45.

1891 New York Species of *Tricholoma.* N. Y. State Mus. Rept., 44:38–64. Bot. ed.

Peck, C. H.

1893 New York Species of *Omphalia*. N. Y. State Mus. Rept., 45:32–42. Bot. ed.

1893a New York Species of *Pluteolus*. N. Y. State Mus. Rept., 46:58–61. Bot. ed.

1893b New York Species of *Galera*. N. Y. State Mus. Rept., 46:61–69. Bot. ed.

1895 Edible and Poisonous Fungi of New York. N. Y. State Mus. Rept., 48:105–241. Pl. A., and col. pls. 1–43.
[2d ed. '97. For the continuation of this paper, see **Peck**, '00a and succeeding bulletins.]

1896 New York Species of *Collybia*. N. Y. State Mus. Rept., 49:32–55. Bot. ed.

1897 *Spathularia* [Key to the New York species]. N. Y. State Mus. Rept., 50:118–119.

1897a New York Species of *Flammula*. N. Y. State Mus. Rept., 50:133–142.

1900 *Odontia* [Key to the New York species]. N. Y. State Mus. Rept., 53:847.

1900a Report of the State Botanist on Edible Fungi of New York, 1895–1899. N. Y. State Mus. Mem., Vol. 3 (No. 4):131–234. Col. pls. 44–68.
[For the first paper see **Peck**, '95.]

1901 *Trametes* [Key to the New York species]. N. Y. State Mus. Rept., 54:169–170.

1907 New York Species of *Hygrophorus*. N. Y. State Mus. Bul., 116:45–67.

1907a New York Species of *Russula*. N. Y. State Mus. Bul., 116:67–98.

1908 New York Species of *Pholiota*. N. Y. State Mus. Bul., 122:141–158.

1909 New York Species of *Lentinus*. N. Y. State Mus. Bul., 131:42–47.

1909a New York Species of *Entoloma*. N. Y. State Mus. Bul., 131:47–54.

1910 New York Species of *Inocybe*. N. Y. State Mus. Bul., 139:48–67.

1910a New York Species of *Hebeloma*. N. Y. State Mus. Bul., 139:67–77.

1911 New York Species of *Hypholoma*. N. Y. State Mus. Bul., 150:73–84.

1911a New York Species of *Psathyra*. N. Y. State Mus. Bul., 150:84–86.

1912 New York Species of *Clitocybe*. N. Y. State Mus. Bul., 157:59–89.
[Account of poisoning by *Pholiota autumnalis*.]

1912a New York Species of *Laccaria*. N. Y. State Mus. Bul., 157:90–93.

1912b New York Species of *Psilocybe*. N. Y. State Mus. Bul., 157:94–105.

Pennington, L. H.

1915 New York Species of *Marasmius*. N. Y. State Mus. Bul., 179:52–79.

1915a *Marasmius* (temperate species). North American Flora, 9:250–286.

Pernot, E. F.

1908 Preserving Wild Mushrooms. Oregon Agr. Exp. Sta. Bul., 98:1–6.

Phillips, W.

1881 A Revision of the Genus *Vibrissea*. Linnean Soc. London Trans., 2 (Ser. 2):1–10.

1887. A Manual of the British Discomycetes etc. 446p. London.

Plunkett, O. A., Young, P. A., and Ryan, R. W.

1923 A Systematic Presentation of New Genera of Fungi. American Microsc. Soc. Trans., 42:43–67.

[A list of names of new families and genera of fungi described since the appearance of volume 22 of Saccardo's Sylloge Fungorum. An accompanying typewritten list continues this paper.]

Pritzel, G. A.

1872 Thesaurus litteraturae botanica etc. 576p. New ed. Leipzig.

Quélet, L., and Bataille, F.

1902 Flora Monographique des Amanites et des Lépiotes. 88p. Paris.

Rabenhorst, L.

1884–1896 Kryptogamen-Flora von Deutschland, Oesterreich und der Schweiz. Vol. 1, Abt. 1, 1884; Abt. 2, 1887; Abt. 3, 1906. 2d ed.

Ramsbottom. J.

1923 A Handbook of the Larger British Fungi. 222p. London.

1927 Fairy Rings. Quekett Microsc. Club Jour., 15 (Ser. 2):231–242.

Rankin, W. H.

1918 Manual of Tree Diseases. 398p. New York.

Rayner, J. F.

1906 Mycology as a Branch of Nature Study. Brit. Mycol. Soc. Trans., for 1905, p. 123–126.

1922 Mycorrhiza in the Ericaceae. Brit. Mycol. Soc. Trans., 8:61–66.

Rea, C.
1922   British Basidiomycetae. A Handbook to the Larger.
       British Fungi. 799 p. Cambridge, Eng.
1927   Appendix to British Basidiomycetae. Additions and Cor-
       rections. Brit. Mycol. Soc. Trans., 12:205–230.
1932   Appendix II to British Basidiomycetae. Trans. Brit.
       Mycol. Soc., 17:35–50, col., pl.

Richon, C., and Roze, E.
1888   Atlas des champignons comestibles et vénéneux de la
       France et des pays circonvoisins, etc. Folio. 265p.,
       72 col. pl. Paris.

Ricken, A.
1915   Die Blätterpilze (Agaricaceae) Deutschlands und der
       angrenzenden Länder, besonders Österreichs und der
       Schweiz. 2 vols., 480p., 112 col. pl. Leipzig.

Ridgway, R.
1912   Color Standards and Color Nomenclature. 43p., 53 col. pl.
       Washington, D. C.

Robinson, W.
——   Mushroom Culture, its Extension and Improvement. 172p.
       London.

Rolfe, R. T., and Rolfe, F. W.
1925   The Romance of the Fungus World. 309p. London.

Rosen, H. R.
1926   A New *Amanita* from Arkansas [*A. arkansana*]. Myco-
       logia, 18:97–99.
1927   A Pink-colored Form of *Polyporus sulphureus* and its
       Probable Relationship to Root-rot of Oaks. Mycologia,
       19:191–194.

Roze, E.
1882–1883   Le Parasitisme du *Morchella esculenta* Pers. sur
       l'Helianthus tuberosus, L. Bul. Soc. Bot. France,
       29:166–167; 30:139–143.

Saccardo, P. A.
1882–1931   Sylloge Fungorum. Vols. 1–25. Padua.
       [See **Plunkett, O. A., Young, P. A., and Ryan, R. W.**]

Sartory, A., and Maire, L.
1918   Synopsis du genre *Collybia,* 226p. Paris
1918a Synopsis du genre *Tricholoma,* 158p. Paris.
[1931]   Monographie du genre *Boletus* Dill. Nancy.

Sass, J. E.
1929   The Cytological Basis for Homothallism and Hetero-
       thallism in the Agaricaceae. Amer. Jour. Bot., 16:663–
       701. Illus. pl. LXIV-LXVII.

Schaeffer, J.

1933–1934 *Russula*-monographic. Annal. Mycol., 31:305–515. Illus.; ibid., 32: 141–243. Illus.

1933 Bestimmungstabelle für die europäischen Täublinge [*Russula*]. Zeitschr. f. Pilzk., 12:48–53, 83–91.

Schäffer, J. C.

1762–1770 Fungorum qui in Bavaria et Palatinatu circa Ratisbonam nascuntur icones. 3 vols., 300 col. pl. and descriptive text. Regensburg. [New edition by C. H. Persoon, 4 vols., 330 col. pl. with text. Erlangen, 1800.]

Schrenk, H. v.

1900 Fungous Diseases of Forest Trees. U. S. Dept. Agr. Yearbook, p. 199–210.

1902 The Decay of Timber and Methods of Preventing it. U. S. Dept. Agr., Bur. Plant Industry Bul., 14:1–96.

Schrenk, H. v., and Spaulding, P.

1909 Diseases of Deciduous Forest Trees. U. S. Dept. Agr., Bur. Plant Industry Bul., 149:1–85.

Schroeter, J.

1897 Helvellineae. In Engler and Prantl, Nat. Pflanzenfam. 1:1:172. Illus.

Seaver, F. J.

1909 Discomycetes of North Dakota. Mycologia, 1:104–114.

1910 Iowa Discomycetes. Contribs. from the N. Y. Bot. Gard., No. 133, p. 41–219.

1914 North American Species of *Aleuria* and *Aleurina*. Mycologia, 6:273–278.

1915 Photographs and Descriptions of Cup-fungi—I. *Peziza*. Mycologia, 7:90–93.

1915a Illustrations and Descriptions of Cup-fungi—II. *Sepultaria*. Mycologia, 7:197–199.

1916 Photographs and Descriptions of Cup-fungi—III. *Peziza domiciliana* and *Peziza repanda*. Mycologia, 8:195–198.

1916a Photographs and Descriptions of Cup-fungi—IV. *Peziza clypeata*. Mycologia, 8:235–238.

1917 Photographs and Descriptions of Cup-fungi.—V. *Peziza proteana* and *Peziza violacea*. Mycologia, 9:1–3.

1917a Photographs and Descriptions of Cup-fungi—VI. *Discina venosa*. Mycologia, 9:53–54.

1918 Photographs and Descriptions of Cup-fungi—VII. The Genus *Underwoodia*. Mycologia, 10:1–3.

1920 Photographs and Descriptions of Cup-fungi.—VIII. *Elvela infula* and *Gyromitra esculenta*. Mycologia, 12:1–5.

1921 Photographs and Descriptions of Cup-fungi—IX. North American Species of *Discina*. Mycologia, 13:67–71.

Seaver, F. J.

1928 The North American Cup-fungi (Operculates). 284p. New York. [Pezizales].

1930 Photographs and Descriptions of Cup-fungi. XI. *Solenopeziza.* Mycologia, 22:122–124.

1930a Photographs and Descriptions of Cup-fungi. XII. Elvelaceae [Helvellaceae]. Mycologia, 22:163–164. Illus.

1931 A Rare Phalloid from the New York Botanical Garden. Mycologia, 23:83–84, pl. 8. [*Colus schellenbergiae*].

1931a Photographs and Descriptions of Cup-fungi. XV. The Giant *Elvela* [*Helvella*]. Mycologia, 23:409–410. Illus.

1934 Another rare Phalloid. Mycologia, 26:273–275. Illus.

Seymour, A. B.

1929 Host Index of the Fungi of North America. 732p. Cambridge, Mass.

Seyot, P.

1930 Les Amanites. Mém. Soc. Sci. Nancy, 1 (1929):104–126. Illus.

Shantz, H. L., and Piemeisel, R. L.

1917 Fungus Fairy Rings in Eastern Colorado and their Effect on Vegetation. U. S. Dept., Agr., Jour. Agr. Research, 11:191–245.

Sharp, W. M.

1933 The Polyporaceae of Monongalia County, West Virginia. Proc. West Virginia Acad. Sci., 6:29–31.

Shope, P. F.

1931 The Polyporaceae of Colorado. Ann. Missouri Bot. Gard., 18:287–408. Illus.

Singer, R.

1932 Monographie der Gattung *Russula*. Beih. Bot. Centralbl. Abt. II, 49:205–380.

Smith, A. H.

1934 New or unusual Agarics from Michigan. Ann. Mycol., 32:471–487. Illus.

1934a Investigations of Two-spored Forms in the Genus *Mycena*. Mycologia, 26:305–331. Illus.

1934b Unusual Agarics from Michigan. Papers Mich. Acad. Sci., 19.205–216. Illus.

Smith, A. L.

1917 The Relation of Fungi to other Organisms. Brit. Mycol. Soc. Trans., 6:17–31.

1920 A Drain-blocking Fungus. Brit. Mycol. Soc. Trans., 6:262–263.

Smith, C. O.

1899 *Agaricus (Psalliota)* of the Champlain Valley. Rhodora, 1:161–164.

Smith, L. B.

1931 Some Common Polypores of New England. Bul. Boston Soc. Nat. Hist., 59:13–20. Illus.

Snell, W. H.

1932 Notes on Boletes. I. *Boletus porphyrosporus.* Mycologia, 24:334–341. Illus.

1933 Notes on Boletes. II. Mycologia, 25:221–232.

1934 Notes on Boletes. III. Mycologia, 26:348–359. Illus.

Solheim, W. G., Young, P. A., and Plunkett, O. A.

1927 A Systematic Presentation of new Genera of Fungi. II. Trans. Amer. Micros. Soc., 46:187–207.
[For Pt. I, see: **Plunkett, O. A.**; see also **Guba, E. F., and Young, P. A.**]

Sowerby, J.

1797–1809 Coloured Figures of English Fungi or Mushrooms. Folio, 3 vols. and supplement, 440 col. pl. with text. London.

Spaulding, P.

1909 The Present Status of the White-pine Blights. U. S. Dept. Agr., Bur. Plant Industry Cir. 35, p. 1–12.

Stevens, F. L.

1913 The Fungi Which Cause Plant Disease. 754p. New York.

Stevenson, J.

1886 Hymenomycetes britannici. British Fungi (Hymenomycetes). 2 vols. Edinburgh and London.

Stone, R. E.

1920 Upon the Audibility of Spore Discharge in *Helvella elastica.* Brit. Mycol. Soc. Trans., 6:294.

Stover, W. G.
1912   The Agaricaceae of Ohio. Ohio State Acad. Sci. Proc., 5:462–577.
1930   A Popular Key to the Distinctive Groups of the Larger Fungi. Ohio Journ. Sci., 30:81–84.

Sumstine, D. R.
1916   A new Species of *Colus* from Pennsylvania. Mycologia, 8:183–184.
1918   Fungi of Chautauqua County, New York. N. Y. State Mus. Bul., 197:111–118.

Swartz, D.
1933   Some Developmental Characters of Species of Lycoperdaceae. Amer. Jour. Bot., 20:440–465, pl. 29–30.

Szemere.
1932   Der tödlich-giftige Heide-Trichterling, *Clitocybe corda* Schulzer. Zeitschr. f. Pilzk., 16 (N. S. 11):92–98. Illus.

Thomas, C. A.
1931   Mushroom Insects, their Biology and Control. Penn. State College, Agr. Exper. Sta., Bul. 270:1–42. Illus.

Thomas, W. S.
1928   Field Book of Common Gilled Mushrooms with a Key to their Identification and Directions for Cooking those that are Edible. New York.

Togashi, K., and Oda, K.
1934   Spore-size Variability in subsequent Spore Prints of some Hymenomycetous Fungi. Trans. Sapporo Nat. Hist. Soc., 13:121–125.

Trelease, W.
1888   Morels and Puff-balls of Madison, Wisc. Wisc. Acad. Sci. Arts and Letters Trans., 7:105.

Tulasne, L. and C.
1863   Selecta Fungorum Carpologia. Vol. 2:1–319. [See the English translation, by W. B. Grove, 1930.]

Ulbrich, E.
1926   Bildungsabweichungen bei Hutpilzen. Verhandl. Bot. Ver. Prov. Brandenburg, 1926 (1):1–104. Illus.

Underwood, L. M.
1896   On the Distribution of the North American Helvellales. Minnesota Bot. Studies, 8:483–500.
1899   Moulds, Mildews and Mushrooms. A Guide to the Systematic Study of Fungi and the Mycetozoa and their Literature. 236p. New York.

Underwood, L. M., and Earle, F. S.
1897   A Preliminary List of Alabama Fungi.   Alabama Agr.
       Exp. Sta. Bul., 80:113–283.
       [Suggestions to collectors of fleshy fungi, p. 271.]

Veselý, R.
1933   Revisio critica Amanitarum europaearum.   Annal. Mycol.,
       31:209–304.   Illus.   [See also **Kavina, K.**, and **Pilat, A.**,
       '34.]

Vittadini, C.
1835   Descrizione dei funghi mangerecci più communi dell'
       Italia e de' velenosi che possono ció medesimi con-
       fondersi.   364p., 44 col. pl.   Milan.

Wehmeyer, L. E.
1926   A Biologic and Phylogenetic Study of the Stromatic
       Sphaeriales.   Amer. Jour. Bot., 13:575–645.

Weiss, H. B.
1922   The Fungous Insect Fauna of a Mesophytic Woods in
       New Jersey.   Proc. Biol. Soc. of Washington (D. C.),
       35:126–128, 2 pls.

Whetzel, H. H.
1918   An Outline of the History of Phytopathology.   130p.
       Philadelphia.
1926   North American Species of *Sclerotinia*.   I.   Mycologia,
       18:224–235.   Illus.

White, E. A.
1905   A Preliminary Report on the Hymeniales of Connecticut.
       Conn. Geol. and Nat. Hist. Surv. Bul., 3:1–81.
1910   Second Report on the Hymeniales of Connecticut.   Conn.
       Geol. and Nat. Hist. Surv. Bul., 15:1–70.

White, V. S.
1901   The Tylostomaceae of North America.   Torrey Bot. Club
       Bul., 28:421–444.
1902   The Nidulariaceae of North America.   Torrey Bot. Club
       Bul., 29:251–280.

Withering, W.
1796   An Arrangement of British Plants.   Vol. 4.   3d ed.
       London.

Wolf, M. M.
1931   The Polyporaceae of Iowa.   Univ. Iowa Studies Nat.
       Hist., Vol. 14, No. 1, 93p.   Illus.

Yates, H. S.
1916   The Comparative Histology of Certain Californian
       Boletaceae.   Univ. California Public. Bot., 6:221–274.

Zeller, S. M.

1915   Notes on *Cryptoporus volvatus.* Mycologia, 7:121–125.
1929   Contribution to our Knowledge of Oregon Fungi. III. Mycologia, 21:97–111. Illus.
1934   *Protogaster,* representing a new Order of the Gasteromycetes. Ann. Missouri Bot. Gard., 21:231–240. Illus.

Zeller, S. M., and Dodge, C. W.

1918   *Rhizopogon* in North America. Missouri Bot. Gard. Ann., 5:1–36.
1918a *Gautieria* in North America. Missouri Bot. Gard. Ann., 5:133–142.
1919   *Arcangeliella, Gymnomyces* and *Macowanites* in North America. Missouri Bot. Gard. Ann., 6:49–59.
1924   *Leucogaster* and *Leucophlebs* in North America. Missouri Bot. Gard. Ann., 11:389–410.
1929   *Hysterangium* in North America. Ann. Missouri. Bot. Gard., 16:83–122. Illus.

Zeller, S. M., and Togashi, K.

1934   The American and Japanese Matsu-takes. Mycologia, 26:544–558. Illus.

GLOSSARY OF TECHNICAL TERMS

A—, prefixed signifies absence; as aseptate, without septa.

Aber'rant, differing in some of its characters from the group in which it is placed; said of an individual, species, genus, etc.

Abnor'mal, not conforming to the usual type; irregular; unnatural.

Abor'tive, imperfect or wanting.

Abrupt', terminating suddenly.

Abstric'tion, separation of one part from another by constriction, especially of spores from their producers (basidia).

Acu'leate, Acu'leated, having prickles; prickle-pointed.

Ad'nate, attached or grown together; said of lamellae broadly attached to the stipe (figure 57k).

Adnexed', applied to lamellae attached to the stipe but not adnate (figure 57f, adnexed with a tooth, or uncinate).

Adpressed', lying close, appressed.

Aeru'ginose, Aeru'ginous, verdigris-green.

Ag'aric, any gill-bearing fungus.

Agglu'tinate, as if glued together; applied to fungi that are firmly attached to a matrix.

Allia'ceous, having the odor of onions.

Aluta'ceous, light leather colored; color of soiled linen; isabelline.

Alve'olate, deeply pitted, so as to resemble honey-comb.

Amphig'enous, (a) growing all around an object; applied to a hymenium which grows on all the surfaces of a fungus, or to fungi which are not restricted to any particular part of the surface of the host; (b) of or pertaining to amphigens.

Amyg'daline, resembling the almond.

Anas'tomosing, intercommunicating or interlacing of veins, lines or any branched system; said of lamellae that are united by transverse veins or partitions (plate 11).

Angus'tate, narrow.

An'nual, completing growth in one year or season.

An'nulate, bearing a ring.

An'nulus, the ring on the stipe of a mushroom formed by the separation of the veil from the margin of the cap (figure 37A, B, D, E, in each at a); see *Veil*.

Ante'rior, in front; denotes a position on the under side of the pileus adjacent to the margin; thus the end of a lamella next the margin is called the anterior end.

A'pex (pl. *A'pices*), the summit; the end furthest from the base or point of attachment.

Ap'ical, relating to the apex or top.

Apic'ulate, tipped with a short and abrupt point.

Apic'ulus (pl. *Apic'uli*), a short, sharp point (figure

54a) ; the point at the end of spores where these were attached to the basidia (figure 24).

Apothe'cium (pl. *Apothe'cia*), in Ascomycetes, an open cup-shaped fructification with the hymenium on its upper concave surface (figure 20p) ; cup.

Appendic'ulate, provided with or having the character of an appendage or appendages; hanging in small fragments, as the ruptured veil sometimes from the margin of the pileus (figure 37D; plate 21).

Ap'planate, flattened out or horizontally expanded.

Appressed', applied closely to the surface or to each other; adpressed.

Approx'imate, near in position; said of lamellae, where they approach the stipe but do not reach it.

Arach'noid, like cobweb (as in *Cortinarius,* figure 57b).

Arbo'real, growing on trees.

Ar'cuate, curved like a bow (gills of *Clitocybe,* figure 57d).

Arena'ceous, Arena'rious, Ar'-enose, sandy; growing in sandy places.

Are'olate, applied to a surface divided into little areas or patches.

Argilla'ceous, resembling or containing a considerable amount of clay; clay-colored; drab.

Ascend'ing, applied to a lamella where its edge forms a line ascending in the direction from the margin of the pileus toward the apex of the stipe, as in conical shaped pilei (figure 57h) ; applied to the partial veil when in the young stage its stipe-attachment is below the level of its marginal one ; in this case a ring formed from it is called inferior.

Ascomyce'tes, group of fungi in which the spores are produced within little sack-like cells, called asci.

As'cospores, spores f o r m e d within an ascus.

As'cus (pl. *As'ci*), microscopic, sack-like cell in which spores, generally eight in number, are developed (figure 3a).

Asep'tate, without partitions or septa.

At'omate, covered with small atoms.

Atro-, in compositions, "black" or "dark."

Atten'uate, becoming gradually narrowed or smaller.

Auranti'acous, orange-colored.

Azo'nate, without zones or circular bands of different color.

Base, the extremity opposite to the apex; the part of an organ nearest its point of attachment; applied to lamellae, (a) the line of attachment to the pileus, (as, connected by veins at the base) ; (b) sometimes used to define the end attached to the stipe (broad or reticulate at the base).

Basidiomyce'tes, group of fungi which has its spores produced on basidia.

Basid'iospore, spore abjointed from the apex of a basidium.

Basid'ium (pl. *B a s i d' i a*), mother cell in the hymenium of Basidiomycetes formed on the end of a hyphal branch and abstricting spores; the spores are generally four in number, each on a sterigma.

but sometimes more, sometimes fewer, and sometimes sessile (figure 3b).

Bi-, prefix meaning "twice."

Bifur'cate, two-forked; divided into two branches (plate 11 [*Cantharellus aurantiacus*] and figure 75).

Bis'ter, Bis'tre, of the color of bister, blackish-brown.

Biolog'ic, Biolog'ical, pertaining to biology or the science of life.

Boot'ed, peronate (like the volva in *Amanita pantherina,* plate 4).

Boss, a knob or short, rounded protuberance; umbo (plate 6, right figure).

Bossed, furnished with a boss.

Bul'bous, said of the stipe of a mushroom when it has a bulb-like swelling at the base (as in *Amanita,* plate 3).

Cadu'cous. See: *Deciduous.*

Caes'pitose, Caes'pitous (see *Cespitose*).

Calyp'tra, hood; applied to that portion of the volva covering the top of the pileus.

Campan'ulate, bell-shaped (figures 57g, 108).

Canes'cent, covered with whitish or gray pubescence (plate 27, on the cap) ; hoary.

Cap, pileus; the expanded umbrella-like receptacle of the toadstool.

Capillit'ium, thread-like tubes or fibers, often branched or combined in a net, interpenetrating the mass of spores within a ripe spore-bearing body—as in *Lycoperdon* (figure 63c, f).

Cap'itate, having a head, or the form of a head.

Carbona'ceous, rigid, blackish, and brittle; like or composed of carbon or coaly matter.

Cartilag'inous, firm and tough; gristly.

Cell, (a) a little cavity, compartment or hollow place; (b) a mass of protoplasm of various size and shape, generally microscopic, with or without a nucleus and enclosing wall, the fundamental form-element of every organized body.

Cell'ulose, the essential constituent of the primary wall-membrane of cells, a secretion from the contained protoplasm.

Ce'paeform, onion-shaped.

Ceruleous. See: *Coeruleous.*

Cespitose, united in tufts (figure 79).

Chan'neled, grooved; hollowed out; trough-like; canaliculate.

Chlam'ydospores, (e n c a s e d spores) are thick-walled resting spores usually formed in rows on hyphae; are regarded as rudiments of sporangia or conidiophores which, interrupted in development, have assumed the form of spores; on germination they usually develop into sporangia or conidiophores.

Chlo'rophyll, the green coloring matter of plants.

Cil'ia (plural of *Cil'ium*), short, straight, parallel hairs, fringing the margin.

Cine'reous, ash-colored.

Cin'nabarine, cinnabar-colored; brilliant red, vermilion.

Cinnamo'meous, c i n n a m o n colored.

Circumscis'sile, opening or dividing by a circular or equatorial line (applied to the volva of Amanitas, see figure 39b).

Cit'rine, Cit'reous, Cit'rinous, lemon-yellow-colored.

Clath'rate, Clath'roid, latticed (figure 59e).

Cla'vate, Clav'iform, club-shaped; gradually thickened towards the top.

Close, said of lamellae when they are close together.

Coeru'leous, Ceru'leous, light blue; sky blue.

Columel'la, a sterile tissue rising column-like in the midst of the capillitium.

Compressed', flattened laterally.

Concave', having a rounded, incurved surface.

Concen'tric, having a common center, as a series of rings, one within the other.

Concol'orous, of a uniform color.

Con'crete, coalescent; united in a coagulated, condensed or solid state; grown together.

Con'fluent, blended into one.

Con'gener, of the same genus or kind.

Conid'ial, pertaining to or of the nature of a conidium or conidia; characterized by the formation of conidia; bearing conidia.

Conid'ium (pl. *Conid'ia*), asexual spore formed singly or in chains by abstriction from the ends of hyphae or hyphal branches; see under "spore."

Co'nifer, a cone bearing tree.

Conif'erous, applied to trees bearing cones.

Con'stant, always present, or always in the same condition.

Constric'ted, contracted so as to be smaller in one or more places than in others.

Con'text, texture; substance.

Contig'uous, near, or in contact.

Contor'ted, distorted, twisted, crooked, or deformed.

Con'vex, elevated and regularly rounded; forming the segment of a sphere or nearly so.

Con'volute, covered with irregular convexities and depressions resembling the convolutions of the brain (like cap of *Gyromitra,* figure 50a).

Coria'ceous, of a leathery texture.

Cor'rugate, Cor'rugated, wrinkled; contracted; puckered; having a wrinkled appearance.

Cor'tex, the bark; the rind; the outer, rind-like layer or layers of some fungus-bodies.

Corti'na, marginal veil of spider-web structure rupturing at or near the stipe (as in *Cortinarius,* figure 57b).

Cor'tinate, provided with or pertaining to a cortina.

Cre'nate, scalloped.

Cren'ulate, minutely crenate.

Creta'ceous, chalky; of the color of chalk.

Crisp, Crisped, Cris'pate, having the surface, especially near the margin, strongly and finely undulate, as the leaves of the Savoy cabbage.

Cris'tate, crested; bearing a ridge, mane or tuft on the top.

Cru'ciate, Cru'ciform, having the form of a cross with equal arms (like basidia, in section, figure 20i).

Cryp'togam, a plant of the order Cryptogamia.

Cryptogam'ic, Cryptog'amous, pertaining or relating to Cryptogamia.

Cu'neate, Cune'iform, wedge-shaped.

Cu'preous, copper-colored.

Cus'pidate, tipped with a sharp, rigid point.

Cu'ticle, a distinct, skin-like layer; cutis, cuticle, pellicle, and epidermis have been used indiscriminately to describe the separable or inseparable skin-like layer sometimes present on the outer surface of the pileus and stipe; of these terms, cuticle is used most commonly.

Cya'neous, bright-blue; azure; lapis lazuli-blue.

Cy'athiform, cup-shaped, shape of a drinking glass slightly widened at the top.

Cylin'dric, Cylin'drical, cylinder-shaped; applied to a branch or stipe having the same or nearly the same diameter throughout, and its cross section circular.

Cystid'ium (pl. *Cystid'ia*), in Hymenomycetes (figure 20b, c); large, unicellular, often inflated structure, between and often projecting beyond the basidia and paraphyses of the hymenium (anther, antheridium, old terms for the same).

Decid'uous, (a) falling off at maturity, or at the end of the season; (b) losing the foliage every year. Caducous.

Decur'rent, applied to lamellae which are prolonged down the stipe (figure 57c, d, e, h, i).

Decurved', curved downward.

Deflexed', bent or turned down.

Dehis'cence, the spontaneous opening of a peridium (in the Gasteromycetes) at maturity to discharge the spores. Also applied to the opening of an ascus to release its spores.

Dehis'cent, opening at maturity to discharge the spores.

Deliques'cent, becoming liquid at maturity (like the gills in *Coprinus,* figure 2d).

Den'tate, toothed.

Dentic'ulate, finely dentate.

Depressed', as if pressed down or flattened; sunk below the level of the surrounding margin.

Descend'ing, applied to a marginal veil when, in the young stage, its marginal attachment is below the level of its stipe-attachment; a ring formed from it is called superior.

Determina'tion, assigned to the proper place in a classification or series.

Diagno'sis, scientific discrimination of any kind; a short distinctive description, as of a plant.

Dichot'omous, regularly dividing by pairs from below upward (of gills, figure 75).

Dimid'iate, applied to lamellae that reach only half way to the stipe; applied to the pileus when it is semi-circular in outline or nearly so.

Disc, (a) any flat, circular, disk-like growth; (b) the central portion of the upper surface of a pileus; (c) the cup-shaped or otherwise variously shaped hymenial surface of a Discomycete.

Discomyce'tes, a group of ascomycetous fungi in which the hymenium is exposed; the fruiting body is cupular, discoid, or clavate, and sometimes convoluted (*Peziza, Helvella, Morchella*).

Dissep'iments, dividing walls; as between the pores in polypores.

Dis'tant, far apart.

Dor'sal, pertaining to the back; to the upper surface of the pileus; opposite to "ventral."

Down, fine, soft pubescence.

E- or *Ex-,* prefix signifying "destitute of," "outside of" or "away from."

Ebur'neous, ivory-white.

Eccen'tric, see *Excentric.*

Ech'inate, furnished with stiff bristles.

Echin'ulate. minutely echinate.

Ecol'ogy, the science of animal and vegetable economy; the study of the phenomena of the life history of organisms, in their reciprocal and individual relations; thus parasitism and symbiosis come under the scope of ecology.

Ecto-, prefix signifying "outside." See: *Endo.*

Egg, a young plant before the rupture of the volva, in Phalloids (figure 58e), Amanitas (figure 37F, G), etc.

Ellip'soid, a solid figure all plane sections of which are ellipses or circles.

Ellipsoi'dal, shaped like an ellipsoid.

Ellip'tic, Ellip'tical, elongate-ovate; more than twice as long as broad; parallel sided in the middle and rounded at both ends.

Emar'ginate, notched at the end; applied to a lamella which has a notch in its margin close to the stipe (figure 57f).

Encrust'ing, forming a crust-like coating.

Ende'mic, native to a country or region. Opposite to *Exot'ic.*

Endo-, Ento-, prefixes signifying "within," "inside." See: *Ecto.*

Endoperid'ium, inner layer of the peridium.

En'dospore, Endospo'rium, the inner coat of a spore.

Entire', having the edge without toothing or division; not divided into parts; continuous.

Epider'mis, see *Cuticle.*

Epithe'cium, the layer sometimes formed above the asci by the concrescent tips of the paraphyses.

E'qual, applied to a stipe of uniform thickness; to lamellae of equal length.

Ero'ded, having small, irregular sinuses on the margin, as if gnawed (gill-edges in *Lentinus,* figure 57e); erose.

Erose', same as *Eroded.*

Es'culent, edible, eatable, not poisonous.

Evanes'cent, fleeting; vanishing; soon disappearing.

E'ven, having no depressions or elevations; not pitted, striate, etc.; different from smooth or glabrous, which see.

Ex-, prefix—see *E-.*

Excen'tric, not central; said of a stipe which is attached to the pileus at some point between the center and the margin.

Exo-, prefix signifying "outside."

Exoperid'ium, outer layer of the peridium.

Ex'ospores, spores which are free, not produced within a sporangium, as basidio-spores.

Exot'ic, foreign, not native. Opposite to *ende'mic.*

Expan'ded, spread out, as a pileus from convex to plane.

Ex'planate, flattened; expanded; applied usually to a part which has been rolled or folded.

Exsicca'ti, dried specimens; especially those published in sets.

Farc'tate, stuffed, which see.

Farina'ceous, covered as if with meal; mealy.

Fas'ciate, Fas'ciated, (a) having broad, parallel bands or stripes; (b) banded or compacted together; (c) exhibiting fasciation.

Fascia'tion, (a) a monstrous, flattened expansion of the stem; (b) condition of being bound or compacted together.

Fascic'ulate, growing in fascicles or clusters.

Fastig'iate, (a) with branches erect and close together; (b) sloping upward to a summit, point or edge.

Ferru'ginous, Ferrugin'eous, iron-rust colored.

Fi'brillar, Fi'brillate, Fi'brillose, Fi'brillous, appearing to be covered or composed of minute fibers.

Fi'brous, covered with or composed of fibers.

Fil'ament, a separate fiber or fibril of any animal or vegetable tissue, as a filament of silk, wool, etc.

Filamen'tous, like a thread; composed of threads or filaments.

Fim'briate, Fim'briated, fringed.

Fis'sured, cleft or split.

Fis'tular, Fis'tulose, tubular, hollow.

Fixed, said of lamellae or spines not readily detached from the underlying tissue.

Flabel'late, Flabel'liform, fan-shaped.

Flac'cid, soft and limber; flabby; without firmness or elasticity.

Flaves'cent, Fla'vous, yellow.

Flesh, inner substance of a fungus-body as distinguished from the cortical and hymenial layers.

Flesh'y, succulent; composed of juicy, cellular tissue.

Flex'uose, Flex'uous, curved or bent alternately in opposite directions.

Floc'ci (pl of *Floc'cus*), flocks or tufts resembling wool.

Floc'cose, woolly; composed of, or bearing, flocci.

Floc'culose, composed of, or bearing, minute flocci.

Free, said of lamellae which are not attached to the stipe (figure 57m); said of any part not attached to another; of spores not inclosed in a special envelope.

Fri'able, crumbling.

Frill, same as armilla.

Fruc'tification, (a) a fruit; any spore-bearing, spore-containing, or seed-containing structure and its spores or seeds; (b) the process of development of a fruit and its attendant parts.

Fuga'cious, fleeting; transitory; falling or fading early.

Fu'gitive, quickly disappearing; evanescent.

Fuligin'eous, Fulig'inous, very dark, opaque brown; smoky; sooty.

Fulves'cent, somewhat tawny.

Ful'vous, tawny, reddish yellow.

Fu'mose, Fu'mous, smoke-colored, fuliginous.

Fun'goid, of, or pertaining to, fungi.

Fungol'ogy, mycology.

Fun'gus (pl. *Fun'gi*), a thallophyte characterized by the absence of chlorophyll and deriving its sustenance from living or dead organic matter.

Fu'nicle, funiculus.

Funic'ulus, in Nidulariaceae, the cord of hyphae attaching a peridiolum to the inner wall of the peridium.

Fur'cate, forked; divided into branches.

Furfura'ceous, covered with bran-like particles, scurfy.

Fusces'cent, somewhat fuscous.

Fus'cous, of a dark, dusky, swarthy color; brown; brown tinged with gray.

Fu'siform, Fu'soid, tapering from the middle to both ends; spindle-shaped.

Gas'teromyce'tes, Gas'tromyce'-tes, a group of Basidiomycetes in which the hymenium is enclosed in a sack-like envelope called the peridium.

Gelat'inous, jelly-like.

Gener'ic (a) pertaining to, of the nature of, or forming a mark of a genus; (b) having the rank or classificatory value of a genus.

Genet'ic, of or pertaining to origin or mode of production.

Ge'nus (pl. *Gen'era*), a classificatory group ranking next above a species containing one or more species.

Geotrop'ic, turning or inclining toward the earth.

Gib'bous, in the form of a swelling; applied to a pileus which is more swollen or convex on one side than the other; lopsided.

Gill, lamella.

Gil'vous, isabelline; color of sole leather or dirty linen.

Gla'brous, smooth; applied to a surface which is destitute of pubescence; a surface may be glabrous or smooth and not even, or vice versa.

Glands, Glan'dules, moist or sticky dots resembling the glands on the epidermis of Phenogams.

Glan'dular, bearing glands.

Glau'cous, covered with pale, green bloom or very fine, white powder easily rubbed off.

Gle'ba, in Gastromycetes, spore-bearing tissue composed of chambers lined with the hymenium and enclosed by the sack-like peridium, as in puffballs, etc.; in Phalloids the peridium or volva ruptures and the gleba is carried up on the stipe-like or clathrate receptacle.

Glo'bose, Glob'ular, Glob'ulose, nearly spherical.

Gloeocystidia, gelatinous or horny cystidia.

Glu'ten, applied to a tenaceous, viscous substance resembling gluten found on the surface of some mushrooms.

Glu'tinous, Glu'tinose, covered with a sticky exudation; viscous; glue-like.

Gran'ular, Gran'ulate, Gran'-ulose, covered with, or composed of, granules.

Gran'ule, (a) a little grain; a fine particle; (b) a synonym of sporule.

Grega'rious, growing in groups, but not in a tufted manner.

Gut'tate, spotted as if with drops of something colored.

Gutt'ula (pl. *Gutt'ulae*), a small drop or drop-like particle; the oil-globule in some spores resembling a nucleus (figure 24).

Gutt'uate, finely guttate; also, containing or composed of fine drops or drop-like particles; said of spores containing an oily, nucleus-like globule or guttula.

Gy'rate, Gy'rose, folded and waved (like the gleba in *Gyrophragmium,* figure 60a); having folds resembling the convolutions of the brain.

Hab'itat, the natural place of growth of a species.

Hausto'orium (pl. *Hausto'ria*), special branch of filamentous mycelium which serves as an organ of adhesion and suction.

Herba'ceous, said of phenogamous plants which perish annually down to (sometimes including) the root.

Herba'rium, a collection of dried plants arranged systematically.

Heteroge'neous, of a structure which is different from adjacent ones; opposite to "homogeneous."

Hirsute', thickly covered with rather long, stiff hairs.

His'pid, beset with stiff bristles.

Hoar'y, covered with short, dense, grayish-white hairs; canescent.

Holo-, a prefix signifying "entire," "whole."

Homoge'neous, alike in structure; opposite to "heterogeneous."

Host, the name given to any plant or animal supporting a parasitic fungus.

Hu'mus, vegetable mold; woody fiber in a state of decay.

Hy'aline, colorless; transparent.

Hygromet'ric, readily absorbing and retaining moisture.

Hygroph'anous, looking watery when moist, opaque when dry.

Hygroscop'ic, having the property of absorbing moisture from the atmosphere; sensitive to moisture.

Hyme'nium, aggregation of spore-mother-cells, with or without sterile cells, in a continuous layer, upon a sporophore; spore-bearing layer (figure 20b, c); hymenial layer.

Hy'menomyce'tes, a group of Basidiomycetes having the hymenium on the free, exposed surface of the sporophore.

Hy'menophore, Hymenoph'orum, portion of a sporophore which bears the hymenium.

Hy'pha (pl. *Hy'phae*), the elementary filament or thread of a fungus; a cylindric, thread-like, branched body developing by apical growth, and usually becoming transversely septate (figure 20e).

Hy'phal, of or pertaining to a hypha.

Hypogae'ous, Hypoge'al, Hypoge'ous, growing under ground.

Hypog'enous, growing on the under surface.

Hypothe'cium, layer of hyphal tissue immediately beneath a hymenium.

Im'bricate, Im'bricated, overlapping like the shingles of a roof (figure 114).

Immar'ginate, without a well-defined margin.

Incar'nate, flesh-colored.

Incised', as if cut into.

Incras'sate, thickened.

Incrus'ting, forming a crust-like coating.

Indehis'cent, applied to a peridium which does not open spontaneously at maturity, the spores within it becoming free by its decay.

Indig'enous, native; not foreign.

Indu'sium, in certain Phalloids, an appendage or veil hanging from the apex of the stipe beneath the pileus (figure 59b).

Infe'rior, below; on under surface; applied to a ring formed from a veil which in the young state has its stipe attachment below the level of its marginal attachment.

Inflexed', bent inward.

Infundib'uliform, funnel-shaped (plate 17).

In'nate, originating within the substance of the plant or matrix; appearing to be within or blended with the substance of a part.

Inorgan'ic, not produced by vital processes; not organic.

Inser'ted, attached; growing immediately from the matrix like a graft from its stock (not rooting).

Insiti'tious, inserted.

Inter-, prefix meaning "between" or "among" or "during."

Inter'stices, spaces between any surfaces or things.

Intra-, prefix meaning "within."

Introduced', applied to plants brought from another country and growing spontaneously.

In'volute, rolled inward (like the margin of the cap in *Paxillus,* figure 57i).

Isabel'line, color of sole-leather, of soiled linen; alutaceous.

Labyrin'thine, Labyrin'thiform, characterized by intricate and sinuous lines; like a labyrinth (as the tubes of *Daedalea,* figure 56e).

Lac'cate, as if varnished or covered with a coat like sealing wax.

Lac'erate, Lac'erated, as if torn.

Lacin'iate, slashed; deeply cut by narrow incisions, more regular and larger than fimbriate.

Lacu'nose, Lacu'nous, bearing scattered, irregular, broadish, but shallow excavations; having or full of lacunae.

Lamel'la (pl. *Lamel'lae*), gill; vertical plate radiating from the stipe on the under surface of a pileus (figure 20 a, f).

La'nate wooly; covered with a wool-like pubescence.

Lan'ceolate, lance-shaped; many times longer than broad and tapering to one or both ends.

Lat'eral, attached to or by one side.

Lateric'eous, Laterit'ious, brick-colored.

La'tex, thick, milky juice.

Lat'ticed, formed by interlacing and crossing lines or columns which leave open spaces between.

Lentic'ular, Len'tiform, shaped like a double, convex lens; lentil-shaped.

Lig'neous, of woody texture.

Liv'id, bluish-black, like the black and blue of a bruise.

Lobed, Lo'bate, having divisions which are large and rounded.

Lu'cid, bright, clear, transparent.

Lu'rid, sordid; dull; dingy; dirty brownish.

Lu'teous, (a) egg-yellow; gold-yellow; (b) like mud or clay.

Lutes'cent, yellowish.

Macro-, in composition, "large" or "long."

Mac'ulate, Mac'ular, Mac'ulose, spotted.

Mar'ginal Veil, see *Veil.*

Mar'ginate, having a well-defined border.

Ma'trix, the substance upon or in which a fungus grows.

Me'dial, applied to ring when situated at about the middle of stipe.

Membrana'ceous, Mem'branous, having the character or appearance of membrane; thin, rather soft, and pliable.

Mica'ceous, covered with glistening, mica-like particles.

Mi'cron, Mi'kron, microscopic unit of measure; 1/1000 of a millimeter; nearly .00004 inch; to convert inches to microns approximately, divide by .00004.

Min'iate, vermilion-colored; of a bright, vivid, red color.

Mold, Mould, (a) fine, soft earth; (b) a general term to describe certain fungus growths of a low type.

Mon'ster, Monstros'ity, a plant or animal having any marked, abnormal development in form. See: *Teratology.*

Mon'strous, of unnatural formation; deviating greatly from the natural form or structure (has no reference to size).

Morphol'ogy, the science of organic form; the science of outer form and internal structure.

Mov'able, applied to a ring which has separated from the stipe and can be moved up and down.

Mu'cid, (a) musty, mouldy; (b) slimy.

Mucilag'inous, Mu'cous, slimy.

Mu'cronate, tipped with an abrupt, short, sharp point.

Multi-, in composition, "many."

Mush'room, see *Toadstool.*

Mu'tualism, symbiosis of two organisms living together and mutually helping and supporting each other.

Myc, Mycet, Myceto, Myco, prefixes signifying "fungus."

Myce'lial, of or pertaining to mycelium.

Myce'lium, vegetative portion of the thallus of fungi, composed of one or more hyphae (figure 19).

Mycolog'ical, relating to fungi.

Mycol'ogist, one who is versed in mycology.

Mycol'ogy, the science of fungi, their structure, classification, etc.

Mycoph'agist, one who eats fungi.

Mycoph'agy, the eating of fungi.

Mycorrhi'za, a composite organ formed by the symbiosis of the rootlets of certain Phenogams, especially of the Cupuliferae and some other forest trees, and a fungus-mycelium which invests and penetrates them; it is believed that the fungus not only derives nourishment from the tree but that it assists the tree in absorbing nourishment from the soil.; fungi comprised in the Oömycetes, Gasteromycetes, Hymenomycetes and Pyrenomycetes may be symbionts of a mycorrhiza, but are capable of an independent existence.

Nak'ed, bare; without covering of any kind, as of an enveloping membrane, pruinose, farinaceous or furfuraceous particles, tomentum, fragments of volva or veil, etc.

Nigres'cent, Nig'ricant, becoming black; also blackish, dusky, fuscous.

Ni'veous, snow-white.

Nod'ule, a little knot or lump.

Nod'ulose, Nod'ulous, bearing nodules.

Non-, not; prefix giving a negative sense to words.

Nu'cleatv, Nu'cleated, having a nucleus or nuclei.

Nu'cleus (pl. *Nu'clei*), (a) a central mass or kernel; (b) a spherical or ellipsoidal mass in the protoplasm of a cell denser and more highly refractive than the rest of the protoplasm, functionally the most important portion of a cell, for in it the process of cell-division begins; (c) the name has been sometimes improperly applied by systematists to the oil-globules or guttulae and the vacuoles within some spores.

Ob-, in composition, "inversely."

Ob'long, two or three times longer than broad with nearly parallel sides.

Obo'vate, inversely ovate, having the broad end upward or toward the apex.

Ob'solete, indistinct; very imperfectly developed; hardly perceptible.

Obtuse', blunt or rounded at the apex.

Ochra'ceous, O'cherous, O'chreous, O'chroid, O'chry, ocher yellow, light yellow with a tinge of brown.

Oecology, see *Ecology.*

Oliva'ceous, olive-green.

Opaque', Opake', mostly used in the sense of dull, not shining.

Oper'culum, a lid-like cover (as in the terminal end of the asci of some [operculate] Ascomycetes, figure 20q).

Organic, pertaining to either living or dead animal or vegetable organisms.

Os'tiole, Osti'olum, the aperture in the top of a perithecium through which spores are discharged (see figure 20r).

O'vate, having a figure the shape of a longitudinal section of an egg.

O'void, egg-shaped—used to describe solids.

Pales'cent, inclining to paleness; becoming pallid.

Pal'lid, of a pale, indefinite color.

Pal'udine, Palu'dinous, Pal'udose, Palus'trine, growing in marshes or swamps.

Papil'iona'ceous, variegated; mottled; marked with different colors; as the lamellae of some species of *Panaeolus* mottled with black spores (figure 35).

Papil'la (pl. *Papil'lae*), a small, nipple-shaped elevation.

Pap'illate, bearing one or more papillae.

Paraph'ysis (pl. *Paraph'yses*), slender, thread-like bodies growing with the asci (figure 20q); sterile, club-shaped cells growing in the hymenium with the basidia.

Par'asite, a plant growing on or in another living body from which it derives all or part of its nourishment.

Parasit'ic, growing on or in and deriving its sustenance from a living plant or animal.

Par'tial Veil, see *Veil.*

Pec'tinate, having resemblance to the teeth of a comb (like the cap-striations in *Russula foetens,* plate 31).

Ped'icel, any short, very small, stem-like stalk.

Ped'icellate, having a pedicel or tiny foot-stalk.

Pel'licle, see *Cuticle.*

Pellu'cid, admitting the passage of light; transparent; translucent.

Pen'dulous, hanging down.

Peren'nial, continuing growth from year to year.

Peridi'olum, Perid'iole, a secondary or interior peridium containing a hymenium (as in *Cyathus,* figure 61d).

Perid'ium (pl. *Perid'ia*), the outer, enveloping coat of the sporophore in angiocarpous fungi, as in puff-balls.

Periph'eral, of, belonging to, or situated on the periphery.

Perithe'cium (pl. *Perithe'cia*), cup-shaped ascocarp with the margin incurved so as to form a narrow-mouthed cavity (figure 20r) ; the case or hollow shell which contains the spores.

Per'onate, booted; said of the stipe when it has a boot-like or stocking-like covering (like the volva in *Amanita pantherina,* plate 4).

Persis'tent, enduring; continuing without withering, decaying or falling off.

Phylog'eny, the history of the evolution of a species or group; tribal history; ancestral development.

Pi'leate, having a cap or pileus.

Pi'leus (pl. *Pi'lei*), the umbrella-like cap or analogous receptacle of many fungi, as in toadstools, morels, etc.; it may be stipitate, sessile, dimidiate, regular, or irregular in form.

Pip-shaped, shape of an apple seed.

Pir'iform, pyr'iform, pear-shaped.

Pi'siform, pea-shaped.

Pith, central stuffing in some stipes.

Pit'ted, covered with pits or small depressions.

Plane, having a flat surface.

Pli'cate, folded like a fan; plaited.

Plum'beous, lead-colored.

Poly-, a prefix meaning "many."

Polyg'onal, having many angles.

Pore, in Pyrenomycetes, same as ostiole; in Hymenomycetes, same as tubulus or tube, as the tubules of polypores; also the mouth of a tubulus.

Po'rose, Po'rous, bearing pores or tubules; pierced with small holes.

Poste'rior, denotes a position on under side of the pileus adjacent to the stipe; the end of a lamella next the stipe is the posterior end.

Proc'ess, an outgrowth or projection from a surface.

Protobasid'ium, basidium divided by transverse septa into four cells, each giving rise to a spore from a laterally inserted sterigma, or a basidium d i v i d e d longitudinally by septa intersecting each other at right angles into four cells, each cell terminating in a long, tubular sterigma (figure 20m, n).

Pro'toplasm, the nitrogenous fluid of variable composition found in living cells; it is the vital substance into which all food is assimilated, and from which all parts of the plant are formed.

Prox'imal, pertaining to the base or extremity of attachment.

Pru'inate, Pru'inose, covered with bloom or powder so as to appear as if frosted.

Pseudo-, prefix s i g n i f y i n g "false" or "spurious."

Pubes'cence, general term to describe hairyness; specifically, covered with short, soft, downy hairs.

Pubes'cent, covered with short, soft, downy hairs; hairy.

Pulvera'ceous, Pulver'ulent, covered as if with powder or dust.

Pul'vinate, cushion-shaped.

Punc'tate, having dots scattered over the surface.

Pyr'iform, see *Piriform.*

Ra'diate, Ra'diating, arranged like the spokes of a wheel.

Rad'icating, rooting; having root-like strands which penetrate the matrix.

Recep'tacle, Receptac'ulum, term o f v a r y i n g signification, usually implying a hollowed out body containing other bodies; (a) same as stroma; (b) same as sporophore; (c) in Phalloids, the stipe and pileus, or the clathrate body which supports the gleba.

Reflexed', Reflec'ted, turned or bent back.

Remote', applied to lamellae where their posterior extremities are distant from the stipe (as in *Lepiota procera,* plate 25).

Ren'iform, kidney-shaped.

Repand', (a) bent or turned up or back (see cap of *Lepiota americana,* plate 24); (b) having a slightly undulating or sinuous margin.

Resu'pinate, attached to the matrix by the back, the hymenium facing outward (as in *Corticium,* figure 2b).

Retic'ulate, Re'tiform, marked with crossed lines like the meshes of a net.

Rev'olute, rolled backward or upward.

Rhi'zomorphs, long, branching or anastomosing, rigid, root-like cords of mycelium with a dark or black exterior, often growing be ween the bark and timber or about and penetrating the roots of dead and living trees, produced by *Armillaria mellea* and various other fungi.

Ri'mose, Ri'mous, covered with cracks (like the cap-surface in *Inocybe* species, figure 65a).

Rim'ulose, Rim'ulous, covered with small cracks.

Ring, annulus; see *Veil.*

Riv'ulose, marked with lines like the rivers on a map.

Root'ing, see *Radicating.*

Rubes'cent, tending to a red color.

Rubig'inous, iron-rust colored; ferrugineous.

Rufes'cent, tending to rufous or dull-red color.

Ru'fous, dull-red, Venetian red.

Ru'gose, wrinkled.

Ru'gulose, minutely rugose.

Sac'cate, in the form of a sack or pouch.

Sanguin'eous, blood-colored.

Sap'id, agreeable to the taste.

Saprophyt'ic, living upon and deriving its sustenance from dead, organic matter.

Sap'rophyte, a plant that lives on decaying, vegetable or animal matter.

Sca'brate, Sca'brous, r o u g h, rugged; especially, rough to the touch.

Scale (=*Squama*). See fig. 65b. Scales and *Amanita*

warts must be carefully differentiated. Scales are a part of the flesh of the cap, whereas *Amanita* warts are superficially attached remains of the volva (see: *Volva*).

Sclero'tium (pl. *Sclero'tia*), hard, black, brownish, or purplish, compact, tuber-like body, which is the resting stage of certain fungi, as in *Collybia tuberosa;* it remains dormant for a time and then sends up shoots which develop into sporophores at the expense of the reserve material.

Scrobic'ulate, pitted.

Scru'pose, rough with little particles.

Semi-, prefix meaning "half" or "partial."

Sep'arable, capable of being detached.

Sep'arating, becoming detached, as lamellae from the stipe, or resupinate fungi from the matrix.

Sep'tate, having partitions.

Sep'tum (pl. *Sep'ta*), partition.

Seric'eous, silky.

Ser'rate, having marginal teeth shaped like saw teeth (like the gill-edges in *Lentinus*, figure 57e).

Ser'rulate, minutely serrate.

Ses'sile, attached by the base; having no stipe or stalk.

Sin'uate, Sin'uose, Sin'uous, tortuous; serpentine; turning or winding in and out: applied to an edge the outline of which is alternately concave and convex; a sinuate lamella has a sudden wave or sinus in its edge near the stipe (figure 57f).

Si'nus, a rounded inward curve between two, projecting lobes.

Smooth, glabrous; destitute of any kind of pubescence; a surface may be uneven and yet smooth.

Sol'itary, growing singly.

Sor'did, of a dingy, dirty hue.

Spadic'eous, date-brown, duller and darker than bay-brown.

Spath'ulate, oblong or rounded and flattened at the top, with a long, narrow, attenuate base.

Spe'cies, an individual or collectively those individuals which differ specifically from all other members of a genus and which do not differ from each other except within narrow limits of variability, and which produce by propagation other individuals of the same kind.

Specif'ic, of, pertaining to, constituting, peculiar to, characteristic of, diagnostic of, designating species or a species; not generic; not of wider application than to a species.

Sphag'num, peat or bog-moss.

Spher'ical, Sphe'roid, of the shape of a ball or globe, or nearly so.

Spore, the reproductive body of Cryptogams analogous to the seed of Phenogams; the terms spores, sporidia, sporules and conidia have been applied somewhat indiscriminately to all spore-bodies; it has been recommended by some authorities and accepted by Saccardo to limit the term spore to the naked spore produced on a basidium (figure 24), sporidium to the spore produced in an ascus (figure 20q), sporule to the spore of imperfect fungi, where enclosed in a perithecium (figure 20r), conidium to the spore of imperfect fungi, where not enclosed in a perithecium or ascus; according to these limitations the terms spermatium, stylospore, clinospore are merged in sporule.

Spo'rophore, branch or portion of thallus which bears spores or spore-mother-cells; said to be simple or filamentous when consisting of a single hypha or branch of a hypha, compound when formed by the cohesion of the ramifications of separate, hyphal branches (the common mushroom is a compound sporophore).

Squa'ma (pl. *Squa'mae*), a scale, or scale-like appendage. See: *Scale.*

Squa'mose, Squa'mous, covered with appressed scales.

Squam'ula, Squam'ule, a small squama.

Squam'ulose, covered with minute scales.

Squar'rose, rough with spreading processes (figure 112).

Stalk, stipe; any stem-like, supporting organ.

Stel'late, star-shaped.

Sterig'ma (pl. *Sterig'mata*), stalk-like branch of a basidium bearing a spore (figure 20c).

Ster'ile, not fertile; producing no spores.

Stipe, stalk of a mushroom.

Stip'itate, having a stipe.

Straight, applied to margin of pileus when not involute.

Stramin'eous, straw-colored.

Stri'a (pl. *Stri'ae*), parallel or radiating lines or markings.

Stri'ate, marked with striae.

Strobil'iform, resembling a pinecone (figure 55c).

Stro'ma (pl. *Stro'mata*), (a) a mass in which another object is embedded; (b) a compact mass of mycelium in the form of a cushion, crust, club or branched expansion upon or in which perithecia or other organs of fructification are borne (as in *Xylaria,* figure 48b).

Stuffed, said of a stipe having a lumen filled with a cottony web or spongy substance; farctate.

Sub-, prefixed signifies "somewhat," "almost" or "under."

Subic ulum, a more or less thin and dense felt of hyphae covering the matrix; upon its surface is spread the hymenium or from it arise stalks supporting sporophores.

Substra'tum, sometimes used in the sense of matrix.

Subterra'nean, under ground.

Su'bulate, su'buliform, awl-shaped.

Sul'cate, grooved.

Sul'cus (pl. *Sul'ci*), groove or furrow.

Sulphu'reous, Sulfu'reous, sulphur-colored.

Super-, Supra-, prefix meaning "above" in position or degree.

Superfic'ial, situated on or close to the surface.

Supe'rior, the upper surface or position; applied to a ring formed from a partial veil which in the young plant has its stipe attachment above the level of its marginal attachment.

Sym'bion, Sym'biont, an organism which lives in a state of symbiosis.

Symbio'sis, the coexistence in more or less mutual interdependence of two different organisms; mutualism; mutual parasitism; commensalism; consortism; with some authors commensalism implies an association less necessary or mutually helpful than symbiosis.

Symbiot'ic, living in that kind of consociation called symbiosis.

Syn'onym, a discarded name for a species or genus; either of two or more names for the same species or genus.

Synon'ymous, expressing the same idea; equivalent in meaning; having the character of a synonym.

Teeth, the hymenium-bearing prolongations of the hymenophore in the Hydnaceae (figure 20h).

Teratol'ogy, the study of abnormal structures; morphology as applied to monstrous growths; not applied to malformations due to disease.

Te'rete, cylindrical or nearly so, having a circular, transverse section.

Terres'trial, growing on the ground.

Tes'selated, arranged in small squares; checkered or reticulated in a regular manner.

Testa'ceous, brick-red.

Tetra-, prefix signifying "four."

Thal'lophyte, one of the so-called "lower Cryptogams," plants in which the vegetative body usually consists of a thallus, which see.

Thal'lus, a vegetative body which is not differentiated into a true root, stem and leaf, has no true vessels or woody fiber; in fungi it is the whole body of the plant not serving directly as an organ of production, i. e., the mycelium, if any, and the sporophore, but not including the hymenial layer.

Tis'sue, an aggregate of similar cells and cell products in a definite fabric.

Toad'stool. "All the fleshy umbrella-shaped fungi are toadstools, and to a small number of the best known edible forms the name mushroom is applied popularly and in commerce; but not a small number of the other toadstools are edible." (W. G. Farlow.)

Tomen'tose, T o m e n' t o u s, densely pubescent with matted wool or tomentum.

Tomen'tum, a species of pubescence consisting of longish, soft, entangled hairs pressed close to the surface.

Torn, said of pores which are superficially rough and jagged as if torn.

Tor'sion, the state of being twisted spirally.

Tor'tuous, bending or turning in various directions.

Tox'ic, poisonous.

Tra'ma, (a) the substance, extending from and homogeneous with the hymenophore, interposed between the two layers of the lamella in Agarics (figure 20b), and between the double membranes of which the dissepiments of the pores are composed in polypores; (b) the hyphal plates forming the walls of the chambers of the gleba, in Gasteromycetes.

Translu'cent, transmitting rays of light without being transparent.

Trans'verse, from side to side.

Trem'elloid, Trem'ellose, of a gelatinous consistency; jelly-like; resembling *Tremella.*

Tri-, prefix meaning "three."

Trun'cate, ending abruptly as if cut off (as in the distal end of the spores of *Lepiota brunnea,* figure 24k).

Tu'baeform, trumpet-shape.

Tube, Tu'bule, in polypores, tube lined with hymenium (figure 20g); same as pore.

Tu'ber, (a) fleshy body, usually of a rounded or oblong form, produced on underground stems, as the potato or artichoke; (b) a genus of underground fungi.

Tu'bercle, any wart-like or knob-like excrescence; a small swelling.

Tuber'cular, Tuber'culate, Tuber'culose, having or covered with tubercules; formed like or forming a tubercle.

Tuber'culiform, shaped like a tubercle.

Tu'berous, rounded and swollen, resembling a tuber.

Tu'mid, swollen, inflated.

Tur'binate, top-shaped; shape of an inverted cone.

Type, (a) a perfect specimen or individual exemplifying the essential characters of the species to which it belongs; (b) the original specimen from which a species was described.

Typ'ical, having the characteristics of the type.

Ul'timate, furthest, last.

Um'ber, Um'brinous, umber-colored.

Umbil'icate, having an umbilicus or central navel-like depression (like the caps of *Omphalia* species).

Umbili'cus, a navel-like depression.

Um'bo, a boss or knob in the center of the pileus (see plates 6 and 25).

Um'bonate, bearing an umbo.

Un'cinate, tipped with a hook (like the stem-end of the gills in figure 57f).

Un'dulate, Un'date, having the surface near the margin alternately concave and convex (see *Hydnum fennicum,* plate 19); waved.

Une'qual, applied to lamellae when of unequal length; to a stipe not of uniform thickness.

Une'ven, said of surfaces that are irregular, striate, sulcate, etc.

Uni-, prefix, meaning "one."

Univer'sal Veil, see *Veil.*

Vag'inate, furnished with or contained in a sheath; sheathed.

Va'riable, said of a species which embraces many individuals which depart more or less from the type of the group.

Va'riegated, marked with different colors; mottled; same as papilionaceous.

Vari'ety, a subdivision of a species with minor characteristics uniformly varying from the type.

Veil, Ve'lum, (a) partial or marginal veil, a special envelope extending from the margin of the pileus to the stipe, enclosing the lamellae, often forming a ring (annulus) on the stipe; (b) universal veil or volva, a special envelope enclosing the entire plant in the young state, either concrete with the cuticle of the pileus, as in *Lepiota*, or discrete, as in *Amanita*, ultimately ruptured by the expanding pileus (figures 37 to 39) ; (c) a membranaceous, fibrous or granulose coating stretched over the mouth of an apothecium or cup, soon breaking up into fragments.

Veins, swollen wrinkles on the sides of, and at the base between, the lamellae, often connected to form cross partitions.

Ve'lum, see *Veil*.

Ve'nate, Veined, Ve'nose, Ve'nous, having veins.

Ven'tral, applied to the 'under side of the pileus ; opposite to "dorsal."

Ven'tricose, swelling out in the middle ; bellying.

Ver'rucose, Verru'ciform, covered with warts.

Verru'culose, minutely verrucose.

Ves'icle, a small bladder or air-cavity.

Vesic'ular, Vesi'culate, Vesic'ulose, Vesi'ulous, composed of or like vesicles.

Vil'lose, Vil'lous, covered with long, soft, weak hairs.

Vi'nous, of the color of red wine.

Viola'ceous, of a violet color.

Vires'cent, green or becoming green.

Vir'gate, (a) streaked ; (b) having wand-like branches.

Vis'cid, moist and sticky.

Vol'va, (a) wrapper ; same as universal veil (see *Veil*) ; the name is often applied to that portion of a discrete volva which is left (after rupturing) either attached in fragments to, or forming a distinct membranous sheath about, the base of the stipe ; (b) the peridium in Phalloids, analogous to the volva in *Amanita*. See: *Scale*.

Wart, any wart-like excrescence ; name applied to the wart-like remains of the volva on the surface of the pileus of some Amanitas (figure 38).

Waved, Wa'vy, see *Undulate*.

Zo'nate, Zoned, marked with concentric bands of color.

Zones, circular bands of color.

APPENDIX
NOMENCLATURAL CHANGES
Compiled by
Robert L. Shaffer

Changes in the scientific names of fungi often puzzle amateur mycologists. A question I frequently encounter, when working with amateurs, goes something like this: "The fungi don't change, so why does almost every book have a different name for the same fungus?"[1] This is sometimes followed by a joking statement to the effect that professional mycologists must have nothing better to do than change names and thereby keep things as confusing as possible for amateurs. An introduction to a list updating the scientific names in Krieger's *Handbook,* an excellent text for amateur mycologists, seems a good place for an explanation.

Nomenclatural changes occur for different reasons and are, therefore, of different kinds. One kind, if it may even be considered a nomenclatural change, results from a misidentification. For example, *Amanita phalloides,* which is the correct name of a well-known European species, once was also widely used for an eastern North American fungus thought to be the same. As it turned out, however, the North American fungus is a distinctly different species, wrongly identified as *A. phalloides* and now correctly called *A. brunnescens.*

To understand better why names usually change, the distinction between two major mycological activities must be recognized. The first is *classification,* which involves placing organisms in a hierarchical sequence of taxonomic groups on the basis of their real or supposed relationships. Among these groups the species is basic; and species are grouped into genera, genera into families, families into orders, orders into classes, and classes into divisions. The other activity is *nomenclature,* which is concerned with applying names to the groups after they have been delimited.

Nomenclature per se is uncomplicated and may be handled objectively, for an International Code of Botanical Nomenclature has been developed and is now followed by most mycologists the world over. The Code aims to provide "a stable method of naming taxo-

---

[1] As a matter of fact, the fungi in all probability *do* change. Like other, better known groups of organisms, they must be constantly evolving through time. This change, however, is very slow; and during the past 300 years, a period that encompasses all of man's significant mycological activities, a change in the fungi themselves has not been detected and must be infinitesimal. It certainly does not underlie the innumerable nomenclatural changes that have occurred in the same period.

nomic groups, avoiding and rejecting the use of names which may cause error or ambiguity or throw science into confusion" and to avoid "the useless creation of names." (The quoted phrases are from the preamble of the 1966 edition of the Code.) The Code establishes the ranks of taxonomic groups, the terms denoting them, and their sequence. It gives directions for coining names for the groups and guidance in the matters of orthography and gender of names. It sets forth technical requirements for valid publication of names; it determines which name must be used when more than one has been applied to a group or when a change in classification is made; and, finally, it lists conditions under which names must be rejected.

Application of the rules of the Code results, of course, in nomenclatural changes. A few examples must suffice. One rule says, to paraphrase, that the correct name of a species[2] must, unless certain exceptions apply, contain the earliest epithet published for the species in accordance with the Code. Therefore, when the name *Clitocybe gibba,* whose epithet dates from 1821, was found to apply to the species usually called *C. infundibuliformis,* a name with an 1836 epithet, the name with the earlier epithet had to be taken up to replace the more familiar and more widely used one. Another rule states that a name (but not necessarily a specific epithet) must be rejected if it has been used previously for another taxonomic group of the same rank. Thus, because *Russula insignis* was used by Quélet in 1888 for a certain species, another species for which Burlingham published the same name in 1915 had to be renamed, in this case *R. burlinghamiae* by Singer in 1938. Both of the foregoing rules stem from the principle of priority of publication, which is one of the bases of the Code. The principle is not applied absolutely, for the Code establishes one date as the starting point of nomenclature for each of the major groups of plants, those names for members of the group published before that date being disregarded. Also, conservation of some widely used names of families and genera that otherwise would not be legitimate is permitted. Other provisions of the Code state that a name must be rejected and may be replaced by another if it was not validly published, if it has been used in more than one sense and has become ambiguous, or if it is based upon a monstrosity.

The kinds of changes discussed so far are, or may be, made independently of classification; however the large majority of no-

---

[2] The name of a species (e.g., *Amanita virosa*) is binary, consisting of the name of the genus to which the species belongs (*Amanita*) and the specific epithet (*virosa*).

menclatural changes result from changes in classification. This is not to say that these nomenclatural changes must not be made in accordance with the Code of Nomenclature. But, except for establishing the ranks of taxonomic groups and the names and sequence of these ranks, the Code itself has nothing to do with classification. Its rules apply only after the decisions on classification have been made.

Unlike nomenclature, classification is highly subjective. The concept of a species, or a genus, or any other taxonomic group may differ from mycologist to mycologist and from year to year. Even after a concept has been established, there remains the difficult practical matter of applying the concept to organisms as they occur in nature, i.e., of recognizing and delimiting taxonomic groups. Different mycologists may attack this problem in different ways and come up with different results.

Systems of classification usually change as the information on the organisms being classified increases, for newer information often gives clues to relationships formerly undetected. In the fungi the recent increase has been mostly in information on morphological and chemical characters of microscopic structures, and the tendency has been to delimit taxonomic groups more and more finely on the basis of these characters. Not unexpectedly, subjectivity also enters here. One mycologist may evaluate and apply the same information differently than another, and thus come up with a different system of classification.

No matter what accounts for differing systems, if the differences are at the generic level, one species may have a different name in each of the systems. For example, Overholts, in *The Polyporaceae of the United States, Alaska, and Canada* (1953), used the name *Polyporus sulphureus* for the chicken mushroom. Bondarzew and Singer also recognized the genus *Polyporus* in their papers on the pore fungi (1941 et seq.), but delimited it more narrowly and considered the species mentioned to belong to another genus named *Laetiporus*. Therefore, they used *Laetiporus sulphureus* for the specific name. It is not true that only one of these names is correct, for each is correct within the framework of its own system of classification. In such cases nomenclatural correctness, as determined by the Code, can be judged only in relation to the system of classification adopted. The supporting evidence and arguments for one system may be better than for another, but one cannot say, in the foregoing example, either that the system adopted by Overholts is correct and that of Bondarzew and Singer is incorrect, or vice versa.

If a difference in systems of classification exists at the specific level, a fungus may also receive different names depending upon the system used. For example, Murrill, in *North American Flora* (1917), recognized two species named *Crepidotus nephrodes* and *C. fulvifibrillosus;* but Hesler and Smith, in their book *North American Species of Crepidotus* (1965), considered the differences between the two insufficient to justify maintaining them. They recognized only one species for which they used the name with the earlier published epithet, *C. nephrodes,* as the Code of Nomenclature requires. (The reverse situation, in which a later mycologist recognizes two or more species where an earlier mycologist recognized only one, is essentially similar, but more common.) Here again one system cannot be termed correct, the other incorrect. If a fungus fits Murrill's concept of the species named *C. fulvifibrillosus,* its correct name under his system differs from its correct name under Hesler and Smith's. It's as simple as that.

At this point, the amateur mycologist is likely to throw up his hands and wonder where to turn when even the doctors disagree. The best advice I can give is to concentrate on knowing the fungi themselves, to be aware of the subjectivity involved in classification, and to recognize the distinctness of nomenclature from, yet its dependence upon, classification. Then follow the classification and nomenclature of the most current authority available for the taxonomic group in question. The fact that another authority disagrees with this classification and, as a result, legitimately uses different names for some taxonomic groups will then be understandable and perhaps less disturbing. Furthermore, with knowing the fungi well will come the ability to judge systems of classification and make an informed choice among them.

In mycology there is now fairly general agreement about classification of taxonomic groups of the higher ranks, but at the levels of family, genus, and species the situation is one of turmoil. The fungi are just not well enough known in all their aspects and in all their diversity to permit one system of classification that is generally agreed upon. Unfortunately, this will be the case for many years to come; but, fortunately, this makes their study very rewarding.

In the following alphabetical list of names from Krieger's book, a specific name, with its author(s), appearing alone is a correct name used by Krieger for a species still recognized as a good species and as belonging to the genus indicated. In some of these cases, the author citation has been added or corrected, or the spelling of the specific name itself has been corrected. Authors' names are abbreviated according to the list on pp. 454-455 of the book; names not appearing there are spelled out completely.

If two names are connected by the symbol ≡, the first (i.e., the one used by Krieger) is incorrect for purely nomenclatural reasons.

If two names connected by the symbol = have the same specific epithet (except perhaps for the endings indicating different gender, e.g., *salmoneum* and *salmoneus, perrara* and *perrarus,* etc.), they are both correct according to the Code. However, the second is expressive of the more modern system of classification in which genera are usually more narrowly delimited.

If two specific names connected by the symbol = have different epithets, either the second name has the earlier epithet or is the correct name for some other nomenclatural reason, or the two species are no longer generally considered different, in which case the second name should be used. In practice, these two situations are not always distinct. If, in addition, the generic names are different, the species is now often placed in the genus indicated by the second name.

Other situations are explained by a brief statement.

A name used by Krieger and missing from the following list could not be located in literature published since the book first appeared. This is not necessarily to say either that the name is incorrect or that the species or variety should not be recognized, but merely that I found no recent evaluation of the name or the species or variety it represents.

Agaricus campestris L. ex Fr.
Amanita bisporigera Atk.
Amanita brunnescens Atk.
Amanita brunnescens var. *pallida* Krieger
Amanita caesarea (Scop. ex Fr.) Pers. ex Schw.
Amanita chlorinosma (Pk.) Sacc.
Amanita citrina (Schaeff.) ex S. F. Gray
Amanita cothurnata Atk.
Amanita flavoconia Atk.
Amanita flavorubescens Atk.
Amanita frostiana (Pk.) Sacc.
Amanita mappa = *Amanita cit-*

rina (Schaeff.) ex S. F. Gray
Amanita mappa var. *citrina* = *Amanita citrina* (Schaeff.) ex S. F. Gray
Amanita muscaria (L. ex Fr.) Pers. ex Hooker
Amanita pantherina (DC. ex Fr.) Secr.
Amanita pantherinoides = *Amanita pantherina* (DC. ex Fr.) Secr.
Amanita phalloides (Vaillant ex Fr.) Secr. The mushroom of the northeastern United States that was called *A. phalloides* by Krieger and others is *Ama-*

nita brunnescens Atk.
Amanita porphyria (A. & S. ex Fr.) Secr.
Amanita rubescens (Pers. ex Fr.) S. F. Gray
Amanita russuloides = *Amanita gemmata* (Fr.) Gill.
Amanita solitaria (Bull. ex Fr.) Secr.
Amanita spissa = *Amanita excelsa* (Fr.) Kummer
Amanita spreta (Pk.) Sacc.
Amanita strobiliformis = *Amanita solitaria* (Bull. ex Fr.) Secr.
Amanita verna (Bull. ex Fr.) Pers. ex Vitt.
Amanita virosa Secr.
Amanitopsis agglutinata=*Amanita agglutinata* (Berk. & Curt.) Lloyd
Amanitopsis farinosa=*Amanita farinosa* Schw.
Amanitopsis nivalis = *Amanita nivalis* Grev.
Amanitopsis strangulata=*Amanita inaurata* Secr.
Amanitopsis vaginata=*Amanita vaginata* (Bull. ex Fr.) Vitt.
Amanitopsis vaginata var. *alba* =*Amanita vaginata* (Bull. ex Fr.) Vitt. var. *alba* Gill.
Amanitopsis vaginata var. *fulva* is now recognized as a species, *Amanita fulva* (Schaeff.) ex Secr.
Amanitopsis volvata = *Amanita volvata* (Pk.) Martin
Anthurus aseroëformis is recognized as a variety, *Anthurus muellerianus* Kalchbr. var. *aseroëformis* E. Fischer.
Apostemidium guernisaci

(Crouan) Boud.
Armillaria caligata = *Tricholoma caligatum* (Viviani) Ricken
Armillaria mellea (Vahl ex Fr.) Kummer
Auricularia auricula-judae= *Auricularia auricula* (L. ex Hooker) Underwood

Bacterium phosphoreum (Cohn) Molisch
Bolbitius vitellinus (Pers. ex Fr.) Fr.
Boletinus appendiculatus Pk.
Boletinus cavipes (Opat.) Kalchbr.
Boletinus paluster (Pk.) Pk.
Boletinus pictus (Pk.) Pk.
Boletinus porosus = *Gyrodon merulioides* (Schw.) Singer
Boletinus spectabilis Pk.
Boletus aereus Bull. ex Fr.
Boletus affinis=*Xanthocomium affine* (Pk.) Singer
Boletus albus=*Suillus placidus* (Bonord.) Singer
Boletus alutarius = *Tylopilus felleus* (Bull. ex Fr.) Karst.
Boletus alveolatus = *Boletus frostii* Russell
Boletus americanus = *Suillus americanus* (Pk.) Snell
Boletus ananas = *Boletellus ananas* (Curt.) Murrill
Boletus auriporus = *Pulveroboletus auriporus* (Pk.) Singer
Boletus badius = *Xerocomus badius* (Fr.) Gilbert
Boletus betula = *Boletellus betula* (Schw.) Gilbert
Boletus bicolor=*Boletus rubel-*

lus Krombh.

Boletus boudieri = *Suillus granulatus* (L. ex Fr.) O. Kuntze

Boletus brevipes = *Suillus brevipes* (Pk.) O. Kuntze

Boletus castaneus = *Gyroporus castaneus* (Bull. ex Fr.) Quél.

Boletus chrysenteron = *Xerocomus chrysenteron* (Bull. ex St. Amans) Quél.

Boletus clintonianus is recognized as a variety, *Suillus grevillei* (Klotzsch) Singer var. *clintonianus* (Pk.) Singer.

Boletus cyanescens = *Gyroporus cyanescens* (Bull. ex Fr.) Quél.

Boletus duriusculus = *Leccinum duriusculum* (Schulz. ex Fr.) Singer

Boletus edulis Bull. ex Fr.

Boletus elbensis = *Suillus aeruginascens* (Secr.) Snell

Boletus elegans = *Suillus elegans* (Schumacher ex Fr.) Snell

Boletus erythropus (Fr. ex Fr.) Secr.

Boletus eximius = *Tylopilus eximius* (Pk.) Singer

Boletus felleus = *Tylopilus felleus* (Bull. ex Fr.) Karst.

Boletus firmus Frost

Boletus frostii Russell

Boletus gracilis = *Porphyrellus gracilis* (Pk.) Singer

Boletus granulatus = *Suillus granulatus* (L. ex Fr.) O. Kuntze

Boletus grisellus = *Boletinus grisellus* Pk.

Boletus griseus Frost

Boletus hemichrysus = *Pulveroboletus hemichrysus* (Berk. &

Curt.) Singer

Boletus laricinus = *Suillus aeruginascens* (Secr.) Snell

Boletus luridus Schaeff. ex Fr.

Boletus luteus = *Suillus luteus* (L. ex Fr.) S. F. Gray

Boletus miniatoolivaceus Frost

Boletus miniatoporus = *Boletus erythropus* (Fr. ex Fr.) Secr.

Boletus ornatipes = *Pulveroboletus retipes* (Berk. & Curt.) Singer

Boletus pachypus = *Boletus calopus* Fr.

Boletus pallidus Frost

Boletus pseudosulphureus Kallenb.

Boletus punctipes = *Suillus punctipes* (Pk.) Singer

Boletus ravenelii = *Pulveroboletus ravenelii* (Berk. & Curt.) Murrill

Boletus retipes = *Pulveroboletus retipes* (Berk. & Curt.) Singer

Boletus rugosiceps = *Leccinum rugosiceps* (Pk.) Singer

Boletus russellii = *Boletellus russellii* (Frost) Gilbert

Boletus sanguineus = *Boletus rubellus* Krombh.

Boletus satanas Lenz

Boletus scaber = *Leccinum scabrum* (Bull. ex Fr.) S. F. Gray

Boletus scaber var. *aurantiacus* is now recognized as a species, *Leccinum aurantiacum* (Bull. ex St. Amans) S. F. Gray.

Boletus scaber var. *niveus* = *Boletus holopus* Rostkovius

Boletus separans Pk.

Boletus sphaerosporus = *Suillus sphaerosporus* (Pk.) A. H. Smith & Thiers

Boletus strobilaceus = Strobilo-myces floccopus (Vahl ex Fr.) Karst.

Boletus subalbellus = Gyroporus subalbellus Murrill

Boletus subluteus = Suillus sub-luteus (Pk.) Snell

Boletus subtomentosus = Xero-comus subtomentosus (L. ex Fr.) Quél.

Boletus versipellis = Leccinum aurantiacum (Bull. ex St. Amans) S. F. Gray

Bovista pila Berk. & Curt.

Bovista plumbea Pers.

Bulgaria inquinans Fr.

Calocera cornea (Fr.) Loudon

Calostoma cinnabarina Desvaux

Calvatia caelata = Calvatia bo-vista (Pers.) Kambly & Lee

Calvatia craniiformis (Schw.) Fr.

Calvatia cyathiformis (Bosc) Morg.

Calvatia gigantea (Batsch ex Pers.) Lloyd

Calvatia saccata = Calvatia exci-puliforme (Pers.) Perdeck

Cantharellus aurantiacus = Cli-tocybe aurantiaca (Wulf. ex Fr.) Studer

Cantharellus cibarius Fr.

Cantharellus cinnabarinus Schw.

Cantharellus floccosus = Gom-phus floccosus (Schw.) Singer

Cantharellus infundibuliformis (Scop.) ex Fr.

Cantharellus lutescens (Pers.) ex Fr.

Cantharellus minor Pk.

Cantharellus muscigenus = Lep-toglossum muscigenum (Bull.

ex Fr.) Karst.

Cantharellus pruinosus Pk.

Cantharellus tubaeformis (Bull.) ex Fr.

Cantharellus umbonatus = Clito-cybe umbonata (Gmelin ex Fr.) Konrad

Catastoma circumscissum = Dis-ciseda candida (Schw.) Lloyd

Cauloglossum transversarium = Rhopalogaster transversarius (Bosc) Johnston

Chlorosplenium aeruginosum = Chlorociboria aeruginosa (Oeder ex S. F. Gray) Seaver

Clavaria abietina = Ramaria ochraceo-virens (Jungh.) Donk

Clavaria argillacea Fr.

Clavaria aurea = Ramaria aurea (Fr.) Quél.

Clavaria botrytis = Ramaria bo-trytis (Fr.) Ricken

Clavaria cinerea = Clavulina cinerea (Fr.) Schroet.

Clavaria cristata = Clavulina cristata (Fr.) Schroet.

Clavaria dichotoma = Clavuli-nopsis dichotoma (Godey) Corner

Clavaria flava = Ramaria flava (Fr.) Quél.

Clavaria formosa = Ramaria formosa (Fr.) Quél.

Clavaria fusiformis = Clavuli-nopsis fusiformis (Fr.) Cor-ner

Clavaria ligula = Clavariadel-phus ligula (Fr.) Donk

Clavaria pistillaris = Clavaria-delphus pistillaris (Fr.) Donk

Clavaria pyxidata = Clavicorona pyxidata (Fr.) Doty

Clavaria stricta = *Ramaria stricta* (Fr.) Quél.

Clavaria vermicularis Fr.

Clitocybe adirondackensis (Pk.) Sacc.

Clitocybe aperta = *Clitocybula aperta* (Pk.) Singer

Clitocybe catinus (Fr.) Quél.

Clitocybe clavipes (Pers. ex Fr.) Kummer

Clitocybe compressipes (Pk.) Sacc.

Clitocybe cyathiformis (Bull. ex Fr.) Kummer

Clitocybe dealbata (Sow. ex Fr.) Kummer. Krieger's use of the name is probably a misidentification of *Clitocybe truncicola* (Pk.) Sacc.

Clitocybe decora=*Tricholomopsis decora* (Fr.) Singer

Clitocybe fragrans (Sow. ex Fr.) Kummer

Clitocybe gigantea=*Leucopaxillus giganteus* (Sow. ex Fr.) Singer

Clitocybe illudens = *Clitocybe olearia* (DC. ex Fr.) Maire

Clitocybe infundibuliformis = *Clitocybe gibba* (Pers. ex Fr.) Kummer

Clitocybe media = *Clitocybe clavipes* (Pers. ex Fr.) Kummer

Clitocybe metachroa (Fr.) Kummer

Clitocybe monadelpha = *Armillaria tabescens* (Scop. ex Fr.) Emel

Clitocybe multiceps = *Lyophyllum decastes* (Fr. ex Fr.) Singer

Clitocybe multiformis = *Lyophyllum multiforme* (Pk.) Bigelow

Clitocybe nebularis (Batsch ex Fr.) Kummer

Clitocybe odora (Bull. ex Fr.) Kummer

Clitocybe pithyophila=*Clitocybe cerussata* (Fr.) Kummer

Clitocybe sinopica (Fr. ex Fr.) Kummer

Clitocybe sinopicoides Pk.

Clitocybe sudorifica = *Clitocybe dealbata* (Sow. ex Fr.) Kummer

Clitocybe tabescens=*Armillaria tabescens* (Scop. ex Fr.) Emel

Clitocybe truncicola (Pk.) Sacc.

Clitocybe viridis = *Clitocybe odora* (Bull. ex Fr.) Kummer

Clitopilus abortivus = *Rhodophyllus abortivus* (Berk. & Curt.) Singer

Clitopilus novaeboracensis = *Rhodocybe novaeboracensis* (Pk.) Singer

Clitopilus orcella = *Clitopilus prunulus* (Scop. ex Fr.) Kummer

Clitopilus prunulus (Scop. ex Fr.) Kummer

Collybia abundans = *Clitocybula abundans* (Pk.) Singer

Collybia acervata (Fr.) Kummer

Collybia albiflavida = *Melanoleuca alboflavidum* (Pk.) Murrill

Collybia albipilata = *Marasmius albipilatus* (Pk.) Singer

Collybia butyracea (Bull. ex Fr.) Kummer

Collybia colorea = *Callistosporium luteoolivaceum* (Berk. & Curt.) Singer

Collybia dryophila (Bull. ex
Fr.) Kummer
*Collybia familia = Clitocybula
familia* (Pk.) Singer
*Collybia longipes = Oudeman-
siella longipes* (Bull. ex St.
Amans) Moser
Collybia maculata (A. & S. ex
Fr.) Kummer
Collybia myriadophylla (Pk.)
Sacc.
*Collybia platyphylla = Tricho-
lomopsis platyphylla* (Pers. ex
Fr.) Singer
*Collybia radicata = Oudeman-
siella radicata* (Relh. ex Fr.)
Singer
Collybia tuberosa (Bull. ex Fr.)
Kummer
*Collybia velutipes=Flammulina
velutipes* (Curt. ex Fr.) Karst.
Colus hirudinosus Cavara &
Séchier
Coprinus atramentarius (Bull.
ex Fr.) Fr.
Coprinus comatus (Müll. ex
Fr.) S. F. Gray
Coprinus micaceus (Bull. ex
Fr.) Fr.
Coprinus plicatilis (Curt. ex
Fr.) Fr.
*Coprinus soboliferus=Coprinus
atramentarius* (Bull. ex Fr.)
Fr.
Coprinus sterquilinus (Fr.) Fr.
Cordyceps capitata (Holmskjold
ex Fr.) Link
Cordyceps militaris (L. ex St.
Amans) Link
Corticium caeruleum (Schrader
ex Fr.) Fr.
*Corticium vagum = Botryoba-
sidium vagum* (Berk. & Curt.)
Rogers
Cortinarius alboviolaceus (Pers.
ex Fr.) Fr.
Cortinarius argentatus (Pers. ex
Fr.) Fr.
Cortinarius armillatus (Fr. ex
Fr.) Fr.
Cortinarius biformis Fr.
Cortinarius camphoratus Fr.
Cortinarius castaneus (Bull. ex
Fr.) Fr.
Cortinarius cinnamomeus (L. ex
Fr.) Fr.
Cortinarius cinnamomeus var.
semisanguineus is now recog-
nized as a species, *Cortinarius
semisanguineus* (Fr.) Gill.
Cortinarius collinitus (Sow. ex
Fr.) Fr.
Cortinarius corrugatus Pk.
Cortinarius cyanites Fr.
Cortinarius distans Pk.
Cortinarius haematochelis
(Bull.) ex Fr.
*Cortinarius intrusus=Conocybe
intrusa* (Pk.) Singer
Cortinarius mucifluus Fr.
Cortinarius scutulatus (Fr.) Fr.
Cortinarius violaceus (L. ex
Fr.) Fr.
*Craterellus cantharellus = Can-
tharellus odoratus* (Schw.)
Fr.
*Craterellus clavatus=Gomphus
clavatus* Pers. ex S. F. Gray
Craterellus cornucopioides (L.
ex Fr.) Pers.
Craterellus dubius Pk.
*Craterellus lutescens = Cantha-
rellus lutescens* (Pers.) ex Fr.
Crepidotus croceitinctus Pk.
*Crepidotus fulvotomentosus =
Crepidotus calolepis* (Fr.)

Karst.
Crepidotus haustellaris (Fr. ex Fr.) Kummer
Crepidotus herbarum (Pk.) Sacc.
Crepidotus tiliophilus = *Simocybe tiliophila* (Pk.) Singer
Cryptoporus volvatus (Pk.) Hubbard
Cyclomyces greenei Berk.

Daedalea quercina L. ex Fr.
Daldinia concentrica (Bolt. ex Fr.) Cesati & de Notaris
Deconica coprophila (Bull. ex Fr.) Karst.
Dictyophora duplicata (Bosc) E. Fischer
Dictyophora ravenelii = *Phallus ravenelii* Berk. & Curt.

Echinodontium tinctorium Ell. & Everh.
Entoloma salmoneum = *Rhodophyllus salmoneus* (Pk.) Sacc.
Entoloma clypeatum = *Rhodophyllus clypeatus* (L. ex Fr.) Quél.
Entoloma cyaneum ≡ *Rhodophyllus murraii* (Berk. & Curt.) Singer
Entoloma cyaneum ≡ *Rhodophyllus violaceus* (Murrill) Singer
Entoloma grayanum = *Rhodophyllus grayanus* (Pk.) Singer
Entoloma jubatum = *Rhodophyllus jubatus* (Fr.) Quél.
Entoloma lividum=*Rhodophyllus sinuatus* (Bull. ex Fr.) Singer
Entoloma nidorosum = *Rhodophyllus nidorosus* (Fr.) Quél.

Entoloma peckianum = *Rhodophyllus peckianus* (Burt) Romagnesi
Entoloma sericeum = *Rhodophyllus sericeus* (Bull. ex Mérat) Quél.
Entoloma sinuatum = *Rhodophyllus sinuatus* (Bull. ex Fr.) Singer
Exidia glandulosa Fr.
Exobasidium mycetophilum (Pk.) Burt is a name applied to the teratological formations on the fruiting bodies of *Collybia dryophila* (Bull. ex Fr.) Kummer.

Fistulina hepatica Schaeff. ex Fr.
Flammula alnicola = *Pholiota alnicola* (Fr.) Singer
Flammula carbonaria = *Pholiota carbonaria* (Fr. ex Fr.) Singer
Flammula sapinea = *Gymnopilus sapineus* (Fr.) Maire
Fomes annosus (Fr.) Cke.
Fomes applanatus=*Ganoderma applanatum* (Pers. ex Wallroth) Patouillard
Fomes fomentarius (L. ex Fr.) Kickx
Fomes igniarius = *Phellinus igniarius* (L. ex Fr.) Quél.
Fomes pinicola (Swartz ex Fr.) Cke.

Galera coprinoides ≡ *Galerella plicatella* (Pk.) Singer
Galera hypnorum ≡ *Galerina hypnorum* (Schrank ex Fr.) Kühner
Galera inculta ≡ *Alnicola inculta*

(Pk.) Singer
Galera lateritia ≡ *Conocybe lactea* (Lange) Métrod
Galera sphagnorum ≡ *Galerina sphagnorum* (Pers. ex Fr.) Kühner
Galera tenera≡*Conocybe tenera* (Schaeff. ex Fr.) Kühner
Geaster hygrometricus ≡ *Astraeus hygrometricus* (Pers.) Morg.
Geaster triplex ≡ *Geastrum triplex* Jungh.
Geoglossum glabrum Pers. ex Fr.
Gloeosporium nervisequum (Fuckel) Sacc. is the name of the imperfect state of *Gnomonia venenata* (Sacc. & Spegazzini) Klebahn.
Gomphidius glutinosus (Schaeff. ex. Fr.) Fr.
Gomphidius nigricans Pk.
Gomphidius viscidus = *Gomphidius˙ rutilus* (Schaeff. ex Fr.) Lundell
Gyrocephalus rufus=*Phlogiotus helvelloides* (Fr.) Martin
Gyromitra brunnea = *Neogyromitra brunnea* (Underwood) Imai
Gyromitra esculenta (Pers.) Fr.
Gyrophragmium delilei Mont.

Hebeloma colvini (Pk.) Sacc.
Hebeloma crustuliniforme (Bull. ex St. Amans) Quél.
Hebeloma pascuense Pk.
Hebeloma sarcophyllum (Pk.) Sacc.
Helvella crispa Fr.
Helvella elastica Bull. ex St. Amans

Helvella infula = *Gyromitra infula* (Schaeff. ex Fr.) Quél.
Helvella lacunosa Afz. ex Fr.
Hirneola auricula-judae=*Auricularia auricula* (L. ex Hooker) Underwood
Hydnum auriscalpium = *Auriscalpium vulgare* S. F. Gray
Hydnum caput-ursi = *Hericium coralloides* (Scop. ex Fr.) S. F. Gray
Hydnum coralloides=*Hericium coralloides* (Scop. ex Fr.) S. F. Gray
Hydnum cyaneotinctum=*Hydnellum caeruleum* (Hornemann ex Pers.) Karst.
Hydnum erinaceus = *Hericium erinaceus* (Bull. ex Fr.) Pers.
Hydnum fennicum (Karst.) Sacc. Krieger's use of this name is a misidentification for *Hydnum scabrosum* Fr.
Hydnum imbricatum Fr.
Hydnum repandum = *Dentinum repandum* (Fr.) S. F. Gray
Hydnum repandum var. *umbilicatum* is now recognized as a species, *Dentinum umbilicatum* (Pk.) Pouzar.
Hydnum septentrionale = *Steccherinum septentrionale* (Fr.) Banker
Hydnum pulcherrimum = *Steccherinum pulcherrimum* (Berk. & Curt.) Banker
Hygrophorus aureus = *Hygrophorus hypothejus* (Fr.) Fr.
Hygrophorus basidiosus (Pk.) Pk.
Hygrophorus borealis Pk.
Hygrophorus cantharellus

(Schw.) Fr.

Hygrophorus ceraceus (Wulf. ex Fr.) Fr.

Hygrophorus chlorophanus (Fr.) Fr.

Hygrophorus coccineus (Schaeff. ex Fr.) Fr.

Hygrophorus coloratus=Hygrophorus speciosus Pk.

Hygrophorus congelatus = Hygrophorus miniatus (Fr.) Fr.

Hygrophorus conicus (Scop. ex Fr.) Fr.

Hygrophorus cuspidatus Pk.

Hygrophorus eburneus (Bull. ex Fr.) Fr.

Hygrophorus flavodiscus Frost

Hygrophorus fuligineus Frost

Hygrophorus immutabilis Pk.

Hygrophorus laetus (Pers. ex Fr.) Fr.

Hygrophorus laricinus Pk.

Hygrophorus laurae Morg.

Hygrophorus laurae var. *decipiens* Pk.

Hygrophorus laurae var. *unicolor* Pk.

Hygrophorus limacinus (Scop. ex Fr.) Fr.

Hygrophorus marginatus Pk.

Hygrophorus mephiticus Pk.

Hygrophorus miniatus (Fr.) Fr.

Hygrophorus nitidus Berk. & Curt.

Hygrophorus peckianus Howe

Hygrophorus pratensis (Pers. ex Fr.) Fr.

Hygrophorus proximus Krieger

Hygrophorus psittacinus (Schaeff. ex Fr.) Fr.

Hygrophorus pudorinus (Fr.) Fr.

Hygrophorus puniceus (Fr.) Fr.

Hygrophorus purpurascens (A. & S. ex Fr.) Fr.

Hygrophorus ruber Pk.

Hygrophorus rubropunctus = Hygrophorus glutinosus Pk.

Hygrophorus russula (Schaeff. ex Fr.) Quél.

Hygrophorus speciosus Pk.

Hygrophorus subviolaceus Pk.

Hygrophorus virgineus (Wulf. ex Fr.) Fr.

Hypholoma aggregatum = Psathyrella velutina (Pers. ex Fr.) Singer

Hypholoma appendiculatum = Psathyrella candolleana (Fr.) Maire

Hypholoma candolleanum = Psathyrella candolleana (Fr.) Maire

Hypholoma capnoides (Fr. ex Fr.) Kummer

Hypholoma elaeodes (Fr.) Gill.

Hypholoma epixanthum (Fr.) Quél.

Hypholoma fasciculare (Huds. ex Fr.) Kummer

Hypholoma incertum is recognized as a form, *Psathyrella candolleana* (Fr.) Maire f. *incerta* (Pk.) Singer.

Hypholoma lacrymabundum = Psathyrella velutina (Pers. ex Fr.) Singer

Hypholoma perplexum = Hypholoma sublateritium (Fr.) Quél.

Hypholoma pyrotrichum = Psythyrella pyrotricha (Holmskjold ex Fr.) Moser

Hypholoma sublateritium (Fr.) Quél.

Hypholoma velutinum=Psathy-

rella velutina (Pers. ex Fr.)
Singer
Hypomyces chrysospermus Tul.
Hypomyces hyalinus (Schw. ex
Fr.) Tul.
*Hypomyces inaequalis = Hypo-
myces hyalinus* (Schw. ex
Fr.) Tul.
Hypomyces lactifluorum (Schw.
ex Fr.) Tul.
Hypomyces transformans Pk.

Inocybe agglutinata Pk.
Inocybe albodisca Pk.
Inocybe castanea Pk.
Inocybe infelix = Inocybe lacera
(Fr.) Kummer
Inocybe infida (Pk.) Earle
Inocybe maritimoides (Pk.)
Sacc.
Inocybe nigrodisca Pk.
Inocybe paludinella (Pk.) Sacc.
*Inocybe rigidipes = Inocybe
calospora* Quél.
Inocybe serotina Pk.
Inocybe squamosodisca Pk.
Inocybe subfulva Pk.
Inocybe subtomentosa Pk.
Inocybe unicolor Pk.
*Ithyphallus impudicus≡Phallus
impudicus* Pers.

*Laccaria amethystina=Laccaria
amethystea* (Bull. ex Mérat)
Murrill
Laccaria laccata (Scop. ex Fr.)
Cke.
Laccaria ochropurpurea (Berk.)
Pk.
Laccaria striatula (Pk.) Pk.
Laccaria tortilis (Bolt. ex S. F.
Gray) Cke.
Laccaria trullisata (Ell.) Pk.

*Lachnocladium ornatipes=Cla-
vulina ornatipes* (Pk.) Corner
*Lachnocladium vestipes = Ra-
mariopsis vestipes* (Pk.) Cor-
ner
Lactarius affinis Pk.
Lactarius chelidonium Pk.
Lactarius camphoratus (Bull. ex
Fr.) Fr.
Lactarius chrysorheus Fr.
Lactarius cilicioides Fr.
Lactarius corrugis Pk.
Lactarius deceptivus Pk.
Lactarius deliciosus (L. ex Fr.)
S. F. Gray
Lactarius glyciosmus (Fr. ex
Fr.) Fr.
Lactarius hygrophoroides Berk.
& Curt.
Lactarius indigo (Schw.) Fr.
Lactarius lignyotus Fr.
Lactarius paludinellus Pk.
Lactarius piperatus (Scop. ex
Fr.) S. F. Gray
*Lactarius plumbeus = Lactarius
turpis* (Weinmann) Fr.
Lactarius resimus (Fr.) Fr.
Lactarius rimosellus Pk.
Lactarius rufus (Scop. ex Fr.)
Fr.
*Lactarius sordidus = Lactarius
turpis* (Weinmann) Fr.
Lactarius subdulcis (Pers. ex
Fr.) S. F. Gray
Lactarius subpurpureus Pk.
Lactarius theiogalus (Bull. ex
Fr.) S. F. Gray
Lactarius torminosus (Schaeff.
ex Fr.) S. F. Gray
Lactarius uvidus (Fr. ex Fr.)
Fr.
Lactarius vellereus (Fr.) Fr.
Lactarius volemus (Fr.) Fr.

Laternea columnata = Clathrus columnatus Nees

Lentinus approximans=Hohenbuehelia approximans (Pk.) Singer

Lentinus haematopus=Lentinus suavissimus Fr.

Lentinus lepideus (Fr. ex Fr.) Fr.

Lentinus spretus Pk.

Lentinus suavissimus Fr.

Lentinus sulcatus Berk.

Lentinus tigrinus (Bull. ex Fr.) Fr.

Lentinus velutinus = Panus badius (Berk.) Singer

Lentinus vulpinus = Lentinellus vulpinus (Sow. ex Fr.) Kühner & Maire

Lentodium squamulosum Morg. is a species in its own right, not an abnormal form of *Lentinus lepideus* (Fr. ex Fr.) Fr.

Leotia lubrica Pers.

Lepiota acerina Pk.

Lepiota acutesquamosa (Weinmann) Kummer

Lepiota americana (Pk.) Sacc.

Lepiota amianthina = Cystoderma amianthinum (Scop. ex Fr.) Fayod

Lepiota badhamii (Berk. & Broome) Quél.

Lepiota cepaestipes = Leucocoprinus cepaestipes (Sow. ex Fr.) Patouillard

Lepiota cepaestipes var. *lutea = Leucocoprinus birnbaumii* (Corda) Singer

Lepiota clypeolaria (Bull. ex Fr.) Kummer

Lepiota cristata (Fr.) Kummer

Lepiota fuscosquamea (Pk.) Sacc.

Lepiota helveola Bres.

Lepiota metulaespora (Berk. & Broome) Sacc. The fungus for which Krieger used this name is now called *Lepiota ventriosospora* Reid.

Lepiota morgani = Chlorophyllum molybdites (Meyer ex Fr.) Mass.

Lepiota naucina = Lepiota leucothites (Vitt.) Orton

Lepiota naucinoides = Lepiota leucothites (Vitt.) Orton

Lepiota procera (Scop. ex Fr.) S. F. Gray

Lepiota pusillomyces = Lepiota seminuda (Lasch) Kummer

Lepiota rhacodes (Vitt.) Quél.

Lycoperdon atropurpureum Vitt.

Lycoperdon calyptriforme=Lycoperdon acuminatum Bosc

Lycoperdon excipuliforme=Lycoperdon perlatum Pers.

Lycoperdon frostii = Lycoperdon pulcherrimum Berk. & Curt.

Lycoperdon gemmatum = Lycoperdon perlatum Pers.

Lycoperdon glabellum = Lycoperdon umbrinum Pers.

Lycoperdon leprosum = Lycoperdon acuminatum Bosc

Lycoperdon molle = Lycoperdon umbrinum Pers.

Lycoperdon pusillum Pers.

Lycoperdon pyriforme Pers.

Lycoperdon separans=Lycoperdon marginatum Vitt.

Lycoperdon subincarnatum Pk.

Lycoperdon wrightii=Lycoperdon curtisii Berk.

Lysurus borealis = *Anthurus borealis* Burt

Marasmius alliatus = *Marasmius scorodonius* (Fr.) Fr.
Marasmius androsaceus (L. ex Fr.) Fr.
Marasmius calopus (Pers. ex Fr.) Fr.
Marasmius capillaris Morg.
Marasmius oreades (Bolt. ex Fr.) Fr.
Marasmius rotula (Scop. ex Fr.) Fr.
Marasmius scorodonius (Fr.) Fr.
Marasmius siccus (Schw.) Fr.
Merulius lacrymans = *Serpula lacrimans* (Wulf. ex Fr.) Karst.
Mitrula phalloides ≡ *Mitrula paludosa* Fr.
Morchella angusticeps Pk.
Morchella bispora = *Verpa bohemica* (Krombh.) Schroet.
Morchella crassipes=*Morchella esculenta* Pers. ex St. Amans
Morchella deliciosa=*Morchella esculenta* Pers. ex St. Amans
Morchella esculenta Pers. ex St. Amans
Morchella hybrida = *Morchella semilibera* (DC. ex Fr.) Lév.
Morchella semilibera (DC. ex Fr.) Lév.
Mutinus caninus (Pers.) Fr.
Mutinus curtisii = *Mutinus elegans* (Mont.) Fischer
Mycena adirondackensis = *Mycena radicatella* (Pk.) Sacc.
Mycena alcalina (Fr. ex Fr.) Kummer
Mycena amabillissima (Pk.) Sacc.
Mycena anomala Beardslee
Mycena atroumbonata = *Mycena hemisphaerica* Pk.
Mycena corticola (Pers. ex Fr.) S. F. Gray
Mycena crocata (Schrader ex Fr.) Kummer
Mycena cyaneobasis = *Mycena subcaerulea* (Pk.) Sacc.
Mycena epipterygia (Scop. ex Fr.) S. F. Gray
Mycena filopes (Bull. ex Fr.) Kummer
Mycena flavifolia Pk.
Mycena galopus (Pers. ex Fr.) Kummer
Mycena haematopus (Pers. ex Fr.) Kummer
Mycena leaiana (Berk.) Sacc.
Mycena luteopallens (Pk.) Sacc.
Mycena odorifera (Pk.) Sacc.
Mycena palustris = *Lyophyllum palustre* (Pk.) Singer
Mycena praelonga (Pk.) Sacc.
Mycena pura (Pers. ex Fr.) Kummer
Mycena sanguinolenta (A. & S. ex Fr.) Kummer
Mycena splendipes = *Mycena viscosa* (Secr.) Maire
Mycena tenerrima (Berk.) Sacc.
Mycena vulgaris (Pers. ex Fr.) Kummer
Mycenastrum corium (Guersent) Desvaux
Myriostoma coliforme (Pers.) Corda

Naucoria firma = *Agrocybe firma* (Pk.) Singer
Naucoria semiorbicularis = *Agrocybe semiorbicularis*

(Bull. ex St. Amans) Fayod
Naucoria sororia Pk. = *Agrocybe sororia* (Pk.)
Naucoria temulenta=Agrocybe temulenta (Fr.) Orton
Nyctalis asterophora ≡ *Asterophora lycoperdoides* (Bull. ex Mérat) S. F. Gray

Omphalia austini ≡ *Mycena austinii* (Pk.) Kühner
Omphalia campanella ≡ *Xeromphalina campanella* (Batsch ex Fr.) Maire
Omphalia gerardiana ≡ *Omphalina gerardiana* (Pk.) Singer
Omphalia gracillima ≡ *Mycena delectabilis* (Pk.) Sacc.
Omphalia lilacifolia ≡ *Mycena lilacifolia* (Pk.) A. H. Smith
Omphalia oculus ≡ *Clitocybula ocula* (Pk.) Singer
Omphalia olivaria ≡ *Omphalina olivaria* (Pk.) Singer
Omphalia pyxidata≡Omphalina pyxidata (Bull. ex Fr.) Quél.
Omphalia striipilea (Fr.) Gill.≡ *Collybia striaepilea* (Fr.) Orton
Otidea leporina ≡ *Scodellina leporina* (Batsch ex Fr.) S. F. Gray
Otidea onotica ≡ *Scodellina onotica* (Pers. ex Fr.) S. F. Gray

Panaeolus campanulatus (Bull. ex Fr.) Quél.
Panaeolus papilionaceus (Bull. ex Fr.) Quél.
Panaeolus retirugis (Fr.) Gill.
Panaeolus solidipes=Panaeolus sepulchralis (Berk.) Sacc.
Panaeolus subbalteatus (Berk. &

Curt.) Sacc.
Panaeolus venenosus = *Panaeolus subbalteatus* (Berk. & Broome) Sacc.
Panus stipticus = *Panellus stipticus* (Bull. ex Fr.) Karst.
Panus strigosus Berk. & Curt.
Paxillus atrotomentosus (Batsch ex Fr.) Fr.
Paxillus involutus (Batsch ex Fr.) Fr.
Paxillus panuoides (Fr. ex Fr.) Fr.
Paxillus rhodoxanthus=Phylloporus rhodoxanthus (Schw.) Bres.
Peziza aurantia=Aleuria aurantia (Fr.) Fuckel
Peziza badia Pers. ex Mérat
Peziza vesiculosa Bull. ex St. Amans
Phallogaster saccatus Morg.
Pholiota adiposa (Fr.) Kummer
Pholiota albocrenulata (Pk.) Sacc.
Pholiota autumnalis = *Galerina autumnalis* (Pk.) A. H. Smith & Singer
Pholiota caperata = *Rozites caperatus* (Pers. ex Fr.) Karst.
Pholiota dura = *Agrocybe dura* (Bolt. ex Fr.) Singer
Pholiota luteofolia = *Gymnopilus luteofolius* (Pk.) Singer
Pholiota marginata = *Galerina marginata* (Batsch ex Fr.) Kühner
Pholiota minima = *Galerina minima* (Pk.) A. H. Smith & Singer
Pholiota praecox = *Agrocybe praecox* (Pers. ex Fr.) Fayod

Pholiota spectabilis = *Gymnopilus junonius* (Fr.) Orton
Pholiota squarrosa (Müll. ex Fr.) Kummer
Pholiota squarrosoides (Pk.) Sacc.
Physalacria inflata (Schw.) Pk.
Pilobolus crystallinus Tode ex van Tiegham
Pleurotus atrocaeruleus = *Hohenbuehelia atrocaerulea* (Fr. ex Fr.) Singer
Pleurotus campanulatus=Resupinatus cyphelliformis (Berk.) Singer
Pleurotus japonicus=Lampteromyces japonicus (Kawamura) Singer
Pleurotus mitis=Panellus mitis (Pers. ex Fr.) Singer
Pleurotus olearius = *Clitocybe olearia* (DC. ex Fr.) Maire
Pleurotus ostreatus (Jacquin ex Fr.) Kummer
Pleurotus petaloides = *Hohenbuehelia petaloides* (Bull. ex Fr.) Schulz.
Pleurotus porrigens = *Pleurotellus porrigens* (Pers. ex Fr.) Kühner & Romagnesi
Pleurotus salignus = *Pleurotus ostreatus* (Jacquin ex Fr.) Kummer
Pleurotus sapidus = *Pleurotus cornucopiae* (Paulet ex Pers.) Rolland
Pleurotus serotinus = *Panellus serotinus* (Schrader ex Fr.) Kühner
Pleurotus striatulus = *Resupinatus striatulus* (Fr.) Murrill
Pleurotus tremulus = *Pleurotellus tremulus* (Schaeff. ex Fr.) Konrad & Maublanc
Pleurotus ulmarius = *Pleurotus tessulatus* (Bull. ex Fr.) Gill.
Pluteus cervinus (Schaeff. ex Fr.) Kummer
Pluteus umbrosus (Pers. ex Fr.) Kummer
Polyporus berkeleyi = *Bondarzewia berkeleyi* (Fr.) Bondarzew
Polyporus betulinus = *Piptoporus betulinus* (Bull. ex Fr.) Karst.
Polyporus caudicinus = *Polyporus squamosus* Mich. ex Fr.
Polyporus cincinnatus = *Laetiporus sulphureus* (Bull. ex Fr.) Bondarzew & Singer
Polyporus confluens = *Scutiger confluens* (A. & S. ex Fr.) Bondarzew & Singer
Polyporus frondosus = *Polypilus frondosus* (Dicks. ex Fr.) Karst.
Polyporus lucidus=Ganoderma lucidum (Leysser ex Fr.) Karst.
Polyporus ovinus = *Scutiger ovinus* (Schaeff. ex Fr.) Murrill
Polyporus pes-caprae=Scutiger pes-caprae (Pers. ex Fr.) Bondarzew
Polyporus rimosus = *Phellinus rimosus* (Berk.) Pilát
Polyporus roseus=Fomes roseus (A. & S. ex Fr.) Cke.
Polyporus schweinitzii=Phaeolus schweinitzii (Fr.) Patouillard
Polyporus squamosus Mich. ex Fr.
Polyporus sulphureus = *Laeti-*

porus sulphureus (Bull. ex Fr.) Bondarzew & Singer
Polyporus umbellatus = *Polypilus umbellatus* (Pers. ex Fr.) Bondarzew & Singer
Polyporus volvatus = *Cryptoporus volvatus* (Pk.) Hubbard
Polysaccum pisocarpium=*Pisolithus tinctorius* (Pers.) Coker & Couch
Polystictus pergamenus = *Hirschioporus pergamenus* (Fr.) Bondarzew & Singer
Polystictus versicolor=*Coriolus versicolor* (L. ex Fr.) Quél.
Poria vaporaria = *Coriolus vaporarius* (Fr.) Bondarzew & Singer
Poronia punctata (L. ex Fr.) Fr.
Psalliota abruptibulba ≡ *Agaricus abruptibulbus* Pk.
Psalliota arvensis ≡ *Agaricus arvensis* Schaeff. ex Secr.
Psalliota bernardii ≡ *Agaricus bernardii* Quél.
Psalliota campestris ≡ *Agaricus campestris* L. ex Fr.
Psalliota campestris, "the cultivated Meadow Mushroom" ≡ *Agaricus bisporus* (Lange) Pilát
Psalliota diminutiva ≡ *Agaricus diminutivus* Pk.
Psalliota haemorrhoidaria ≡ *Agaricus haemorrhoidarius* Schulz.
Psalliota halophila ≡ *Agaricus halophilus* Pk.
Psalliota maritima ≡ *Agaricus halophilus* Pk.
Psalliota micromegatha≡*Agari-*

cus micromegathus Pk.
Psalliota perrara ≡ *Agaricus perrarus* Schulz.
Psalliota placomyces ≡ *Agaricus placomyces* Pk.
Psalliota rodmani ≡ *Agaricus bitorquis* (Quél.) Sacc.
Psalliota silvatica ≡ *Agaricus silvaticus* Schaeff. ex Secr.
Psalliota silvicola ≡ *Agaricus silvicola* (Vitt.) Pk.
Psalliota subrufescens ≡ *Agaricus subrufescens* Pk.
Psalliota villatica ≡ *Agaricus villaticus* Brondeau
Psathyrella atomata (Fr.) Quél.
Psathyrella graciloides = *Psathyrella subatrata* (Fr.) Gill.
Pseudobalsamia microspora = *Diehliomyces microsporus* (Diehl & Lambert) Gilkey
Psilocybe conissans = *Psathyrella subcernua* (Schulz.) Singer
Psilocybe foenisecii=*Panaeolus foenisecii* (Pers. ex Fr.) Schroet.
Psilocybe semilanceata (Fr. ex Secr.) Kummer
Psilocybe spadicea=*Psathyrella spadicea* (Schaeff. ex Fr.) Singer
Psilocybe uda = *Hypholoma udum* (Pers. ex Fr.) Kühner
Puccinia graminis Pers.

Queletia mirabilis Fr.

Rhizina inflata = *Rhizina undulata* Fr. ex Fr.
Rhizopogon rubescens Tul.
Rhytisma acerinum (Pers. ex

St. Amans) Fr.

Rozites caperatus (Pers. ex Fr.)
Karst.

Russula abietina Pk.

Russula adusta (Pers. ex Fr.)
Fr.

Russula alutacea (Pers. ex Fr.)
Fr.

Russula compacta Frost

Russula crustosa Pk.

Russula cutifracta = *Russula
cyanoxantha* (Schaeff. ex
Secr.) Fr.

Russula densifolia (Secr.) Gill.

Russula emetica (Schaeff. ex
Fr.) Pers. ex S. F. Gray

Russula foetens (Pers. ex Fr.)
Pers. ex Fr.

Russula foetentula Pk.

Russula fragilis (Pers. ex Fr.)
Fr.

Russula furcata = *Russula het-
erophylla* (Fr.) Fr.

Russula magnifica = *Russula
polyphylla* Pk.

Russula mariae Pk.

Russula nigricans (Bull. ex
Mérat) Fr. The species for
which Krieger used this name
is probably that now called
Russula dissimulans Shaffer.

Russula ochrophylla Pk.

Russula palustris Pk.

Russula pectinatoides Pk.

Russula rubra (Lam. ex Fr.)
Fr.

Russula rugulosa Pk.

Russula sordida = *Russula al-
bonigra* (Krombh.) Fr.

Russula turci Bres.

Russula variata Banning

Russula virescens (Schaeff. ex
Zantedschi) Fr.

Russula viridella Pk.

Russula xerampelina (Schaeff.
ex Secr.) Fr.

Sarcoscypha floccosa = *Antho-
peziza floccosa* (Schw.) Kanouse

Sarcosphaera coronaria = *Sarcosphaera eximia* (Durieu &
Lév.) Maire

Schizophyllum commune Fr.

Scleroderma aurantium Pers.

Scleroderma geaster Fr.

Scleroderma verrucosum =
Scleroderma lycoperdoides
Schw.

Scleroderma vulgare = *Scleroderma aurantium* Pers.

Sclerotinia tuberosa (Hedwig ex
Fr.) Fuckel

Simblum sphaerocephalum
Schlechtendahl

Sparassis crispa Fr.

Sparassis herbstii = *Sparassis
spathulata* (Schw.) Fr.

Sparassis spathulata (Schw.)
Fr.

Spathularia clavata = *Spathularia flavida* Fr.

Spathularia velutipes Cke. &
Farlow

Sphaerobolus stellatus Pers.

Stereum purpureum (Pers. ex
Fr.) Fr.

Strobilomyces annamiticus =
Boletellus emodensis (Berk.)
Singer

Strobilomyces floccopus (Vahl
ex Fr.) Karst.

Strobilomyces floccosus = *Strobilomyces floccopus* (Vahl ex
Fr.) Karst.

Strobilomyces pallescens=*Bole-*

tellus ananas (Curt.) Murrill

*Strobilomyces strobilaceus =
Strobilomyces floccopus* (Vahl ex Fr.) Karst.

Stropharia aeruginosa (Curt. ex Fr.) Quél.

Stropharia coronilla (Bull. ex Fr.) Quél.

Stropharia epimyces = Psathyrella epimyces (Pk.) A. H. Smith

Stropharia melasperma = Stropharia melanosperma (Bull. ex Fr.) Gill.

Stropharia semiglobata (Batsch ex Fr.) Quél.

Stropharia stercoraria = Stropharia semiglobata (Batsch ex Fr.) Quél.

Stropharia umbonatescens = Stropharia luteonitens (Fr.) Quél.

Thelephora anthocephala (Bull.) ex Fr.

Thelephora terrestris Ehrhart ex Fr.

Trametes pini = Phellinus pini (Thore ex Fr.) Pilát

Tremella frondosa Fr.

Tremella lutescens Fr.

Tremella mesenterica Fr.

Tremella vesicaria = Tremella reticulata (Berk.) Farlow

Tremellodon gelatinosum ≡ Pseudohydnum gelatinosum (Fr.) Karst.

Tricholoma albiflavidum = Melanoleuca alboflavidum (Pk.) Murrill

Tricholoma argyraceum (Bull. ex St. Amans) Gill.

Tricholoma atrosquamosum

(Chevallier) Sacc.

Tricholoma brevipes = Melanoleuca brevipes (Bull. ex Fr.) Patouillard

Tricholoma columbetta (Fr.) Kummer

Tricholoma equestre = Tricholoma flavovirens (Pers. ex Fr.) Lundell

Tricholoma flavescens = Tricholomopsis flavescens (Pk.) Singer

Tricholoma flavobrunneum (Fr.) Kummer

Tricholoma imbricatum (Fr. ex Fr.) Kummer

Tricholoma leucocephalum (Fr.) Quél.

Tricholoma microcephalum = Melanoleuca microcephalum (Karst.) Singer

Tricholoma nudum = Lepista nuda (Bull. ex Fr.) Cke.

Tricholoma orirubens Quél.

Tricholoma panaeolum = Lepista luscina (Fr. ex Fr.) Singer

Tricholoma personatum = Lepista personatum (Fr. ex Fr.) Kummer

Tricholoma portentosum (Fr.) Quél.

Tricholoma putidum = Lyophyllum putidum (Fr.) Singer

Tricholoma resplendens (Fr.) Karst.

Tricholoma rutilans = Tricholomopsis rutilans (Schaeff. ex Fr.) Singer

Tricholoma saponaceum (Fr.) Kummer

Tricholoma sejunctum (Sow. ex Fr.) Quél.

Tricholoma sordidum = Lepista

sordidum (Fr.) Singer

Tricholoma sulphureum (Bull. ex Fr.) Kummer

Tricholoma terreum (Schaeff. ex Fr.) Kummer

Tricholoma transmutans = *Tricholoma flavobrunneum* (Fr.) Kummer

Tricholoma vaccinum (Pers. ex Fr.) Kummer

Tricholoma variegatum=*Tricholomopsis rutilans* (Schaeff. ex Fr.) Singer

Trogia faginea=*Plicatura crispa* (Pers. ex Fr.) Rea

Tylostoma mammosum=*Tulostoma brumale* Pers.

Underwoodia columnaris Pk.

Urnula craterium (Schw. ex Fr.) Fr.

Urnula geaster = *Chorioactis geaster* (Pk.) Kupfer

Verpa digitaliformis = *Verpa conica* Swartz ex Pers.

Vibrissea truncorum Fr.

Volveria bombycina ≡ *Volvariella bombycina* (Schaeff. ex Fr.) Singer

Volvaria gloiocephala is recognized as a variety, *Volvariella speciosa* (Fr. ex Fr.) Singer var. *gloiocephala* (DC. ex Fr.) Singer.

Volvaria loveiana ≡ *Volvariella surrecta* (Knapp) Singer

Volvaria speciosa ≡ *Volvariella speciosa* (Fr. ex Fr.) Singer var. *speciosa*

Volvaria volvacea ≡ *Volvariella volvacea* (Bull. ex Fr.) Singer

Wynnea americana Thax.

Xylaria hypoxylon ≡ *Xylosphaera hypoxylon* (L.) ex Dumortier

Xylaria polymorpha ≡ *Xylosphaera polymorpha* (Pers. ex Mérat) Dumortier

INDEX

(Heavy-faced page numbers indicate where descriptions are given. Names of fungi in heavy-face type are new to science.)

[535]

A CATALOGUE OF
SELECTED DOVER BOOKS
IN ALL FIELDS OF INTEREST

A CATALOGUE OF SELECTED DOVER BOOKS IN ALL FIELDS OF INTEREST

CELESTIAL OBJECTS FOR COMMON TELESCOPES, T. W. Webb. The most used book in amateur astronomy: inestimable aid for locating and identifying nearly 4,000 celestial objects. Edited, updated by Margaret W. Mayall. 77 illustrations. Total of 645pp. 5⅜ x 8½.
20917-2, 20918-0 Pa., Two-vol. set **$10.00**

HISTORICAL STUDIES IN THE LANGUAGE OF CHEMISTRY, M. P. Crosland. The important part language has played in the development of chemistry from the symbolism of alchemy to the adoption of systematic nomenclature in 1892. ". . . wholeheartedly recommended,"—Science. 15 illustrations. 416pp. of text. 5⅝ x 8¼. 63702-6 Pa. **$7.50**

BURNHAM'S CELESTIAL HANDBOOK, Robert Burnham, Jr. Thorough, readable guide to the stars beyond our solar system. Exhaustive treatment, fully illustrated. Breakdown is alphabetical by constellation: Andromeda to Cetus in Vol. 1; Chamaeleon to Orion in Vol. 2; and Pavo to Vulpecula in Vol. 3. Hundreds of illustrations. Total of about 2000pp. 6⅛ x 9¼.
23567-X, 23568-8, 23673-0 Pa., Three-vol. set $32.85

THEORY OF WING SECTIONS: INCLUDING A SUMMARY OF AIR-FOIL DATA, Ira H. Abbott and A. E. von Doenhoff. Concise compilation of subatomic aerodynamic characteristics of modern NASA wing sections, plus description of theory. 350pp. of tables. 693pp. 5⅜ x 8½.
60586-8 Pa. $9.95

DE RE METALLICA, Georgius Agricola. Translated by Herbert C. Hoover and Lou H. Hoover. The famous Hoover translation of greatest treatise on technological chemistry, engineering, geology, mining of early modern times (1556). All 289 original woodcuts. 638pp. 6¾ x 11.
60006-8 Clothbd. $19.95

THE ORIGIN OF CONTINENTS AND OCEANS, Alfred Wegener. One of the most influential, most controversial books in science, the classic statement for continental drift. Full 1966 translation of Wegener's final (1929) version. 64 illustrations. 246pp. 5⅜ x 8½.(EBE)61708-4 Pa. **$5.00**

THE PRINCIPLES OF PSYCHOLOGY, William James. Famcus long course complete, unabridged. Stream of thought, time perception, memory, experimental methods; great work decades ahead of its time. Still valid, useful; read in many classes. 94 figures. Total of 1391pp. 5⅜ x 8½.
20381-6, 20382-4 Pa., Two-vol. set **$17.90**

YUCATAN BEFORE AND AFTER THE CONQUEST, Diego de Landa. First English translation of basic book in Maya studies, the only significant account of Yucatan written in the early post-Conquest era. Translated by distinguished Maya scholar William Gates. Appendices, introduction, 4 maps and over 120 illustrations added by translator. 162pp. 5⅜ x 8½.
23622-6 Pa. $3.00

THE MALAY ARCHIPELAGO, Alfred R. Wallace. Spirited travel account by one of founders of modern biology. Touches on zoology, botany, ethnography, geography, and geology. 62 illustrations, maps. 515pp. 5⅜ x 8½.
20187-2 Pa. $6.95

THE DISCOVERY OF THE TOMB OF TUTANKHAMEN, Howard Carter, A. C. Mace. Accompany Carter in the thrill of discovery, as ruined passage suddenly reveals unique, untouched, fabulously rich tomb. Fascinating account, with 106 illustrations. New introduction by J. M. White. Total of 382pp. 5⅜ x 8½. (Available in U.S. only)   23500-9 Pa. $5.50

THE WORLD'S GREATEST SPEECHES, edited by Lewis Copeland and Lawrence W. Lamm. Vast collection of 278 speeches from Greeks up to present. Powerful and effective models; unique look at history. Revised to 1970. Indices. 842pp. 5⅜ x 8½.   20468-5 Pa. $9.95

THE 100 GREATEST ADVERTISEMENTS, Julian Watkins. The priceless ingredient; His master's voice; 99 44/100% pure; over 100 others. How they were written, their impact, etc. Remarkable record. 130 illustrations. 233pp. 7⅞ x 10 3/5.   20540-1 Pa. $6.95

CRUICKSHANK PRINTS FOR HAND COLORING, George Cruickshank. 18 illustrations, one side of a page, on fine-quality paper suitable for watercolors. Caricatures of people in society (c. 1820) full of trenchant wit. Very large format. 32pp. 11 x 16.   23684-6 Pa. $6.00

THIRTY-TWO COLOR POSTCARDS OF TWENTIETH-CENTURY AMERICAN ART, Whitney Museum of American Art. Reproduced in full color in postcard form are 31 art works and one shot of the museum. Calder, Hopper, Rauschenberg, others. Detachable. 16pp. 8¼ x 11.
23629-3 Pa. $3.50

MUSIC OF THE SPHERES: THE MATERIAL UNIVERSE FROM ATOM TO QUASAR SIMPLY EXPLAINED, Guy Murchie. Planets, stars, geology, atoms, radiation, relativity, quantum theory, light, antimatter, similar topics. 319 figures. 664pp. 5⅜ x 8½.
21809-0, 21810-4 Pa., Two-vol. set $11.00

EINSTEIN'S THEORY OF RELATIVITY, Max Born. Finest semi-technical account; covers Einstein, Lorentz, Minkowski, and others, with much detail, much explanation of ideas and math not readily available elsewhere on this level. For student, non-specialist. 376pp. 5⅜ x 8½.
60769-0 Pa. $5.00

THE SENSE OF BEAUTY, George Santayana. Masterfully written discussion of nature of beauty, materials of beauty, form, expression; art, literature, social sciences all involved. 168pp. 5⅜ x 8½. 20238-0 Pa. $3.50

ON THE IMPROVEMENT OF THE UNDERSTANDING, Benedict Spinoza. Also contains *Ethics, Correspondence,* all in excellent R. Elwes translation. Basic works on entry to philosophy, pantheism, exchange of ideas with great contemporaries. 402pp. 5⅜ x 8½. 20250-X Pa. $5.95

THE TRAGIC SENSE OF LIFE, Miguel de Unamuno. Acknowledged masterpiece of existential literature, one of most important books of 20th century. Introduction by Madariaga. 367pp. 5⅜ x 8½.
20257-7 Pa. $6.00

THE GUIDE FOR THE PERPLEXED, Moses Maimonides. Great classic of medieval Judaism attempts to reconcile revealed religion (Pentateuch, commentaries) with Aristotelian philosophy. Important historically, still relevant in problems. Unabridged Friedlander translation. Total of 473pp. 5⅜ x 8½. 20351-4 Pa. $6.95

THE I CHING (THE BOOK OF CHANGES), translated by James Legge. Complete translation of basic text plus appendices by Confucius, and Chinese commentary of most penetrating divination manual ever prepared. Indispensable to study of early Oriental civilizations, to modern inquiring reader. 448pp. 5⅜ x 8½. 21062-6 Pa. $6.00

THE EGYPTIAN BOOK OF THE DEAD, E. A. Wallis Budge. Complete reproduction of Ani's papyrus, finest ever found. Full hieroglyphic text, interlinear transliteration, word for word translation, smooth translation. Basic work, for Egyptology, for modern study of psychic matters. Total of 533pp. 6½ x 9¼. (USCO) 21866-X Pa. $8.50

THE GODS OF THE EGYPTIANS, E. A. Wallis Budge. Never excelled for richness, fullness: all gods, goddesses, demons, mythical figures of Ancient Egypt; their legends, rites, incarnations, variations, powers, etc. Many hieroglyphic texts cited. Over 225 illustrations, plus 6 color plates. Total of 988pp. 6⅛ x 9¼. (EBE)
22055-9, 22056-7 Pa., Two-vol. set $20.00

THE STANDARD BOOK OF QUILT MAKING AND COLLECTING, Marguerite Ickis. Full information, full-sized patterns for making 46 traditional quilts, also 150 other patterns. Quilted cloths, lame, satin quilts, etc. 483 illustrations. 273pp. 6⅞ x 9⅝. 20582-7 Pa. $5.95

CORAL GARDENS AND THEIR MAGIC, Bronsilaw Malinowski. Classic study of the methods of tilling the soil and of agricultural rites in the Trobriand Islands of Melanesia. Author is one of the most important figures in the field of modern social anthropology. 143 illustrations. Indexes. Total of 911pp. of text. 5⅝ x 8¼. (Available in U.S. only)
23597-1 Pa. $12.95

THE PHILOSOPHY OF HISTORY, Georg W. Hegel. Great classic of Western thought develops concept that history is not chance but a rational process, the evolution of freedom. 457pp. 5⅜ x 8½.   20112-0 Pa. $6.00

LANGUAGE, TRUTH AND LOGIC, Alfred J. Ayer. Famous, clear introduction to Vienna, Cambridge schools of Logical Positivism. Role of philosophy, elimination of metaphysics, nature of analysis, etc. 160pp. 5⅜ x 8½. (USCO)   20010-8 Pa. $2.50

A PREFACE TO LOGIC, Morris R. Cohen. Great City College teacher in renowned, easily followed exposition of formal logic, probability, values, logic and world order and similar topics; no previous background needed. 209pp. 5⅜ x 8½.   23517-3 Pa. $4.95

REASON AND NATURE, Morris R. Cohen. Brilliant analysis of reason and its multitudinous ramifications by charismatic teacher. Interdisciplinary, synthesizing work widely praised when it first appeared in 1931. Second (1953) edition. Indexes. 496pp. 5⅜ x 8½.   23633-1 Pa. $7.50

AN ESSAY CONCERNING HUMAN UNDERSTANDING, John Locke. The only complete edition of enormously important classic, with authoritative editorial material by A. C. Fraser. Total of 1176pp. 5⅜ x 8½.
20530-4, 20531-2 Pa., Two-vol. set $16.00

HANDBOOK OF MATHEMATICAL FUNCTIONS WITH FORMULAS, GRAPHS, AND MATHEMATICAL TABLES, edited by Milton Abramowitz and Irene A. Stegun. Vast compendium: 29 sets of tables, some to as high as 20 places. 1,046pp. 8 x 10½.   61272-4 Pa. $17.95

MATHEMATICS FOR THE PHYSICAL SCIENCES, Herbert S. Wilf. Highly acclaimed work offers clear presentations of vector spaces and matrices, orthogonal functions, roots of polynomial equations, conformal mapping, calculus of variations, etc. Knowledge of theory of functions of real and complex variables is assumed. Exercises and solutions. Index. 284pp. 5⅝ x 8¼.   63635-6 Pa. $5.00

THE PRINCIPLE OF RELATIVITY, Albert Einstein et al. Eleven most important original papers on special and general theories. Seven by Einstein, two by Lorentz, one each by Minkowski and Weyl. All translated, unabridged. 216pp. 5⅜ x 8½.   60081-5 Pa. $3.50

THERMODYNAMICS, Enrico Fermi. A classic of modern science. Clear, organized treatment of systems, first and second laws, entropy, thermodynamic potentials, gaseous reactions, dilute solutions, entropy constant. No math beyond calculus required. Problems. 160pp. 5⅜ x 8½.
60361-X Pa. $4.00

ELEMENTARY MECHANICS OF FLUIDS, Hunter Rouse. Classic undergraduate text widely considered to be far better than many later books. Ranges from fluid velocity and acceleration to role of compressibility in fluid motion. Numerous examples, questions, problems. 224 illustrations. 376pp. 5⅝ x 8¼.   63699-2 Pa. $7.00

THE AMERICAN SENATOR, Anthony Trollope. Little known, long unavailable Trollope novel on a grand scale. Here are humorous comment on American vs. English culture, and stunning portrayal of a heroine/villainess. Superb evocation of Victorian village life. 561pp. 5⅜ x 8½.
23801-6 Pa. $7.95

WAS IT MURDER? James Hilton. The author of *Lost Horizon* and *Goodbye, Mr. Chips* wrote one detective novel (under a pen-name) which was quickly forgotten and virtually lost, even at the height of Hilton's fame. This edition brings it back—a finely crafted public school puzzle resplendent with Hilton's stylish atmosphere. A thoroughly English thriller by the creator of Shangri-la. 252pp. 5⅜ x 8. (Available in U.S. only)
23774-5 Pa. $3.00

CENTRAL PARK: A PHOTOGRAPHIC GUIDE, Victor Laredo and Henry Hope Reed. 121 superb photographs show dramatic views of Central Park: Bethesda Fountain, Cleopatra's Needle, Sheep Meadow, the Blockhouse, plus people engaged in many park activities: ice skating, bike riding, etc. Captions by former Curator of Central Park, Henry Hope Reed, provide historical view, changes, etc. Also photos of N.Y. landmarks on park's periphery. 96pp. 8½ x 11. 23750-8 Pa. $4.50

NANTUCKET IN THE NINETEENTH CENTURY, Clay Lancaster. 180 rare photographs, stereographs, maps, drawings and floor plans recreate unique American island society. Authentic scenes of shipwreck, lighthouses, streets, homes are arranged in geographic sequence to provide walking-tour guide to old Nantucket existing today. Introduction, captions. 160pp. 8⅞ x 11¾. 23747-8 Pa. $7.95

STONE AND MAN: A PHOTOGRAPHIC EXPLORATION, Andreas Feininger. 106 photographs by *Life* photographer Feininger portray man's deep passion for stone through the ages. Stonehenge-like megaliths, fortified towns, sculpted marble and crumbling tenements show textures, beauties, fascination. 128pp. 9¼ x 10¾. 23756-7 Pa. $5.95

CIRCLES, A MATHEMATICAL VIEW, D. Pedoe. Fundamental aspects of college geometry, non-Euclidean geometry, and other branches of mathematics: representing circle by point. Poincare model, isoperimetric property, etc. Stimulating recreational reading. 66 figures. 96pp. 5⅝ x 8¼.
63698-4 Pa. $3.50

THE DISCOVERY OF NEPTUNE, Morton Grosser. Dramatic scientific history of the investigations leading up to the actual discovery of the eighth planet of our solar system. Lucid, well-researched book by well-known historian of science. 172pp. 5⅜ x 8½. 23726-5 Pa. $3.50

THE DEVIL'S DICTIONARY. Ambrose Bierce. Barbed, bitter, brilliant witticisms in the form of a dictionary. Best, most ferocious satire America has produced. 145pp. 5⅜ x 8½. 20487-1 Pa. $2.50

HISTORY OF BACTERIOLOGY, William Bulloch. The only comprehensive history of bacteriology from the beginnings through the 19th century. Special emphasis is given to biography-Leeuwenhoek, etc. Brief accounts of 350 bacteriologists form a separate section. No clearer, fuller study, suitable to scientists and general readers, has yet been written. 52 illustrations. 448pp. 5⅝ x 8¼. 23761-3 Pa. $6.50

THE COMPLETE NONSENSE OF EDWARD LEAR, Edward Lear. All nonsense limericks, zany alphabets, Owl and Pussycat, songs, nonsense botany, etc., illustrated by Lear. Total of 321pp. 5⅜ x 8½. (Available in U.S. only) 20167-8 Pa. $4.50

INGENIOUS MATHEMATICAL PROBLEMS AND METHODS, Louis A. Graham. Sophisticated material from Graham *Dial*, applied and pure; stresses solution methods. Logic, number theory, networks, inversions, etc. 237pp. 5⅜ x 8½. 20545-2 Pa. $4.50

BEST MATHEMATICAL PUZZLES OF SAM LOYD, edited by Martin Gardner. Bizarre, original, whimsical puzzles by America's greatest puzzler. From fabulously rare *Cyclopedia*, including famous 14-15 puzzles, the Horse of a Different Color, 115 more. Elementary math. 150 illustrations. 167pp. 5⅜ x 8½. 20498-7 Pa. $3.50

THE BASIS OF COMBINATION IN CHESS, J. du Mont. Easy-to-follow, instructive book on elements of combination play, with chapters on each piece and every powerful combination team—two knights, bishop and knight, rook and bishop, etc. 250 diagrams. 218pp. 5⅜ x 8½. (Available in U.S. only) 23644-7 Pa. $4.50

MODERN CHESS STRATEGY, Ludek Pachman. The use of the queen, the active king, exchanges, pawn play, the center, weak squares, etc. Section on rook alone worth price of the book. Stress on the moderns. Often considered the most important book on strategy. 314pp. 5⅜ x 8½. 20290-9 Pa. $5.00

LASKER'S MANUAL OF CHESS, Dr. Emanuel Lasker. Great world champion offers very thorough coverage of all aspects of chess. Combinations, position play, openings, end game, aesthetics of chess, philosophy of struggle, much more. Filled with analyzed games. 390pp. 5⅜ x 8½. 20640-8 Pa. $5.95

500 MASTER GAMES OF CHESS, S. Tartakower, J. du Mont. Vast collection of great chess games from 1798-1938, with much material nowhere else readily available. Fully annotated, arranged by opening for easier study. 664pp. 5⅜ x 8½. 23208-5 Pa. $8.50

A GUIDE TO CHESS ENDINGS, Dr. Max Euwe, David Hooper. One of the finest modern works on chess endings. Thorough analysis of the most frequently encountered endings by former world champion. 331 examples, each with diagram. 248pp. 5⅜ x 8½. 23332-4 Pa. $3.95

THE COMPLETE BOOK OF DOLL MAKING AND COLLECTING, Catherine Christopher. Instructions, patterns for dozens of dolls, from rag doll on up to elaborate, historically accurate figures. Mould faces, sew clothing, make doll houses, etc. Also collecting information. Many illustrations. 288pp. 6 x 9. 22066-4 Pa. $4.95

THE DAGUERREOTYPE IN AMERICA, Beaumont Newhall. Wonderful portraits, 1850's townscapes, landscapes; full text plus 104 photographs. The basic book. Enlarged 1976 edition. 272pp. 8¼ x 11¼.
23322-7 Pa. $7.95

CRAFTSMAN HOMES, Gustav Stickley. 296 architectural drawings, floor plans, and photographs illustrate 40 different kinds of "Mission-style" homes from *The Craftsman* (1901-16), voice of American style of simplicity and organic harmony. Thorough coverage of Craftsman idea in text and picture, now collector's item. 224pp. 8⅛ x 11. 23791-5 Pa. $6.50

PEWTER-WORKING: INSTRUCTIONS AND PROJECTS, Burl N. Osborn. & Gordon O. Wilber. Introduction to pewter-working for amateur craftsman. History and characteristics of pewter; tools, materials, step-by-step instructions. Photos, line drawings, diagrams. Total of 160pp. 7⅞ x 10¾. 23786-9 Pa. $3.50

THE GREAT CHICAGO FIRE, edited by David Lowe. 10 dramatic, eye-witness accounts of the 1871 disaster, including one of the aftermath and rebuilding, plus 70 contemporary photographs and illustrations of the ruins—courthouse, Palmer House, Great Central Depot, etc. Introduction by David Lowe. 87pp. 8¼ x 11. 23771-0 Pa. $4.00

SILHOUETTES: A PICTORIAL ARCHIVE OF VARIED ILLUSTRA-TIONS, edited by Carol Belanger Grafton. Over 600 silhouettes from the 18th to 20th centuries include profiles and full figures of men and women, children, birds and animals, groups and scenes, nature, ships, an alphabet. Dozens of uses for commercial artists and craftspeople. 144pp. 8⅜ x 11¼.
23781-8 Pa. $4.50

ANIMALS: 1,419 COPYRIGHT-FREE ILLUSTRATIONS OF MAM-MALS, BIRDS, FISH, INSECTS, ETC., edited by Jim Harter. Clear wood engravings present, in extremely lifelike poses, over 1,000 species of animals. One of the most extensive copyright-free pictorial sourcebooks of its kind. Captions. Index. 284pp. 9 x 12. 23766-4 Pa. $8.95

INDIAN DESIGNS FROM ANCIENT ECUADOR, Frederick W. Shaffer. 282 original designs by pre-Columbian Indians of Ecuador (500-1500 A.D.). Designs include people, mammals, birds, reptiles, fish, plants, heads, geometric designs. Use as is or alter for advertising, textiles, leathercraft, etc. Introduction. 95pp. 8¾ x 11¼. 23764-8 Pa. $4.50

SZIGETI ON THE VIOLIN, Joseph Szigeti. Genial, loosely structured tour by premier violinist, featuring a pleasant mixture of reminiscences, insights into great music and musicians, innumerable tips for practicing violinists. 385 musical passages. 256pp. 5⅝ x 8¼. 23763-X Pa. $4.00

TONE POEMS, SERIES II: TILL EULENSPIEGELS LUSTIGE STREICHE, ALSO SPRACH ZARATHUSTRA, AND EIN HELDENLEBEN, Richard Strauss. Three important orchestral works, including very popular *Till Eulenspiegel's Marry Pranks,* reproduced in full score from original editions. Study score. 315pp. 9⅜ x 12¼. (Available in U.S. only)
23755-9 Pa. $8.95

TONE POEMS, SERIES I: DON JUAN, TOD UND VERKLARUNG AND DON QUIXOTE, Richard Strauss. Three of the most often performed and recorded works in entire orchestral repertoire, reproduced in full score from original editions. Study score. 286pp. 9⅜ x 12¼. (Available in U.S. only)
23754-0 Pa. $8.95

11 LATE STRING QUARTETS, Franz Joseph Haydn. The form which Haydn defined and "brought to perfection." *(Grove's).* 11 string quartets in complete score, his last and his best. The first in a projected series of the complete Haydn string quartets. Reliable modern Eulenberg edition, otherwise difficult to obtain. 320pp. 8⅜ x 11¼. (Available in U.S. only)
23753-2 Pa. $8.95

FOURTH, FIFTH AND SIXTH SYMPHONIES IN FULL SCORE, Peter Ilyitch Tchaikovsky. Complete orchestral scores of Symphony No. 4 in F Minor, Op. 36; Symphony No. 5 in E Minor, Op. 64; Symphony No. 6 in B Minor, "Pathetique," Op. 74. Bretikopf & Hartel eds. Study score. 480pp. 9⅜ x 12¼. 23861-X Pa. $10.95

THE MARRIAGE OF FIGARO: COMPLETE SCORE, Wolfgang A. Mozart. Finest comic opera ever written. Full score, not to be confused with piano renderings. Peters edition. Study score. 448pp. 9⅜ x 12¼. (Available in U.S. only) 23751-6 Pa. $12.95

"IMAGE" ON THE ART AND EVOLUTION OF THE FILM, edited by Marshall Deutelbaum. Pioneering book brings together for first time 38 groundbreaking articles on early silent films from *Image* and 263 illustrations newly shot from rare prints in the collection of the International Museum of Photography. A landmark work. Index. 256pp. 8¼ x 11.
23777-X Pa. $8.95

AROUND-THE-WORLD COOKY BOOK, Lois Lintner Sumption and Marguerite Lintner Ashbrook. 373 cooky and frosting recipes from 28 countries (America, Austria, China, Russia, Italy, etc.) include Viennese kisses, rice wafers, London strips, lady fingers, hony, sugar spice, maple cookies, etc. Clear instructions. All tested. 38 drawings. 182pp. 5⅜ x 8.
23802-4 Pa. $2.75

THE ART NOUVEAU STYLE, edited by Roberta Waddell. 579 rare photographs, not available elsewhere, of works in jewelry, metalwork, glass, ceramics, textiles, architecture and furniture by 175 artists—Mucha, Seguy, Lalique, Tiffany, Gaudin, Hohlwein, Saarinen, and many others. 288pp. 8⅜ x 11¼. 23515-7 Pa. $8.95

THE CURVES OF LIFE, Theodore A. Cook. Examination of shells, leaves, horns, human body, art, etc., in *"the* classic reference on how the golden ratio applies to spirals and helices in nature . . . . "—Martin Gardner. 426 illustrations. Total of 512pp. 5⅜ x 8½.   23701-X Pa. **$6.95**

AN ILLUSTRATED FLORA OF THE NORTHERN UNITED STATES AND CANADA, Nathaniel L. Britton, Addison Brown. Encyclopedic work covers 4666 species, ferns on up. Everything. Full botanical information, illustration for each. This earlier edition is preferred by many to more recent revisions. 1913 edition. Over 4000 illustrations, total of 2087pp. 6⅛ x 9¼.   22642-5, 22643-3, 22644-1 Pa., Three-vol. set **$28.50**

MANUAL OF THE GRASSES OF THE UNITED STATES, A. S. Hitchcock, U.S. Dept. of Agriculture. The basic study of American grasses, both indigenous and escapes, cultivated and wild. Over 1400 species. Full descriptions, information. Over 1100 maps, illustrations. Total of 1051pp. 5⅜ x 8½.   22717-0, 22718-9 Pa., Two-vol. set **$17.00**

THE CACTACEAE,, Nathaniel L. Britton, John N. Rose. Exhaustive, definitive. Every cactus in the world. Full botanical descriptions. Thorough statement of nomenclatures, habitat, detailed finding keys. The one book needed by every cactus enthusiast. Over 1275 illustrations. Total of 1080pp. 8 x 10¼.   21191-6, 21192-4 Clothbd., Two-vol. set **$50.00**

AMERICAN MEDICINAL PLANTS, Charles F. Millspaugh. Full descriptions, 180 plants covered: history; physical description; methods of preparation with all chemical constituents extracted; all claimed curative or adverse effects. 180 full-page plates. Classification table. 804pp. 6½ x 9¼.   23034-1 Pa. **$13.95**

A MODERN HERBAL, Margaret Grieve. Much the fullest, most exact, most useful compilation of herbal material. Gigantic alphabetical encyclopedia, from aconite to zedoary, gives botanical information, medical properties, folklore, economic uses, and much else. Indispensable to serious reader. 161 illustrations. 888pp. 6½ x 9¼. (Available in U.S. only)   22798-7, 22799-5 Pa., Two-vol. set **$15.00**

THE HERBAL or GENERAL HISTORY OF PLANTS, John Gerard. The 1633 edition revised and enlarged by Thomas Johnson. Containing almost 2850 plant descriptions and 2705 superb illustrations, Gerard's *Herbal* is a monumental work, the book all modern English herbals are derived from, the one herbal every serious enthusiast should have in its entirety. Original editions are worth perhaps $750. 1678pp. 8½ x 12¼.   23147-X Clothbd. **$75.00**

MANUAL OF THE TREES OF NORTH AMERICA, Charles S. Sargent. The basic survey of every native tree and tree-like shrub, 717 species in all. Extremely full descriptions, information on habitat, growth, locales, economics, etc. Necessary to every serious tree lover. Over 100 finding keys. 783 illustrations. Total of 986pp. 5⅜ x 8½.   20277-1, 20278-X Pa., Two-vol. set **$12.00**

GREAT NEWS PHOTOS AND THE STORIES BEHIND THEM, John Faber. Dramatic volume of 140 great news photos, 1855 through 1976, and revealing stories behind them, with both historical and technical information. Hindenburg disaster, shooting of Oswald, nomination of Jimmy Carter, etc. 160pp. 8¼ x 11. 23667-6 Pa. $6.00

CRUICKSHANK'S PHOTOGRAPHS OF BIRDS OF AMERICA, Allan D. Cruickshank. Great ornithologist, photographer presents 177 closeups, groupings, panoramas, flightings, etc., of about 150 different birds. Expanded *Wings in the Wilderness*. Introduction by Helen G. Cruickshank. 191pp. 8¼ x 11. 23497-5 Pa. $7.95

AMERICAN WILDLIFE AND PLANTS, A. C. Martin, et al. Describes food habits of more than 1000 species of mammals, birds, fish. Special treatment of important food plants. Over 300 illustrations. 500pp. 5⅜ x 8½. 20793-5 Pa. $6.50

THE PEOPLE CALLED SHAKERS, Edward D. Andrews. Lifetime of research, definitive study of Shakers: origins, beliefs, practices, dances, social organization, furniture and crafts, impact on 19th-century USA, present heritage. Indispensable to student of American history, collector. 33 illustrations. 351pp. 5⅜ x 8½. 21081-2 Pa. $4.50

OLD NEW YORK IN EARLY PHOTOGRAPHS, Mary Black. New York City as it was in 1853-1901, through 196 wonderful photographs from N.-Y. Historical Society. Great Blizzard, Lincoln's funeral procession, great buildings. 228pp. 9 x 12. 22907-6 Pa. $8.95

MR. LINCOLN'S CAMERA MAN: MATHEW BRADY, Roy Meredith. Over 300 Brady photos reproduced directly from original negatives, photos. Jackson, Webster, Grant, Lee, Carnegie, Barnum; Lincoln; Battle Smoke, Death of Rebel Sniper, Atlanta Just After Capture. Lively commentary. 368pp. 8⅜ x 11¼. 23021-X Pa. $11.95

TRAVELS OF WILLIAM BARTRAM, William Bartram. From 1773-8, Bartram explored Northern Florida, Georgia, Carolinas, and reported on wild life, plants, Indians, early settlers. Basic account for period, entertaining reading. Edited by Mark Van Doren. 13 illustrations. 141pp. 5⅜ x 8½. 20013-2 Pa. $6.00

THE GENTLEMAN AND CABINET MAKER'S DIRECTOR, Thomas Chippendale. Full reprint, 1762 style book, most influential of all time; chairs, tables, sofas, mirrors, cabinets, etc. 200 plates, plus 24 photographs of surviving pieces. 249pp. 9⅞ x 12¾. 21601-2 Pa. $8.95

AMERICAN CARRIAGES, SLEIGHS, SULKIES AND CARTS, edited by Don H. Berkebile. 168 Victorian illustrations from catalogues, trade journals, fully captioned. Useful for artists. Author is Assoc. Curator, Div. of Transportation of Smithsonian Institution. 168pp. 8½ x 9½. 23328-6 Pa. $5.00

SECOND PIATIGORSKY CUP, edited by Isaac Kashdan. One of the greatest tournament books ever produced in the English language. All 90 games of the 1966 tournament, annotated by players, most annotated by both players. Features Petrosian, Spassky, Fischer, Larsen, six others. 228pp. 5⅜ x 8½. 23572-6 Pa. $3.50

ENCYCLOPEDIA OF CARD TRICKS, revised and edited by Jean Hugard. How to perform over 600 card tricks, devised by the world's greatest magicians: impromptus, spelling tricks, key cards, using special packs, much, much more. Additional chapter on card technique. 66 illustrations. 402pp. 5⅜ x 8½. (Available in U.S. only) 21252-1 Pa. $5.95

MAGIC: STAGE ILLUSIONS, SPECIAL EFFECTS AND TRICK PHO-TOGRAPHY, Albert A. Hopkins, Henry R. Evans. One of the great classics; fullest, most authorative explanation of vanishing lady, levitations, scores of other great stage effects. Also small magic, automata, stunts. 446 illus-trations. 556pp. 5⅜ x 8½. 23344-8 Pa. $6.95

THE SECRETS OF HOUDINI, J. C. Cannell. Classic study of Houdini's incredible magic, exposing closely-kept professional secrets and revealing, in general terms, the whole art of stage magic. 67 illustrations. 279pp. 5⅜ x 8½. 22913-0 Pa. $4.00

HOFFMANN'S MODERN MAGIC, Professor Hoffmann. One of the best, and best-known, magicians' manuals of the past century. Hundreds of tricks from card tricks and simple sleight of hand to elaborate illusions involving construction of complicated machinery. 332 illustrations. 563pp. 5⅜ x 8½. 23623-4 Pa. $6.95

THOMAS NAST'S CHRISTMAS DRAWINGS, Thomas Nast. Almost all Christmas drawings by creator of image of Santa Claus as we know it, and one of America's foremost illustrators and political cartoonists. 66 illustrations. 3 illustrations in color on covers. 96pp. 8⅜ x 11¼. 23660-9 Pa. $3.50

FRENCH COUNTRY COOKING FOR AMERICANS, Louis Diat. 500 easy-to-make, authentic provincial recipes compiled by former head chef at New York's Fitz-Carlton Hotel: onion soup, lamb stew, potato pie, more. 309pp. 5⅜ x 8½. 23665-X Pa. $3.95

SAUCES, FRENCH AND FAMOUS, Louis Diat. Complete book gives over 200 specific recipes: bechamel, Bordelaise, hollandaise, Cumberland, apri-cot, etc. Author was one of this century's finest chefs, originator of vichyssoise and many other dishes. Index. 156pp. 5⅜ x 8. 23663-3 Pa. $2.75

TOLL HOUSE TRIED AND TRUE RECIPES, Ruth Graves Wakefield. Authentic recipes from the famous Mass. restaurant: popovers, veal and ham loaf, Toll House baked beans, chocolate cake crumb pudding, much more. Many helpful hints. Nearly 700 recipes. Index. 376pp. 5⅜ x 8½. 23560-2 Pa. $4.95

ILLUSTRATED GUIDE TO SHAKER FURNITURE, Robert Meader. Director, Shaker Museum, Old Chatham, presents up-to-date coverage of all furniture and appurtenances, with much on local styles not available elsewhere. 235 photos. 146pp. 9 x 12. 22819-3 Pa. $6.95

COOKING WITH BEER, Carole Fahy. Beer has as superb an effect on food as wine, and at fraction of cost. Over 250 recipes for appetizers, soups, main dishes, desserts, breads, etc. Index. 144pp. 5⅜ x 8½. (Available in U.S. only) 23661-7 Pa. $3.00

STEWS AND RAGOUTS, Kay Shaw Nelson. This international cookbook offers wide range of 108 recipes perfect for everyday, special occasions, meals-in-themselves, main dishes. Economical, nutritious, easy-to-prepare: goulash, Irish stew, boeuf bourguignon, etc. Index. 134pp. 5⅜ x 8½. 23662-5 Pa. $3.95

DELICIOUS MAIN COURSE DISHES, Marian Tracy. Main courses are the most important part of any meal. These 200 nutritious, economical recipes from around the world make every meal a delight. "I . . . have found it so useful in my own household,"—*N.Y. Times.* Index. 219pp. 5⅜ x 8½. 23664-1 Pa. $3.95

FIVE ACRES AND INDEPENDENCE, Maurice G. Kains. Great back-to-the-land classic explains basics of self-sufficient farming: economics, plants, crops, animals, orchards, soils, land selection, host of other necessary things. Do not confuse with skimpy faddist literature; Kains was one of America's greatest agriculturalists. 95 illustrations. 397pp. 5⅜ x 8½. 20974-1 Pa. **$4.95**

A PRACTICAL GUIDE FOR THE BEGINNING FARMER, Herbert Jacobs. Basic, extremely useful first book for anyone thinking about moving to the country and starting a farm. Simpler than Kains, with greater emphasis on country living in general. 246pp. 5⅜ x 8½. 23675-7 Pa. $3.95

PAPERMAKING, Dard Hunter. Definitive book on the subject by the foremost authority in the field. Chapters dealing with every aspect of history of craft in every part of the world. Over 320 illustrations. 2nd, revised and enlarged (1947) edition. 672pp. 5⅜ x 8½. 23619-6 Pa. $8.95

THE ART DECO STYLE, edited by Theodore Menten. Furniture, jewelry, metalwork, ceramics, fabrics, lighting fixtures, interior decors, exteriors, graphics from pure French sources. Best sampling around. Over 400 photographs. 183pp. 8⅜ x 11¼. 22824-X Pa. $6.95

ACKERMANN'S COSTUME PLATES, Rudolph Ackermann. Selection of 96 plates from the *Repository of Arts,* best published source of costume for English fashion during the early 19th century. 12 plates also in color. Captions, glossary and introduction by editor Stella Blum. Total of 120pp. 8⅜ x 11¼. 23690-0 Pa. $5.00

THE ANATOMY OF THE HORSE, George Stubbs. Often considered the great masterpiece of animal anatomy. Full reproduction of 1766 edition, plus prospectus; original text and modernized text. 36 plates. Introduction by Eleanor Garvey. 121pp. 11 x 14¾.   23402-9 Pa. **$8.95**

BRIDGMAN'S LIFE DRAWING, George B. Bridgman. More than 500 illustrative drawings and text teach you to abstract the body into its major masses, use light and shade, proportion; as well as specific areas of anatomy, of which Bridgman is master. 192pp. 6½ x 9¼. (Available in U.S. only)
22710-3 Pa. **$4.50**

ART NOUVEAU DESIGNS IN COLOR, Alphonse Mucha, Maurice Verneuil, Georges Auriol. Full-color reproduction of *Combinaisons ornementales* (c. 1900) by Art Nouveau masters. Floral, animal, geometric, interlacings, swashes—borders, frames, spots—all incredibly beautiful. 60 plates, hundreds of designs. 9⅜ x 8-1/16.   22885-1 Pa. **$4.50**

FULL-COLOR FLORAL DESIGNS IN THE ART NOUVEAU STYLE, E. A. Seguy. 166 motifs, on 40 plates, from *Les fleurs et leurs applications decoratives* (1902): borders, circular designs, repeats, allovers, "spots." All in authentic Art Nouveau colors. 48pp. 9⅜ x 12¼.
23439-8 Pa. **$6.00**

A DIDEROT PICTORIAL ENCYCLOPEDIA OF TRADES AND IN-DUSTRY, edited by Charles C. Gillispie. 485 most interesting plates from the great French Encyclopedia of the 18th century show hundreds of working figures, artifacts, process, land and cityscapes; glassmaking, paper-making, metal extraction, construction, weaving, making furniture, clothing, wigs, dozens. of other activities. Plates fully explained. 920pp. 9 x 12.
22284-5, 22285-3 Clothbd., Two-vol. set **$50.00**

HANDBOOK OF EARLY ADVERTISING ART, Clarence P. Hornung. Largest collection of copyright-free early and antique advertising art ever compiled. Over 6,000 illustrations, from Franklin's time to the 1890's for special effects, novelty. Valuable source, almost inexhaustible.
Pictorial Volume. Agriculture, the zodiac, animals, autos, birds, Christmas, fire engines, flowers, trees, musical instruments, ships, games and sports, much more. Arranged by subject matter and use. 237 plates. 288pp. 9 x 12.
20122-8 Clothbd. **$15.00**

Typographical Volume. Roman and Gothic faces ranging from 10 point to 300 point, "Barnum," German and Old English faces, script, logotypes, scrolls and flourishes, 1115 ornamental initials, 67 complete alphabets, more. 310 plates. 320pp. 9 x 12.   20123-6 Clothbd. $15.00

CALLIGRAPHY (CALLIGRAPHIA LATINA), J. G. Schwandner. High point of 18th-century ornamental calligraphy. Very ornate initials, scrolls, borders, cherubs, birds, lettered examples. 172pp. 9 x 13.
20475-8 Pa. **$7.95**

GEOMETRY, RELATIVITY AND THE FOURTH DIMENSION, Rudolf Rucker. Exposition of fourth dimension, means of visualization, concepts of relativity as Flatland characters continue adventures. Popular, easily followed yet accurate, profound. 141 illustrations. 133pp. 5⅜ x 8½.
23400-2 Pa. $2.75

THE ORIGIN OF LIFE, A. I. Oparin. Modern classic in biochemistry, the first rigorous examination of possible evolution of life from nitrocarbon compounds. Non-technical, easily followed. Total of 295pp. 5⅜ x 8½.
60213-3 Pa. $5.95

PLANETS, STARS AND GALAXIES, A. E. Fanning. Comprehensive introductory survey: the sun, solar system, stars, galaxies, universe, cosmology; quasars, radio stars, etc. 24pp. of photographs. 189pp. 5⅜ x 8½. (Available in U.S. only)
21680-2 Pa. $3.75

THE THIRTEEN BOOKS OF EUCLID'S ELEMENTS, translated with introduction and commentary by Sir Thomas L. Heath. Definitive edition. Textual and linguistic, notes, mathematical analysis, 2500 years of critical commentary. Do not confuse with abridged school editions. Total of 1414pp. 5⅜ x 8½. 60088-2, 60089-0, 60090-4 Pa., Three-vol. set $19.50

Prices subject to change without notice.

Available at your book dealer or write for free catalogue to Dept. GI, Dover Publications, Inc., 31 East 2nd St. Mineola., N.Y. 11501. Dover publishes more than 175 books each year on science, elementary and advanced mathematics, biology, music, art, literary history, social sciences and other areas.